The Legacy of the New Wave in French Cinema

The Legacy of the New Wave in French Cinema

Douglas Morrey

BLOOMSBURY ACADEMIC
NEW YORK • LONDON • OXFORD • NEW DELHI • SYDNEY

BLOOMSBURY ACADEMIC
Bloomsbury Publishing Inc
1385 Broadway, New York, NY 10018, USA
50 Bedford Square, London, WC1B 3DP, UK

BLOOMSBURY, BLOOMSBURY ACADEMIC and the Diana logo
are trademarks of Bloomsbury Publishing Plc

First published in the United States of America 2020

Copyright © Douglas Morrey, 2020

For legal purposes the Acknowledgements on p. vii constitute an extension
of this copyright page.

Cover design by Louise Dugdale
Cover image: Film *Boy Meets Girl*, Mireille Perrier, 1984,
© Winstar Cinema/Courtesy Everett Collection / Mary Evans

All rights reserved. No part of this publication may be reproduced or transmitted
in any form or by any means, electronic or mechanical, including photocopying,
recording, or any information storage or retrieval system, without prior
permission in writing from the publishers.

Bloomsbury Publishing Inc does not have any control over, or responsibility for,
any third-party websites referred to or in this book. All internet addresses given in
this book were correct at the time of going to press. The author and publisher regret
any inconvenience caused if addresses have changed or sites have ceased to exist,
but can accept no responsibility for any such changes.

A catalog record for this book is available from the Library of Congress.
Names: Morrey, Douglas, author.
Title: The legacy of the new wave in French cinema / Douglas Morrey.
Description: New York, NY : Bloomsbury Academic, 2019. | Includes
bibliographical references and index.
Identifiers: LCCN 2019008335 (print) | LCCN 2019015824 (ebook) | ISBN
9781501311901 (ePDF) | ISBN 9781501311918 (ePub) | ISBN 9781501311932 (pbk.) |
ISBN 9781501311949 (hardback)
Subjects: LCSH: New wave films–France–History and criticism.
Classification: LCC PN1993.5.F7 (ebook) | LCC PN1993.5.F7 M67 2019 (print) |
DDC 791.430944–dc23
LC record available at https://lccn.loc.gov/2019008335

ISBN:	HB:	978-1-5013-1194-9
	PB:	978-1-5013-1193-2
	ePDF:	978-1-5013-1190-1
	eBook:	978-1-5013-1191-8

Typeset by Integra Software Services Pvt. Ltd.

To find out more about our authors and books visit www.bloomsbury.com
and sign up for our newsletters.

CONTENTS

List of Figures vi
Acknowledgements vii

Introduction 1

1 The Post-New Wave of the 1970s: Eustache, Doillon, Garrel 13

2 The *cinéma du look* 45

3 The *jeune cinéma français* of the 1990s 89

4 The Old New Wave 131

5 Contemporary Auteur Directors in France 185

Conclusion 231

Bibliography 236
Index 254

FIGURES

1.1 The *ménage à quatre* in *Les Doigts dans la tête* (1974): Roselyne Vuillaume, Christophe Soto, Ann Zacharias and Olivier Bousquet. Courtesy MK2 27

1.2 Mireille Perrier in *Elle a passé tant d'heures sous les sunlights* (1985). Courtesy France Inter 36

2.1 Expressionist space in *Diva* (1981): Richard Bohringer, Frédéric Andréi and Thuy An Luu. Courtesy StudioCanal/Optimum World 65

2.2 Denis Lavant in *Mauvais Sang* (1986). Courtesy Artificial Eye 70

3.1 Mathieu Amalric and Marianne Denicourt in *Comment je me suis disputé (Ma vie sexuelle)* (1996). Courtesy Cahiers du cinéma 104

3.2 David Douche and Marjorie Cottreel in *La Vie de Jésus* (1997). Courtesy Blaq Out 115

4.1 Lucy Russell in *L'Anglaise et le Duc* (2001). Courtesy Potemkine 156

4.2 Bohdan Litnianski and his wife in *Les Glaneurs et la Glaneuse* (2000). Courtesy Artificial Eye 166

5.1 Ernst Umhauer in *Dans la maison* (2012). Courtesy eOne 206

5.2 Ludivine Sagnier and Rasha Bukvic in *Les Bien-Aimés* (2011). Courtesy New Wave Films 211

ACKNOWLEDGEMENTS

I am grateful to the British Academy Small Grants scheme for funding some of the early stages of research into this book and to the University of Warwick for providing periods of study leave in order to pursue the research.

Material from this book was presented at conferences in Regina, Paris, York, Warwick, Atlanta, Aberdeen, Glasgow, Dublin, Manchester, Oxford, Bloomington, Bangor and Cork. I am grateful to all those colleagues who came to hear my talks and offered feedback.

At one such conference at the very beginning of this project, I met the woman who was to become my wife. Shortly before I submitted the manuscript, we celebrated our son's second birthday. My thanks are due to the two of them for everything else.

Introduction

This is not another book about the French New Wave. Rather, this book seeks to trace the aesthetic, industrial, discursive and ideological legacy of the New Wave in the half-century and more since the movement ended. The New Wave is widely regarded to have been one of the most revolutionary shifts in the history of filmmaking and film theorizing not just in France but in all of world cinema. This book will attempt to pin down key concepts, practices, attitudes and stylistic markers that have been inherited from the New Wave by looking at a series of case studies drawn from each decade of the intervening period. In order to do this, we must first establish a consensual understanding of what the New Wave was.

The Nouvelle Vague has received more critical commentary than practically any other period or trend in film history (one exception might be film noir), and this Introduction will endeavour to condense that broad scholarship into a short summary that will serve as a point of reference in the chapters to follow. Michel Marie called the New Wave 'unique in the history of French cinema' while Antoine de Baecque opined that it was 'the first film movement to have fixed with such acuity the mythology of a particular moment in history'.[1] While the importance of the New Wave is rarely questioned, its parameters are much more open to debate. In the strictest definition, it only lasted from the beginning of 1959 until the end of 1960.[2] Many critics and cinephiles, however, use the term much more loosely to refer to the films of key New Wave directors for the whole of the 1960s, if not beyond. Indeed, James Monaco notes that 'colloquially, "New Wave" soon degenerated into a synonym for "Avant-Garde"'.[3] In an effort to bring some clarity to this vague usage, this Introduction will outline the social and industrial contexts behind the French New Wave, consider some of its key representational trends, review important theoretical concepts attributed to the movement and identify its associated elements of film style before summarizing the structure of this book.

The period between 1945 and 1960 in France saw a vast and very rapid increase in the population which grew more than it had in the previous one hundred years.[4] The country's rural exodus also meant that Paris grew disproportionately and its built environment was transformed during this period.[5] The post-war baby boom led to a large and very distinct generation of young people, the first 'to be understood in its entirety as a sociological phenomenon'.[6] A generational conflict grew between an older generation who had experienced wartime France and who occupied positions of power, and the youth often regarded as spoiled, entitled and apathetic.[7] Despite the growing population, box office receipts were in decline at the cinema as economic growth and prosperity offered different leisure opportunities.[8] The audience for cinema became younger and better educated, making it more of an 'intellectual' pastime.[9] Meanwhile, the French cinema of the 1950s had failed to renew itself, its institutions largely controlled by ageing directors, technicians, screenwriters and actors.[10] Intellectual life in post-war France was broadly divided between a Marxist left and the 'right-wing anarchist' Hussards, and the filmmakers of the New Wave tended to gravitate towards the latter, in particular through the journal *Arts* where much of their early criticism was published.[11] These critics tended to focus on style over ideology and were dedicated to the romantic cult of the artist.[12] But the New Wave was also facilitated by the arrival in power of the Gaullists through state financial aid as well as the symbolic support of André Malraux's Ministry of Culture.[13]

The New Wave was suspicious of big-budget cinema. Several key players (Chabrol, Truffaut, Barbet Schroeder) used small familial inheritances to set up their own production companies and, supported by adventurous producers like Georges de Beauregard, Pierre Braunberger and Anatole Dauman, were able to work with more creative freedom.[14] There was also a flourishing culture of mutual aid (both financial and practical) between New Wave filmmakers.[15] Social capital was therefore also important in the French New Wave: Louis Malle, for instance, was able to get *Ascenseur pour l'échafaud* (1958) made in large part because of his friendships with, among others, Jacques Cousteau, Roger Nimier and Boris Vian.[16] At the same time, this film, along with Chabrol's debut *Le Beau Serge* (1959), benefited from the state-funded *prime à la qualité* awarded to deserving screenplays.[17] Although relatively modest, this financial assistance could contribute significantly to the production of a small-budget film.[18] Small budgets made it easier for films to break even at the box office, which allowed filmmakers to keep working and helps explain the prolific careers of key directors like Godard and Chabrol during the 1960s.[19] These reduced budgets account for some of the key aesthetic principles of the New Wave such as working with a reduced crew on location and using direct sound recording where possible.[20] Shooting outside the studio allowed for greater realism, greater rapidity and greater spontaneity. As Neupert puts it: 'Shooting a movie was suddenly casual and fun.'[21]

To an extent, New Wave films dispensed with traditional storytelling. Truffaut noted that these films were united by a refusal of theatrical intrigues and expository scenes.[22] In extreme examples, like the films of Jean-Luc Godard, scenes could be reduced to 'incomplete shards of action'.[23] The focus of scenes was often deliberately shifted away from narratively significant acts towards apparently minor details or 'dead' time.[24] The received rules of continuity editing might be deliberately flouted, rendering space and time confused.[25] Far from the goal-directed protagonists of classical narrative cinema, New Wave films were often 'peopled with characters who either [did] not know what they [were] supposed to be doing or [were] impotent to achieve their goal'.[26] Character motivations could be left deliberately hazy.[27] The use of small budgets tended to preclude the casting of major stars and so the New Wave gradually gave rise to a new generation of film actors.[28] They displayed a variety of novel performance styles, often deliberately exaggerated (Léaud, Brialy, Belmondo, Karina, Lafont), elsewhere determinedly naturalistic (Bardot) or oddly inexpressive (Aznavour, Subor).[29] These varied styles repeatedly encouraged an interrogation of the relationship between cinema and reality, or truth and lies. James Monaco observes that one of the key recurring questions of the French New Wave is: 'Are films more important than life?'[30] References to, and quotations from, the cinema of the past (both recent and more distant) are extremely common in New Wave films.[31] The male characters of these films are, much like their critic-directors, often neurotic fetishists obsessed with cinema – hence Sellier's characterization of the New Wave as a cinema in the 'first person masculine singular'.[32] She adds that most of the male stars of the movement (Belmondo, Brialy, Ronet, Trintignant) serve as 'the filmmaker's alter egos rather than icons designed for the adoration of women filmgoers' (contrast Alain Delon, who was never really associated with the New Wave).[33] It is nonetheless true that there are a striking number of New Wave films in which women drive the action, and these films tended to be the most successful with popular audiences.[34] The New Wave came to be associated with 'a new representation of the relations between men and women, and the exploration of sexual desire'.[35] The movement developed a reputation for representing the increasing sexual liberalization of French society, something that became particularly associated with the figure of Brigitte Bardot.[36] The New Wave debunked the myth of a love that lasts a lifetime and, in the process, worked to develop a new 'politics of intimacy'.[37] Nonetheless, this often took place at the narrative expense of women's dignity, freedom or even lives, especially if they were working-class characters.[38] We must also remember the massive gender bias in production during this period: 'of the 150 filmmakers who made their first full-length fictional film between 1957 and 1962, there isn't a single woman' (Varda's first feature was made in 1955) – and this despite the increasing feminization of other cultural fields in France like literature and popular music.[39]

It is possible to see the French New Wave as being created, in significant part, by rather shy and very obsessive male film enthusiasts who had carefully worked out their cinematic preferences, and their own distinctive narrative of film history, through many hours spent in dark film theatres. These were the young men who wrote polemical and highly influential film criticism, first in *Arts* and then in *Cahiers du cinéma* during the 1950s. One striking feature of this writing was the way it 'combined connoisseurship with direct effrontery':[40] these critics often did have an encyclopaedic knowledge of film history, but they would also use their platform to make sweeping ex cathedra judgements on contemporary films, frequently favouring obscure or minor works, many of which are now largely forgotten. There was a kind of dandyism in these critics' celebration of the marginal.[41] More than that, though, this criticism could become a kind of quasi-mystical discourse, as though the cinephiles were 'touched by aesthetic grace'.[42] It is in this context that we need to understand the famous *politique des auteurs* which, as Monaco notes, involved 'working out the relationship between the historical dimension and the personal dimension' of film criticism.[43] Arguably, what these critics valued was not the technical skill of filmmakers or even such relatively objective criteria as stylistic originality, narrative economy, aesthetic coherence, etc.; rather, 'the main determinant of who was an auteur was the director's world view which he expressed through the material he was working with'.[44]

As Hess suggests, this led the *Cahiers* critics to value in particular directors whose work could be seen to conform to a broad structural narrative depicting the movement of a solitary figure into relationship with others (and ultimately with God). In this vision of cinema as particularly suited to the representation of a spiritual quest, we see further evidence of the near-mystical conception of the seventh art and its devotees. Among the consequences of the *politique des auteurs* upon the critics' subsequent work as directors were a marked tendency towards explicit authorial intervention into the film in terms of self-conscious stylistic effects, plus a tendency for critics of the New Wave to interpret the films with a close eye on the director's biography.[45]

A closely related concept to the *politique des auteurs* is that of mise en scène, which Jim Hillier describes as 'a – perhaps *the* – central and essential concept in *Cahiers* and in later criticism influenced by *Cahiers*'[46] and that James Tweedie calls 'the single most important legacy of French new wave cinema'.[47] As the name, taken from theatrical staging, suggests, mise en scène is first of all a spatial concept: 'a network of relationships, an architecture of connections, an animated complex that seems suspended in space'.[48] Yet mise en scène is a notoriously slippery, some would say hopelessly vague, concept 'abused to the point of nonsense', as Emilie Bickerton notes.[49] For mise en scène was also required to represent 'a distinctive tableau put in place by the director, which in turn presented a coherent and unique world view', hence working in tandem with the *politique des auteurs*.[50] In the words of André Bazin, mise en scène is 'the very matter of the auteur film'.[51] Mise en scène thus becomes a kind of shorthand for discussing the operation of a cinema perceived as personal. As James Monaco says of Truffaut, the purpose of this approach to filmmaking is 'to capture the *quality* of life [...], not its historical details [...], to increase the quotient of honesty and clarity in film and thereby decrease the distance between author and observer'.[52] Mise en scène, in other words, names the process of giving shape to the raw material of life that provides the basic *stuff* of cinema.[53] Jean-Luc Godard himself suggested that the New Wave could be defined, at least in part, by a new relationship between fiction and reality;[54] and it is often suggested that the movement rendered the distinction between fiction and documentary film much more permeable.[55] This helps to explain the contempt for the screenplay among directors like Godard, Rivette and Varda: a carefully elaborated screenplay tends to work against the openness to the real and sense of spontaneity sought by most New Wave directors. The reason the films of the French New Wave continue to excite new viewers today, suggests Marie, is that they managed so successfully (indeed 'miraculously') to capture the unique and authentic 'present moment' of their time.[56] Indeed, a central argument of James Tweedie's book is that it was mise en scène that allowed the New Wave to apprehend on screen a key moment of cultural transition in France, affecting the spaces of work and play, the bodies and attitudes of young people and the rhythms of speech and movement.[57]

If mise en scène remains arguably a somewhat vague and idealistic notion, it is nonetheless possible to point to some practical aspects of film style that became particularly associated with the French New Wave. The use of light-sensitive film stock allowed for filming in low-light conditions, which facilitated the move out of the studio into the naturalism of ordinary daylight. While the first films of the New Wave were nearly all made in black and white, subsequent works made use of colour film, sometimes to add a further degree of naturalism and sometimes, on the contrary, to give a deliberately stylized formalist touch to the mise en scène (especially in the films of Godard).[58] Likewise, the use of sound could both add authenticity (through direct recording or the use of contemporary youth slang and syntax) and provide a further element of stylization. Michel Marie talks about a 'generalized mise en scène of the voice' in the New Wave:[59] the dialogue track is often separated, in one way or another, from the image, giving a new autonomy to the individuality of voices, sometimes creating the soundtrack as a kind of 'second narrative' that competes with, or reflects, the story told in the image.[60] Music was also important: jazz was ubiquitous, following the success of Miles Davis's original score for *Ascenseur pour l'échafaud*, but several directors also obtained effects on pace and mood by including pre-recorded pop songs, often in extenso. The use of music points to one of the most important, but least recognized, elements leading to the aesthetic success of New Wave films: their control of rhythm. The best-known directors and films of the Nouvelle Vague are frequently associated with a fast rhythm. James Monaco writes that 'Truffaut often seems to be almost embarrassed to hold a shot too long',[61] while Godard's early work can sometimes come across like 'an elegy to speed'.[62] The jump cut, particularly associated with À bout de souffle, came to be seen as an emblem of the New Wave but, as critics have demonstrated, that film and others from the movement are actually marked by the rhythmic combination of long takes with jump cuts and by a cracking pace that, from time to time, grinds to a halt to focus on the small details of character, dialogue and relationships.[63] In Godard's work, and elsewhere, this rhythmic alternation often tends to be played out in the dynamic interaction of interior and exterior space. For Tweedie, the rhythms of New Wave films reflect the unique historical conjuncture of France at the turn of the 1960s:[64] cities that, on the surface, are changing rapidly, with the increasing presence of automobiles, the proliferation of construction sites and fast-evolving sexual morals; while, at the same time, residents continue to appreciate the pleasures of strolling in ancient streets, quoting art and literature from previous centuries, and the age-old movement of approach and withdrawal of young lovers. But the rhythm of New Wave films is also affected by the fundamental philosophy of cinema espoused by its practitioners: the tension and release, acceleration and arrest of these films reflect a conception of cinema as at once visceral and intellectual, material and spiritual. The movement from rarefied contemplation in confined rooms to ecstatic play on the streets of Paris is one of the most original distinguishing features of the French New Wave and an important aspect of its legacy.

As we mentioned at the outset of this Introduction, the idea that the New Wave has been highly influential is widespread in film studies. For Michel Marie, the New Wave was 'an aesthetic revolution that marked all of film history'.[65] James Monaco suggested that the movement 'has left us with a cinema forever changed, enlarged, more powerful, more eloquent, more acute'.[66] Inevitably, French filmmakers in particular have had to negotiate this massive inheritance: Jill Forbes suggests that for two or three decades after the New Wave, filmmakers felt the 'constant necessity' to position themselves 'positively or negatively in relation to the Nouvelle Vague'.[67] While it is beyond the scope of this book, the New Wave is generally regarded as having had significant international reach too. Marie sees the late 1960s peak of European art cinema (Bergman, Buñuel, Fellini, Pasolini) as stemming directly from the international reception of the French New Wave.[68] Indeed, for Tweedie, the New Wave has to be understood as an international phenomenon: cinematic new waves occur (Tweedie compares more recent examples in Taiwan and China) when a distinctive local artistic tradition rubs up against the growing cultural significance of the global economy on a nation's youth, in particular, and these new waves subsequently require an international film-festival circuit in order to reach their, naturally globalized, audience.[69] The New Wave arguably remains unique, however, in terms of the ongoing reach of the particular conception of cinema that it so vividly brought to widespread attention. As Jim Hillier recognizes, it is commonly considered that 'film criticism and theory as we know it today – and even filmmaking too – owe almost everything to French film criticism' of the *Cahiers* school.[70] The concept of the director as auteur can be seen to have 'helped usher film study into academic institutions'[71] and indeed one can discern the ways in which film history itself is often now accessed second-hand through the films and the writings of the French New Wave.[72] Some elements of auteurist film culture, like the published interview with the director invited to interpret and explain his or her own work, have become so naturalized that it is easy to forget their novelty at the time of the New Wave.[73] Even if one dislikes the New Wave and sees its exponents as little more than talented self-publicists, one is obliged to recognize the persistence of this model in directorial careers today.[74]

This book is not intended to constitute an industrial or economic history of French cinema since the New Wave.[75] While the New Wave undoubtedly had certain long-term structural influences over the French industry – in particular enshrining a principle of regular renewal of talent and a certain cult of the first film[76] – many aspects of the industry, and especially the perennially popular genres of the comedy, the crime thriller and the historical drama, have felt little real impact from the New Wave. Indeed, the Nouvelle Vague, and the state support that facilitated it, can be seen to have created, in France, 'a media "at two speeds," a "commercial" cinema, on the one hand, and an "auteur" cinema on the other'.[77]

This book focuses on the latter, looking in particular at tendencies, trends or 'movements' in French cinema since the 1960s that have either taken the New Wave explicitly as model or have been positively or negatively compared to the New Wave by critics. I take one case study from each decade since the 1960s and ask of it three key questions: How did the filmmakers associated with this movement situate themselves in relation to the New Wave in their own discourse around their filmmaking practice? To what extent, and in what ways, did French critics refer to the New Wave in the reception of these films, and what was the purpose and tone of these references? Finally, what influences or echoes from the New Wave can be detected in the narrative, thematic or formal material of the films themselves and what value do they have in the different context in which the later films were made? This study therefore involves evaluating the place of these works (both the New Wave films and their successors) within the history of French cinema and, accordingly, one of the key methodologies deployed will be evaluative criticism. However, since the generation of the New Wave can be seen largely to have invented the terms of evaluative criticism in cinema (Chad Newsom argues that they 'created the most important, influential body of evaluative film criticism in our discipline's history'[78]), this can understandably not be considered an objective or 'neutral' approach. The introduction to Philippe Mary's book, for instance, implies that a sociological and an aesthetic approach to film history and criticism must be mutually exclusive.[79] I reject this disciplinary purism and believe that evaluative criticism can have an important place in an historical account of cinema. How do we explain the fact that today's undergraduate students continue to react with enthusiasm and interest to the films of the French New Wave? The reason cannot only be to do with the uniqueness of the historical conjuncture (as Tweedie's argument might imply, at its nadir), because nobody suggests that television documentaries of the same era would work just as well in the classroom. Nor can the appeal of the New Wave be explained away by the symbolic force of the discourse surrounding the movement and its filmmakers, otherwise why wouldn't students react as positively to *Une femme est une femme* (1961) and *Les Carabiniers* (1963) as they do to *À bout de souffle* (1960) and *Le Mépris* (1963)? In other words, a historical study that seeks to account for the lasting success and influence of cultural phenomena like fiction films must, at some stage, engage with the qualities inherent to those works that explain their success and render them, by some observable criteria, *more* successful than others.[80] The goal of this book is certainly not to imply that the films of the New Wave were 'better' than all those that have been made in France since that time. But it does seek to determine which qualities explain the lasting appeal of those films and to question how far they might be specific to a particular cultural context and era and how far and how successfully they can be appropriated and recycled by subsequent generations of filmmakers.

The first chapter of this book focuses on the immediate post-New Wave of the 1970s of Jean Eustache, Philippe Garrel and Jacques Doillon, a generation of relatively muted, inward-looking filmmaking in France, somewhat paralysed by the unsurpassable model of the Nouvelle Vague and grief over the failure of May 1968. Chapters 2 and 3 look at two examples of 'movements' in French cinema that were measured against the model of the New Wave: the so-called *cinéma du look* of the 1980s, often dismissed as a commercial phenomenon without real artistic depth; and the *'jeune cinéma français'* of the 1990s, the fruit of several decades of state support and film education in France that gave rise to a generation of significant film directors and performers. Chapter 4 considers the ongoing influence exerted over French cinema by the New Wave directors, showing how Jean-Luc Godard, Agnès Varda and Éric Rohmer, in their seventies or eighties, all engaged in high-profile experiments with digital filmmaking which, at the same time, served to position them as something like the gatekeepers of the memory of cinema. Finally, Chapter 5 looks at three case studies of successful contemporary auteurs, showing how, in every case, a certain measuring up against the New Wave in terms of direct reference or pastiche seems to have become a rite of passage in the early career of French auteur directors, an obligatory paying of debts that paves the way for a more personal, but internationally focused career.

Notes

1. Michel Marie, *La Nouvelle Vague: Une école artistique* (Paris: Nathan, 1997), 5. Antoine de Baecque, *La Nouvelle Vague: Portrait d'une jeunesse* (Paris: Flammarion, 1998), 115.
2. Marie, *La Nouvelle Vague*, 15.
3. James Monaco, *The New Wave: Truffaut, Godard, Chabrol, Rohmer, Rivette* (New York: Oxford University Press, 1976), vii.
4. Richard Neupert, *A History of the French New Wave Cinema* (Madison: University of Wisconsin Press, 2002), 6.
5. James Tweedie, *The Age of New Waves: Art Cinema and the Staging of Globalization* (Oxford: Oxford University Press, 2013), 83–4.
6. Geneviève Sellier, *Masculine Singular: French New Wave Cinema*, trans. by Kristin Ross (Durham, NC: Duke University Press, 2008), 11. For statistics on the baby boom, see Richard Ivan Jobs, *Riding the New Wave: Youth and the Rejuvenation of France after the Second World War* (Stanford: Stanford University Press, 2007), 23–4.
7. de Baecque, *La Nouvelle Vague*, 43–6.
8. Neupert, *A History of the French New Wave Cinema*, 7–8.
9. Ibid., 10–11.
10. See Marie, *La Nouvelle Vague*, 19, and Philippe Mary, *La Nouvelle Vague et le cinéma d'auteur: Socio-analyse d'une révolution artistique* (Paris: Seuil, 2006), 32 and 37–40.
11. See Antoine de Baecque, *L'Histoire-Caméra* (Paris: Gallimard, 2008), 142–52, and Marc Dambre, 'Arts and the Hussards in Their Time', *Film Criticism* 39: 1 (2014), 9–32.
12. Sellier, *Masculine Singular*, 129.
13. de Baecque, *L'Histoire-Caméra*, 169–72.
14. See, for instance, Neupert, *A History of the French New Wave Cinema*, 126–7, 255–6; Mary, *La Nouvelle Vague et le cinéma d'auteur*, 141, 156.
15. Neupert, *A History of the French New Wave Cinema*, 128.
16. Ibid., 95.
17. Marie, *La Nouvelle Vague*, 49–50.
18. Neupert, *A History of the French New Wave Cinema*, 39.
19. Ibid., 188, 245.

20 Marie, *La Nouvelle Vague*, 63.
21 Neupert, *A History of the French New Wave Cinema*, 40.
22 Quoted in Marie, *La Nouvelle Vague*, 88.
23 Neupert, *A History of the French New Wave Cinema*, 214.
24 Ibid.
25 Ibid., 216–19.
26 Geoffrey Nowell-Smith, *Making Waves: New Cinemas of the 1960s* (New York: Continuum, 2008), 104.
27 Neupert, *A History of the French New Wave Cinema*, 107–8 and 214.
28 Ibid., 39.
29 Marie, *La Nouvelle Vague*, 90, 94, 100.
30 Monaco, *The New Wave*, 126.
31 de Baecque, *La Nouvelle Vague*, 130–1.
32 Sellier, *Masculine Singular*, 84.
33 Ibid., 100.
34 Neupert, *A History of the French New Wave Cinema*, 112; Sellier, *Masculine Singular*, 67.
35 Sellier, *Masculine Singular*, 61.
36 Marie, *La Nouvelle Vague*, 89; de Baecque, *La Nouvelle Vague*, 24; Jobs, *Riding the New Wave*, 203.
37 de Baecque, *La Nouvelle Vague*, 52; Monaco, *The New Wave*, 39.
38 Sellier, *Masculine Singular*, 149–50.
39 Ibid., 6, 14.
40 Chad R. Newsom, '*Cahiers du cinéma* and Evaluative Criticism', *The Cine-Files* 2 (2012).
41 de Baecque, *La Nouvelle Vague*, 32.
42 Mary, *La Nouvelle Vague et le cinéma d'auteur*, 122.
43 Monaco, *The New Wave*, 9.
44 John Hess, 'La Politique des auteurs (Part one): World View as Aesthetics', *Jump Cut* 1 (1974).
45 Marie, *La Nouvelle Vague*, 68; Neupert, *A History of the French New Wave Cinema*, 163.
46 Jim Hillier, 'Introduction', in *Cahiers du cinéma, Vol 1: The 1950s: Neo-Realism, Hollywood, New Wave*, ed. Jim Hillier (London: Routledge and Kegan Paul/BFI, 1985), 9.
47 Tweedie, *The Age of New Waves*, 25.
48 Jacques Rivette, 'The Essential', in *Cahiers du cinema, Vol 1: The 1950s: Neo-Realism, Hollywood, New Wave*, ed. Jim Hillier (London: Routledge and Kegan Paul, 1985), 134. Originally published as 'L'Essentiel', *Cahiers du cinéma* 32 (February 1954), 44.

49 Emilie Bickerton, *A Short History of Cahiers du cinéma* (London: Verso, 2009), 45.
50 Ibid., 27.
51 Quoted in Mary, *La Nouvelle Vague et le cinéma d'auteur*, 115. Mary's quotation of Bazin is not referenced.
52 Monaco, *The New Wave*, 23.
53 de Baecque, *La Nouvelle Vague*, 118. For this reason, it is not straightforward to summarize something like a distinctively New Wave approach to the practice of mise en scène. Readers seeking a more detailed discussion of this most elusive concept are encouraged to consult Jacques Aumont, *Le Cinéma et la mise en scène* (Paris: Armand Colin, 2010) and Adrian Martin, *Mise en scène and Film Style: From Classical Hollywood to New Media Art* (London: Palgrave Macmillan, 2014).
54 Jean-Luc Godard, *Jean-Luc Godard par Jean-Luc Godard, tome 1: 1950–1984* (Paris: Cahiers du cinéma, 1998), 223.
55 Marie, *La Nouvelle Vague*, 64.
56 Ibid., 115.
57 Tweedie, *The Age of New Waves*, 52.
58 Neupert, *A History of the French New Wave Cinema*, 235.
59 Marie, *La Nouvelle Vague*, 72.
60 de Baecque, *La Nouvelle Vague*, 93.
61 Monaco, *The New Wave*, 35.
62 Mary, *La Nouvelle Vague et le cinéma d'auteur*, 69.
63 de Baecque, *La Nouvelle Vague*, 126; Tweedie, *The Age of New Waves*, 102–3.
64 Tweedie, *The Age of New Waves*, 53.
65 Marie, *La Nouvelle Vague*, 116.
66 Monaco, *The New Wave*, 11.
67 Jill Forbes, *The Cinema in France after the New Wave* (London: BFI/Macmillan, 1992), 3.
68 Marie, *La Nouvelle Vague*, 111.
69 Tweedie, *The Age of New Waves*, 6.
70 Hillier, 'Introduction', 1.
71 Newsom, '*Cahiers du cinéma* and Evaluative Criticism'.
72 Marie, *La Nouvelle Vague*, 116.
73 Mary, *La Nouvelle Vague et le cinéma d'auteur*, 116.
74 Sellier explores this perception of the New Wave, *Masculine Singular*, 2–3.
75 Readers seeking this kind of account might consult Michael Temple and Michael Witt (eds), *The French Cinema Book*, second edition (London: Palgrave/BFI, 2018), Susan Hayward, *French National Cinema*, second edition (London: Routledge, 2005), Laurent Creton, *Économie du cinéma*, fifth edition (Paris: Armand Colin, 2014).

76 Marie, *La Nouvelle Vague*, 113.
77 Sellier, *Masculine Singular*, 36.
78 Newsom, '*Cahiers du cinéma* and Evaluative Criticism'.
79 Mary, *La Nouvelle Vague et le cinéma d'auteur*, 13.
80 For a robust defence of the role of evaluation in criticism, see Noël Carroll, *On Criticism* (London: Routledge, 2009).

1

The Post-New Wave of the 1970s: Eustache, Doillon, Garrel

It has been widely acknowledged, by filmmakers and critics alike, that the generation of auteur directors that immediately followed the New Wave (principally Jean Eustache, Philippe Garrel and Jacques Doillon, but also others including Chantal Akerman and Benoît Jacquot) were overwhelmingly influenced by two factors: first, by the ideals and aesthetics of the Nouvelle Vague itself; and second, by the revolutionary turmoil, utopian aspirations and subsequent disappointments surrounding the events of May 1968 in France. It is worth asking, therefore, what the nature of the relationship is between the French New Wave and May 1968. There is regrettably not room in this book to explore this question in the detail that it merits, but a few key points are important to establish at the outset of this chapter. As we saw in the Introduction to this book, most historians now regard the majority of the New Wave as apolitical at best and, in some cases, tainted by its associations with charismatic figures on the political right. It is therefore not realistic to see any meaningful influence of the New Wave over the more explicitly political strikes and demonstrations of May 1968 organized by Marxist trade unions. On the other hand, if the events of May are understood primarily as a spontaneous movement of self-expression begun by young people (the students of Parisian universities) and aimed at a general decalcification of French social life, then the model of New Wave cinema, in which young people test the boundaries of their newfound freedoms, can indeed be taken as an important precursor to the spirit of May.

In the world of French cinema specifically, two events are particularly associated with the spring of 1968, both of them involving a leading role for New Wave filmmakers. Firstly, a precursor to the insurrections of May occurred with the 'Affaire Langlois' that took place between February and April 1968 around the Cinémathèque Française. Although the Cinémathèque was largely state-funded, the Ministry of Culture grew increasingly impatient with its chaotic organization and account-keeping under the idiosyncratic leadership of Henri Langlois and eventually imposed a new director.[1] For the New Wave directors, Langlois's Cinémathèque was the sacrosanct space in which they had learned their craft and they took a central role in opposing the state-sanctioned changes, particularly as the plan involved discontinuing the screenings where so many of these young cinephiles had first met and shared their ideas. Alain Resnais presided over a Comité de Défense de la Cinémathèque while Truffaut orchestrated a campaign to persuade international directors to boycott the institution. Godard and Chabrol organized pickets outside the Cinémathèque, the rough police dispersal of which helped to turn public opinion against the patrician state, thus contributing to prepare the ground for the unrest of May.[2] It was during that turbulent month that the Cannes Film Festival was scheduled, as it is every year. It opened on 10 May 1968, a date that came to be known as the 'Night of the Barricades' in Paris, because of the makeshift blockades erected by rioting students. Under such circumstances, many felt that a glamorous festival on the Riviera was incongruous and inappropriate, and it was François Truffaut who travelled to Cannes to deliver an official communiqué calling for the closure of the festival in solidarity with the striking workers and students.[3] Although many jury members resigned immediately, a skeleton festival continued for over a week during which Truffaut, Godard and Jean-Pierre Léaud were involved in physical scuffles in an attempt to prevent the projection of *Peppermint Frappé*, a film that director Carlos Saura had withdrawn from competition in support of the protestors.[4]

While these may be relatively minor footnotes in the wider history of the May 1968 movement in France, for committed young cinephiles they demonstrated that the generation of the New Wave was, at worst, in sympathy with the ideals of May and, at best, could be seen as its standard bearers. Indeed, several New Wave directors made significant changes to their own filmmaking practice following the national soul-searching of that spring, changes that lasted for most of the subsequent decade. Most famously, Godard abandoned 'bourgeois' commercial filmmaking altogether, working with the collective Dziga Vertov Group to produce films with an explicitly revolutionary message for distribution to factories and universities. Jacques Rivette made some of his most challenging film experiments, full of improvised performance and narrative deconstruction. Agnès Varda made political documentaries in the United States and Cuba before returning to France to make a film about the women's movement, *L'une chante, l'autre pas* (1977). More generally, it might be argued that the young people who took to the streets in France in May 1968 were 'the children of the New

Wave and of Jean-Luc Godard'.[5] Antoine de Baecque argues that given its youthfulness and rapidity for much of the 1960s, the cinema in France may have played an important role in shaping the imaginary worlds of young people, somewhat as rock and pop music did for the youth of Britain and America. 'Jean-Luc Godard offered young people images of revolt, fragments of film with which to envisage a different world and attempt a revolution in black and white or vivid colour.'[6]

Jean Eustache: *La Maman et la Putain*

The cinema of Jean Eustache and in particular his magnum opus *La Maman et la Putain* (1973) have been frequently interpreted as a reaction to the legacy of May 1968 in French social and cultural life. Indeed, Jean Douchet has gone so far as to call *La Maman et la Putain* 'undeniably the only "May-'68" film in French cinema'.[7] The events of May 1968 caused such upheaval in France that they remained an essential point of reference for many years. For those artists, intellectuals and activists who were invested in the movement, whether ideologically or emotionally or both, the aftermath of '68 was often experienced as a disappointing comedown, a retreat from radical utopian ideals and a retrenchment in more traditional values and modes of social organization. May 1968 is referred to in this spirit in certain key dialogues (or, more properly, monologues) of *La Maman et la Putain*. At one point, the protagonist Alexandre (Jean-Pierre Léaud) recalls being in a crowded cafe one day in May when everyone began to cry because a tear gas canister had exploded nearby. At that moment, he says, 'Before my eyes, a hole opened up in reality' ('Sous mes yeux, une brèche s'était ouverte dans la réalité'). Since we learn nothing, in the film, about Alexandre's life prior to 1968, his experience of May can be taken as crucially formative. Seemingly disappointed by life in France post-'68, he does not work, refusing any active economic contribution to society and expressing contempt for those who do work, arguing that they are merely 'pretending'. Alexandre's break-up with his ex-girlfriend Gilberte (Isabelle Weingarten) is couched in similar terms. At the beginning of the film, Gilberte announces that she is planning to marry another man, who happens to be bourgeois, wealthy and respectable. Alexandre accuses her of betraying herself as well as him, suggesting that she is seeking to erase the memory of the past 'like France after the Liberation, like France after May '68'. The significance of his words is heightened by a cut from a two-shot to a close-up of Alexandre's face and he intones, 'You are picking yourself up like France after May '68, my love.'[8]

Elsewhere in the film, Alexandre says that he feels as though everything that has happened in the world in the last few years (so we might understand since 1968) is somehow 'directed against him'. He is dismissive of contemporary trends in music (Alexandre only listens to classical music and pre-war French *chansons*) and cinema (at one point he reads sardonically from a review of current political film release, Elio Petri's *La classe operaia va in paradiso* [1971]). Alexandre is out of time. As Alain Philippon puts it, he inhabits a kind of '"no man's time" between the ghosts of a past generation and the uncertain shadows of a future that is hard to imagine'.[9] His disdain for contemporary arts is accompanied by a sense that a certain cultural levelling has rendered it difficult to assess the value of any phenomenon. When Alexandre tells a friend (Jacques Renard) about a young woman he has briefly met, the friend insists that it is impossible to assume anything about her social background on the basis of her appearance. These days, he opines wistfully, everything is the same ('Tout est pareil'). This lament for the lack of distinction in the cultural life of the 1970s goes hand in hand with what various commentators have identified as a certain dandyism displayed by Alexandre and that reflects the behaviour of Eustache himself. Like Eustache, Alexandre dresses with a degree of ostentation, wearing his hair long and often accessorizing with dark glasses and more than one neck scarf. In addition, although basically without income, Alexandre enjoys demonstrating his financial largesse, for instance borrowing money in order to take Véronika (Françoise Lebrun) to an expensive restaurant, with the memorable line, 'Not having any money is no reason to eat poorly.'[10] One of the clearest manifestations of this dandyism is Alexandre's insistence on using the formal mode of address 'Vous' with his two lovers, Véronika and Marie (Bernadette Lafont), even though he uses the informal 'Tu' with everyone else, and the two women address each other as 'Tu'.

The use of 'Vous' appears as a deliberate rejection of the spirit of egalitarian solidarity established by May 1968 in favour of an almost aristocratic discourse. Faced with the indistinction that has become the cultural legacy of 1968, this return to an almost archaic mode of address appears as the only way to underline the uniqueness of the relation to the loved one.[11] Critics have wondered, however, whether this rather mannered behaviour may not signal a hypocritical abandonment of the values of May 1968, what Keith Reader calls 'an exhausted retreat into the style of reactionary nostalgia'.[12] Elsewhere, evoking the Liberation, Alexandre regrets that he never knew an era in which young women swooned before men in uniform. Today they are more likely to be impressed by sports cars and men in suits. But, as Susan Weiner points out, this can be seen as a typical strategy of reactionary politics: evoking an older (and more authoritarian) era as a defence against one's diminishing importance in the present. Alexandre's nostalgia is 'transparently a commentary on his own invisibility in late capitalist culture': in a context in which authority is conferred by education, employment and wealth, Alexandre, for all his rhetoric, is effectively worthless in the eyes of society.[13]

Jean Eustache's relationship to May 1968 is, therefore, a complex and ambiguous one: on the one hand, the events of May remain a vital point of reference in *La Maman et la Putain*, implying a turning point in French cultural life; on the other hand, the insidious sense of failure, cynicism and surrender that pervades *La Maman*, and other films by Eustache, suggests regret at the way in which the radical possibilities of May became corrupted and co-opted by the mechanisms of consumerism whereby the aspiration to egalitarianism gave way to a reality of homogenization. Eustache's reaction to this turn of events combines a potentially progressive critique of social conformism with a nostalgia for quasi-aristocratic values – Katia Kaupp detected in the film 'a flavour of the old right with a twist of Célinian resentment'.[14] This attitude – what the French often refer to as 'right-wing anarchism' – is familiar from the work of various New Wave filmmakers, most obviously Godard and Chabrol, although elements of it can sometimes be discerned, too, in Truffaut and Rohmer. As we saw in the Introduction to this book, during their formative years as critics in the 1950s, at *Cahiers du cinéma* and especially at *Arts*, the core New Wave gang was often close to the right-wing literary coterie known as the Hussards.

What, then, is the relationship of Jean Eustache to the French New Wave? Eustache grew up in a working-class family in the provincial town of Pessac in South-West France where the cinema provided one of his principal distractions and offered the vision of alternative lifestyles. Shortly after his arrival in Paris in 1958, Eustache married Jeanne Delos who, in 1961, began working as secretary at *Cahiers du cinéma*. It was through his wife, therefore, that Eustache initially came into contact with the critics and filmmakers of the New Wave in the offices of the *Cahiers*. Indeed, according to various contemporary accounts, Eustache's first short film, *Les Mauvaises Fréquentations* (1963), was financed by money that his wife 'borrowed' from the coffers of the famous magazine.[15] In addition to being around ten years younger than most of the *Cahiers* crowd, Eustache also came from a more modest background. Jean Douchet has described the disruption caused by 'the intrusion of this lout [*voyou*] into our petit-bourgeois world'[16] and notes that the world of the poor is evoked with more sympathy and understanding in Eustache's films than in those of the New Wave directors, most of whom came from comfortable or wealthy backgrounds.[17] Later in his career, Eustache benefited from the financial and practical support of New Wave filmmakers. Jean-Luc Godard paid for the film stock and sound mixing of Eustache's *Le Père Noël a les yeux bleus* (1967), using part of the budget for his own film *Masculin féminin* (1966),[18] while Luc Moullet produced *La Rosière de Pessac* (1968) and *Le Cochon* (1970).[19]

For some contemporary critics, *La Maman et la Putain* failed to measure up to the successes of the New Wave. Jean-Louis Bory found it 'old-fashioned' compared to recent works by Éric Rohmer or Jacques Rivette.[20] Some assumed that the film's unusual length (215 minutes) reflected an uncritical amassing of detail.[21] The extended gaze at his chosen material led some to see Eustache as engaged in a dull and rather naïve naturalism, far from the unpredictable stylistic quirks of the New Wave directors. But, as Jean Douchet suggests, the stylization employed by Eustache is 'of the kind that can't be seen', a lesson he suggests the director learned from Robert Bresson.[22] Alain Philippon concurs, proposing that if *La Maman et la Putain* can be seen as naturalist at all, it is in the manner of 'Rouch filmed by Bresson'.[23] Cinematic naturalism has typically been associated, at least since Italian neorealism, with the depiction of the lives of poor people, an approach that often implies a somewhat patronizing gaze by the bourgeois filmmaker. But, as mentioned above, Eustache's own experience of poverty allowed him to depict the lives of others with greater fraternity, and indeed he saw himself as a properly 'popular' filmmaker.[24] François Truffaut, of course, was also from a modest background but, as Jean Douchet observes, there is a lightness and an escapist quality to Truffaut's cinema whereas time weighs heavily on Eustache's characters, 'such that each change of shot is marked by gravity'.[25] For Colette Dubois, finally, Eustache's cinema is characterized not by a style – which would be too subject to the vagaries of fashion – but rather by 'the permanence of an *attitude* with regard to the subject filmed', an attitude of 'calculated distance, of care in the approach, of respect'.[26]

La Maman et la Putain's most obvious debt to the French New Wave probably lies in its casting. Eustache employs two actors irrevocably associated with New Wave directors: Bernadette Lafont, most famous for her roles in early films by Claude Chabrol, plays Marie while Jean-Pierre Léaud, the eponymous hero of Truffaut's Antoine Doinel series, incarnates Alexandre. The latter role was written for Léaud, and Susan Weiner suggests that the character of Alexandre draws significantly on the persona built up by the actor over the course of the Doinel series: like Antoine, Alexandre lacks 'professional and financial power' but still manages to 'charm and seduce', thanks to his physical energy and verbal dexterity.[27] Some critics see Léaud's performance style as 'fake' or 'false' ('Léaud joue faux', wrote Jean-Louis Bory[28]), and indeed, as Alain Philippon points out, this would not be a bad description of his method if it could be stripped of its pejorative connotations.[29] In a commentary on his work with the actors, Eustache remarked that Léaud constructs 'a veritable mise-en-scène' around himself and that, if his delivery of dialogue sometimes appears stilted or monotone, it is because his speech is always 'premeditated', 'the reading back of a thought that has already been recorded'.[30] Michel Marie argues that in *La Maman et la Putain*, Léaud attains a tragedy and a pathos that he had never before succeeded in expressing[31] and critics likewise found a new maturity and commitment in Bernadette Lafont's performance.[32] Eustache was undoubtedly well aware of his New Wave models when working with these actors, and he seems to have had a relationship of fairly explicit rivalry with them. Lafont reports that when, during the pre-production of *La Maman et la Putain*, she was offered the lead role in Truffaut's *Une belle fille comme moi* (1972), Eustache became very jealous, fearing that she would be 'completely ruined by this comedy'.[33]

The situation of *La Maman et la Putain* – in which one man is in love with two women and an uneasy friendship is established between the three, frequently disrupted by scenes of jealousy – has led critics to compare it to that of Truffaut's *Jules et Jim* (1962), in which the genders are reversed.[34] More generally, the focus on the intimate relations of couples – both physical and emotional, and largely taking place in the private spaces of apartments and bedrooms – is typical of the New Wave. *La Maman et la Putain* is sometimes taken as the model for a kind of 'chamber cinema' that was subsequently emulated by French filmmakers determined to make movies despite miniscule budgets (directors including Philippe Garrel and Jacques Doillon, but also the likes of Chantal Akerman and Benoît Jacquot).[35] But it is important to note how much this tendency also owes to the New Wave. For all their reputation of filming on the streets of Paris, New Wave directors – and most especially Godard – often set their most important scenes precisely in bedrooms and apartments and used them to examine in detail the developing or declining intimate relation between a couple.

Various elements of film style, and a variety of more or less explicit cultural references, also bespeak Eustache's debt to the New Wave. The use of music in *La Maman et la Putain*, exclusively diegetic, is unusual in allowing songs to be played in full. This has its most dramatic effect near the end of the film when Marie listens to Édith Piaf's 'Les Amants de Paris' alone after Alexandre has taken Véronika home, eventually burying her face in her hands at the realization that she is now excluded from the couple of Parisian lovers evoked by Piaf. It has been remarked that the use of singers from the 1930s (Piaf, Fréhel, Damia) links Eustache's film to the classic French realist cinema of, for instance, Jean Renoir, Marcel Pagnol or Sacha Guitry.[36] But, while songs often featured in this cinema, they were commonly performed by characters in the diegesis and thus contributed to the spectacle of the film. Including full-length songs from a diegetic source (radio or record player) but that are *not* performed 'live' is unusual in cinema because it interrupts the narrative flow. Sometimes diegetic music may, so to speak, become non-diegetic as it accompanies a montage of images or action from another space. But it is very unusual simply to arrest narrative development long enough to show characters doing nothing other than listening to music. One notable example, however – and another sign of Eustache's debt to the New Wave – is the scene in Godard's *Une femme est une femme* (1961) in which Anna Karina listens to a Charles Aznavour song in a cafe.

Une femme est une femme is also referenced in *La Maman et la Putain* when Alexandre makes his bed by holding the sheets up in front of him then falling forward on to the mattress. When Véronika expresses surprise,

Alexandre explains that he once saw it done in a film. The reference is not specified but devotees of the New Wave will remember Anna Karina performing the same trick in *Une femme est une femme*. 'That's what films are for', Alexandre explains in a famous line, 'To teach you how to live, how to make a bed.' Some critics have questioned the extent of Eustache's debt to the New Wave, pointing out that his film style – like that of Garrel – reaches much further back to connect with silent cinema, 'a power to the image that comes from primitive cinema'.[37] It is striking that, with the exception of Bernadette Lafont, Eustache's actresses (Françoise Lebrun and Isabelle Weingarten in *La Maman et la Putain*) have an almost anachronistic look reminiscent of silent film heroines, their round pale faces emphasized by dark make-up around their eyes and mouth somewhat in the manner of Lilian Gish or Mary Pickford. In addition, rejecting the sometimes frenetic editing and camera movement of Godard and Truffaut, Eustache favours simple, static camera set-ups, often placing the camera more or less directly facing the actors for close-ups, two-shots and simple shot/counter-shot formations.[38] While these allusions to silent cinema in Eustache are certainly real, we should not lose sight of the fact that the New Wave, too, made frequent, affectionate reference to the techniques of silent cinema. The bed-making example from *Une femme est une femme* cited above can itself be seen as a nod towards the tradition of visual gags in burlesque cinema. Godard and Truffaut famously revived editing and camera techniques such as irises and masking that had been out of fashion in cinema for decades, while Agnès Varda included an entire pastiche of a silent film in *Cléo de 5 à 7* (1961). Godard's tendency, discussed above, to film characters in the quiet appreciation of other works of art – Anna Karina listening to Aznavour or watching *La Passion de Jeanne d'Arc* (1928) in *Vivre sa vie* (1962) – allows him to train his camera in close-up on silently emoting faces in a way that is obviously a tribute to an earlier era of cinema.

La Maman et la Putain thus owes a lot to the French New Wave in terms of its approach to its subject and its film style. But how do the gender politics of Eustache's film compare to those of his New Wave forebears? The film is, as we have seen, centred around Alexandre and his relations with not two but three women: the early scenes concentrate on his desperate attempts to win back Gilberte and, at one point, he admits to Véronika that she entered his life at the precise moment when, in despair over Gilberte, he had decided to fall in love with the first woman he met. This type of remark implies that women are almost interchangeable for Alexandre,[39] an impression augmented by the similarity in appearance between Gilberte and Véronika, as well as a third woman whom Alexandre half-heartedly attempts to charm while waiting for Véronika, and who is played by Marinka Matuszewski, the real-life model for Véronika in this largely autobiographical film. Alexandre's double standards are comically laid bare by the film: he has no apparent scruples about living with Marie while courting Véronika and at the same time trying to get back together with Gilberte; yet he becomes furious when Marie sees other men, provoking an argument after a man named Philippe telephones the apartment and later walking out of a dinner party in a childish sulk when he learns that this same Philippe is invited.

Alexandre raises hypocrisy to a kind of ethical stance. At one point, when Véronika remarks that he doesn't seem very at ease with himself, he asserts that people who consider it important to be in agreement with themselves (*'être d'accord avec soi-même'*) are altogether 'bovine'. Alexandre is essentially unable to make up his mind, which is why, as he admits, he has 'never left anyone'; but the inevitable corollary is that 'people are always leaving me'. As Natacha Thiéry puts it, Alexandre is unable to choose the object of his desire, no doubt so that he won't have to undergo the pain of losing it.[40] Colette Dubois also notes that Alexandre seems, above all, interested in 'deferring the moment of choice', and that, if he is apparently unable to leave Marie, it is because this would mean leaving the indefinitely suspended moment of their intimacy: 'To leave Marie would be to leave the studio, to leave the film, to return to the world, to choose.'[41] Yet the film gradually moves towards what Susan Weiner sees as an unmasking of Alexandre's 'neediness and insecurity'.[42] Jill Forbes interprets Alexandre as basically a fantasist, living in a world that effectively recognizes no existence for women outside the context of male desire. It is 'a world in which women fall for men at the drop of a hat and stay with them despite – and often in proportion to – their mistreatment'; in short, concludes Forbes, this is 'the pornographic imagination run riot'.[43]

While there is perhaps some truth to this assessment in the early scenes of the film, it is to reckon without the increasing emasculation of Alexandre as the narrative progresses. And the rather misleading reference to pornography obscures a less obvious but nonetheless potent influence over *La Maman et la Putain*: the cinema of Éric Rohmer. Alain Philippon, who notes that Eustache was present on the set of Rohmer's *La Boulangère de Monceau* (1963), sees the older director as a more important influence over Eustache than either Godard or Truffaut.[44] Eustache's sound recordist, Jean-Pierre Ruh, argues that the atmosphere of 'veracity' achieved with direct sound was 'the most important thing in Eustache's cinema' and suggests that this may, in fact, have influenced the later work of Rohmer.[45] The crudity of language and sentiments in Eustache's work may seem a world apart from Rohmer's uniquely chaste films, yet both directors depict situations in which characters paint themselves into a corner through their self-deluding verbal pirouettes. *La Maman et la Putain* in particular is reminiscent of Rohmer's *Six Moral Tales* in which male protagonists try to convince themselves that they are sophisticated and irresistible seducers when, in fact, their behaviour often reveals their very conventional social aspirations as well as their complete misreading of women's intentions.

But, if *La Maman et la Putain*'s treatment of gender relations reaches back to the New Wave and, via Rohmer, to older traditions of representing and analysing love and sex, Eustache's film is also very much of its time in its depiction of 'open' relationships. As Francis Vanoye remarks, the couple, in Eustache's work, is regarded as desirable, since it marks the realization of the loving union, but also as contemptible, since it implies mindless conformity to social convention,[46] a situation which goes some way towards explaining Alexandre's hesitation in his relationships. As we have seen, Alexandre and Marie live together while each pursuing relations with other people, and many of the film's most memorable scenes document the difficulties of this non-monogamous lifestyle, each partner either pretending to be indifferent about the other's conquests or pleased on his/her behalf, while jealousy simmers just beneath this polite surface and tempers are short whenever other lovers are evoked. Vanoye suggests that, in the wake of 1968 and its rhetoric of the liberation of desire, this kind of open relationship became almost compulsory for a certain sector of society for whom the traditional married couple was dismissed as an example of the tyranny of bourgeois morality. *La Maman et la Putain* implies a situation in which non-monogamy has become a new doxa, in many ways just as inflexible and damaging as the old.[47] As Alain Philippon puts it: 'The mistake was in believing that political slogans [*des mots d'ordre*] could regulate the disorder of feelings.'[48]

If the film's attitude towards non-monogamy thus appears deeply ambivalent, how should we understand its depiction of Véronika who, after all, is presented as an unusually sexually 'liberated' young woman? Véronika talks openly about her very active sex life and her multiple partners, at one point claiming, 'I can fuck anybody.'[49] She is not remotely bashful when it comes to discussing sex or having it, unlike Alexandre who is too self-conscious to accept her offer of open-air sex by the Seine. In many ways, Véronika can be interpreted as a strong and positive female presence in the film, if only because she gradually loosens Alexandre's discursive – and, by extension, perspectival – stranglehold over the narrative. This begins with a series of counter-shots of Alexandre's interlocutor which serve subtly to undermine the authority of his monologues.[50] As the film goes on, Alexandre is ultimately reduced to silence by Véronika,[51] in what Keith Reader calls a 'usurpation of phallogocentrism'.[52] At the same time, however, there is a repeated sense, in the film, that Véronika's sexuality is not simply the fact of a young woman enjoying her body and her freedom; instead, it is presented as something slightly pathological. Alexandre and Marie agree that Véronika is 'a little lost' ('*un peu paumée*'); her repeated tales of seduction at the hands of doctors and interns in the hospital where she works imply that she is being exploited by older men; and sometimes her sexual activity seems less an expression of desire than of displaced anger: asked what she did with her afternoon when Alexandre wouldn't keep her company, Véronika replies, 'I went to fuck or get fucked.' This narrative undermining of Véronika's sexual freedom is reinforced in her long, tearful monologue at the end of the film in which she insists she is not interested in sex, which she describes as 'shitty' and 'sordid', and says that the only beautiful thing in the world is a couple who love each so much they want to create a child in their image. This, insists Véronika, is the only condition under which love is 'valid', and any couple who does not want this is not really a couple, 'c'est une merde'. As Keith Reader neatly summarizes this scene, Véronika '"twin-tracks" a discourse of disillusioned sexual liberation with one of Catholic orthodoxy on sex and procreation, endlessly attempting to drive away the *maman/ putain* dichotomy that endlessly forces its way back into her vocabulary'.[53]

Given the trajectory of Véronika in the narrative, it would certainly be possible to read *La Maman et la Putain* as an anti-feminist film that rejects women's sexual freedom and re-inscribes the primacy of marriage and children as social goals. Indeed, Jean-Louis Bory condemned it as 'the most misogynist film imaginable'.[54] For Marie-Odile Briot, the fact that Alexandre's ex, Gilberte, is revealed to have had an abortion, while Véronika ends the film by announcing her pregnancy, can be read as a metaphorical reversal of the gains of women's liberation.[55] Others have argued that Véronika's final monologue can be read as an inchoate feminist rejection of the discourse of sexual liberation, of the kind that would be set out in subsequent years by the likes of Sheila Jeffreys, on the grounds that it ultimately serves the interests of acquisitive male desire by compelling women to be sexually promiscuous or face social stigma.[56] For Martine Pierquin, with this speech Véronika is 'rebelling against a new form of sexual exploitation masquerading as emancipation'.[57] The uncertainty over the film's position in relation to these questions is augmented by the deeply ambiguous final scene of *La Maman et la Putain*. Jean-François Buiré has remarked that the endings of films by Eustache are 'never satisfying',[58] and Reader notes of *La Maman* that it does not so much end as *stop*, 'almost as if it had run out of footage'.[59] In the final scene, Alexandre accompanies Véronika home whereupon she announces that she may be pregnant; he asks her to marry him and she accepts. However, what might, from this description, appear to be a traditional romantic conclusion is fatally undermined by its presentation. Véronika is drunk and abusive, telling Alexandre 'You disgust me'. His initial response is to leave, before returning and yelling, in aggressive desperation, 'Do you love me?! Will you marry me?!' Véronika responds with hysterical laughter before accepting, then promptly announces she is going to be sick and orders Alexandre not to look at her. The camera focuses on Alexandre as he sinks to the floor, panting, before the credits roll. The prospect of marriage and children, as presented in this scene, is far from the 'beautiful' image evoked in Véronika's preceding monologue; instead, they imply a resignation or exhausted surrender, encapsulated in the image of vomiting (which almost seems to suggest, following Reader, that the film has *had enough of itself*). Certainly *La Maman et la Putain* has none of the happy futurity of the traditional romantic movie ending since, as Susan Weiner rightly asserts, 'the married life of Alexandre and Véronika is simply unimaginable on screen'.[60]

Jacques Doillon: *Les Doigts dans la tête*

Released in 1974, *Les Doigts dans la tête* was Jacques Doillon's second feature but, following the collective political work *L'An 01* of the previous year (written by the comic artist Gébé, based on his own *bande dessinée*, and containing sequences directed by Alain Resnais and Jean Rouch), *Les Doigts* can be considered Doillon's first truly personal *film d'auteur*, one that contains the germ of his entire career.[61] Like *La Maman et la Putain*, *Les Doigts dans la tête* is very much a film of its time since its narrative is based around two ideas, or social phenomena, that were 'in the air' in the early 1970s: so-called free love and open relationships, on the one hand, and, on the other hand, the tense labour relations that existed in France in the aftermath of the social movements of May 1968. Christophe (Christophe Soto), a young baker, is going out with the young woman, Rosette (Roselyne Vuillaume), who serves customers in the bakery where he works. When he meets an outgoing young Swedish girl, Liv (Ann Zacharias), Christophe defends his right to pursue a relationship with her as well, impatiently telling Rosette, 'We're not married.' Liv's Swedishness evokes stereotypes of the advanced liberalism and sexual promiscuity assumed to pertain in Scandinavia, and Christophe discovers she lives in a sort of commune in which a young woman is not embarrassed to take a shower while a boy she doesn't know urinates in the same bathroom. Despite being a year or two younger than Christophe and his friends, Liv comes across as 'twice as experienced' and seems to find some of their behaviour a little conventional, not to say parochial: when Rosette announces that she spends most of her free time visiting her family in Bourges, Liv declares this to be 'sad'. As in *La Maman et la Putain*, Rosette feels obliged to put up with her rival for fear of appearing old-fashioned yet suffers acute jealousy; at one point, when Christophe and Liv make love in a bed next to her, she experiences an anxiety attack in which she is unable to breathe, an evident expression of her emotional distress.

This narrative of liberal sexuality becomes linked to the question of labour relations when Christophe is late for work after first spending the night with Liv. When his boss summarily dismisses him, Christophe decides to protest by occupying his room in the building above the bakery and the two young women join him in solidarity, along with Christophe's friend Léon (Olivier Bousquet), thereby establishing a curious, and increasingly tense, *ménage-à-quatre*. Several details of this scenario are typical of the post-'68 era in France and in French cinema: Christophe's meetings with the union delegate from the CGT (Pierre Fabien) who enumerates his rights; the willingness of these young people to mount a symbolic protest against the injustice of management (Rosette herself goes on strike in support of Christophe's cause); and their fear of reprisals (at one point, hearing noises on the roof above, they imagine a police raid may be in progress). As René Prédal points out, what is also new to the post-'68 context is the attitude of these young people to work: their protest is more than a request for improved working conditions but less than a call for socialist revolution. It is rather, as in May 1968 itself, an expression of their dissatisfaction at the idea of living to work and the marking of a deliberate halt in order to try and think through alternatives.[62] As Christophe puts it at one point, 'I want to start living. I'm not going to spend my whole life in a bakehouse.' Unlike *La Maman et la Putain*, though, this questioning of the role and ideology of work is not accompanied, in Doillon's film, by a contempt for active members of society. Instead, as René Prédal puts it, *Les Doigts dans la tête* depicts 'the fragile awakening of a class consciousness that is within reach of ordinary people'.[63] One critic even found the film to evoke the 'populist intimacy' of 1930s French films from the era of the Popular Front.[64]

Upon its release, *Les Doigts dans la tête* was associated with a set of other contemporary French films that were loosely grouped together under the label of a 'new naturalism' (*Le Nouveau Naturel*). While some critics may have been briefly tempted to label this trend a 'new New Wave',[65] the majority of the films and filmmakers associated with this label were, as Prédal points out, quickly forgotten.[66] Not unlike Eustache, Doillon tends to favour simple camera set-ups and unadorned locations that minimize the distraction from the performers (a further instance of the 'chamber cinema' evoked in the preceding section) and, in the 1970s in particular, he worked with many unknown or non-professional actors (although, in his later career, he would collaborate with many prominent names from French cinema and theatre). To an extent, this style has been born of economic necessity, since Doillon has kept up a very regular production schedule since the beginning of his career, invariably investing all profits from his films into subsequent projects. Thus the relative success of *L'An 01* facilitated the production of *Les Doigts dans la tête* but on a low budget using non-professional actors and black-and-white super 16 mm film stock, frugal choices that Doillon would make again in the future when more generous funding was not forthcoming.[67] It would be a mistake, however, to associate Doillon with a kind of semi-improvised, shot-from-the-hip naturalism. It is certainly true that the dialogues and performances of *Les Doigts* appear much more believable than the stylized monologues of *La Maman et la Putain*, but they are not, for all that, the result of improvisation. Doillon has developed a reputation for recording multiple takes of each scene, often as many as fifteen, and for being very precise and demanding in his direction of actors. Indeed, Nicolas Livecchi reports that Doillon always budgets for a large amount of film stock in order to facilitate these additional takes, even when the otherwise limited budgets restrict the availability of machinery, crew members, etc.[68] The repeated takes allow Doillon and his performers to eliminate that which is false or redundant in a scene and to focus in on the essential. They also require the actor to abandon his preconceived ideas about a character and arrive at a final representation that combines his sense of the character with that of the director.[69] The results can appear deceptively spontaneous and unrehearsed: contemporary critics noted that the performers 'never appear to be acting'.[70] But, as Prédal remarks, Doillon is less concerned with capturing a raw reality than with honing the emotional truth of characters, situations and faces,[71] and this tends to involve a degree of theatrical artifice as in the somewhat contrived situation of the four young people in Les Doigts dans la tête who lock themselves in a room together.[72] It is the theatricality of this situation, notes Prédal, that allows the film to move away from the sociological document (about the professional and sexual struggles of young people in France in the early 1970s) and focus instead on the psychological complexity of their emotional reality. Thus, we witness the largely unspoken anguish of Christophe's hesitation between two women, concealed beneath his easy charm and bravado; Rosette's internal conflict between her desire to hold on to Christophe and her attempts to preserve her dignity and self-respect; Liv's well-intentioned, but somewhat naïve and disingenuous attempt to make the peace within the group without ever quite grasping the extent of her own responsibility for the conflict; and finally Léon's simmering bitterness and anger at the casual cruelty with which his friend courts two women while they seemingly refuse to recognize his own status and feelings as a desiring adult. François Truffaut, in an article on Les Doigts dans la tête, noted that the lesson of Italian Neorealism and the French New Wave is that naturalism for its own sake in the cinema dates as quickly as news reports; only those films concerned to develop a style of their own may resist the passage of the years.[73] It is the attention with which Doillon seeks out the emotional truth in the faces, voices and bodies of his young performers that guarantees the undiminished freshness of Les Doigts dans la tête after four decades.

It is nonetheless this appearance of naturalism that perhaps most immediately distances Doillon from the New Wave filmmakers. Films of the French New Wave often included elements of naturalism and almost documentary-realism, but these would typically be inserted alongside other stylistic quirks that served to distance the spectator from the events shown (Godard) or to create jarring, often humorous shifts in tone (Truffaut). Elsewhere in the New Wave, elements of naturalism were combined with carefully contrived narratives that undermined the credibility of the world on screen (Rivette). If anything, Doillon's unadorned style is perhaps closest to that of Éric Rohmer among New Wave filmmakers, yet Doillon does not share Rohmer's moralism. What Doillon inherits from the New Wave,

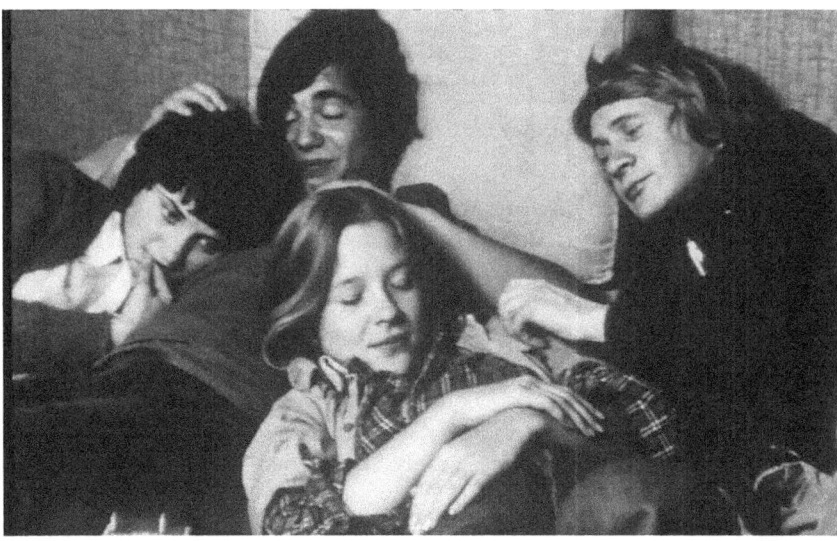

FIGURE 1.1 *The* ménage à quatre *in* Les Doigts dans la tête *(1974): Roselyne Vuillaume, Christophe Soto, Ann Zacharias and Olivier Bousquet. Courtesy MK2.*

finally, can perhaps be summarized in three points. First, Doillon adopts a production model made popular by the likes of Godard and Chabrol and, like those directors, his principal aim seems to be to continue making films as regularly as possible by using the income from one film to launch a subsequent project with minimal delay. To this end, Doillon, like many of the New Wave filmmakers, set up his own production company – Lola Films – as soon as he was able to do so and which he uses to finance those personal projects that attract less interest from more mainstream production companies. Second, Doillon shares with Truffaut an interest in depicting and exploring on film the lives of children and young people, a tendency established with *Les Doigts dans la tête* and his next film, a commission to direct an adaptation of Joseph Joffo's popular novel *Un sac de billes* about the experiences of two Jewish children during the Occupation (the film was released in 1975). Finally, and perhaps most importantly, Doillon shares with Jacques Rivette a certain method of working with actors. Although very demanding, neither has the tyrannical reputation with actors sometimes associated with Godard, for instance. In both Doillon and Rivette, there is an openness to the actor that tends to include the performer as a full participant in the creative process, building the character, and often the narrative, in collaboration. In this sense, the encounter on the film set – what happens when actor A meets actor B in a particular setting – effectively becomes the subject of the film, since the unpredictable reactions and personal responses of each performer are incorporated into the film.

Philippe Garrel: *Elle a passé tant d'heures sous les sunlights*

Philippe Garrel has become a semi-legendary figure in post-New Wave French cinema, even though (or perhaps because) the dozen or so films he made in the first decade of his directorial career are rarely seen. Like Eustache and Doillon, Garrel has demonstrated a single-minded commitment to making films that pays little heed to the industry's usual (above all financial) requirements for a career in cinema. Garrel directed his first feature film *Marie pour mémoire* (1967), aged just nineteen. The film was awarded the Grand Prix at the Festival de Hyères amid controversy between jury, journalists and public. Garrel continued to make films throughout the 1970s, despite working, for the most part, effectively without a producer or a distributor: the films were largely self-funded or made with money borrowed from friends or admirers and screened only at the Cinémathèque or in a single cinema (La Pagode) that supported Garrel's work.[74] Sally Shafto has pointed out that the 'incomplete credits for [Garrel's] early films stress all the more his individual authorship and creative genius',[75] somewhat in the manner of Jean-Luc Godard who, in the credits for *Bande à part* (1964), famously defined his own contribution with the immodest title 'JEAN LUC CINÉMA GODARD'. It is nonetheless true that, in the depths of the 1970s, Garrel, in addition to being the director of his films, was also the producer, the scriptwriter, the director of photography and camera operator, and the editor. During that same period he continued to make films even without the most basic technical capabilities, filming without sound and without new film stock. As Philippe Azoury remarks, that Garrel continued steadily to work in these conditions for a decade without any clear prospect of them improving is a testament to his extraordinary tenacity and dedication.[76] Like Eustache, Garrel seems to raise poverty to a virtue, in what Shafto identifies as an almost biblical respect for austerity, no doubt inherited from Garrel's background in a bohemian, artistic family (his father was an actor, having begun in the theatre, and his godfather a puppeteer).[77] Poverty becomes a kind of ethical stance for Garrel, what Anne-Marie Faux calls 'an absolute moral commitment', which has seen him consistently refuse to accept funding from a state that he sees as politically and ethically anathema.[78] Garrel comes across, in this first decade of his career, as a kind of 'monk of cinema'[79] or, in the words of Joshka Schidlow, he is the sort of *poète maudit* for whom the very notion of success appears suspect.[80]

The sense of Garrel as a kind of martyr is linked not only to his poverty and his refusal to compromise his artistic integrity but also to well-known accounts of his drug use – several films of the late 1960s and 1970s are understood to have been conceived or made under the influence of LSD. As a result of this drug use, during the production of *La Cicatrice intérieure*

(1972) Garrel was arrested and hospitalized in Italy where he was subjected to electroshock therapy.[81] In addition, during this period, Garrel famously had turbulent and destructive relationships with the actresses who appeared in his films, in particular Nico, who was addicted to heroin, and Jean Seberg, who committed suicide by overdose of barbiturates in 1979. While Garrel's filmmaking in the 1970s thus reflects a difficult, and sometimes tragic, personal life, it can also be read as a reflection of France in the years after May 1968.

Garrel began making films around 1968 – indeed his footage shot on the streets of Paris during the events of May, *Actua I*, has achieved legendary status as the greatest film produced during the movement but subsequently lost – and the experience of May was a formative one for him and for his cinema, just as it was for Eustache. Garrel's persistence with his singular filmmaking project, his refusal to compromise or collaborate with the mainstream industry, can be interpreted as a fidelity to the spirit of '68, as well as to the idealism of adolescence.[82] As Philippe Azoury comments, there is, in the films of the 1970s, a retrenchment or turning within 'a vitrified contemplation' that resonates with the sense of disappointment, betrayal and isolation following the defeat of the ideals of May.[83] After he emerged from this singularly withdrawn cinema in the 1980s, Garrel would frequently make (more or less oblique) reference to May 1968 in his films: most famously in *Les Amants réguliers* (2005) but also, for instance, in the character of *Le Vent de la nuit* (1999), who evokes his memories of the time only reluctantly and in evident pain, and who will take his own life at the end of the film. In *Elle a passé tant d'heures sous les sunlights* (1985), the film we will discuss at length in this section, Garrel, who appears in the film, asks another man if he has read Daniel Cohn-Bendit's book about May 1968, *Le Grand Bazar*.[84] He adds, 'He's a journalist now', as though to condemn the recuperation of revolutionary ideals by the industry of spectacle. The same sentiment is conveyed in the subsequent scene in which Jacques Bonnaffé, in the voice of a radio announcer commenting on a horse race or a football match, describes a scene that resonates with memories of 1968, of police chasing insurrectionaries who try to take refuge in apartment buildings.

Despite the sense of drug-induced torpor and post-euphoric comedown that surrounds Garrel's films of the 1970s, there is, paradoxically, in this period, an evident desire to make films quickly (hence the surprisingly high rate of productivity), one consequence of which is that, however abstract, poetic and out-of-time some of these films may appear, with hindsight they can be viewed as 'eyewitness accounts of an era'.[85] What's more, it is this method of self-reliance forged in the hardship of the 1970s, a method that involves shooting in a single take in order to save film, shooting in sequence and editing concurrently with the filming (in case the production should collapse at any moment), that has allowed Garrel to continue working quickly and cheaply and, above all, independently, now that he has joined a more mainstream film industry.[86] Still, Garrel cautions that an artistic career is necessarily 'subject to contingencies' and that we should always be wary of conflating the rhythms of creation with the artificial rhythms of a marketplace avid for new product.[87] Probably the only model in French cinema (perhaps in world cinema) for Garrel's approach to filmmaking – for its combination of speed, originality and independence – is that of Jean-Luc Godard. Garrel has openly and repeatedly acknowledged Godard's decisive influence over him and his work. He relates how it was upon seeing *Alphaville* (1965) at the age of sixteen that he discovered his vocation as a filmmaker, realizing, in the same moment, his inevitable marginality within the film industry.[88] For instance, Garrel argues that Godard found a unique solution for filmmaking which was to design his shots, plan his narrative and communicate dialogue to actors as he arrived on set each morning, thereby managing to avoid the calcification of his cinema into preset forms and modes.[89] A reference to Godard appears in *Elle a passé tant d'heures sous les sunlights* when Bonnaffé, in voice-over, remarks that Godard succeeded in bringing the whole history of classical painting together with Picasso, an allusion to *Passion* (1982). Garrel has also suggested that *Sunlights*, as a film about filmmaking, is closer to *Passion* than to Truffaut's *La Nuit américaine* (1973), because he is concerned to show 'the workers of cinema'.[90] Sally Shafto goes as far as to suggest that Garrel sets himself up as a Christ-like figure in relation to Godard's status as God-the-father, 'rewriting the rules of cinema';[91] the idea might seem far-fetched, but is consonant with the martyrdom of Garrel's self-representation, indicated above. At the same time, however, Garrel displays an ongoing solidarity with his peers from the post-New Wave of the 1970s – Eustache, Doillon and also Chantal Akerman – all of whom are evoked in *Elle a passé tant d'heures sous les sunlights*.

Garrel states that this solidarity with fellow artists who are 'making cinema in impossible conditions' became more conscious after the death of Jean Eustache who (he insists) was killed by 'the system'.[92] Garrel goes to visit Akerman at one point in the film (her voice is heard but no image seen) and later talks at length with Doillon about the film underway; meanwhile, Eustache is evoked in an aside, referred to as a 'genius' and *La Maman et la Putain* held up as a masterpiece comparable to *La Règle du jeu* (1939).

As may already have become clear, Garrel, like Eustache, works with what, in the literary field, has come to be known as 'autofiction', the tight weaving together of fiction and autobiography in such a way that it becomes difficult to separate what is real from what is imaginary. Garrel takes this approach a step further than Eustache, however, in that the performers in his films are often the same people who have played a role in the dramas of his life. Thus Garrel himself frequently appears in his films, alongside his father Maurice and his son Louis; he has also regularly filmed his lover Nico and the mother of his children Brigitte Sy. The basic narrative situation of *Elle a passé tant d'heures sous les sunlights* can be seen to reflect Garrel's passage between these two women, from a drug-addicted former lover to a new partner with whom he fathers a son (Louis Garrel was born in 1983).[93] The Nico character, played by Anne Wiazemsky, is named Christa (Nico's birth name) and is seen, in a couple of condensed scenes, under the influence of, and undergoing withdrawal from, heroin. The film also includes a lengthy montage sequence soundtracked by one of Nico's most famous songs, 'All Tomorrow's Parties', a sequence which depicts the loss of a woman since it condenses into a few shots scenes of Marie (Mireille Perrier) meeting, embracing and driving away with Lou (Lou Castel) while the (unnamed) Jacques Bonnaffé character runs helplessly after the car.

As Philippe Azoury remarks, however, if the narrative of *Sunlights* is based on real events, the different people, episodes and times evoked in the film coexist and overlap in a confusing way that suggests the present continues to be inhabited by the past.[94] Azoury further suggests that it is often Garrel's most nakedly autobiographical films (like *Sunlights*) that have the most complicated and 'undateable' time frame.[95] The paradoxical result is that Garrel's cinema is built almost exclusively around memory and introspection while refusing simply to look backwards, instead re-inscribing past events with the urgency of the present.[96] As we remarked above regarding the films of the 1970s, however much Garrel's films may sometimes come across as self-absorbed and withdrawn from the mainstream of society, they nonetheless appear distinctly of their time, like documentary portraits of people and places.

The confusion of fact and fiction, past and present, is found repeatedly in *Sunlights* and becomes increasingly tangled as the film goes on. For instance, when Marie commits suicide at the end of the film, a character whose role had appeared roughly equivalent to that of Brigitte Sy in Garrel's life is revealed also to contain elements of Jean Seberg (Garrel notes a principle endorsed by Proust according to which, for a female character to be convincing, she should be based on two different women[97]). Garrel himself is effectively doubled in the film, represented by Bonnaffé, whose character breaks up with Christa and fathers a child with Marie, but also appearing more or less as himself in certain scenes; indeed, it is unclear whether the Garrel who appears on screen should be taken as another character in the fiction or as the film's real-life director providing a kind of meta-commentary on the work. *Sunlights* thus incessantly confuses the fictional space of the film narrative with the factual arena of Garrel's biography, but also with the present reality of the film's shooting. For instance, having seen Anne Wiazemsky as Christa breaking up with the Bonnaffé character and withdrawing from heroin, we subsequently see her, out of character, discussing her role with Garrel. Wiazemsky protests that it is cruel and inappropriate to make her play a character who is 'a million miles away from me' and, what's more, 'a very unpleasant woman', and, although Nico's (stage) name is never mentioned, Wiazemsky and Garrel evoke verifiable incidents from the singer's life such as an apparently racist assault on a black woman in New York whose corrective cosmetic surgery had to be paid for by Andy Warhol.[98] As Philippe Azoury points out, the choice of Wiazemsky to play a character based on Nico is indeed counter-intuitive given their lack of physical resemblance and their very different backgrounds; however, the choice can perhaps be explained by the fact that Wiazemsky was Godard's partner for some of the same years that Nico was with Garrel and could therefore relate to the idea of living with a demanding and uncompromising filmmaker.[99]

The uncertainty of the relation between fact and fiction is heightened in those scenes featuring Garrel's filmmaking friends. Jacques Doillon appears in a lengthy series of scenes towards the end of the film in which he engages in apparently personal discussions with Garrel, talking notably about their desire to film their own children, sometimes against the wishes of the child's mother. Doillon's reference to his daughter Lola and his film *La Femme qui pleure* (1979) give this exchange a kind of seal of authenticity. But when Garrel subsequently confesses to Doillon that he is falling in love with Mireille Perrier, the actress who plays Marie in *Sunlights*, is this a kind of true public declaration to Perrier or rather a contrived attempt to add another layer to the complicated interpenetration of fiction and reality? Similarly, when Garrel goes to see Chantal Akerman and she asks where he got the money to make his film, Garrel replies that he made the money by dealing heroin. Here, then, Garrel appears to use a documentary-like scene to introduce an element of fiction, unless, as Azoury comments, this is a kind of double bluff whereby Garrel exploits the 'enormity' of the situation in order to confess an unspeakable truth.[100] This episode is further complicated by the fact that, in the preceding scene, Garrel is seen in a car at night with Lou Castel, hiding nervously from passing police. Immediately after the police have passed, however, Lou begins to tie a tourniquet around his arm as though to inject drugs while Garrel's panicked voice cries 'Cut! Cut!' Scenes like these drive home the significance of the juxtaposition and interpenetration of life and cinema in *Sunlights*. If only we could control life like we control a film, this scene seems to say, by yelling 'Cut!' when things get out of hand. The film documents the way in which Garrel (and/or his surrogate, Bonnaffé) seeks to do just that by transforming elements of life into cinema. But in the process, cinema risks destroying life by injuring those we love with its indiscreet gaze (Garrel telephones 'Christa' at one point and tells her 'I'm going to do this film without you because I love you and cinema destroys life, you know?'). Garrel has admitted that Nico 'would quite rightly reproach me for making a film about our life instead of trying to make her more comfortable'.[101] Cinema is used as a means of corralling, controlling life; in the process cinema destroys life. And yet the lesson of Garrel's cinema – like that of Godard, of Eustache or of Doillon – is that cinema is only truly cinema when it *surprises us with life*, when something or someone on the set or in front of the camera betrays a moment of truth that could not have been scripted, precisely when cinema enables us to see life more acutely. This interlocking spiral of life and cinema that is central to Garrel's work – and most thoroughly explored in *Elle a passé tant d'heures sous les sunlights* – is a key lesson learned from Jean-Luc Godard and the French New Wave. It is the subject, for instance, of a celebrated text by Godard entitled 'Pierrot mon ami' in which he compares the real and the imaginary in cinema to the two sides (which are at the same time only one) of a Möbius strip.[102]

We have established, then, that Garrel's understanding of the relations between cinema and life, Garrel's living of cinema and filming of life, is largely inherited from his admiration for Godard and reflects, for instance, Godard's own on-screen use of his life partners (Anna Karina, Anne Wiazemsky, Anne-Marie Miéville) or his tendency, since the late 1970s, to shoot most of his films in the immediate environs of his own home on the shores of Lake Geneva. At a more microscopic level, however, how does Garrel's cinema appropriate or extend filmmaking techniques, stylistic tropes and methods of narrative organization from Godard or the rest of the New Wave? First, at the level of narrative structure – as was already implied by the discussion of autofiction above – Garrel's films, and especially *Elle a passé tant d'heures sous les sunlights*, tend to be very disordered (Adrian Martin calls the film 'forbiddingly convoluted'[103]). *Sunlights* contains a half-buried narrative frame about a theatre director making an adaptation of *Snow White*. Eight minutes into the film, over a close-up of Mireille Perrier's face, Garrel in voice-over reads a text that introduces this narrative. The director is referred to in the third person; he has been offered the chance to direct *Snow White* for the Comédie Française, but the prospect reminds him of Christa (the reference to Snow White might evoke the spectre of heroin or of Nico's famously pale skin). Afraid that he would simply be exploiting his love for her, but that this would not serve to bring her back, the director ultimately turns down the offer. This text is read so quickly, however, and in Garrel's rather mumbled delivery, that it would be difficult for most spectators, on first viewing, to catch all the details. But this text is repeated later, around forty-five minutes into the film, in a scene in which Bonnaffé and Perrier/Marie are sat in a theatre auditorium while Garrel paces the aisles beside them. Bonnaffé reads, from a script, but slowly and with more signs of emotion, the same text (give or take a few minor changes to phrasing) that Garrel had read earlier. This repetition seems to establish the *Snow White* episode as central to the narrative, and yet, aside from these two scenes, and one or two other dialogue evocations, we learn nothing more about it. What's more, this repetition serves further to confuse matters since it is unclear whether Bonnaffé or Garrel is supposed to be the director in question.

We might assume, then, that *Elle a passé tant d'heures sous les sunlights* is a film (by Philippe Garrel) about Philippe Garrel making a film about a director (Jacques Bonnaffé) trying, and failing or refusing, to stage a play based on *Snow White*. In practice, however, this narrative is evoked only to be largely ignored; it serves only as a pretext for lengthy scenes documenting the interaction between the lovers Bonnaffé and Christa or Bonnaffé and Marie, many of which dissolve into long, enraptured gazes in close-up on the faces of the actors (especially Mireille Perrier). One of Philippe Azoury's conclusions, expressed on the last page of his book on Garrel, is that Garrel is one of cinema's great manipulators of time, comparable to figures like Alain Resnais, Orson Welles, Stanley Kubrick, Marguerite Duras or Michelangelo Antonioni. For Azoury, however, Garrel's singularity compared to these cinematic modernists is in uniting this difficult structural exploration of time with an over-riding concern for sensuality, for physical intimacy and pleasure.[104] In Garrel, in other words, the complex interpenetration of different times is achieved above all with the goal of reviving the treasured memory of intense physical proximity and emotional intimacy with a lover. It is this sensuality, I would suggest, that helps to explain the repetition of certain scenes in *Sunlights*. For the above-mentioned text about Snow White is only one of several episodes that are repeated in the film, typically without the same time delay between them. For instance, in one scene, Bonnaffé comes to see Christa after she has given up heroin and they stand at the window having a conversation. They talk wistfully of the past, Christa saying that her only regret is not to have had a child with him, while he says sadly, 'It's only now that we'd be capable of living together, now that we no longer are.' The scene is played once in long shot, the couple framed in the window but filmed as though from across a street or courtyard. Then it is played again, still framed in the window, but this time in medium close-up. The couple repeat their dialogue with slightly different lines, but covering the same sentiments. Now this kind of repetition is not uncommon in Godard's work of the 1960s, in particular. Godard will frequently have an actor perform the same line twice in a single take and then keep both deliveries of the line in the final edit; he might film the same scene or line from a different angle or include a redundant overlap across a cut, so that a line spoken at the end of one shot is repeated at the beginning of the next. In Godard's work, these practices are typically interpreted as deliberate efforts at distanciation, reminding the spectator of the artificial nature of cinema while also (in the mid-1960s work in particular) interrogating the peculiarly alienating effects of having to communicate through the inevitable *différance* of language. In Garrel, repetition seems to have a rather different intent, based around his work with memory. It suggests, on the one hand, the unreliability of memory (the fact that the dialogue differs slightly from one take to the next implies the partiality of memory); but, more than that, it speaks to the desire to hold on to, and replay in the mind, cherished memories, to relive precious moments with a lover. Fabrice Revault d'Allonnes, who sees separation as the central subject of all Garrel's work, argues that the form of his films is constantly fighting against the disappearance of loved ones, seeking to hold on to them, while at the same time 'fatally, registering the inexorable, irremediable character of their disappearance'.[105]

Another technique that Garrel has learned from Godard – one that is fundamental throughout almost all of Godard's work in cinema – is the disjunction between image and sound: the combining of an image with a sound that is unexpected or apparently unrelated, or a time lag whereby what we see in the image will only be explained on the soundtrack later, or vice versa. An example of this comes just five minutes into *Elle a passé tant d'heures sous les sunlights*. We see a close-up of Christa lying unconscious with a needle and a spoon next to her. On the soundtrack we hear the sounds of Bonnaffé apparently entering the apartment: footsteps, an opening door, the unzipping of a garment. However, instead of discovering Christa, Bonnaffé's voice reads a poetic text addressed from one lover to another: 'To find again your absent gaze ... A form that changes like fire ... In pain I caress the words that you wrote to me.' In the subsequent shot, we see Bonnaffé leave a building with a rumpled piece of paper in hand, pause and look up. Next we see him and Christa fighting over the drugs paraphernalia he has found. The implication, then, is that Bonnaffé comes home and, unaware that Christa is drugged and unconscious in the bedroom, finds a letter addressed to him. It is only after leaving the building that he makes the connection to a possible overdose, returns and finds Christa and the drugs. However, the film has not yet set up the space of the apartment, or the living arrangements of the couple, in such a way as to make this clear, and the narrative sense of the scene can only be deduced in retrospect. In the absence of a shot of Bonnaffé discovering the letter, the shot of Christa and accompanying voice-over instead have a romanticizing effect, presenting drug use as a response to, or flight from, disappointment and anguish over a lover; and this sense is augmented by the calm beauty of the shot's composition.

This disjunction between sound and image is partly responsible for what Philippe Azoury calls the 'magical' moments in Garrel's work, which he sees as related to 'the way in which his images detach themselves from the narrative and install a zone of silence and suspension around themselves'.[106] This occurs, Azoury notes, most especially with close-up images of faces which are no longer tied to the screenplay, or to the film industry, or to questions of technical expertise, but instead are an expression of the special intimacy between the filmmaker and his model.[107] In this, adds Azoury, Garrel is in the lineage of directors like Godard, but also Robert Bresson or Jean-Marie Straub, whose principal goal in filmmaking is not to tell original stories or to invent unusual situations, but rather to understand what it means to give figuration to 'a feeling, an act, a relationship'.[108] In this sense, argues Kent Jones, it is 'probably more useful to think of his work in terms of events rather than shots'.[109] A similar 'magical' effect can sometimes be generated by surprising actors with unexpected instructions or ideas at the moment of filming. During the filming of *Sunlights*, Garrel would pass notes to his performers in envelopes or film them during supposed 'breaks' on set in order to capture their surprise and incomprehension before the camera.[110] This kind of desire to provoke accidents on set that may be captured on camera and give more life to the film is a fundamental aspect of the work of those New Wave directors (Godard, Rivette) who work without a predetermined screenplay, writing scenes from day to day.

Perhaps above all, however, the technique that makes Garrel's films most distinctive, and that contributes to the strange 'detachment' of many of his images, is his appeal to silent film aesthetics. As we argued in the section on Eustache above, the majority of the New Wave filmmakers were interested in silent cinema, acknowledged its historical significance and, from time to time, included homages of one kind or another to silent cinema in their own films. Garrel has gone further, however, than perhaps any other contemporary director in making silent film aesthetics a central part of his filmmaking enterprise.[111] From the very beginning of his career (his second feature, *Le Révélateur*, 1968, is silent) Garrel has made several entire films that are silent and regularly included lengthy silent sequences in his films. As we suggested in the introduction to this section, Garrel's recourse to silence was partly a result of his determination to keep making films in the

FIGURE 1.2 *Mireille Perrier in* Elle a passé tant d'heures sous les sunlights *(1985)*. *Courtesy France Inter.*

absence of funding but, as Azoury argues, it can also be interpreted as a kind of self-imposed austerity related to Garrel's post-1968 rejection of the mainstream film industry, 'as if the first cord that needed to be cut was that of language, which still belongs to reason',[112] where reason is assumed, in the fever of psychotropic experimentation, to be complicit with bourgeois ideology. But the imposition of silence also provides a lesson in narrative economy that will serve Garrel even after he can afford to use sound again. As Azoury puts it, Garrel went without words for so long that he is unlikely suddenly to feel the need to tell all.[113] A good example of this narrative economy is the previously mentioned sequence accompanied by Nico's 'All Tomorrow's Parties'. In this wordless sequence, we see Marie, in close-up, driving by herself; she stops the car and, through a windscreen trickling with raindrops, we see her embrace Lou; we then see Jacques Bonnaffé, through the rear window, chasing hopelessly after the car and eventually being left behind; finally, the camera films Marie and Lou together in the car, Marie resting her head thoughtfully on the dashboard while Lou drives. This short sequence then serves to demonstrate that Marie leaves Bonnaffé for Lou; it documents Bonnaffé's despair and Marie's uncertainty (in the final shot of the sequence, her smiles are interspersed with a more wistful gaze in which it is possible to discern an element of regret or sadness). What is important to Garrel, though, is to capture the emotion of the moment – and something of the timelessness of the triangular structure – rather than to offer narrative explanations: we never know why Marie chooses to leave Bonnaffé, or what attracts her to Lou, or indeed who Lou is, his relations to the other characters in the film. The accompanying song by Nico does not really add anything to our understanding of the scene (the lyrics are not some kind of commentary on what we see), but instead, as suggested earlier, helps to collapse together different times and different figures in Garrel's life. The fact that the sequence can be understood above all as silent is underlined by the fact that the images continue in silence for a further two minutes after the song ends.

Philippe Azoury remarks that in some of Garrel's 1970s films, silence does not appear as a result of some aspirational communion with the great artists of early cinema, but instead is testimony to Garrel's withdrawal into an extreme form of introspection, a sign that the film no longer has the strength to communicate, that communication itself has become 'extinguished, impossible'.[114] In the later films, too, and notably *Elle a passé tant d'heures sous les sunlights*, silence sometimes seems to carry similar connotations of exhaustion or surrender. In *Sunlights*, the proportion of silent material increases as the film goes on until silent footage seems to dominate much of the last forty-five minutes or so of the film. There is a long silent scene of Bonnaffé and Marie in an apartment together, the camera watching them perform everyday activities like sleeping, drinking coffee, bathing. This is followed by the previously discussed 'All

Tomorrow's Parties' sequence, filmed as silent but accompanied by music. The section featuring Doillon also appears in this part of the film, much of it consisting of silent shots of the director or images of Garrel and Doillon talking without sound. When we do hear them talk, there is often the impression that the spectator is eavesdropping on a private conversation whose relationship to the film narrative is unclear. There are other long silent shots here of Garrel himself and of Lou Castel. The gathering silence tends to give the impression that the film is falling apart before our eyes, collapsing into irrecuperable fragments that can no longer or will no longer be forced into making narrative sense. For Fabrice Revault d'Allonnes, both Garrel's characters and his films give the impression of being 'at the end of their rope': *au bout du rouleau*, at the end of their roll, literally so in the case of films made on scraps of recuperated film stock.[115] In Azoury's words, *Sunlights* becomes 'a film without an anchor, without a centre, lost in its own interlocking mechanism'.[116] The silence also adds a dreamlike quality to much of the film, and the condensing of different periods, different characters, different spaces and lives lends something of the structure of dreams to the narrative. Azoury has called Garrel a 'filmmaker of sleep' (*'cinéaste du sommeil'*): his work often features characters in states of semi-alertness, not just asleep, but intoxicated, withdrawn, numbed by emotional pain.[117] Garrel admits that he organized *Sunlights* around five of his own dreams, although he suggests this accounts for the film's 'failure', since 'people don't like dreams in the cinema'.[118] The final revelation of Marie's suicide both acts as a kind of jolting awake for the spectator – since it marks a sudden return to narrative event after at least half an hour of floating in semi-narrative images – and confirms the dream-logic of the film, since there is no clear narrative motivation for Marie to kill herself, the suicide instead appearing as the crystallization of several elements peripheral to the narrative: Christa/Nico's flirtation with overdose; Garrel's extratextual relationship with Jean Seberg; and the generally pervading atmosphere of loss, hopelessness and emotional exhaustion that comes to envelop the film. If the recalcitrant narrative of *Elle a passé tant d'heures sous les sunlights* can best be described as a film about making a film about the failure to stage a play, then the film stages its own failure through its gradual renunciation of narrative – except in the most schematic and condensed images of despair – and its subsiding into silence.

Conclusion

Compared to the high profile of the Nouvelle Vague, the post-New Wave of the 1970s was wilfully marginal. Indeed, several of the key 1970s films of these three directors, including *La Maman et la Putain*, are still not available on disc. It is possible to see a kind of snobbery in this deliberate marginalization, an aggressive rejection of the mainstream, reflected in the almost aristocratic notions sometimes espoused by Jean Eustache. A parallel scale of value is set up whereby artistic integrity is sacrosanct and commercial success is regarded with suspicion: true recognition cannot be expected during the artist's lifetime, as Garrel repeatedly insists. The artist thus necessarily becomes a kind of martyr. This is an unapologetically Romantic view of the artist's role in society. Romanticism also colours the treatment of gender relations in these films. All of them demonstrate the fallout of sexual liberation, since they show characters who are emotionally attached to more than one lover and struggling with the logistic and moral complications of these arrangements. What we witness is the way in which social or political values of sexual freedom and emotional non-exclusivity are repeatedly undermined by the resurgence of discourses drawn from Christian and Romantic traditions stressing relationships of possession, rapture and dependence vis-à-vis the loved one. In other words, these films are *both* documents of changing social morals in post-1968 France *and* deeply personal self-portraits by artists who consider themselves to be totally marginal in relation to that society. But this, in itself, is perhaps an important legacy of the French New Wave: the best films of that movement are at once chronicles of an era of massive social change and highly individual, often partly autobiographical, reflections of an artistic subjectivity. This gives the lie to the arguments of a historian like James Tweedie who seems to see their social significance as the key to the lasting value of these films.[119] All New Wave films reflect social change in one way or another, but it is only those that also contain an irreducibly personal element that continue to resonate with contemporary viewers as compelling works of art. The New Wave created a model for an artistically successful auteur film that is at once an indulgent self-portrait and a self-effacing documentary about the time, place and conditions of its making. The films of the post-New Wave were sometimes seen as more 'naturalistic' than those of their 1960s precursors, but this is an inaccurate label, disregarding the extensive work of writing undertaken by Eustache or of rehearsal by Doillon. Rather than a 'naturalism' of situations, gestures or speech, these filmmakers are seeking to capture something closer to the emotional truth of an event; they are first and foremost, as Azoury suggests of Garrel, figuring a feeling.[120] Eustache, Doillon and Garrel are the inheritors, via the New Wave, of a Bazinian conception of cinema as betraying the truth of life. Hence the recurring rhetoric, in Eustache and Garrel, as in Godard or Truffaut, whereby cinema is conflated and confused with life, and vice versa. As Colette Dubois puts it, 'it is as though life were only interesting in its capacity to become cinema, as though the spectacle of life would only take on its true value when edited, framed and projected'.[121]

Notes

1. On the build-up to the *Affaire Langlois*, see Laurent Mannoni, *Histoire de la Cinémathèque Française* (Paris: Gallimard, 2006), 334–59.
2. Ibid., 370–9.
3. Kieron Corless and Chris Darke, *Cannes: Inside the World's Premier Film Festival* (London: Faber & Faber, 2007), 128.
4. Ibid., 133–4.
5. Antoine de Baecque, *Godard: Biographie* (Paris: Grasset, 2010), 423.
6. Ibid.
7. Jean Douchet, 'Le premier artiste d'après la Nouvelle Vague', *Cahiers du cinéma* 523, special supplement *Eustache* (April 1998), 5.
8. 'Tu te relèves comme la France après Mai 68, mon amour.'
9. Alain Philippon, *Jean Eustache* (Paris: Cahiers du cinéma, 1986), 42.
10. Eustache himself, it seems, made it 'a point of honour to remain broke': whenever he had money he would spend it quickly in restaurants, hotels and casinos. See Marc Cerisuelo, 'Être fauché', in *Le Dictionnaire Eustache*, ed. Antoine de Baecque (Paris: Éditions Léo Scheer, 2011), 104.
11. See Angie David, 'Dandysme', and André Habib, 'Vouvoiement', both in *Le Dictionnaire Eustache*, 74–5 and 306–7.
12. Keith Reader, '"Pratiquement plus rien d'intéressant ne se passe": Jean Eustache's *La Maman et la Putain*', *Nottingham French Studies* 31: 1 (1993), 95.
13. Susan Weiner, 'Jean-Pierre Léaud's Anachronism: The Crisis of Masculinity in Jean Eustache's *La Maman et la putain*', *L'Esprit créateur* 42: 1 (2002), 47–8.
14. 'un soupçon de vieille droite et un zeste de rogne célinienne'. Katia D. Kaupp, 'Le réalisateur le plus "antifestival" va représenter la France à Cannes', *Le Nouvel Observateur*, 14 May 1973.
15. See Antoine de Baecque, 'Delos, Jeanne', in *Le Dictionnaire Eustache*, 79–80.
16. See Antoine de Baecque, 'Autodidacte', in *Le Dictionnaire Eustache*, 28.
17. Michel Marie, '*Cahiers du cinéma*', in *Le Dictionnaire Eustache*, 51.
18. See Michel Marie, 'Autoproduction', and Marc Cerisuelo, 'Godard, Jean-Luc', in *Le Dictionnaire Eustache*, 30–2 and 128–9.
19. Samuel Douhaire, 'Moullet, Luc', in *Le Dictionnaire Eustache*, 202–3.
20. Jean-Louis Bory, 'Romance d'un jeune homme pauvre', *Le Nouvel Observateur*, 14 May 1973.
21. Henry Rabine, 'Cannes: Un film français discutable et discuté', *La Croix*, 18 May 1973.
22. Douchet, 'Le premier artiste d'après la Nouvelle Vague', 4.
23. Alain Philippon, 'L'amour absolu du cinéma', *Cahiers du cinéma* 336 (May 1982), 39.

24 Philippon, *Jean Eustache*, 18.
25 Douchet, 'Le premier artiste d'après la Nouvelle Vague', 4.
26 Colette Dubois, *La Maman et la Putain de Jean Eustache* (Crisnée: Yellow Now, 1990), 33 (original emphasis).
27 Weiner, 'Jean-Pierre Léaud's Anachronism', 43.
28 Bory, 'Romance d'un jeune homme pauvre'.
29 Philippon, 'L'amour absolu du cinéma', 40.
30 'relisant une pensée déjà inscrite', Stéphane Lévy-Klein, 'Entretein avec Jean Eustache (à propos de *la Maman et la Putain*)', *Positif* 157 (March 1974), 53.
31 Michel Marie, 'Acteurs', in *Le Dictionnaire Eustache*, 17.
32 See Louis Chauvet, 'Ce nouveau mal de la jeunesse', *Le Figaro*, 17 May 1973, and Rabine, 'Cannes'.
33 Patrick Leboutte and Charles Tatum, Jr., interview with Bernadette Lafont, in Dubois, *La Maman et la Putain de Jean Eustache*, 100.
34 See, for instance, Jill Forbes, 'Psychoanalysis as Narrative in Films by Jean Eustache', *French Cultural Studies* 14: 3 (2003), 253.
35 See Philippe Azoury, 'Garrel, Philippe', in *Le Dictionnaire Eustache*, 124.
36 Michel Marie, 'Fréhel', in *Le Dictionnaire Eustache*, 120.
37 Azoury, 'Garrel, Philippe', 123.
38 Martine Pierquin, '*La Maman et la Putain/The Mother and the Whore*', in *The Cinema of France*, ed. Phil Powrie (London: Wallflower, 2006), 135.
39 As Avril Dunoyer remarks, 'Baiser', in *Le Dictionnaire Eustache*, 34.
40 Natacha Thiéry, 'Désir', in *Le Dictionnaire Eustache*, 81.
41 Dubois, *La Maman et la Putain de Jean Eustache*, 12, 25.
42 Weiner, 'Jean-Pierre Léaud's Anachronism', 44. For Jean-Louis Bory, Alexandre is 'a derisory conqueror, powerless to truly possess [women]', 'Romance d'un jeune homme pauvre'.
43 Forbes, 'Psychoanalysis as Narrative', 254–5.
44 Philippon, *Jean Eustache*, 12–13.
45 Quoted in Dubois, *La Maman et la Putain de Jean Eustache*, 116.
46 Francis Vanoye, 'Couples', in *Le Dictionnaire Eustache*, 70.
47 Ibid., 71.
48 Philippon, *Jean Eustache*, 36. More than just slogans, *mots d'ordre* are watchwords by which members of a political party or revolutionary cell are expected to abide. The term had a particular currency during the political meetings of May 1968.
49 The satirical paper *Le Canard enchaîné* called her 'a Stakhanovite of fuckery' ('une Stakhanoviste du baisage')! Michel Duran, '*La Maman et la Putain* (Eustache ou rasoir?)', *Le Canard enchaîné*, 23 May 1973.
50 Claire Clouzot, 'Contre-emploi et défense', *Le Monde*, 29 April 1982.
51 Weiner, 'Jean-Pierre Léaud's Anachronism', 44.

52 Reader, 'Pratiquement plus rien d'intéressant ne se passé', 93.
53 Ibid., 92.
54 Bory, 'Romance d'un jeune homme pauvre'.
55 Marie-Odile Briot, 'Le cycle infernal de la féminité (Sur *La Maman et la Putain*)', *Positif* 157 (March 1974), 55.
56 See, for instance, Sheila Jeffreys, *Anticlimax: A Feminist Perspective on the Sexual Revolution* (London: The Women's Press, 1990).
57 Pierquin, '*La Maman et la Putain*', 137.
58 Jean-François Buiré, 'Au bordel! Au bordel! Au bordel!', in *Le Dictionnaire Eustache*, 24.
59 Reader, 'Pratiquement plus rien d'intéressant ne se passé', 92.
60 Weiner, 'Jean-Pierre Léaud's Anachronism', 49.
61 René Prédal, *Jacques Doillon, trafic et topologie des sentiments* (Paris/Condé-sur-Noireau: Éditions du Cerf/Éditions Corlet, 2003), 43.
62 Ibid., 45.
63 Ibid., 42.
64 Albert Cervoni, 'Un "néo-réalisme" français', *France Nouvelle*, 16 December 1974.
65 See Jean de Baroncelli, '*Les Doigts dans la tête* de Jacques Doillon', *Le Monde*, 9 December 1974.
66 Prédal, *Jacques Doillon*, 42–3.
67 Ibid., 13, 19.
68 Nicolas Livecchi, *L'Enfant acteur: De François Truffaut à Steven Spielberg et Jacques Doillon* (Brussels: Les Impressions Nouvelles, 2012), 194.
69 Prédal, *Jacques Doillon*, 22–3, 26.
70 Louis Chauvet, review of *Les Doigts dans la tête*, *Le Figaro*, 9 December 1974. José Bescos also remarked that 'everything, here, appears improvised', '*Les Doigts dans la tête*', *Pariscope*, 11 December 1974.
71 Prédal, *Jacques Doillon*, 33.
72 Doillon would employ similar situations of theatrical confinement in later works: in *La Femme qui pleure* (1979), four characters are stuck in a house together; *La Drôlesse* (1979) is about the developing relationship between a kidnapper and his captive; *La Fille prodigue* (1981) focuses closely on a father–daughter relationship.
73 Quoted in Prédal, *Jacques Doillon*, 50.
74 Philippe Azoury, *Philippe Garrel, en substance* (Paris: Capricci, 2013), 18.
75 Sally Shafto, 'Artist as Christ/Artist as God-the-Father: Religion in the Cinema of Philippe Garrel and Jean-Luc Godard', *Film History* 14: 2 (2002), 145.
76 Azoury, *Philippe Garrel*, 64.
77 Shafto, 'Artist as Christ', 151.
78 Anne-Marie Faux, 'Éloge de la pauvreté', in *Philippe Garrel*, ed. Jacques Déniel (Pantin: Studio 43, 1988), 24.

79 Shafto, 'Artist as Christ', 149.
80 Joshka Schidlow, ' … Ou qui se détruit', *Télérama*, 2 October 1985.
81 Azoury, *Philippe Garrel*, 25.
82 Garrel stresses that one significant difference between him and the generation of the New Wave is that he began filming in adolescence, and therefore on the margins of society, whereas the New Wave directors, aged around thirty when they made their first films, had already been admitted into society. See Philippe Garrel and Thomas Lescure, *Une caméra à la place du coeur* (Aix-en-Provence: Amiranda/Institut de l'image, 1992), 35.
83 Azoury, *Philippe Garrel*, 26.
84 Daniel Cohn-Bendit, *Le Grand Bazar* (Paris: Belfond, 1975).
85 Azoury, *Philippe Garrel*, 201.
86 Ibid., 140–1. For Garrel's own description of this method, see Garrel and Lescure, *Une caméra à la place du coeur*, 100.
87 See Alain Philippon, 'Les ministères de l'art', in *Philippe Garrel*, ed. Jacques Déniel (Pantin: Studio 43, 1988), 19.
88 Garrel and Lescure, *Une caméra à la place du coeur*, 34.
89 In Azoury, *Philippe Garrel*, 128.
90 Garrel and Lescure, *Une caméra à la place du coeur*, 147.
91 Shafto, 'Artist as Christ', 146.
92 Garrel and Lescure, *Une caméra à la place du coeur*, 38.
93 Adrian Martin argues that Brigitte Sy and Nico represent two incarnations among a small handful of female archetypes who recur across Garrel's work (Jean Seberg represents a third model, the others being casual lovers and prostitutes). See 'A Cinema of Intimate Spectacle: The Poetics of Philippe Garrel', *Cineaste* 34: 4 (2009), 40.
94 Azoury, *Philippe Garrel*, 155.
95 Ibid., 184.
96 Ibid., 14, 188.
97 Ibid., 132.
98 On this incident, see Simon Reynolds, 'From the Velvets to the Void', *The Guardian*, 15 March 2007.
99 Azoury, *Philippe Garrel*, 152. Wiazemsky had also played the 'Nico role' in Garrel's *L'Enfant secret* (1979). Garrel refers to this casting as 'a French princess playing a German worker', Garrel and Lescure, *Une caméra à la place du coeur*, 86.
100 Azoury, *Philippe Garrel*, 234.
101 Garrel and Lescure, *Une caméra à la place du coeur*, 89.
102 Jean-Luc Godard, 'Pierrot mon ami', in *Jean-Luc Godard par Jean-Luc Godard, Tome 1: 1950–1984* (Paris: Cahiers du cinéma, 1998), 259–63. For a commentary on this text, see Douglas Morrey, *Jean-Luc Godard* (Manchester: Manchester University Press, 2005), 25.

103 Martin, 'A Cinema of Intimate Spectacle', 39.
104 Azoury, *Philippe Garrel*, 244.
105 Fabrice Revault d'Allonnes, 'Séparations (Gare, elle ...)', in *Philippe Garrel*, ed. Jacques Déniel (Pantin: Studio 43, 1988), 29.
106 Azoury, *Philippe Garrel*, 46.
107 Ibid., 66.
108 Ibid., 186.
109 Kent Jones, 'Sad and Proud of It: The Films of Philippe Garrel', *Film Comment* 33: 3 (1997), 25.
110 Azoury, *Philippe Garrel*, 121; Garrel and Lescure, *Une caméra à la place du coeur*, 98.
111 In order to appreciate Garrel's uniqueness in this regard, one only has to reflect on the difference between Garrel's use of silent images, scattered throughout his career, and recent pastiches of silent cinema like *The Artist* (Michel Hazanavicius, 2011) or *Tabu* (Miguel Gomes, 2012), however accomplished and affectionate they may be.
112 Azoury, *Philippe Garrel*, 22.
113 'Garrel ne s'est pas tant de fois passé de mots pour soudain se croire obligé de tout dire.' Ibid., 69.
114 Ibid., 89.
115 Revault d'Allonnes, 'Séparations (Gare, elle ...)', 30.
116 'un film sans ancre, sans centre, perdu dans son propre jeu d'emboîtement délirant', Azoury, *Philippe Garrel*, 237.
117 Ibid., 56. Adrian Martin concurs that 'Garrel is a poet of sleep to rival, even surpass, Murnau', 'A Cinema of Intimate Spectacle', 39. Kent Jones, meanwhile, notes 'a sense of peace' and a 'becalmed feeling' given off by Garrel's films, one that stems from the definitive resignation to marginality. 'Sad and Proud of It', 27.
118 Garrel and Lescure, *Une caméra à la place du coeur*, 143.
119 See James Tweedie, *The Age of New Waves: Art Cinema and the Staging of Globalization* (Oxford: Oxford University Press, 2013). Tweedie's argument is set out in detail in the Introduction to this book.
120 Azoury, *Philippe Garrel*, 186.
121 Dubois, *La Maman et la Putain de Jean Eustache*, 40.

2

The *cinéma du look*

In the early 1980s, a handful of French directors released distinctive debut features that were widely identified as marking a significant departure from the majority of French film production and in particular from the broadly social-realist aesthetic that has a strong tradition in French auteur filmmaking. Like the films of the New Wave, these features tended to revolve around youthful protagonists and incorporated aspects of generic fiction, notably bringing their own idiosyncratic concerns to narrative structures and tropes borrowed from the crime genre. But the *cinéma du look*, as its name implies, became most famous for its distinctive mise en scène: highly stylized sets, original costumes and carefully designed colour schemes. When married to the films' relative lack of concern for narrative realism, this led some critics to label them 'mannered' and even 'baroque'. While the *cinéma du look* shares some of the youthful energy of the New Wave, then, its approach to production design is arguably very different, rejecting the shot-from-the-hip spontaneity of many of the Nouvelle Vague's fast-and-loose shooting schedules and on-set practices in favour of meticulously planned creation in the studio. The prime movers of the *cinéma du look* have had very different career trajectories: Jean-Jacques Beineix abandoned filmmaking after six features in order to work in lobbying and promotion of French film abroad; Luc Besson has become one of the most commercially successful of contemporary French filmmakers, but he has done so largely by refusing any specificity to French cinema and working in a transnational arena that has led to the production of international action-movie franchises like *Taken* (begun in 2008); only Leos Carax has maintained a distinctive authorial identity in French cinema, but he has done so at the cost of productivity: just five features in thirty years, with a gap of nearly a decade between *Les Amants du Pont-Neuf* (1991) and *Pola X* (1999), then well over a decade until *Holy Motors* (2012). Despite the irreducible differences between them, however, these filmmakers together constituted – if not a movement, exactly – a distinct trend within French cinema of the early to mid-1980s that was recognized within the French and, to some extent, the international film press. This chapter will consider how the reception of key films from the *cinéma du look* – *Diva* (Beineix, 1981), *Subway* (Besson, 1985) *Boy Meets Girl* (Carax, 1984) and *Mauvais Sang* (Carax, 1986) – invokes the memory of the New Wave for the sake of both positive and negative comparison, focusing notably on the depiction of youth, but particularly on the conception of the auteur director which is perhaps the New Wave's most obvious legacy to subsequent generations of filmmakers. The chapter will explore the differences between the two movements by discussing their shared interest in, but diverse, treatment of urban space: where the New Wave became famous for its location shooting on the streets of Paris, the *cinéma du look* is associated with often artificial and claustrophobic sets. Finally, the chapter will suggest, partly as a result of this use of space, that the *cinéma du look*'s chief failing, in comparison to the New Wave, can be found in its less successful grasp of rhythm. As was evoked in the Introduction, it is a central argument of this book that the French New Wave displayed a particularly sensitive and successful awareness of cinematic rhythm. This is not simply a question of the technical skill applied to editing but also reflects broader structuring elements of the films, as well as key components of individual scenes such as dialogue, music and mise en scène. Yvette Bíro has suggested that the 'rhythmic design' of films needs to be understood as a dialectic of 'turbulence and flow'. She argues that human experience as a whole is characterized by the necessary tension between 'smooth continuity', through which we seek stability and repetition, and moments of 'sudden confusion' followed by 'an inevitable reordering or regrouping'.[1] It is thus entirely natural that works of narrative art should build their rhythm around this interplay of turbulence and flow. Bíro goes on to note that works of modern (especially European) cinema have frequently sought to interrupt their flow through narrative digression, and she asserts that the pleasures of digressive narrative may be so fundamentally satisfying because they are, as it were, atavistically tied to the rhythms of sexual congress: 'its dramatic arc is the natural model for the narrative [...] digression preceding catharsis, an attempt to hold back the final closure'.[2] This chapter seeks, through a comparison of the rhythmic design of *cinéma du look* films with examples from the New Wave, to better understand the rhythmic sophistication of the Nouvelle Vague, demonstrating how such vital components as its spatial organization (i.e. its mise en scène) and its use of music feed into its control of turbulence and flow.

The New Wave and the *cinéma du look*

Beineix and *Diva*

Diva was rarely compared explicitly to the New Wave.[3] The film has a variety of influences: explicit references within *Diva* to other works of cinema history include *Citizen Kane* (Orson Welles, 1941), in the long shots of Gorodish (Richard Bohringer) with his enormous jigsaw puzzle, and *The Seven Year Itch* (Billy Wilder, 1955) when a woman's skirt is blown up as she crosses a grill over the underground. In terms of its more general narrative development and stylistic tropes, critics compared *Diva* more to the classic French cinema of the 1930s and 1940s than to the New Wave. It was seen to resemble *Drôle de drame* (Marcel Carné, 1937) or a film by Jean Cocteau.[4] In general, it is interesting to compare the films of the *cinéma du look* to the French poetic realist cycle of the late 1930s: Marie-Thérèse Journot points out that critics of both eras tended to admire the striking images of these films while finding them highly artificial.[5] Alain Bergala has suggested the influence, over the 'mannerist' style of the *cinéma du look*, of Jean-Pierre Melville more of a fellow traveller of the New Wave than a member of the movement proper.[6] In particular, the cold, metallic colour scheme of Melville's late features, dominated by blues, silvers and greys, is revived in *Diva*. At the same time, as Journot remarks, this mise en scène has a number of precursors in painting, from the Neue Sachlichkeit of 1920s Germany, through American hyperrealism and photorealism, to the work of Jacques Monory.[7] Jean-Jacques Beineix himself claimed to have 'no particular antecedents', although he demonstrated his awareness of French film history when he ended the same interview by asserting that a 'new wave was coming' to shake French cinema out of its routine.[8] But the difference between Beineix and the New Wave, suggests Raphaël Bassan, is that unlike Godard, for instance, Beineix has no particular interest in situating himself in film history or in spawning his own disciples.[9] In Bassan's interpretation, Beineix recognizes that the cinema of the 1980s must necessarily be constructed from a recycling of existing elements that it brings nothing inherently new and therefore will not have imitators of its own: along the same lines, Fredric Jameson famously called *Diva* 'the first French postmodernist film'.[10] Going further than Bassan, David Russell, writing in the UK, suggested that 'European cinema', defined as 'a cinema oriented towards mental rather than action images', was 'to all intents and purposes already dead'.[11] It is this context that explains the 'mannerism' of the *cinéma du look*: Marie-Thérèse Journot remarks that if a form is regarded as effectively exhausted, then novelty can only be achieved by superficial flourishes on top of existing templates. It is in this sense, too, that we can understand the frequent comparison made between the *cinéma du look* and the aesthetics of advertising: Journot goes on to remark that there is little real scope for originality in advertising, tied as it is to the marketing of a commercial product, so all the creativity of the form tends to lie in precisely this kind of superficial mannerism.[12]

Curiously, given this insistence of the director and other commentators on the film's recycling of supposedly moribund forms, the release of *Diva* in France was met by a number of extravagant claims by critics as to its absolute originality. *Diva* 'could not be compared to any other film', declared *L'Humanité*.[13] *La Croix* agreed that the film was 'unlike anything we've seen before' and took the spectator 'from surprise to astonishment'.[14] 'Not only are we not bored', gushed Annie Coppermann in *Les Échos*, 'we are perpetually surprised'.[15] The hyperbole perhaps reached its summit with Pierre Billard in *Le Point* who promised readers that *Diva* contained 'some of the most astonishing images ever seen on screen'[16] while Marie-Élisabeth Rouchy in *Le Matin* predicted that the effect of the film would be like a bomb going off in the cinema.[17] More sober voices were rare, but among them *Cahiers du cinéma* cautiously suspected that the film was more canny than uncanny.[18] Those critics who admired the originality of *Diva* were quick to label Beineix an auteur. The status of auteur director is so coveted in the French film establishment that reviewers are eager to display their own critical acuity by identifying auteurs from their very first films.

Thus *Pariscope* declared that Beineix had 'delivered a masterstroke with his first film',[19] while Annie Coppermann closed her review with the simple but telling affirmation: 'This is what we call a *film d'auteur.*'[20] *Le Figaro* went further, arguing that Beineix had succeeded in turning a *film de commande* into a *film d'auteur*, that is in taking the commercial proposition of a producer (Irène Silberman suggested to Beineix that he adapt Delacorta's source novel) and turning it into a personal project, in other words precisely the strategy of artistic appropriation that the New Wave critics admired in the great directors of classical Hollywood.[21] 'Every sequence carries his signature', insisted Pierre Billard,[22] while by December 1984, when Beineix had only made one other film, the critical and commercial disaster that was *La Lune dans le caniveau* (1983), *Le Matin* could blithely describe *Diva* as an 'already mythical' film.[23]

Given all these critical plaudits, one of the most puzzling aspects of the reception of *Diva* was a certain tendency to present the film as a victim of critical persecution. Interviewed a year after *Diva*'s initial release, Beineix admitted that he had been upset by the 'violence' and the 'sarcasm' with which his film had been greeted in the press.[24] We might simply suspect the director of being oversensitive about his own work, if it were not for the fact that other critics also complained of the film's unfair treatment. *Pariscope* lamented that it had been 'shot down in flames'[25] while *Le Point* saw a criminal 'conspiracy of silence' around the season's most original film.[26] But this view is simply not borne out by the evidence of the press reviews of *Diva*. Naturally there were individual differences between reviewers, and not all critics were as ecstatic in their praise as Pierre Billard. Some found the narrative confusing and many remarked on the excessive stylization of the mise en scène (as we shall see in the section below). The overall consensus, however, was that *Diva* was a highly original work by a talented young director whose subsequent efforts were awaited with considerable anticipation. In addition, *Diva* was commercially successful. After a modest initial run, the film continued to play in two cinemas, steadily attracting around one thousand spectators a week for almost a year until it won four César awards and garnered a new audience, finishing with a very respectable 1,500,000 total spectators in France.[27] Under the circumstances, one cannot reasonably claim any 'conspiracy' against the film. How, then, do we explain these complaints? Marie-Thérèse Journot offers an intriguing interpretation when she suggests that the traditional romantic conception of the artist as revolutionary, fighting against the establishment's arbiters of good taste, had effectively been overturned by the late twentieth century: the art of rupture and revolution had become the 'official' art, sanctioned by the media and the academy (in the context of French cinema, it was no doubt largely the New Wave that was responsible for this inversion). In this new context, then, it is paradoxically the artist who is most in tune with the public, and rejected by the intelligentsia, who can claim the status of *artiste maudit*.[28] But, while Beineix in interviews repeatedly stated his sense of being 'in tune' with youth (for instance through his embracing of the advertising aesthetic), an opinion seemingly corroborated by *Diva*'s slow-burn, word-of-mouth success at the box office,[29] the evidence of the film's reception shows, as we have seen, that it was anything but 'rejected' by the French intelligentsia. In the end, we can perhaps only conclude that the status of auteur in French cinema remains so dominant as a category of interpretation and so essential as a strategy of identification for directors, while also remaining stubbornly tied to the romantic conception of the *artiste maudit*, that a certain persecution complex becomes an obligatory attitude to adopt for young directors, a kind of rite of passage, even where the evidence of critical and commercial reception belies their expressed concerns. We might note, for instance, that Leos Carax, too, criticized the 'cowardly irony' with which his first film was greeted in the press whereas, in fact, the overwhelming response was the designation of an astonishing new auteur and a warm welcome for what was seen as a genuinely poetic evocation of youthful romance.[30]

Besson and *Subway*

Of all the *cinéma du look* directors, and indeed perhaps of all the French filmmakers discussed in this book, Luc Besson is probably the least susceptible to this image of the *artiste maudit*. Besson does insist, like so many other directors, on his profession as a kind of calling: 'There was never any question of me doing anything else', he says.[31] For the most part, however, Besson avoids discussion of the poetics of cinema or of his own artistic philosophy to focus on practical and technical aspects of filmmaking. He notes that he filled most roles on a film set – sound recordist, assistant camera operator, assistant editor – on his way to becoming a director, because he felt it necessary to have a technical grasp of all aspects of cinema production before presuming to oversee a whole film.[32] Indeed, journalists tend to stress his calm, confident demeanour on set and his technical competence: 'his mastery shines through in every shot', said *Pariscope*.³³ Nor is Besson one for discussing the canon of film history and its influence on his work. He claims to watch around 300 films a year but 'mostly mediocre ones, because you learn more from a bad film than from a good one'.³⁴ From early in his career, Besson takes the role of producer as seriously as that of director. He was his own executive producer for *Subway* and speaks proudly of his efficient shooting schedule and lack of unnecessary expenses; if the film went slightly over budget, Besson absorbed the extra costs himself.³⁵ Overall, Besson's discourse around *Subway* already demonstrates the mindset of the pragmatic global producer he would become and whose chief concern is simply with *getting films made*. He appears largely uninterested in critical judgements and, if he gamely admits that *Subway* is 'full of mistakes', he simply chalks it up to inexperience.³⁶

If Luc Besson's self-conception as a filmmaker apparently owes little to the New Wave, however, *Subway* shares with the films of Godard and Truffaut a taste for generic hybridity, combining elements, as Susan Hayward remarks, of 'the thriller, the comic-thriller, the musical and fantasy'.³⁷ The shifts in genre lead to ruptures of tone, somewhat as in *Tirez sur le pianiste* (Truffaut, 1961), with the suspense of pursuit giving way to comic exchanges or to musical interludes. Marie-Thérèse Journot suggests that such breaks in tone may be one of the main reasons for the success of *cinéma du look* films, since they inject novelty into a genre (the thriller) that otherwise affords little room for surprise, except through the escalation of violence³⁸ (and it is worth adding that the *cinéma du look* generally is very restrained in its representation or evocation of violence, as was the New Wave). However, where the New Wave mixed together elements of those classical Hollywood genres that its own practitioners had sought to rehabilitate in their criticism (the crime thriller, the musical, melodrama), Besson often appeals to popular genres that are still regarded with some disdain by the critical establishment. *Cahiers du cinéma* noted that *Subway*, in places, resembled a film by Walter Hill or John Carpenter (contemporary equivalents of the second-tier American auteur directors, like Robert Aldrich or Raoul Walsh, admired by the New Wave critics), but mixed with some of the worst clichés of the French police comedy.³⁹ As such, suggests Phil Powrie,⁴⁰ Besson is arguably less an inheritor of the New Wave than a sign of the continuity of popular genres in French, and world, cinema; fantasy and adventure genres (Besson also proclaims his love of Walt Disney and *Raiders of the Lost Ark* [Spielberg, 1981]⁴¹) have a perennial currency among youth and popular audiences who defy fashion and critical orthodoxy.

This willing association with film genres tied to young people can also be seen in Besson's own description of *Subway* as 'a kids' film, a vanilla ice cream'.⁴² Besson has also described the film's marginal figures hiding out in the Paris underground as 'lost children'[43] and characterized the plot as being largely concerned with adolescence: the missed adolescence of Héléna (Isabelle Adjani), trapped in a loveless marriage, who seeks rejuvenation and escape alongside eternal youth Fred (Christophe Lambert).[44] As we have seen, the *cinéma du look* was often associated, through its 'advertising aesthetic', with the tastes, values and style of young people, but Raphaël Bassan argues that we should not see these as carefree images of leisure and nightlife but rather as 'desperate visions of stifled individuals'[45] (in *Subway* the constraints on freedom are literalized as the protagonists are driven underground). As we saw in the Introduction to this book, one of the chief and abiding interests of the French New Wave has been its recording of the lives, the fashions and the concerns of a generation of young people. The focus on young people is thus one of the key points of comparison between the New Wave and the *cinéma du look*, since the protagonists of all the films discussed in this chapter are assumed to be in their early twenties.

There are a number of key differences, however, between the generation of the early 1960s, in France, and that of the early 1980s (the latter being, in many cases, the children of the former). The New Wave depicted the children of France's post-war baby boom, benefiting from unprecedented (and so far unrepeated) sustained economic growth but seeking to distinguish themselves from their parents' generation, seen as tainted by the legacy of the Second World War, and to grasp new freedoms, especially in the sexual arena. By contrast, as Susan Hayward points out, the economic and cultural context of the early 1980s was defined by recession, austerity and unemployment, leaving young people with much less faith in the future.[46] The clash of generations is often central to the New Wave: it is explicit in Truffaut's Antoine Doinel series, but also implicit in the early films of Rohmer and Chabrol, in the protagonists' fumbling attempts to elaborate their own moral code. In the films of the *cinéma du look*, however, parents are often absent: in *Subway*, Fred's father died when he was a child, while *Mauvais Sang* opens with the announcement of Alex's father's death. For Hayward, this reflects the rise in divorce rates and single-parent families in French society of the time.[47] She goes on to point out that, as the traditional family fails, the surveillance of young people becomes a public concern, mediated through technology.[48] This is, in effect, the subject of *Subway*: a group of young people seek to create their own alternative community underground but are constantly pursued by a police force whose size is exaggerated in extended shots of them trooping down narrow staircases. The response of young people to this surveillance, continues Hayward, citing the work of Dick Hebdige, is a kind of self-conscious display that highlights the extent to which youth has become spectacle in our culture. There are elements of punk to the *cinéma du look*, and to *Subway* in particular, most notably Héléna/Adjani's spiky hairstyle (described by the character as 'Iroquois') that became an icon of the film and that she wears to a high-society dinner from which she exits with the petulant declaration: 'Sir, your dinner is crap, your house is crap, and you can all go fuck yourselves.'[49] Like punk, the *cinéma du look* is not a political movement but rather an inarticulate cry of indignation from a generation denied the spoils of consumerism by virtue of the previous generation's mismanagement of the economy. It is a generation that no longer believes in the possibility of radical political change (sufficiently disillusioned by the failures of the late 1960s and 1970s) but remains contemptuous of the mainstream, nine-to-five working lifestyle.

Leos Carax

Of the different directors associated with the *cinéma du look*, Leos Carax clearly had, from the beginning, the strongest commitment to a personal filmmaking style and, as such, his work was seized upon with particular effusion by a French film press eager to identify new auteur directors. Serge Daney wrote of *Boy Meets Girl*: 'This is a real first film and (let's take a gamble on him) a real auteur.'[50] In *Cahiers du cinéma*, Marc Chevrie declared: 'We can feel from the very first shots that this is a born filmmaker.'[51] Much stress was placed on Carax's youth: he was only twenty-three when he made *Boy Meets Girl*, considerably younger than the filmmakers of the New Wave were when they made their first films (mostly around thirty). It was repeatedly suggested (as in the citation from Daney above) that, given Carax's young age, the film constituted a kind of extraordinary *gamble*: it was a gamble for the director to expose his naïve sensibility in this way; it was a gamble for the producers to take a risk on such a youngster; and it was a gamble for critics to proclaim their belief in Carax's artistic identity on the basis of this one uneven, and sometimes clumsy, film.[52] Carax was frequently compared to Arthur Rimbaud, the legendary French poet whose revolutionary verse was mostly written before he was seventeen and who abandoned literature at the age of nineteen in search of travel and adventure. Carax encouraged these comparisons by naming his second film *Mauvais Sang*, after a poem by Rimbaud and having the main character, Alex (Denis Lavant), speak Rimbaud's last words ('When will I be transported aboard?') shortly before his death at the end of the film. As Daney remarks, *Boy Meets Girl* is a film whose author apparently has more experience of cinema than of real life, but who crams his limited experience of life into the film in his eagerness to make cinema.[53] As a result, *Boy Meets Girl* is made up of quotations from favourite films, books and music, lengthy discussions of artistic aspirations and suicidal impulses and hastily conceived, imperiously experienced young love. Hervé Guibert remarked, in *Le Monde*, that it was refreshing to find, on film, many of the most awkward, naïve and embarrassing qualities of youth and not simply the freshness and charm beloved of much teen romance.[54] The film evidently contains a number of autobiographical echoes: the protagonist, Alex (Carax's real first name), becomes a kind of alter ego for the director (as he will in the subsequent films *Mauvais Sang, Les Amants du Pont-Neuf* and *Holy Motors*): in *Boy Meets Girl*, the character is an aspiring filmmaker and his tendency to retreat into silence and his fascination with pinball are similarly familiar from Carax's life story.

According to his own anecdotes, Leos Carax left school at sixteen and descended into a period of silent contemplation. He claims not to have spoken between the ages of sixteen and eighteen, instead devoting all his time to pinball and cinema-going before finally acquiring his own film camera.[55] Elements of this biography feed into the Alex of *Mauvais Sang* who was nicknamed 'Langue Pendue'[56] by his parents because he was 'a dangerously silent child' and who, in adulthood, has mastered the trick of ventriloquizing (a literal trick, in the film, because achieved with voice-over). As Alex says in the film, 'People always talk about keeping silent, but that's wrong: it's the silence that keeps us.'[57] The pendant to Carax's silence is mythomania and self-mythologizing: when he isn't refusing to talk about himself and his films, he sometimes makes up improbable stories: in his first interview with *Le Monde* he was evasive about his birth date and claimed that 'Leos Carax' was his real name, taken from a Mexican province where he supposedly had his origins.[58] As *Cahiers du cinéma* put it, 'There is in Carax the force of silence, at each stage of a film, before, during and after; a secret to be preserved and which incites his own myth.'[59] Various collaborators attest to this secrecy and silence that is part of Carax's method of working. Jean-Yves Escoffier, the director of photography on *Mauvais Sang*, says he received little information during the writing stage 'because it was very secretive'.[60] Juliette Binoche claims that she received most direction for her character of Anna not from Carax's words but from his gaze.[61] Carax chooses not to show rushes to his actors during shooting because 'making a film is a secret', and the longer the secret is preserved, the more the actor's 'appetite for the character' and willingness to take risks grow.[62] Once a film is released, Carax further 'cultivates his mystery' through his resistance to having his photograph taken or distributed and his reluctance to grant interviews.[63] So much so that, two weeks after the release of *Mauvais Sang*, *Libération* published a short text entitled 'Le silence de Leos Carax' remarking upon the enigmatic silence of the director around his much discussed film: 'There is in this silence all the arrogance of an orphan, a filmmaker persuaded of the death of cinema, a Godardian kid who forces himself to keep quiet lest he say too much.'[64] (Carax would eventually grant a single, long interview to *Cahiers du cinéma*, published in the December 1986 issue.) Most commentators, far from dwelling on the apparent shyness that such silence would seem to imply, tend to stress Carax's single-mindedness and sense of purpose. Critics speak of his 'total investment' and 'crazy energy',[65] his 'insane demands' and his 'iron will'.[66] After all, an unusual level of tenacity would have been required to get films like *Boy Meets Girl* and *Mauvais Sang* made in the first place. Serge Toubiana expresses his astonishment that someone 'so young, so frail and so alone' could succeed in imposing on a producer a project as 'strange' as *Mauvais Sang*.[67] And Serge Daney asserts that only French cinema could produce 'a filmmaker as *determined* as Carax'.[68] In *Cahiers du cinéma*, Alain Philippon remarked that Carax's second film resembles both a first film and a final film, so stubborn is the director's insistence that things be done a certain way.[69] Carax's obstinacy on set has been noted by collaborators. Jean-Yves Escoffier mentions 'moments of extreme tension' and 'extreme severity' from the 'stormy' Leos who 'would never give up' when things appeared not to be working.[70] The director's single-minded dedication to his vision allegedly led him to feed his actors exclusively on vegetables during the shooting of *Mauvais Sang* in an effort to give them a paler complexion.[71] Carax himself relates this conviction back to his adolescent discovery of cinema, the one thing that gave him a sense of total clarity: 'In the cinema, I have always had an absolute certainty, on seeing a film, of its integrity or otherwise. When you're alone in a dark room aged sixteen with that certainty, alone and sure, that gives you an untold strength.'[72]

Carax goes as far as to say, 'I was born in a dark room' (i.e. a cinema), and he adds, 'I made cinema in order to become an orphan.'[73] (In a similar way, when Alex learns of the death of his father in *Mauvais Sang*, he exclaims, with a kind of relief, 'Finally an orphan!') Carax's rhetoric here is very close to that of the New Wave filmmakers, all of whom, in the 1950s, used obsessive cinema-going as a way of escaping unhappy family lives (Truffaut) or unwanted family associations (Godard, Rohmer) and who created, first, a phantasmatic family out of their cinematic idols and, subsequently, a real new family made up of the friends and associates encountered through their own filmmaking. 'Cinema was my only friend and my only school', says Carax of his adolescence.[74] Discovering the cinema by exploring the works of individual directors or actors was how Carax expressed his autonomy and shaped his own tastes and identity. 'That's how you start living', he stresses.[75] As already hinted above, the fact that Carax began filmmaking at such a young age, with relatively little life experience, inevitably meant that his first films were full of references and homages to other works of cinema, and critics of *Boy Meets Girl* and *Mauvais Sang* were quick to enumerate the most obvious influences. Carax objected to this practice, however, complaining that it was like being 'buried under proper names'. In his eyes, it wasn't a question of 'references' or 'influences' so much as a debt of love.[76] He complained that journalists were simply scoring points by spotting these similarities whereas, for him, the filmmakers he admired had literally 'saved his life'.[77] It remains the case, however, that Carax's cinema is unusually dense in citations and intertextual echoes. Reviewers of *Mauvais Sang*, in particular, were struck by Carax's propensity to incarnate a kind of memory of the whole of cinema. *France-Soir* suggested that 'his mind is a computer containing everything the cinema has ever created'.[78] *Le Quotidien de Paris* described *Mauvais Sang* as 'an encyclopedia of cinema'[79] and *La Croix* talked about it 'summarizing a century of film art'.[80] Alain Bergala diagnosed, in Carax and other filmmakers of the 1980s (including international examples like Wim Wenders and Jim Jarmusch), an overwhelming sense of *coming after* film history: not just cinema's classical era but also its modern era associated with the French and other new waves. Carax is thus a representative of a postmodern cinema employing a kind of 'generalized recycling', in which the whole of film history is available for plunder in the mode of 'self-service'. Bergala sees television as largely responsible for this development, with its tendency to 'disconnect films from any origin, to divest them of a singular aura'.[81] Not only are the images of the films recycled, but there is a sense in which emotion itself, through its association with canonical citations, can only ever be second-hand, never quite experienced directly. Thus, as Alban Pichon points out, to talk about childhood, Carax cites Céline, to evoke pain he uses Samuel Fuller; Cocteau or René Char are invoked to signify love, and Léo Ferré turns up to express solitude.[82]

If Carax's cinema draws inspiration from the whole of film history, however, the influence of the French New Wave is impossible to ignore in his work and, in particular, the model of Jean-Luc Godard, described by Serge Daney as 'a god for Carax'.[83] The influence of the New Wave is visible in Carax's drawing on autobiographical material (a strategy employed at times by both Godard and Truffaut); in his tendency to work with the same troupe of actors (Lavant, Binoche, Mireille Perrier) as well as other personnel (Escoffier, producer Alain Dahan, editor Nelly Quettier); but perhaps most of all, as Michel Pérez points out,[84] in the stress on the sheer pleasure of cinema – for both filmmakers and spectators – the sense of wonder at what the medium can do. From Godard, Carax borrows a narrative structure characterized by lengthy mid-sections set in domestic interiors, typically focusing on an extended dialogue between a man and a woman. As in Godard, too, these dialogues are often closer to monologues or at least obey a different cadence than everyday speech. Carax's tendency to dislocate sounds from images draws on one of the basic lessons of Godard's cinema, and the use of music is also similar between the two directors: both contemporary popular and canonical classical music are used, sometimes cutting abruptly in and out on the soundtrack, elsewhere playing in extenso in such a way as to hold up narrative development. Carax's taste for citation is of course itself an inheritance of Godard and the two directors have many of the same points of reference in literature (Céline, Aragon, Rimbaud, Ramuz) and cinema (Cocteau, Bresson, Hawks). A number of critics saw *Boy Meets Girl* as potentially equivalent to *À bout de souffle* as 'the emblematic film of a generation'.[85]

The specific moments from Carax's first two features that recall films by Godard are so numerous that it is perhaps most simple to present them as a list:

Boy Meets Girl

- Carax repeatedly uses sounds (car horns, a whistling kettle, thunder) to drown out dialogue in a way that Godard has always done.
- Mireille (Mireille Perrier) has a page from Tintin stuck to her wall, reminiscent of the newspaper clippings, art prints and cartoons seen on walls in Godard's 1960s films.
- In a sequence set in a cafe, a pinball machine threatens to dominate the entire scene through its loud noises and the beauty of its flashing lights, as in *Vivre sa vie* (1962).
- In the cafe, bit-part players are responsible for some of the film's more humorous encounters, such as Monsieur Bouriana who exasperatedly spells out his name over the telephone: 'B like Bouriana, O like Ouriana, U like Uriana, etc.' This recalls Godard's career-long taste for cameos and impromptu routines, and particularly the surreal but rather hard-edged encounters of his films from the early 1980s which effectively depicted the abrasiveness of social life in late capitalism.
- A sequence in which one man makes photocopies while another looks on and repeatedly interjects 'Faster!' is similarly reminiscent of early 1980s Godard, both in the attempt to find unexpected beauty in contemporary technology (the flashing lights of the photocopier caught in rich black and white) and in the barked imperatives to which social intercourse has been reduced.
- When Alex tries to steal some records he is chased in a stylized and comical manner by the shop employees in a way that recalls Godard's pantomime fight sequences in films like *Bande à part* (1964) and *Pierrot le fou* (1965), themselves gesturing back to burlesque silent cinema.
- Alex and Lise's (Julie Delpy) discussion of oral sex takes place over deliberately de-eroticizing images of a stairwell and corridors, not unlike the cold treatment of sex in *Vivre sa vie*.
- *Boy Meets Girl* contains a long and bleakly humorous party sequence that is clearly inspired by the party at the beginning of *Pierrot le fou*. In *Pierrot*, Ferdinand (Jean-Paul Belmondo) is

introduced to Samuel Fuller (playing himself) who talks, through an interpreter, about his philosophy of cinema. In *Boy Meets Girl*, Alex encounters a deaf-mute man who relates, through a sign-language interpreter, his memories of working in silent cinema.

- Like Marianne (Anna Karina) in *Pierrot le fou*, Mireille in *Boy Meets Girl* is closely associated with a pair of scissors with which she appears to be contemplating suicide when Alex first sees her; which she uses to cut her own hair; and which will ultimately be the cause of her (accidental?) death at the end of the film.
- Mireille's self-administered hair cut is not unlike the boyish cut sported by Jean Seberg in *À bout de souffle*.
- Favouring disorienting, non-naturalistic lighting like Godard, Carax has the artificial light come and go in the kitchen where Alex and Mireille get to know each other.
- At one point, during this conversation, extreme close-ups of parts of Alex's face are positioned in the frame in front of parts of Mireille's face in a fragmentation that recalls *Une femme mariée*.

Mauvais Sang

- The opening minutes of *Mauvais Sang* are unmistakeably Godardian. The film opens with a voice-over recording of C-F Ramuz (a writer hailing from the same part of Switzerland as Godard) reading his own text about the love between a young boy and girl, a recording that Godard would later use in *Histoire(s) du cinéma* (1998).[86] The plot exposition invokes generic cues (faked suicides, guns, blackmail) and schematic dialogue ('If you don't pay, you'll pay') without ever setting out the stakes of the narrative in a clear and logical manner, comparable to the famous apartment sequence in *Pierrot le fou* in which Marianne repeats 'I'll explain everything' while explaining next to nothing. The very flat mise en scène, featuring extreme close-ups of faces and sometimes the backs of people's heads against bold-coloured backgrounds is also reminiscent of the Godard of the mid-to-late 1960s, as are the occasional close-ups on newspaper type. Meanwhile, Michel Piccoli, who plays Marc in *Mauvais Sang*, is of course familiar from *Le Mépris* (1963).
- The subsequent sequence of Alex and Lise in a sun-dappled forest idyll, but interrupted by distant gunfire, is further reminiscent of *Pierrot le fou*.

- Juliette Binoche is coiffed in this film with a bob like Anna Karina in *Vivre sa vie*, itself a reference back to Louise Brooks.
- In Alex's room, we see extreme close-ups on a revolver that recall those in *À bout de souffle* when Michel Poiccard (Belmondo) shoots the policeman.
- *Mauvais Sang*'s plot, about a disease ('STBO') that attacks people who make love without feeling, is of course a reference to the developing AIDS crisis, as reviewers noted, but it also recalls *Alphaville*'s (1965) critique of a society from which emotion has been banished. The repeated close-ups on a flashing yellow headlight, interspersing shots of news headlines about STBO, evoke the car headlamp that Godard used to incarnate the supercomputer Alpha-60.
- *Mauvais Sang* contains further examples of comical fight sequences and of Godardian musical interludes (songs by Serge Reggiani and David Bowie). It also features an amorous fight with shaving foam that is reminiscent of the domestic play-fights in *Une femme est une femme* (1961).
- Marc's assistant Hans is played by Hans Meyer who had a minor role as a gang enforcer in *Pierrot le fou* and, in places, he makes the same mysterious, slow gestures with his splayed hands around his face that he made before beating Ferdinand in Godard's film.

After Godard, perhaps the most powerful influence over Carax is exerted by Philippe Garrel, himself profoundly indebted to Godard, as we saw in the previous chapter. Following the release of *Boy Meets Girl*, *Cahiers du cinéma* organized a meeting between Carax and Garrel in which they discussed their shared New Wave inheritance and their philosophy of cinema. Garrel subsequently cast Mireille Perrier in *Elle a passé tant d'heures sous les sunlights* (1985), having discovered her in Carax's film. Carax has arguably inherited Garrel's almost puritanical attitude to cinema, his refusal to see his artistic vision diluted and his mistrust of the mainstream film industry. Like Garrel, Carax is wary of granting interviews, seemingly in part out of a generalized mistrust of speech and language that relates back to his adolescent withdrawal into silence. But this also translates into a love of silent cinema that Carax shares with Garrel. In their joint interview, Carax expresses his admiration for Griffith, King Vidor and Jean Epstein[87] and he showed Juliette Binoche examples of Lilian Gish performances in preparation for her role as Anna.[88] As Jean-Luc Douin remarked, Carax seems to be seeking 'the mobility of expression of the faces of silent film stars',[89] and in doing so he includes, in both *Boy Meets Girl* and *Mauvais Sang*, shots of characters speaking without sound, a recurring strategy in Garrel's work.

Specific references to silent cinema in Carax include the superimposition of a woman's face over the Seine at the beginning of *Boy Meets Girl* that borrows from *Coeur fidèle* (Jean Epstein, 1923); Alex's staggering, swaying walk, matched to that of a toddler, in *Mauvais Sang*, in homage to *Limelight* (Chaplin, 1952); and the scene, channelling Buster Keaton, in which Alex uses the full extent of a telephone cord to lean out into the street and crane his neck up to Anna's window. At the same time, as Alban Pichon remarks,[90] the use of film editing to convey Alex's various tricks and sleights of hand recalls Georges Méliès's exploitation of early cinema as an art of illusion.

Another point of comparison between Carax and Garrel is that, for both, cinema is conceived, from the beginning, as a method of meeting women and as a means of documenting relationships with women. Carax admits that he bought his first film camera during his silent adolescent phase in order to meet a girl he liked: he cast the girl in his film and their first conversation took place with the camera rolling.[91] There are similar stories about Garrel's beginnings in filmmaking and the director famously documented on film his own intense relationship with Nico. Again, the New Wave serves as a model here, most particularly Godard's relationship with Anna Karina, displayed across seven feature films, although Truffaut and Chabrol also had well-known liaisons with some of their actresses. Extrapolating from these commonalities, Carax suggests that the couple is at the heart of art history: 'all movements, all waves', he suggests, 'were simply people who were in love at the same moment'.[92]

Garrel likewise compares this tendency to the history of painters' relationships with their models, citing Ingres and Georges de la Tour as examples.[93] The somewhat seedy associations of these directors exploiting cinema as a way of meeting attractive young women are offset by the relative bashfulness of Carax and Garrel when it comes to filming their actresses. Carax expresses his distaste for the vast majority of nudity in cinema, affirming that the filmmakers responsible are guilty of criminal disrespect for women.[94] On the contrary, he suggests that it is precisely when directors are in a relationship with their actress that they are least likely to show them naked: 'Anna Karina was never naked in a film by Godard', he points out.[95] This sense of a cinema of love coinciding with a respect for the image of women is conveyed by a scene in *Mauvais Sang* in which Alex is suddenly lovestruck by the vision of a woman while riding on a bus. The filming of this sequence, involving unnatural lighting, a series of extreme camera angles, character blocking and reflections in windows and mirrors, means that we never get a clear look at this woman; as Jean-Luc Douin puts it, 'This woman's face does not belong to us.'[96] We assume that the woman is Anna but, when the same musical theme from Benjamin Britten that accompanies the scene in the bus recurs towards the end of the film, as Alex is travelling in a car with Anna and glimpses another woman in white rounding a corner, the film raises the possibility that we, and perhaps Alex himself, have been mistaken in this identification. All the same, romantic love and the idea of love at first sight repeatedly coloured the rhetoric with which *Mauvais Sang* was discussed. Jean-Yves Escoffier suggested that the film itself was 'in love' with its actors, given the attentiveness of the camera to the emotion on the characters'/actors' faces.[97] Juliette Binoche declared, 'I fell in love with cinema while making this film.'[98] But reviewers too discussed *Mauvais Sang* as they might a nascent love affair: Michel Boujut suggested the film left him 'trembling with emotion, with a tight throat and shining eyes'[99] while *La Vie ouvrière* was dumbstruck like a teenager in love for the first time: 'We would have to invent new words in order to convey the atmosphere of *Mauvais Sang*.'[100]

Urban space in the *cinéma du look*

As was suggested in the Introduction, one point of connection between the New Wave and the *cinéma du look* is the depiction of the urban lifestyles of young people living in Paris. The experience of living in Paris underwent significant shifts during this period. In the 1950s, a housing crisis was identified in the French capital, largely brought about by rent controls, which meant that available property in the city was small, scarce and poorly maintained.[101] As a result, a major programme of slum clearance and new building was undertaken. Between 1954 and 1974, twenty-five per cent of the architecture in Paris was destroyed and rebuilt, and the number of workers living within the city declined by forty-four per cent, forced out by increasing rents to live in the hastily constructed housing projects of the suburbs.[102] Post-war France saw the age of 'rationalized' architecture, most famously inspired by the work of Le Corbusier: large blocks of standardized housing, often erected at some distance from the businesses and services of the city. The avant-garde in France at the time, and most notoriously the situationists, were highly critical of this new urbanism, decrying the loss of the character and community of the old city. They saw rationalized architecture as the projection of an imaginary 'social hierarchy without conflict' and the new urbanism as representing 'the totalitarian tendency of modern capitalism's organization of life':[103] 'life definitively partitioned in closed blocks, in surveilled societies; the end of chances for insurrection; automatic resignation'.[104] The situationists famously prescribed a playful re-appropriation of urban space through aimless drifting (*dérive*) through the city, interrupting the habitual trajectories of the capitalist working week and ignoring the privileged sites of the society of spectacle in favour of forgotten corners of Paris where it might still be possible to have unexpected encounters.

As is well known, the films of the French New Wave became famous for their use of location shooting in Paris. These films offered occasional glimpses of tourist sites like the Eiffel Tower or Notre Dame, but mostly chose to document the 'real Paris', the cafes, streets and riverbanks, the hotels and attic rooms frequented by young people in the early 1960s. I believe this aesthetic choice was partly a felicitous outcome of the housing crisis in Paris at the time: as a result of the poor quality accommodation available, young people chose to do much of their socializing, not to mention in some cases their intellectual work, in cafes and other public locations. It is also the case that characters in French New Wave films spend a considerable amount of time walking the streets of the city in a way that is not without recalling the principles of the situationist *dérive*. As James Tweedie comments, 'In the ambulatory cinema of the new wave, the contortions of plot are often mere pretexts as the directors pursue a less programmed ideal, with the protagonists set loose in an uncontrollable mass of other bodies, buildings, shops, automobiles, street signs, and movie marquees.'[105] It would be a mistake to overstate the connection between the New Wave and the situationists: the latter movement was radical in its rejection of contemporary culture and would have considered the New Wave just another product of the all-consuming capitalist spectacle. Even Godard, the most politicized of the New Wave filmmakers, was famously eviscerated in a critique published in the *Internationale situationniste*.[106] That said, there are a number of parallels to be drawn between the situationist discourse on urbanism and the New Wave's use of Parisian space. First, a number of key New Wave films feature long scenes of characters wandering aimlessly, on foot, through the city: most especially *Le Signe du Lion* (Rohmer, 1962) and *Cléo de 5 à 7* (Varda, 1961), which François Penz has described as 'the yardstick against which all other films must be measured' in terms of 'topographical coherence' (i.e. the fidelity and accuracy with which the film represents space as it exists on the ground).[107] Second, a number of New Wave films depict young people at play in the city: the truanting Antoine Doinel (Jean-Pierre Léaud) in *Les 400 coups* (Truffaut, 1959) or the partying students in Chabrol's *Cousins* (1959) and *Godelureaux* (1961). Third, some New Wave films, while filmed on location, take a ludic approach to the depiction of urban space, using editing to conflate spaces that are not geographically contiguous, as in *Paris nous appartient* (Rivette, 1961), or to draw attention to the elision of space (*Une femme est une femme*, Godard, 1961). Fourth, in his work of the later 1960s, Godard, in particular, would be openly critical of the alienating effects of the urban redesign of Paris (*Alphaville*, 1965; *2 ou 3 choses que je sais d'elle*, 1966).

In a bold new interpretation, James Tweedie has suggested, in a recent book, that this moment of urban modernization effectively provides the whole basis for the New Wave and, furthermore, that it can be generalized to other geographical and historical contexts (Tweedie compares the Nouvelle Vague to the Taiwanese New Wave of the 1980s and 1990s and the 'Fifth Generation' filmmakers of contemporary China). The conditions of a cinematic new wave, according to Tweedie, are as follows: (1) a demographic shift resulting in a young population where youth becomes 'the principal agent of social and cultural change'; (2) rapid urbanization giving rise to new 'paradigms for the organization of social space and belonging'; (3) accelerated globalization and marketization in which the indigenous population is exposed to the cultural products and ideologies of the world at large; and (4) an international art cinema or festival market to promote and disseminate the films, meaning that, paradoxically, 'they enter the global network of art cinema by producing images that allude to the tradition of realist filmmaking and in the process document a locality present in front of the camera'.[108] Tweedie argues that the New Wave's most important legacy, in formal terms, is the idiosyncratic conception of mise en scène developed in the 1950s by the *Cahiers du cinéma* critics who went on to become the directors of the Nouvelle Vague (a conception discussed in some detail in the Introduction to this volume). These critics-cum-directors, asserts Tweedie, dismissed narrative and were largely uninterested in editing, instead seeing the specificity of cinema in mise en scène, conceived as 'a phenomenon of bodies, objects, and space recorded with the incomparable precision and fidelity of the camera'.[109] It is this understanding and prioritizing of mise en scène that allowed the New Wave to capture the processes of social and cultural change underway in the France of the late 1950s and 1960s, and the key techniques of location shooting and the long take have subsequently been adopted by filmmakers in other national contexts undergoing similar waves of modernization (these techniques thereby becoming a kind of *lingua franca* of international art or festival cinema). The implication of Tweedie's argument is then that the enduring popularity of the Nouvelle Vague is not attributable to any great formal innovation but is largely due to the status of these films as documents:

> The films of the French and other new waves capture a glimpse of a future on the threshold of its arrival; they inhabit a landscape constructed in one social and economic system and experience a moment of transition; they reveal, in other words, the present when the walls from the past are being dismantled and the new façades are about to be unfurled.[110]

How, then, does the *cinéma du look* compare to these older examples? If Tweedie is right (and, although one may wish to argue about the specific historical differences in his three case studies, the broad strokes of his comparison are surely valid), then this would seem to imply that films set in Paris in the 1980s necessarily cannot be as compelling as the New Wave films in their depiction of space because the social context was less turbulent. By the 1980s, France's transition to a post-industrial economy was complete but the unprecedented economic growth of the post-war years had foundered in recession, and the growth of the population had slowed dramatically. The *cinéma du look* cannot share the New Wave's dramatic clash of generations, values, lifestyles and architectures, because, by the 1980s, the old Paris is simply no longer there, the working-class community has been marginalized along with its housing and its jobs. There is a single scene in *Diva* in which Jules delivers a benefit cheque to an old lady in a run-down apartment building; she is disappointed with the amount, having misunderstood that her allocation would be raised due to a local road-widening project. But this tokenistic effort at social comment appears so exceptional in *Diva* (accounting for less than thirty seconds of its 117-minute runtime) that the woman is clearly treated as a slightly comical figure, an anachronism held over from an earlier era that is all but extinct.

In what follows, I want to argue, following Tweedie's example, that the films of the *cinéma du look* have aged much more quickly than those of the New Wave in part because they do not have the same value as documents. Where the mise en scène of the Nouvelle Vague was designed to show how real people lived in real places, the famously stylized mise en scène of these 1980s films sought to create somewhat fantastical spaces carved out from the real. Ironically, then, the real spaces of the 1960s manage to look fresher today than the fantasy spaces of the 1980s. *Diva* presents several significant locations, both interior and exterior. The principal interiors are the living spaces of the protagonist Jules (Frédéric Andréi) and his friend and helper (almost in the manner of the classic folktale) Gorodish. Given Fredric Jameson's appellation of *Diva* as 'the first French postmodernist film',[111] it is significant that both of these lofts are reclaimed industrial spaces, an automotive garage in one case and an apparently renovated factory by a canal in the other. Other repurposed industrial spaces in the film include the lighthouse that has become a holiday home-cum-hideaway for Gorodish and friends and the disused warehouse in which Gorodish entraps the corrupt police chief Saporta (Jacques Fabbri). These are no longer spaces of work, but rather of leisure and consumption, where the characters eat, drink, flirt and listen to music. In keeping with postmodernism's much-discussed dissolving of frontiers (between old and new, popular and elite, working class and bourgeois, etc.)[112] these are also spaces in which inside and outside are confused: Jules rides his moped all the way into what is, effectively, his living room, and his home is decorated with the shells of crashed cars. Meanwhile, Alba (Thuy An Luu) roller-skates around Gorodish's loft.

Distinctions of public and private are also fluid in these spaces: Gorodish's bathtub is not enclosed in a room, but sits in the centre of the open-plan loft; and at Jules's place, there seems to be little to stop intruders from riding up to his 'apartment' in the industrial elevator (as happens several times during the film). A blurring of the boundaries between work and leisure, public and private, etc., was central to the situationist critique of space and time under capitalism.[113] The difference, however, is that where situationism sought to expose and condemn the ways in which capitalist imperatives structure our most basic modes of existence – our manner of inhabiting space and time – the postmodernist dissolving of boundaries represents, on the contrary, the ultimate victory of capitalism: work invades our homes, putting an end to privacy and 'downtime', while the iconography of play is imported into the workplace in an effort further to mask the oppressive nature of labour relations.[114] *Diva* demonstrates no critical awareness of this trend, instead simply presenting its spaces as examples of urban cool, the real-estate equivalent of 'distressed' jeans, or what Jules, at one point, calls 'le désastre de luxe'.

Diva's reputation for excessive stylization is largely attributable to these two sets, described as 'staggering' by one critic and 'aggressively original' by another,[115] so much so that they could easily become distracting or irritating. Both sets have almost matching blue-and-white or blue-and-silver colour schemes augmented by frequent bluish lighting. In addition, Gorodish's loft has an almost underwater feel generated by the centrepieces of a large wave machine and a huge jigsaw of a seascape (in addition to the bath), and, at one point, he wears a snorkel while chopping onions. While being self-consciously stylized, these are also pointedly intertextual spaces: Jules's garage features a large wall mural containing the image of teenagers racing 1950s cars in an apparent reference to the 'chickie run' scene in *Rebel without a Cause* (Ray, 1955) and the recurring images of Gorodish's massive jigsaw recall the one played by the lonesome Susan Alexander in *Citizen Kane* (1941). Also, while Gorodish's interior design is certainly minimalist, in places, the wilful complication of the mise en scène in *Diva* evokes the high expressionism of a Fritz Lang with its vertical lines, bars, reflections and trompe-l'oeil surfaces. In a scene like the one in which an injured Jules hides out from murderous pursuers in an amusement arcade, this aesthetic might conceivably be taken to reflect the protagonist's mental distress, as it often did in 1930s Germany or 1940s film noir; in the scene in Gorodish's kitchen, however, a clear justification for the shot is much harder to find.

The lack of psychological motivation for this mise en scène is matched by the absence of any clear social explanation for these living spaces. It is perhaps believable that the middle-aged Gorodish should be wealthy enough to afford his luxury loft, but the source of his income remains largely mysterious. Over the course of the narrative, he succeeds in extorting money by playing two sets of crooks off against each other, and it is implied that his secret (again, in true 'postmodern' style) lies in tapping in to flows of information, being in the right place at the right time and turning his foes' aggression against them (he never actually kills anyone in the film, merely tricks them into killing themselves or each other). On the other hand, Jules's occupation of his garage space remains entirely enigmatic. The garage is apparently not in commercial use, although it appears to have been so until recently. The wrecked cars are not there to be mended, but as ornaments and collector's items – Jules proudly points out one, a Rolls Royce Corniche, that

FIGURE 2.1 *Expressionist space in* Diva *(1981): Richard Bohringer, Frédéric Andréi and Thuy An Luu. Courtesy StudioCanal/Optimum World.*

collided with a palm tree in Monaco. There is an evocation here of an earlier era of luxury and hedonism, and the deaths of figures like Roger Nimier and Albert Camus, but no explanation of how such an artefact comes to be in the Paris apartment of a junior postal worker. The logic of collectibles pertains elsewhere in the film too. When Jules goes to stay with some colleagues from the Post Office, their apartment displays the more realistic cramped conditions of the urban working class, yet comes across as equally stylized since virtually every surface is covered with aeroplanes: pictures, posters and postcards, toys and models, even the pieces of bread the friend dips in his bowl of coffee are shaped like little planes. Then, too, the prostitute that Jules visits has a small collection of black mannequins in her apartment. And how does a prostitute (who, we later learn, is effectively performing slave labour) afford an apartment off Avenue Foch in the extremely bourgeois sixteenth arrondissement? If the apartment belongs to her pimp, why does she show off to Jules about the system of revolving lights she has bought, which casts a similar atmospheric light to the ones found in Jules's and Gorodish's homes and which provides a neat visual match to the wheel that turns the elevator cables in the former.

We might conclude that *Diva* is simply not trying to portray realistic spaces. Yet much of the thriller plot unfolds in the bustling arena of Parisian public transport facilities, specifically St Lazare station and the metro. I would argue, however, that the potential sense of threat is undercut in these scenes because the distancing effect of the film's extreme stylization militates against any suspension of disbelief. As Alain Bergala noted, in these films, natural locations seem to be filmed like theatrical sets.[116] It is unclear whether Beineix chose to make narrative use of the French national postal service and railway because their branded colour schemes of blue-and-yellow and blue-and-white matched his chosen visual design or whether the mise en scène of *Diva* was elaborated around these commercial brands; what is clear is the relative chromatic consistency between the 'stylized' interior scenes and the 'realistic' ones outside. The film's set-piece action scene in which Jules is chased into the underground, riding his moped downstairs, along moving walkways and on and off subway trains becomes thus, for me, a dull and repetitive formal exercise, empty of any suspense since the metro comes across not as a real space containing vulnerable citizens but as something like an amusement park. David Berry calls it 'a ludic space', the metro's 'maze of corridors [becoming] a metonymic structure for the convolutions of the plot';[117] or, as Fredric Jameson puts it, 'a strange new exhilaration' becomes 'conveniently breathable at all the interstices of daily life in late capitalist space'.[118] The same effect is achieved, this time even more clearly, in a later chase, when Jules runs into an underground car park on the Avenue Foch then, passing through a door, finds himself literally in an amusement arcade. The postmodern city comes across as what Zygmunt Bauman called a 'managed playground' where inhabitants are shuttled from one dedicated leisure space to another, their status insistently confirmed as spectators rather than meaningful social actors.[119]

The injured Jules telephones Gorodish and Alba from this amusement arcade and his friend arrives just in time to neutralize Jules's assailant, a matter of minutes, since the villain is already scouring the arcade for Jules while the latter is on the phone. Given that Gorodish takes the call at home, however, this is geographically impossible since, if his building is next to a canal, then it is most likely to be situated in the nineteenth arrondissement (i.e. on the other side of the city entirely) or else somewhere in the suburbs. By this stage of the film, however, such considerations of spatial realism have long since ceased to hold much meaning. As mentioned above, the deliberate dislocation of Parisian space was something that New Wave director Jacques Rivette enjoyed doing in films like *Paris nous appartient*, but there is a striking difference of effect between this example and *Diva*. Rivette took everyday Parisian locations and gave them an eerie, labyrinthine quality, implying a sinister conspiratorial logic at work behind the scenes of daily life; in *Diva*, Beineix achieves something like the opposite of this: scenes portraying the intrusion of organized crime and mysterious networks into the spaces of daily life are, by virtue of their stylization and their spatial trickery, stripped of their menace and rendered as inoffensive entertainment.

The underground railway that provides the setting for *Diva*'s most conspicuous action sequence constitutes the set of practically the whole of *Subway*. Fred, on the run from both police and private security, hides out in the Paris metro and discovers an entire community of misfits, oddballs and petty criminals. The film presents the underground as a labyrinthine space of connecting tunnels and corridors of which the public station platforms are only the most visible fraction. At the beginning of the film, Fred evades his pursuers by apparently jumping into the path of an oncoming train, only to escape via a maintenance trough beneath the train that then connects to a hidden corridor. A handful of very long, repetitive shots, such as the one in which a squadron of police officers descend a seemingly endless staircase, contribute to this sense of a space that is infinitely larger than it initially appears. To an extent, the metro risks becoming a temporal labyrinth too since, in the absence of daylight, it is difficult to tell how much time has elapsed, although the blackmail narrative tends to militate against this effect by imposing deadlines, while the coming and going of the public on the platforms is a clear enough indication of the time of day. In addition, though, Besson deliberately avoided showing billboards or posters within the metro in an effort to resist situating the film too obviously in time and space.[120] Again, here, the contrast with the New Wave is striking. Films of the Nouvelle Vague often made considerable efforts to demonstrate that they were set in a specific time and place: Godard famously included footage of Eisenhower's visit to Paris in September 1959 in *À bout de souffle* while Varda used actual radio broadcasts from 21 June 1961 in *Cléo de 5 à 7*. These indicators of historical specificity have allowed the films to remain fresh and fascinating documents of a transitional time, where the efforts at timeless stylization in the *cinéma du look* now seem all too tied to the 1980s but without telling us much about life in Paris at the time.

While much of *Subway* was shot in the real Paris metro during its night-time hours of closure to the public, some of the sequences taking place in hidden parts of the underground network were filmed on specially constructed studio sets. The set designer for *Subway* was Alexandre Trauner, famous for his work on the classic French poetic realist films of the 1930s and 1940s. Critics were quick to point out, in particular, Trauner's work on Marcel Carné's *Les Portes de la nuit* (1946) for which he famously rebuilt the Barbès metro station in the studio. As we have already seen, connections have been made by critics between poetic realism and the *cinéma du look* in terms of the tendency of both movements to privilege sets and atmosphere over narrative verisimilitude. While it is certainly true that *Subway* often favours the local colour of this underground community over the progression of the narrative, certainly in the early scenes, and while it is also true that critics found very obvious flaws in the screenplay of Besson's film, this is perhaps to do a disservice to poetic realism since the films of Carné, in particular, were always extremely tightly plotted whereas critics could point to 'immense gaps' in the screenplay of *Subway* or suggest that the order of the reels could be mixed up without affecting the narrative cohesion.[121] Still, it is perhaps the influence of Trauner and poetic realism that leads, in

Subway as in *Diva*, to an expressionist mise en scène of filtered light, high contrast and the division of the frame by various bars and lines.

As in *Diva*, though, a clear justification for this expressionist mise en scène is not easy to find. As is well known, the 'moody' aesthetic of poetic realism has been retrospectively interpreted as a reflection of the social crises in the France of the 1930s: the betrayal of the working class and the descent into factionalism and conflict.[122] Is it possible to offer a similar social interpretation of the *cinéma du look*? Hayward's reading in terms of disenfranchised youth is probably the most thoroughly elaborated example of such an analysis but I am not ultimately persuaded of its pertinence.

Consider the use of the underground space in *Subway*, for instance in the scene – very comparable to the chase in *Diva* – in which a roller-skating purse snatcher is chased by police. A charitable reading of this scene, and the wider film, might suggest that these young people are re-appropriating the space of the metro and, in an almost situationist sense, resisting the rigid psychogeography imposed by the authorities and re-imagining the underground as a space of play and contestation. But the problem with this reading is, in the end, that life in the metro *looks like too much fun*; somewhat as in *Diva*, the subway is presented as one big playground. Now this is not to suggest that a situationist *dérive* shouldn't be fun – au contraire – but it should also incorporate at least some critical awareness of the prescribed usage of space and of the politico-economic base that governs this superstructure. Without this awareness, the playfulness of *Subway* becomes, as one critic put it, 'a gratuitous and rather vain game'.[123] There is little sense, in the film, of the underground as a space in which real economic relations are played out. In *Cahiers du cinéma*, Michel Chion suggested that this was largely because the general public – the daily users of the metro – are mostly absent from the film. Chion points out a scene in which the police commissioner (Michel Galabru) arrests the roller-skating thief on a subway train by handcuffing him to the hand rail; curiously, there is no reverse shot here to show the reaction of other passengers in the carriage.[124] The public is relegated to the margins of the film. Again, one could attempt a charitable reading by suggesting that *Subway* overturns the traditional social hierarchy such that law-abiding, productive citizens become all but invisible whereas outlaws occupy centre stage. But one obvious blind spot in this reading is the glaring absence, among this underground community, of any of the people who *actually* live in the metro in real life, i.e. the homeless human residue of liberal capitalism. As Marie-Thérèse Journot has argued, in the *cinéma du look* marginalization is always an individual affair, often with romantic motivation, as in the case of Fred whose retreat to the subway is sparked by his ill-conceived and apparently hopeless infatuation with wealthy socialite Héléna. There is a kind of tragic glamour to the fractured lives of these characters for which society is never rendered responsible.[125]

Leos Carax's use of space, perhaps unsurprisingly given all we already know about the director's proximity to Godard and Garrel, is much closer to that of the original New Wave, at least in *Boy Meets Girl*. The film begins by the Seine, with unstable, hand-held camerawork establishing the river and passing boats, where Alex meets his friend Thomas (Christian Cloarec) who he discovers has betrayed him by sleeping with Alex's girlfriend Florence. Alex gets his revenge by pushing Thomas into the river, the action filmed in long shot and appearing almost as an afterthought, Alex running back after having initially left the scene. This opening scene clearly sets up the film as being closely tied to its Parisian locations, and this sense is strengthened when Alex reveals, behind a picture on the wall of his room, a hand-drawn map of the city annotated with the dates of various first experiences: first kiss, first theft, first lie to 'F' and, following the encounter with Thomas, first attempted murder. The sense of Parisian space as something to be exhaustively mapped and catalogued while, at the same time, being full of mystery and intrigue is familiar from the films of Jacques Rivette. In particular, Alex's diagram recalls the way in which a map of Paris is fitted together with a spiral-shaped children's game, the *jeu de l'oie*, in *Le Pont du Nord* (1981).[126] At the same time, the inhabiting of space by young people is considerably more realistic in *Boy Meets Girl* than in the other films of the *cinéma du look*. Both Alex and Mireille live in small rooms or apartments, sparsely furnished with domestic essentials (hot plate, fridge) and a handful of luxuries (a record player and a telephone for Mireille, a television and a typewriter for Alex), and Alex has to bang on the wall when disturbed by noise from his neighbours. The rest of the film takes place in the exterior locations accessible to penniless young people – cafes, phone booths, record shops, the metro, the stairwells and corridors of friends' apartment buildings – plus the glimpse of a more affluent society in the party where Alex and Mireille meet, but which he has gatecrashed after stealing an invitation. The only rather less plausible set in the film is the large plate-glass window out of which Mireille stares and in front of which she dies at the end of the film. This huge window seems inconsistent with the small apartment in which Mireille apparently lives earlier in the film and comes across as a kind of symbolic representation of cinema, since the window is approximately the size of a cinema screen through which Mireille watches the lovers in a neighbouring building.

This final set in *Boy Meets Girl* looks forward, however, to *Mauvais Sang* in which the use of space is considerably more artificial and stylized. The film is ostensibly set in Paris but almost no identifiable locations are seen. Many of the exterior locations are in unspecified suburbs, such as the forest where we first see Alex and Lise or the private airfield from which the protagonists go skydiving. Sequences presumably taking place within the city are filmed either with such a tight focus that no landmarks are visible (as in Alex's card hustles on the street) or in anonymous modern buildings that could be anywhere (the theft of the vaccine from Darley-Wilkinson). The majority of the film is set in Marc's living space which features a very contrived décor, evidently inspired by the stylized colour schemes of Godard's mid-to-late 1960s films. Everything in this building is apparently black, white or red, save for occasional touches of blue.

The walls are decorated, on their lower half, with crazy black-and-white tiling and, on their upper half, with a black-and-white paint effect somewhere between marble and mould, the two halves separated by a red picture rail. Key furnishings (the dining table, the bed linen, the radiator) are all in the same bright red hue, which are further matched to Anna's cardigan and nail polish. Like the space at the end of *Boy Meets Girl*, Marc's place in *Mauvais Sang* seems to feature a picture window on to the street; at one point, as Marc and Alex fight, their faces are squashed against the glass. But 'the street' is self-evidently a studio set, itself decorated in the same palette of black, white and grey with touches of red, such as the signs for the hotel opposite. It is in this décor that many of the film's set-piece performances happen, such as Alex's dance/run along the street to David Bowie's 'Modern Love' (against a series of black, grey and red façades); Alex's impromptu toppling of a (white) Volkswagen Beetle; his Keatonesque hanging on the telephone cord or his Chaplinesque tottering walk (against a wall painted in red and white stripes). More than anything, this 'street' comes to resemble a set from a Hollywood musical: a space with only the most superficial resemblance to an actual city but in fact transparently designed as a backdrop for dancing and acrobatic performance.

Carax's use of artificial sets would continue in his subsequent films: he famously had the entire Pont Neuf and surrounding façades reconstructed

FIGURE 2.2 *Denis Lavant in* Mauvais Sang *(1986). Courtesy Artificial Eye.*

in the south of France in order to film *Les Amants du Pont Neuf*. This anecdote, together with television footage of the extraordinary set, featured prominently in Guy Debord's last film, *Guy Debord, son art et son temps* (1995), completed by Brigitte Cornand after Debord's death. In this deeply melancholic film, Carax's set signifies the irrevocable loss of Debord's beloved Paris, its definitive supplanting by what the former situationist had come to call 'integrated spectacle', a victory so complete for alienated capital that it has become impossible even to remember anything predating the spectacle.[127] Other commentators have also noted the prevalence of spectacle and play in the postmodern city. David Harvey remarks that with the dismantling of traditional industries and the increasing mobility of capital, cities are obliged to work hard to attract investment.[128] One consequence of this process, as Nezar AlSayyad notes, is that municipalities will invest in 'creating spectacular events and spaces of consumption, at the expense of services for the poor'[129] – hence the dazzling surfaces and the recurrent sense of playfulness in the *cinéma du look*. But, whereas the films of the New Wave, like the situationists, appropriated urban space with ludic intent, there is sometimes a sense, in these films of the 1980s, of characters being played by the city, inserted into joyless circuits of consumption like balls in a pinball machine. The problem with the playful spectacle in the *cinéma du look* is that it prevents encounters. If the aimless drift of the situationist *dérive* nonetheless had a goal, it was to facilitate encounters, with places and people that the drifter would otherwise never come across. One of the enduring charms of New Wave films is the frequency with which the protagonists run up against minor characters, extras and passers-by, who may provide moments of comic relief or philosophical reflection before disappearing from the world of the film. With the exception of *Boy Meets Girl*, clearly the most directly beholden of all these films to the Nouvelle Vague, the *cinéma du look* rarely allows for such unnecessary encounters. This is in the image of a leisure society criticized by the situationists for its tendency to segregate populations, control movements and limit horizons. The openness to incident, the sense that anything might happen, is perhaps what has been most noticeably shut down between the New Wave and the *cinéma du look*.

Rhythm

In the preceding section, we have lent considerable credence to James Tweedie's argument that much of the lasting charm and value of the French New Wave rests in its capturing of a key moment of cultural transition, a phenomenon made possible through the New Wave directors' privileging of mise en scène above other elements of film practice. There are limits, however, to the usefulness of this argument. After all, if the value of the Nouvelle Vague lay exclusively, or mainly, in its status as document, then why haven't simple television reportages of the same period aged as gracefully? The lasting appeal of the New Wave is, of course, one of the principal concerns of this book, and we will not attempt to summarize all of its contours here. One factor in the movement's ongoing aesthetic success, however, may be the films' deft command of rhythm, an aspect that is largely absent from Tweedie's account. Tweedie claims, somewhat hastily, that the New Wave critics were largely dismissive of the significance of montage[130] and opines that 'if the new wave consisted exclusively of jump cuts and rough camera work, the ostentatious stylistic gestures most readily attributable to the auteur, it would have ceded its prominent position in film history to the next new thing and faded into obscurity long ago'.[131] Now rhythm in the cinema is by no means exclusively a question of editing. Various theorists, and notably Russian pioneers like Eisenstein and Tarkovsky, have argued that rhythm is generated as much by the content of individual shots as it is by the length of shots or the relationship between shots.[132] But Tweedie's dismissive account of editing tends to downplay its importance in the New Wave not just in terms of arguably modish techniques like the jump cut but more significantly in terms of the overall organization of narrative space. This is unfortunate because I would argue that the use of space in the New Wave was key to these films' engagement of rhythm. In New Wave films, exterior and interior spaces often interact rhythmically: in a very classical division of space, the outside is the arena of encounter with others, of confrontation with authority, of seduction and discovery, whereas interiors provide occasions for introspection, the development of romance or domestic conflict. The canonical example of this is Godard's *À bout de souffle* where the thriller narrative is played out in the streets and the long interior scenes make space for the slow dance of seduction between Michel and Patricia as well as for moments of existential doubt and despair. Similar control of dramatic rhythm can equally be found in films by Truffaut and Chabrol. My suggestion, then, is that in the *cinéma du look*, partly because of the conflation of inside and outside, all of this tends to be confused and the result is not so much a postmodern liberation of social boundaries as a flattening of social space that has an unfortunately deadening effect on dramatic rhythm. It is also important to note that in many New Wave films, and especially those of Godard, the interior scenes are just as gripping as the outdoor 'action' sequences, but for different reasons linked to the playfulness of dialogue, the depth of cultural reference or the complex evolution of sentiments. In the *cinéma du look*, I suggest, the homogenization of space is matched by a certain homogenization of rhythm.

Diva has a remarkably slow, ponderous rhythm for what is, ostensibly, a thriller. There is no dialogue for the first six and a half minutes of the film while Jules watches Cynthia Hawkins, the titular diva (played by

Wilhelmenia Higgins Fernandez), performing an aria. As Phil Powrie has commented, 'It is easy to forget how startling the opening of the film was for audiences at the time, who would have been expecting a police thriller, but were given a poignant (and then largely unknown) opera aria accompanied by a series of dizzy camera movements'.[133] Indulging his erotic obsession with the diva, Jules makes an illicit recording of her recital and steals the dress she performs in. But, if an unlikely romance between the two is a key subplot to the film – indeed, less a subplot than one of two central plots – it develops painfully slowly since a full thirty-six minutes have elapsed before the relationship is sparked by Jules returning the dress. The sequence that marks the centre of their ambiguous courtship, when the pair go on a date and wander the streets of Paris in the early dawn light, is similarly leisurely in its pacing, all dialogue replaced by romantic, Satie-esque piano music. What is supposed to be a wordless idyll, however, risks coming across as merely awkward since the imbalance between this internationally famous American opera star and a shy young postal worker is such that the relationship is never really plausible. Meanwhile, the locations for this sequence have such a picture-postcard tourist familiarity – the Arc de Triomphe, the Jardins du Luxembourg, the Place de la Concorde – that there is little sense of anything personal in this encounter.

Carina Yervasi remarked upon the 'strange contrast' between these 'contemplative moments' and 'the rapidity with which the plot structure develops' in *Diva*.[134] In truth, however, this is not so strange. Laura Mulvey showed, several decades ago, that the arrest of narrative development by moments of erotic contemplation was a key characteristic of narrative cinema, especially in Hollywood.[135] Arguably, this dialectic is central to the sustain-and-release of tension that generates the rhythm of major American genres like film noir. What is striking about *Diva*, I would argue against Yervasi, is that the thriller narrative develops with the same lethargic pace as the hesitant romantic scenes between Jules and Cynthia. The metro chase, for instance, is a series of lengthy shots of running through corridors and up and down stairs that becomes so monotonous it is as though the characters are running on the spot. Meanwhile the metro, as suggested in the section above, becomes just another tourist site: a shiny backdrop but without the social depth that could give meaning and urgency to the stunts occurring within it. Despite its excellent premise (the confusion of two tape recordings: Jules's illicit recording of Cynthia and a confession indicting a police commissioner for his involvement in a prostitution ring, the latter having come into Jules's possession without his knowledge), *Diva* struggles to generate suspense. Key scenes in the development of the crime plot are bungled. At the point when commissioner Saporta meets his henchmen in an empty car park, the spectator does not yet know his secret criminal identity. The scene attempts to maintain this confusion by filming Saporta backlit, out of focus and in blurry reflections in extreme close-up, yet there is no attempt to disguise his voice and his references to his 'team', to the 'dossier' on Jules and to 'my cops' leave little room for doubt. Elsewhere, attempts to inject humour into the crime narrative fall woefully flat, such as the scene in which an old working-class couple play a fairground wheel-of-fortune and witness the murder of the stallholder, Krantz (Jean-Jacques Moreau), a police informer. Such scenes succeed only in dissuading us from taking seriously the plot or the supposed danger to Jules. Marie-Thérèse Journot, remarking upon the slow pace of *Diva*, notes a tendency for Beineix to employ long sequences that end gradually rather than abruptly, static shots or very slow tracks and scenes with minimal action.[136] It is curious, under the circumstances, that more reviewers didn't complain about the slowness of *Diva*; where they were critical at all, it tended to be of the excess in the film's visual design. But the two phenomena are undoubtedly related: as Journot argues, when images recur in *Diva* – for instance, the insistent colour scheme, the taste for shiny and reflective surfaces, repeated figures of statues – it is not because they have any narrative significance (as might be the case with recurrent images in Hitchcock, for instance) but rather as 'the leitmotif of a melody'.[137] Detached in this way from narrative progression, the mise en scène of *Diva* tends to be apprehended as a series of fixed images (and arguably this is how it remains in the memory) rather than as a series of actions captured in a logical sequence of shots. This was indeed how the film was received, at least judging by the critical reaction, but the result is frustratingly lifeless.

By contrast, the opening shot of *Subway* seems to promise a dynamic and exciting film. Besson's film opens on a frontal shot through the windscreen of a car driven by Fred, who searches the floor for a cassette to put in the stereo. Through the rear window of the car, however, we see a large Mercedes approaching at speed, evidently in pursuit of Fred. The two cars chase each other into Paris (where the streets are curiously deserted despite the apparent daylight: a further example of the playground-Paris of the *cinéma du look* from which real danger for real citizens seems oddly absent), and Fred eventually drives straight down the steps of an entrance to the metro. As Marie-Thérèse Journot points out, however, this breathtaking opening scene turns out to be the only rapid sequence in the whole film.[138] Once Fred is below ground, the pace slows considerably and the emphasis tends to be more on the strange atmosphere generated by the almost-expressionist sets, the filtered light and the curious inhabitants of the subway. Perhaps more accurately, periodic action sequences, when Fred and his pals are chased through the underground corridors either by the police or by the hired men of Héléna's husband, are interspersed with lengthy scenes effectively documenting the largely idle life underground. The somewhat disjointed effect, together with the use of music – in the opening sequence, it is almost as though the chase cannot begin in earnest until Fred puts the tape in the car stereo and presses play – led a number of critics to see in *Subway* an aesthetic of the music video (or *le clip*, in French). It was repeatedly observed that Besson had already directed a video for Isabelle Adjani's single 'Pull Marine' and *Subway* was seen as simply a prolonging of that same logic. The film was 'a music video in Cinemascope'[139] or 'an inexplicably extended video clip'.[140] Yann Plougastel in *L'Événement du jeudi* also saw the film as 'clipesque' with its 'chases among pipes and smoke, hammering rock'n'roll and lighting through metallic blinds'.[141] What is striking here is the extent to which the association of these visual cues with the cinema (German Expressionism via film noir) has apparently been superseded, in the popular cultural imaginary, by their status as clichés from music videos.

Raphaël Bassan complained, no doubt with some justification, that there was a large part of anachronistic snobbery in these criticisms, a refusal to allow filmmakers to use the visual language of their age in creating their art.[142] In a similar way, David Russell pointed to Beineix's almost exclusive use of artificial light when filming the interiors of *Diva* suggesting that it was a way of documenting a world increasingly colonized by consumer capitalism. 'We see [this kind of lighting] every day', he wrote. 'In glossy magazines, fashion photography, shop windows, car showrooms, amusement arcades, shopping precincts, restaurants ... Beineix has simply made of it a new kind of daylight – the daylight in which the images of our culture live and breathe.'[143] This is all the more true in the case of *Subway*, of course, since the majority of the film takes place underground where there *is* no natural light.

Even a cursory familiarity with music video is sufficient to demonstrate that the films discussed in this chapter actually share few of its characteristics.[144] Still, music looms large in the *cinéma du look* and often plays a central role in generating the films' aesthetic organization. In his early films, Luc Besson worked closely with the composer Éric Serra who Gérard Dastugue argues can be considered 'as much an auteur of Besson's films as Besson himself',[145] and it is often possible to see music 'preceding the image' in the conception and realization of Besson's films.[146] We can see this composition led by music in several scenes in *Subway*. After Fred befriends the underground community he is taken to a secret birthday party. As he and the roller skater (Jean-Hugues Anglade) approach the door bass guitar notes sound, which could be taken as non-diegetic until they grow louder when the door opens. A long, slow track around the room eventually reveals the bassist (played by Éric Serra himself) with a friend playing bongos. Fred talks to the guitarist about his idea of setting up a band. The music stops during this conversation and during the subsequent rendition of 'Happy birthday' as the lights are turned out and a cake presented. The blowing out of the candles cues a cut to a dark tunnel shot from the front of a moving subway train as music – now non-diegetic – plays that is similarly heavy on bass notes (although generated by synthesizer). The lighter notes of a melody appear as the train emerges from the tunnel to show a crowd of rush-hour commuters on the platform, thus designating the arrival of morning, and this melody then soundtracks a montage of the daytime metro which culminates in the roller skater's theft of a handbag. It is clear, in other words, how the transition between sequences and the tone of certain scenes is introduced by the music.

Another good example is the scene in which Héléna spends the night in the metro. Fred and the skater break into a station bar and find some champagne but Héléna is in a bad mood having realized that Fred's threatened blackmail was actually just a ruse to attract her into his world. 'Well you're not going to get me!' she declares sulkily, but meanwhile the skater has put a tape into his ghetto blaster. The song that plays ('Lucky Guy' by Rickie Lee Jones) is thus 'diegetic', yet evidently post-synchronized since the sound is richer and fuller than you would expect of a portable tape player in the cavernous space of the Châtelet-Les Halles RER station. Héléna suggests a dance and the camera cuts to a long shot of her and Fred against the empty grey station corridors then tracks in to stop at a head-and-shoulders medium close-up of the two of them just as the vocal begins ('Oh, he's a lucky guy ... '). There ensues a combative yet flirtatious exchange between the two that is among the better pieces of dialogue writing in *Subway*:

FRED: Why do I love you?
HÉLÉNA: Because I'm a terrific girl.
FRED: Why don't you love me?
HÉLÉNA: I don't feel up to it.
FRED: Are you lazy?
HÉLÉNA: Yes.
FRED: Who makes the dinner at your place?
HÉLÉNA: The cook.
FRED: And who makes the beds?
HÉLÉNA: The maid.
FRED: And who makes love?[147]
HÉLÉNA: ...

The roller skater cuts in just in time to prevent Héléna from answering this last impertinent question. After a while, a slow dissolve leads to a frontal shot of these three, plus the drummer (Jean Réno) watching Big Bill (Christian Gomba) apparently doing some welding on the rails of the track, the flying sparks causing lighting effects to flicker off the faces of the characters as they share a joint. Finally, the music fades and another dissolve takes us to the next morning. In addition to resembling a music video, with a romantic sequence accompanying a love song, this scene also suggests the influence of the Hollywood musical genre over *Subway*. As in a musical, it is the song that gives direction, pace and tone to the scene, a song that is ostensibly diegetic but actually added in post-production for maximum effect. But, furthermore, the pattern of Fred and Héléna's relationship is familiar from musicals: Héléna seemingly takes an instant dislike to Fred, and it is only upon dancing with him that she begins to soften; it is as though the music knows the direction of their relationship ('he's a lucky guy ... ') before the characters do. The use of music does, in sum, give a certain *élan* to passages of *Subway* and is often largely responsible for many of the most successful sequences. It remains the case, unfortunately, that these well-conceived musical sequences are separated by longueurs filled out with an implausible, uninvolving plot and rather uninspiring dialogue. Rather than a music video extended to feature length, *Subway* resembles a succession of short clips but whose rhythm and dynamism cannot be sustained for the whole film. The music-video format after all tends to militate against spectator identification and narrative cohesion, precisely because the focus needs to remain on the song and not the story.[148]

This same criticism – of a feature film as a disjointed and inconsistent series of 'clips' – has on occasion also been made of Leos Carax's work. Dominique Jamet described *Mauvais Sang* precisely as 'a succession of clips, or episodes of a comic strip, that are practically independent of one another [...] – Alex packs his suitcase, Alex does a parachute jump, Alex does card tricks – with moments of brilliance, but also long tunnels of boredom'.[149] Carax belongs to the age of music video just as much as Beineix and Besson, and his work is clearly also inspired by it. But Fergus Daly and Garin Dowd suggest that Carax is seeking to avoid the expected emotional associations of musical sequences and to 'reclaim' the form from the entertainment industry, exploiting it as 'an experimental possibility' for cinema.[150] The extent to which this is successful varies considerably between individual sequences. The 'Holiday in Cambodia' sequence in *Boy Meets Girl* is indeed innovative and unusual. Mireille seemingly tunes her radio to find the Dead Kennedys song and then disappears into the kitchen. The camera tracks in slowly and a vague sense of menace gathers out of the combination of this movement and the harsh metallic guitars in the song's intro. Mireille emerges in medium-close profile and slaps herself in the face, before starting to spin her head rapidly as the vocals begin – somewhere between a stretch, a dance and a self-flagellation. The track has thus gathered ominous overtones when it is interrupted by the apartment's intercom buzzer as Mireille's partner, Bernard, calls up from the street. As the scene continues, the sound of the Dead Kennedys track modulates realistically when the camera cuts between the apartment and the street below. Alex approaches and stares at Bernard as he talks to Mireille but the spectator gradually realizes that the words heard on the soundtrack – an increasingly cruel tirade to Mireille ('I have convinced myself that you stink', he says at one point) – do not match the movements of Bernard's mouth into the intercom and, when he signs off the conversation with 'See you later, my angel, I won't be late', it appears that we have been listening instead to his unspoken thoughts. The end of the song coincides with the click as the intercom phone is hung up, so the track effectively determines the duration of the scene, yet in all other respects this sequence is unlike either music videos or the traditional uses of music in cinema. The song does not provide an interlude from plot development nor does it fade into the background to allow further development, and the lyrics have no real relation to the scene at hand. If anything, the music is a distraction from an important scene setting up the triangular relationship between Mireille, Bernard and Alex and that is further complicated by the ambiguous provenance of Bernard's words and their unfriendly tone. The spectator is, in short, uncertain how to interpret this sequence, yet the angry and urgent music of Dead Kennedys lends it a nervous edge that seems ultimately appropriate to its observation of the ugly and conflicted sentiments underlying relationships.

By comparison, the famous 'Modern Love' sequence in *Mauvais Sang* appears altogether conventional. Here, Alex interrupts his long conversation/flirtation with Anna to turn on the radio. The station he finds first plays Serge Reggiani's 'J'ai pas de regrets' while Alex goes outside to smoke a cigarette. Then the announcer introduces David Bowie's 'Modern Love'. As the track begins, Alex seems to bend over and grip his belly (he will subsequently complain that a leaden feeling in his stomach is the legacy of the fifteen months he spent in prison) then stumbles left to right across the frame, both Alex and the camera gathering pace as first the beat, then the vocal and melody come in. Eventually, Alex sprints, leaps, spins and cartwheels along the street to the song, by now clearly no longer diegetic since he has covered too much ground to be able still to hear the radio. While Denis Lavant's performance is uniquely energetic and the tracking shot is impressive for its speed and length, this is ultimately a very conventional use of music. The song cuts out after the first chorus, which is fairly standard for the use of pre-existing pop songs in film: long enough for the audience to recognize and enjoy the track, but not so long as to become a distraction from the narrative. Meanwhile, given the context within Alex's long night with Anna, the title of the song (clearly announced by the radio presenter) and Alex's ebullient canter, the sequence obviously depicts romantic exhilaration of the most familiar kind. But, at the same time, the sequence stands somewhat outside the narrative, as though it were a stand-alone music video (if it is so frequently mentioned by commentators on the film, it is no doubt largely because its parenthetic status makes it stand out in the memory from the rest of the film).

Marc Chevrie has suggested that Leos Carax makes 'a cinema of postures, of speeds, of rhythms, and hence of musicality'.[151] If this is true of individual sequences, however, like the 'Modern Love' episode, it is not necessarily clear that this 'musicality' operates successfully at the level of whole films. Marie-Thérèse Journot notes that because Carax tends to work with 'autonomous sequences', the narrative can place them one after another without ever engendering a tempo. 'Time becomes immobile' in these films.[152] This partly accounts for the other-worldly tone that takes hold of Carax's films, particularly *Mauvais Sang* but, while this is certainly unique, it does not always make for an aesthetically successful film. As briefly mentioned earlier in this chapter, the structure of *Mauvais Sang* (and to a somewhat lesser extent *Boy Meets Girl*) can be seen to be modelled on many of the 1960s films of Jean-Luc Godard, with a long domestic scene bookended by a sketchily drawn thriller plot. The pattern is familiar from *À bout de souffle*, *Le Petit Soldat* or *Pierrot le fou* (where the only difference is that the domestic scenes take place outdoors). Jean-Luc Macia notes that for the first forty-five minutes of *Mauvais Sang*, the rhythm is generated by the proliferation of formal ideas and the restless experimentation: 'Carax seems to review everything it is possible to do with a hyper-mobile camera, changing lenses and nervy editing.'[153] The long scene between Alex and Anna thus comes across as 'an indispensable moment of respiration' in a film otherwise made up of 'more or less panicky gasps for breath'.[154] These two descriptions could ably be applied to any of the Godard films mentioned above, but my own sense is that Carax's films are less successful at sustaining rhythm and spectator engagement across these changes of pace.

It may be that Tweedie's argument can again be invoked here to explain the more urgent appeal of the New Wave film. What is perhaps most gripping about the various apartment sequences of the Nouvelle Vague, and of Godard's cinema in particular, is not the eternal clash of man and woman but precisely the historically situated nature of their sparring. As Tweedie himself notes regarding the famous Hôtel de Suède sequence in *À bout de souffle*, 'what unfolds alongside the verbal interaction between Michel and Patricia is a more revealing drama involving two bodies interacting with each other and their surroundings'.[155] More specifically, we could point to all the ways in which the outside world infiltrates the hotel room, reminding the characters, and the viewer, of the cultural context: this is done through the continual patter of the radio and through the detritus of newly mass-produced cultural artefacts. Paperbacks, records and poster reproductions of paintings place Patricia and Michel within a singular moment of cultural awareness where the global cultural heritage was sufficiently disseminated to be the object of popular discussion but also sufficiently manageable in scope to be encompassed within a totalizing vision or philosophy, precisely the moment in film history that allowed the New Wave to be born from the apprehension, distillation and irreverent recuperation of a half-century of cinema. Meanwhile, the scene in the Hôtel de Suède documents the faltering evolution of gender relations, showing Patricia's hesitant embrace of her liberated sexuality and career ambitions alongside Michel's self-conscious macho bluster and Patricia's fear of pregnancy. If all of this comes to life in *À bout de souffle*, however, it is also because of Godard's command of the rhythm of editing which, here, just as in the scenes outside, although less ostentatiously, combines long takes with jump cuts, allowing the time and space to observe this social transformation while maintaining a playfulness and energy throughout the scene.[156] Rather than the simple good luck implied by Tweedie's conception of the New Wave (which, at its nadir, amounts to having been in the right place at the right time), it is this combination of a felicitous cultural context with a dynamic and very conscious control of rhythm that I suggest accounts for the New Wave's specificity and names what is most sadly lacking from the *cinéma du look*.

Conclusion

The *cinéma du look* shares with the French New Wave a handful of key characteristics, in particular its interest in youthful protagonists and a certain wayward approach to film genre, especially its creative appropriation of the crime thriller. With the exception of Carax, the most obviously indebted to the New Wave, the films of the *cinéma du look* directors were, in fact, rarely compared to the Nouvelle Vague. Surprisingly, French cinema of the 1930s is a more common point of reference, from the poetic realist echoes in *Diva* and *Subway* to Carax's affection for Julien Duvivier. However, compared to their New Wave forebears, these directors of the 1980s show little apparent interest in situating themselves in film history: even Carax's cinephile discourse seems often to present 'the cinema' as a totalizing whole in which he immerses himself, rather than separating out clear categories, canons, paradigms and turning points in relation to which he might position his own work. In other words, the *cinéma du look* arrives at a postmodern moment in which the whole of film history has become a kind of undifferentiated library from which directors may borrow and quote at will, yet the films themselves demonstrate little sense of arriving at a particular moment in history with a peculiar inheritance or a distinct importance. However much they may lift ideas from film history, though, it is hard not to be struck by the hyperbole with which these films were greeted as staggeringly original works of art. No doubt this tells us more about the French film press of the time than it does about the films themselves: an age of increased competition between newspapers and magazines, but also between films on the market, disseminated in greater number, such that even slightly inventive films are more likely to stand out, whereas journalists seek to outdo each other with eye-catching critiques and rush to identify the next major trend.

Arguably, too, the increased ease of access to film history, via television and video cassettes, leads ironically to a faster forgetting of the past since it is just not realistic to absorb all the available material and still keep abreast of current developments, which remains the journalist's raison d'être. One reason for the excess in the critical appraisal of the *cinéma du look* may therefore have been the increasingly short memories of film critics in France, a tendency that has only accelerated in the decades since the 1980s (this question will be addressed further in Chapter 4).

It is no doubt a critical fallacy to suggest that any one era, or decade, is 'more historical' than another. Nonetheless, the sociocultural circumstances of the New Wave and the *cinéma du look* remain very different: the Nouvelle Vague is associated with economic growth and a young and expanding population, with a generational shift marked by a cultural openness and sexual liberation imported from abroad; the *cinéma du look*, on the other hand, arrives at a time of economic recession, slowed demographic growth and family breakdown, the long-term consequences of the 'glorious' post-war decades. If the location shooting and the casually inclusive mise en scène of the New Wave give us, still today, some indication of the physical changes, the social confidence and the sense of possibility in the France of the early 1960s, the films of the *cinéma du look*, for all their polished surfaces, often come across as frustratingly enclosed and inward-looking. The stress on spectacle and surface glamour is perhaps representative of the 'flexible accumulation' of postmodern capitalism,[157] yet the confusion of public and private, inside and outside spaces in these films, is achieved without real critical awareness or social perspicacity, granting us little sense, in the end, of how young people actually lived in the 1980s. The rather leaden rhythm that finally condemns these films is perhaps an effect of this social detachment: the absence of any appreciable sense of how the real might actually impinge upon and shape the lives of these protagonists leaves the films fatally lacking in urgency.

Notes

1 Yvette Bíro, *Turbulence and Flow in Film: The Rhythmic Design* (Bloomington: Indiana University Press, 2008), 6.

2 Ibid., 33.

3 The exceptions to this rule can be found in American film criticism where the term 'New Wave' is often used so loosely – in the broadest sense of 'an arty French film' – that it has only the most minimal ties to the historical movement that interests us in this book. Thus, the *Herald Tribune* called *Diva* 'an offbeat French New Wave film', Lynn Darling, 'The Curious Case of the Film *Diva*', *Herald Tribune*, 6 August 1982. This elasticity of terminology sometimes sneaks into more academic writing: Ernece B. Kelly describes *Diva* as 'old and conservative wine carefully poured into a shiny bottle with New Wave labels', '*Diva*: High Tech Sexual Politics', *Jump Cut* 29 (1984), available at: http://www.ejumpcut.org/archive/onlinessays/JC29folder/Diva.html, accessed 27 August 2014, citation at p. 2 of 7.

4 See, for instance, Claude Baignères, 'La quête de l'absurde', *L'Aurore*, 17 March 1981 and Pierre Billard, 'Ne ratons pas le premier métro', *Le Point*, 23 March 1981.

5 Marie-Thérèse Journot, *Le Courant de 'l'esthétique publicitaire' dans le cinéma français des années 80: La modernité en crise: Beineix, Besson, Carax* (Paris: L'Harmattan, 2004), 119.
6 Alain Bergala, 'D'une certaine manière', *Cahiers du cinéma* 370 (April 1985), 13.
7 Journot, *Le Courant de 'l'esthétique publicitaire'*, 75–6, 82.
8 'cette nouvelle vague arrive', Claire Devarrieux, 'La métaphore de l'alpiniste', *Le Monde*, 9 April 1981.
9 'Beineix ne cherche ni à faire école ni à prendre date avec l'Histoire', Raphaël Bassan, 'Trois néobaroques français: Beineix, Besson, Carax, de *Diva* au *Grand Bleu*', *La Revue du cinéma* 449 (May 1989), 49.
10 Fredric Jameson, '*Diva* and French Socialism', in *Signatures of the Visible* (New York: Routledge, 1990), 55.
11 David Russell, 'Two or Three Things We Know about Beineix', *Sight & Sound* 59: 1 (1989–1990), 47.
12 Journot, *Le Courant de 'l'esthétique publicitaire'*, 142–3.
13 F. M., 'Une histoire farfelue, ou les aventures d'un jeune postier', *L'Humanité*, 11 March 1981.
14 Jean Rochereau, 'La cantatrice et le postier', *La Croix*, 14 March 1981.
15 Annie Coppermann, 'La Diva', *Les Échos*, 17 March 1981.
16 Billard, 'Ne ratons pas le premier métro'.
17 Marie-Élisabeth Rouchy, 'Irène Silberman: priorité au spectacle', *Le Matin*, 11 March 1981.
18 This is my own free translation of a line in the review: 'il est clair que l'*étrangeté* y est beaucoup plus *familière* qu'*inquiétante* … ', literally 'the strangeness in the film is clearly more familiar than disturbing', but 'l'inquiétante étrangeté' is the French translation of Freud's *Unheimlich*, rendered in English as 'the uncanny'. Guy Patrick Sainderichain, '*Diva*', *Cahiers du cinéma* 322 (April 1981), 66.
19 André Halimi, 'Un cinéma nouveau', *Pariscope*, 18 March 1981.
20 Coppermann, 'La Diva'.
21 Marie-Noëlle Tranchant, 'La passion du cinéma selon Jean-Jacques Beineix', *Le Figaro*, 8 March 1982.
22 Billard, 'Ne ratons pas le premier métro'.
23 Éric de Saint Angel, '*Diva* chez soi', *Le Matin*, 25 December 1984.
24 Devarrieux, 'La métaphore de l'alpiniste'.
25 José-Maria Bescos, '*Diva*', *Pariscope*, 25 March 1981.
26 Billard, 'Ne ratons pas le premier métro'.
27 Phil Powrie, *Jean-Jacques Beineix* (Manchester: Manchester University Press, 2001), 35.
28 Journot, *Le Courant de 'l'esthétique publicitaire'*, 155.

29 Journot suggests that word-of-mouth recommendations may be a more important source of information for young people than for other groups of spectators, *Le Courant de 'l'esthétique publicitaire'*, 156–7.
30 See Leos Carax, 'Journal d'un cinéaste par Leos Carax', *Libération*, 22 November 1984.
31 Martine Planells, '*Subway*, sur le quai des adolescences', *Le Quotidien de Paris*, 27 January 1985.
32 Ibid.
33 José-Maria Bescos, '*Subway*', *Pariscope*, 10 April 1985.
34 Joshka Schidlow, 'Luc Besson tourne *Subway*: Métro, boulot, rigolo', *Télérama*, 23 January 1985.
35 Benoît Heimermann, 'Luc Besson en seconde', *Le Matin*, 12 April 1985.
36 Olivier Seguret, '*Subway*, ça rame', *Libération*, 10 April 1985.
37 Susan Hayward, *Luc Besson* (Manchester: Manchester University Press, 1998), 40.
38 Journot, *Le Courant de 'l'esthétique publicitaire'*, 32–3.
39 Michel Chion, 'L'âge du capitaine', *Cahiers du cinéma* 373 (June 1985), 77.
40 Phil Powrie, 'Of Suits and Men in the Films of Luc Besson', in *The Films of Luc Besson: Master of Spectacle*, ed. Susan Hayward and Phil Powrie (Manchester: Manchester University Press, 2006), 76.
41 Heimermann, 'Luc Besson en seconde'.
42 Ibid. Anecdotally, it is perhaps worth pointing out that works by Luc Besson are often among the only French films that British undergraduates have seen before coming to university, especially *The Fifth Element* (1997) and *Léon* (1994), as well as his great successes as producer, *Taxi* (Gérard Pirès, 1998) and *Taken* (Pierre Morel, 2008).
43 Quoted in Hayward, *Luc Besson*, 36.
44 Planells, '*Subway*, sur le quai des adolescences'. We might note that Michel Chion was unconvinced by the inconsistently infantilized Fred, 'expected to play the tough outlaw and the sexual innocent, the equation doesn't add up', 'L'âge du capitaine', 77.
45 Bassan, 'Trois néobaroques français', 48.
46 Hayward, *Luc Besson*, 23.
47 Ibid., 27.
48 Ibid., 79.
49 'Monsieur le préfet, votre dîner est nul, votre baraque est nulle, et je vous emmerde tous.' Héléna's dramatic departure from this dinner party, a kind of social suicide, has interesting parallels to Ferdinand's (Jean-Paul Belmondo) flight from a stultifying soirée in *Pierrot le fou* (Godard, 1965). However, while Godard renders the alienating effect of this party through coloured filters, disorienting edits and non-naturalistic dialogue, the scene in *Subway* is filmed in relatively classical frontal mid-shots of the characters.

50 Serge Daney, 'Leos Carax, première fois', *Libération*, 17 May 1984.
51 Marc Chevrie, '*Boy meets girl*, de Leos Carax', *Cahiers du cinéma* 360–1 (summer 1984), 73.
52 See Claire Devarrieux, untitled introduction to dossier on *Boy Meets Girl*, *Le Monde*, 15 November 1984.
53 Daney, 'Leos Carax, première fois'.
54 Hervé Guibert, '*Le Monde* rencontre un film de Leos Carax', *Le Monde*, 15 November 1984.
55 Hervé Guibert, 'Le réalisateur: Une star pure et dure', *Le Monde*, 15 November 1984.
56 In the film subtitles, this name is rendered as the ironic 'chatterbox' but the original French means literally 'hung' or 'suspended tongue'.
57 'Garder le silence, comme on dit. C'est faux: c'est le silence qui nous garde.' It is perhaps worth pointing that the chiastic structure of this affirmation is very reminiscent of some of Jean-Luc Godard's wordplay, in particular his famous quip (from *Une femme mariée* [1964]) that 'Regarder, c'est garder deux fois' (difficult to translate: 'To regard is to guard again' or literally: 'To look is to keep twice').
58 Guibert, 'Le réalisateur'.
59 Marc Chevrie, introduction to Leos Carax, 'La beauté en révolte', *Cahiers du cinéma* 390 (December 1986), 25.
60 Jean-Yves Escoffier, 'La cérémonie du plan', *Cahiers du cinéma* 389 (November 1986), 25.
61 Juliette Binoche, 'A comme Anna', *Cahiers du cinéma* 389 (November 1986), 24.
62 Carax, 'La beauté en révolte', 27.
63 Danièle Heymann, 'Feux d'artifices', *Le Monde*, 28 November 1986.
64 'Il y a dans ce silence toute l'arrogance d'un orphelin, un cinéaste persuadé de la mort du cinéma, un gamin godardien trop bavard qui se force à se taire.' Louis Skorecki, 'Le silence de Leos Carax', *Libération*, 9 December 1986.
65 Gérard Vaugeois, '*Boy Meets Girl* de Leos Carax', *L'Humanité-Dimanche*, 30 November 1984.
66 Jean Roy, 'Une volonté de fer', *L'Humanité*, 26 November 1986.
67 In Marie-Élisabeth Rouchy and Raphaël Sorin, 'Les *Cahiers* et Carax', *Le Matin*, 26 November 1986.
68 Serge Daney, 'Sang neuf', *Libération*, 26 November 1986, original emphasis.
69 Alain Philippon, 'Sur la terre comme au ciel', *Cahiers du cinéma* 389 (November 1986), 15.
70 Escoffier, 'La cérémonie du plan', 30.
71 Journot, *Le Courant de 'l'esthétique publicitaire'*, 91.
72 Carax, 'La beauté en révolte', 32.
73 Guibert, 'Le réalisateur'.

74 Jeanine Baron, 'Leos Carax: "Le cinéma a été ma seule école"', *La Croix*, 22 November 1984.
75 Philippe Garrel and Leos Carax, 'Dialogue en apesanteur', *Cahiers du cinéma* 365 (November 1984), 39.
76 Guibert, 'Le réalisateur'.
77 Baron, 'Leos Carax'.
78 Robert Chazal, '*Mauvais Sang*', *France-Soir*, 26 November 1986.
79 Anne de Gaspéri, '*Mauvais Sang* ne saurait mentir', *Le Quotidien de Paris*, 26 November 1986.
80 Jean-Luc Macia, 'Un trop-plein de cinéma', *La Croix*, 28 November 1986.
81 Bergala, 'D'une certaine manière', 15.
82 Alban Pichon, *Le Cinéma de Leos Carax: L'expérience du déjà-vu* (Paris: Le Bord de l'eau, 2009), 212.
83 Daney, 'Leos Carax, première fois'.
84 Michel Pérez, 'Leos Carax: Les habits neufs du cinéma français', *Le Matin*, 23 November 1984.
85 Joshka Shidlow, '*Boy Meets Girl*: L'amour à vingt ans', *Télérama*, 21 November 1984.
86 Alban Pichon has noted that the influence of Godard upon Carax has at times worked in reverse. Aside from this example from *Histoire(s) du cinéma*, Pichon points to Godard's *King Lear* (1987) which features Carax in a minor role alongside Julie Delpy, herself familiar from *Mauvais Sang*. *Le Cinéma de Leos Carax*, 188.
87 Garrel and Carax, 'Dialogue en apesanteur', 39.
88 Binoche, 'A comme Anna', 23.
89 Jean-Luc Douin, 'La maladie d'amour', *Télérama*, 26 November 1986.
90 Pichon, *Le Cinéma de Leos Carax*, 161.
91 Garrel and Carax, 'Dialogue en apesanteur', 38.
92 Carax, 'La beauté en révolte', 28–9.
93 Garrel and Carax, 'Dialogue en apesanteur', 38.
94 Carax, 'La beauté en révolte', 29.
95 Ibid.
96 Douin, 'La maladie d'amour'.
97 Escoffier, 'La cérémonie du plan', 26.
98 Binoche, 'A comme Anna', 22.
99 Michel Boujut, 'L'amour qui va vite mais qui dure longtemps', *L'Événement du jeudi*, 27 November 1986.
100 'DB', '*Mauvais Sang*', *La Vie ouvrière*, 8 December 1986.
101 Bernard Marchand, *Paris, histoire d'une ville: XIXe-XXe siècle* (Paris: Seuil, 1993), 251–7.

102 See James Tweedie, *The Age of New Waves: Art Cinema and the Staging of Globalization* (Oxford: Oxford University Press, 2013), 14, and Simon Sadler, *The Situationist City* (Cambridge, MA: The MIT Press, 1999), 55.
103 Raoul Vaneigem and Guy Debord quoted in Sadler, *The Situationist City*, 16.
104 Internationale lettriste, quoted in Sadler, *The Situationist City*, 50.
105 Tweedie, *The Age of New Waves*, 87.
106 Internationale situationniste, 'Le rôle de Godard', *Internationale situationniste* 10 (1966).
107 François Penz, 'From Topographical Coherence to Creative Geography: Rohmer's *The Aviator's Wife* and Rivette's *Pont du Nord*', in *Cities in Transition: The Moving Image and the Modern Metropolis*, ed. Andrew Webber and Emma Wilson (London: Wallflower, 2008), 126.
108 Tweedie, *The Age of New Waves*, 19–20.
109 Tweedie, *The Age of New Waves*, 26.
110 Ibid., 30.
111 Jameson, '*Diva* and French Socialism', 55.
112 E.g., Fredric Jameson, *Postmodernism, or the Cultural Logic of Late Capitalism* (Durham, NC: Duke University Press, 1991), 1–54.
113 Sadler, *The Situationist City*, 25.
114 The notion of the dissolving of boundaries, especially spatial and temporal (surface/depth, past/present, inside/outside, open/closed), is implicit throughout Fredric Jameson's account of the postmodern. See Jameson, *Postmodernism*, 1–54.
115 'des décors ahurissants', Coppermann, 'La Diva'; 'd'une originalité agressive', Robert Chazal, '*Diva*: Amour et bel canto', *France-Soir*, 16 March 1981.
116 Alain Bergala, 'Le vrai, le faux, le factice', *Cahiers du cinéma* 351 (September 1983), 7.
117 David Berry, 'Underground Cinema: French Visions of the Metro', in *Spaces in European Cinema*, ed. Myrto Konstantarakos (Exeter: Intellect, 2000), 14.
118 Jameson, '*Diva* and French Socialism', 60–1.
119 Quoted in Nezar AlSayyad, *Cinematic Urbanism: A History of the Modern from Reel to Real* (New York: Routledge, 2006), 137.
120 Marie-Noëlle Tranchant, 'L'heure du choix', *Le Figaro*, 7 March 1985.
121 Seguret, '*Subway*, ça rame'; Pierre Murat, 'Ticket chic, effet choc', *Télérama*, 17 April 1985.
122 The best source on poetic realism is Dudley Andrew, *Mists of Regret: Culture and Sensibility in Classic French Film* (Princeton: Princeton University Press, 1995).
123 'un jeu gratuit et un peu vain', Gérard Vaugeois, '*Subway* de Luc Besson', *L'Humanité-Dimanche*, 12 April 1985.
124 Chion, 'L'Âge du capitaine', 76.

125 Journot, *Le Courant de 'l'esthétique publicitaire'*, 30–1.
126 For more detail on this, see Douglas Morrey and Alison Smith, *Jacques Rivette* (Manchester: Manchester University Press, 2009), 61–9.
127 On 'integrated spectacle', see Guy Debord, *Commentaires sur la société du spectacle* (Paris: Folio, 1988), 21–5.
128 David Harvey, *The Condition of Postmodernity: An Enquiry into the Origins of Cultural Change* (Oxford: Blackwell, 1990), 295–6.
129 AlSayyad, *Cinematic Urbanism*, 124.
130 Tweedie, *The Age of New Waves*, 26–7.
131 Ibid., 50.
132 For an interesting and detailed consideration of these questions, see Michael Pigott, *Time and Film Style*, unpublished PhD thesis, University of Warwick, 2009.
133 Powrie, *Jean-Jacques Beineix*, 66.
134 Carina L. Yervasi, 'Capturing the Elusive Representations in Beineix's *Diva*', *Literature/Film Quarterly* 21: 1 (1993), 41.
135 Laura Mulvey, 'Visual Pleasure and Narrative Cinema', *Screen* 16: 3 (1975), 6–18.
136 Journot, *Le Courant de 'l'esthétique publicitaire'*, 92–3.
137 Ibid., 107.
138 Ibid., 95–6.
139 Gilles Le Morvan, 'Les néons du néant', *L'Humanité*, 10 April 1985.
140 Michel Pérez, '*Subway* de Luc Besson: Le métro aux heures creuses', *Le Matin*, 12 April 1985.
141 Yann Plougastel, '*Subway*', *L'Événement du jeudi*, 11 April 1985.
142 Bassan, 'Trois néobaroques français', 46.
143 Russell, 'Two or Three Things We Know about Beineix', 45.
144 For a detailed assessment of these characteristics, see the landmark book by Carol Vernallis, *Experiencing Music Video: Aesthetics and Cultural Context*, New York: Columbia University Press, 2004. Some of the key features of music video identified by Vernallis could be summarized as follows: music video is generally non-narrative, lacking the proleptic cause-effect organization of most fiction films and instead being organized around the music; editing in music videos tends to be faster than in most feature films and deliberately foregrounded, often with a proliferation of graphic matches. Music videos tend to favour extreme camera angles and generalized camera movement. Direct address to the camera is de rigueur and locations tend to be generic rather than specific.
145 Gérard Dastugue, 'Musical Narration in the Films of Luc Besson', in *The Films of Luc Besson: Master of Spectacle*, ed. Susan Hayward and Phil Powrie (Manchester: Manchester University Press, 2006), 43.
146 Ibid., 44.

147 F: Pourquoi est-ce que je vous aime? H: Parce que je suis une fille formidable. F: Pourquoi est-ce que vous ne m'aimez pas? H: J'ai pas le courage. F: Vous êtes fainéante? H: Oui. F: Qui c'est qui fait la cuisine chez vous? H: La cuisinière. F: Et le ménage? H: La femme de ménage. F: Et l'amour?

148 Vernallis, *Experiencing Music Video*, 3–4.

149 Dominique Jamet, 'Elle court, elle court la maladie d'amour … ', *Le Quotidien de Paris*, 1 December 1986.

150 Fergus Daly and Garin Dowd, *Leos Carax* (Manchester: Manchester University Press, 2003), 76.

151 Chevrie, '*Boy Meets Girl*'.

152 Journot, *Le Courant de 'l'esthétique publicitaire'*, 100.

153 Macia, 'Un trop-plein de cinéma'.

154 Michel Pérez, 'Un accès de fièvre de croissance', *Le Matin*, 28 November 1986.

155 Tweedie, *The Age of New Waves*, 107.

156 On the mixing of shot lengths in *À bout de souffle* and its contribution to the film's overall rhythm, see Michel Marie, *À bout de souffle* (Paris: Nathan, 1999), 65–78, and, specifically on the Hôtel de Suède sequence, 85–93.

157 'Flexible accumulation' is David Harvey's term for the flows of postmodern capital, detached from the vertically integrated industries and dedicated sites of industrial capitalism. See *The Condition of Postmodernity*, 147.

3

The *jeune cinéma français* of the 1990s

What was the *jeune cinéma français*?

Probably the most significant movement to have been identified in French cinema since the New Wave is the so-called *jeune cinéma français* that emerged in the 1990s.[1] No other development in French cinema in the past six decades has seen the emergence of so many significant new filmmakers while also demonstrating a degree of thematic and stylistic consistency between their works and generating a large amount of media and academic attention. One of the most striking features of French cinema in this period is the sheer number of debut features released every year. The number rose from 26 in 1990 to 39 in 1992; by the end of the decade, it had reached 62.[2] By the mid-1990s, one film in every two made in France was either a director's first or second film.[3] A total of 329 new filmmakers emerged in France in the decade between 1988 and 1997; by 2002 the number had reached 622.[4] Naturally not all of these nascent directors would go on to have successful careers in filmmaking, and even an industry as buoyant as the one in France cannot support this many directors working regularly in the production of feature films for theatrical distribution. As commentators have noted, getting a first film made in France is a relatively easy proposition; having it distributed and exhibited for long enough so that audiences will take note is quite another matter.[5] Claude-Marie Trémois suggests that only one in three new filmmakers in France will survive long enough to make a second feature,[6] although René Prédal points out that the audiovisual sector beyond cinema is large enough to accommodate most of these practitioners in some capacity, albeit without fame.[7]

Indeed, it is this broader audiovisual landscape, and in particular French television, that can be seen as largely responsible for the extraordinary fertility of French cinema. Government quotas oblige television channels in France to devote 60 per cent of their broadcast time to European programming, of which 40 per cent must be French. Given the vitality of French cinema compared to most other European nations, in practice some 50 per cent of films shown on television in France are French and, since the large networks broadcast around 400 films per year, a lot of new product is needed in order to keep audiences interested.[8] It is in this way that the French television channels – especially TF1 and Canal Plus, but also Arte, France 3 and M6 – have become the biggest drivers of the constant renewal in French film production. The overwhelming preference of French viewers for television over cinema – more than three hours per day are devoted to the small screen on average compared to two or three trips to the cinema per year[9] – is one of the main reasons behind a change in culture in French filmmaking. Big-budget 'event' movies – what would once have been regarded as 'Saturday-night cinema' – are now very rare in French production, this section of the market having been almost entirely abandoned to Hollywood blockbusters.[10] One result of this shift is that practically any French film can claim to represent 'auteur cinema' since the boundary between this category and mainstream/popular cinema in France has become extremely porous.[11]

Given the large number of new directors emerging in France in the 1990s, any attempt to identify their influences must necessarily contain a degree of reductive generalization. Still, two discernable trends or groupings have been identified in French cinema of the period. In the type of films commonly designated by the label *jeune cinéma*, the most frequently cited influences are a set of maverick directors famous for their fiercely independent approach to film production and the appearance of a semi-improvisational style in their finished works: John Cassavetes, Jacques Doillon and, especially, Maurice Pialat, with whom young filmmakers like Cédric Kahn and Cyril Collard worked as assistant director.[12] The status of these directors as fellow travellers with, or inheritors of, the New Wave is well established albeit not without controversy. There is, however, a significant strain in French filmmaking that emerged in the 1990s that draws inspiration much more from American models like Martin Scorsese and the Coen brothers than from any French precursors. This trend has been observed in directors like Mathieu Kassovitz, Gaspar Noé and Jean-Pierre Jeunet who arguably resist an identifiably 'French' style in the interest of appealing to the widest possible global audience.[13] Occasionally, a director's career has been able to straddle both these styles, as in the work of Olivier Assayas, whose early films anticipated the *jeune cinéma* with their focus on French youth before *Irma Vep* (1996) inaugurated a more 'international' style in the director's work. Given the focus of this study, the discussion that follows will concentrate on the first group of filmmakers and the evidence for a New Wave heritage in their work. We will return to the question of an international style in contemporary French cinema, and look in more detail at Assayas's work, in the last chapter of this book.

What characterizes the *jeune cinéma français* of the 1990s? By 2002, three books had been published on the phenomenon and a number of critics had attempted to list the key thematic and stylistic features of the movement. The most useful of these lists is probably that produced by Claude-Marie Trémois who identifies a set of eight 'constants' in these films. These are a sense of urgency, both within the diegesis and in the director's desire to get his or her film made; a capturing or distillation of the spirit of the age; narratives designed as 'chronicles' of contemporary life; a tendency towards wandering (both in and of the narrative); elements, or at least the appearance, of improvisation; a taste for long takes; openness of narratives; an attempt to incorporate an ethics of the gaze.[14] We will consider most of these points in detail in the course of this chapter, but what is immediately striking is the extent to which all of these 'constants' are tropes regularly associated with the New Wave. René Prédal suggests that, as a whole, the *jeune cinéma* can be characterized by a 'new interior realism', that is to say a taste for intimacy, an interest in the relationships of couples and small groups, and little details of behaviour rather than large-scale dramatic scenes.[15] The counterpart to this intimate realism, however, is a set of clichés that come to be associated with a cinema too easily dismissed as 'navel-gazing'. Prédal himself identifies many of these clichés: characters who are unlucky in love or solipsistic rebels; a camera that insistently scrutinizes the actors' faces; inevitable scenes of domestic crisis, predictably repressed desires and 'the obligatory dose of homosexuality'.[16] Worse still, Olivier de Bruyn has suggested that what he calls the 'vindictive intimacy' of these films goes hand in hand with a certain refusal of the outside world, a lack of interest in other people.[17] But the very fact that clichés like this can be identified, even if they may be an unfair representation of the films, is itself a demonstration that a coherent movement in French cinema was seen to exist in the 1990s.

The New Wave can be seen, as *Cahiers du cinéma* suggested in 1993, as a kind of 'year zero' for the *jeune cinéma*.[18] Claude-Marie Trémois sets the tone for her book on the *jeune cinéma* when she suggests that the movement began with *Un monde sans pitié* (Éric Rochant, 1989) 'exactly thirty years after *À bout de souffle*'.[19] One notable point of comparison between the two film movements is that each introduced a new generation of actors into French cinema, and the performers of the *jeune cinéma* are sometimes as devoted to the New Wave as the directors. This is the case with Mathieu Amalric whose energetic, impertinent, loquacious performance style owes much to Jean-Pierre Léaud. Amalric remembers discovering *Baisers volés* (Truffaut, 1968) at the Cinémathèque: 'Never has any other film given me such *joie de vivre*.'[20] The exchange of actors is an important factor in determining the relations between the New Wave and the *jeune cinéma* since actresses first revealed by Arnaud Desplechin (Marianne Denicourt and Jeanne Balibar) were subsequently cast in later films by Jacques Rivette (*Haut bas fragile*, 1995, and *Va savoir*, 2001), while actors associated with the New Wave (Léaud, Bernadette Lafont and Bulle Ogier) appear in *Personne ne m'aime* (Marion Vernoux, 1994). The emergence of a distinctive generation of actors also helps to position the themes of filiation and the transmission between generations as central to the concerns of the *jeune cinéma*. Parental figures are absent, failing or inadequate role models in these films as they were for so much of the New Wave.[21]

Noël Herpe, however, has suggested that comparisons between the *jeune cinéma* and the New Wave are simplistic and based on a romanticized opposition, which was already at the heart of the original Nouvelle Vague, between a supposed 'cinema of the real' on one hand and a cinema of 'manipulation and mastery' on the other (the latter represented, in the context of the 1990s, by Jacques Audiard most notably). For Herpe there is here a kind of 'post-Bazinian mysticism' in which an 'exclusive cult of the real' equates to cinematic freedom.[22] Herpe is of course right to denounce this kind of facile antagonism in film history, but his criticism does not, in itself, obviate the usefulness of a comparison between the New Wave and the *jeune cinéma*. In fact, all of the films discussed in this chapter challenge the simplistic equation between 'the real' and freedom or innovation in film form, just as all the best films of the New Wave did before them. Indeed, the necessary interdependence of the real (improvisation, documentary, location shooting) and the artificial (trickery, contrivance, self-consciousness) is one of the most basic lessons of the Nouvelle Vague.

As mentioned above, Claude-Marie Trémois dates the beginning of the *jeune cinéma* from the release of *Un monde sans pitié* in 1989, a moment she equates to the shock of *À bout de souffle*, Godard's New Wave manifesto released in 1960. It is true that Rochant's film shares some elements with Godard's: an irresponsible young male hero interested mainly in the seduction of young women; a setting in the streets of Paris which come to figure as the protagonist's home; a certain energy and volubility expressed especially in the dialogue.[23] But, if *Un monde sans pitié* may have laid down a blueprint for a certain strain of *jeune cinéma* in France, the film has acquired none of the lasting value of *À bout de souffle* (it is, regrettably, not even available on DVD), and Rochant shows no signs of developing the career longevity of a Jean-Luc Godard. One reason why the New Wave is always held up as the canonical example of a coherent film movement is that despite its various important precursors, the start date of the New Wave proper is easy to identify in the spring of 1959 with the release of Claude Chabrol's first two features shortly preceding the presentation of *Les Quatre Cents Coups* at Cannes in May. The beginning of the *jeune cinéma français* is much more nebulous and a number of other start points, in addition to *Un monde sans pitié*, can be posited. René Prédal argues that 'Arnaud Desplechin, Cédric

Kahn and Xavier Beauvois definitively imposed the existence of this current in 1992'.[24] Other commentators point to the significance of a series of telefilms commissioned by La Sept/Arte in 1994 entitled *Tous les garçons et les filles de leur âge* and which served as a showcase for nine (relatively) young French directors.[25] Yet, while one or two of the directors involved became closely associated with the *jeune cinéma* (Cédric Kahn, Laurence Ferreira Barbosa), others had been around since the 1970s (Chantal Akerman, André Téchiné) or established themselves in the 1980s (Olivier Assayas, Claire Denis) while Olivier Dahan would not find success until the 2000s. Still others see 1995 as the key date, when the magazine *L'Express*, which famously first coined the term 'La Nouvelle Vague', entitled its coverage of the Cannes Film Festival 'La nouvelle Nouvelle Vague'.[26] Arguably, however, one important criterion for a film movement is international recognition, and I would suggest that it was at least the mid-1990s before the English-speaking world became aware of the *jeune cinéma*, thanks to films like *Comment je me suis disputé* and *Irma Vep*, and the shape and character of the movement for Anglophone critics has been significantly inflected by the first international successes of Bruno Dumont and the Dardenne brothers in 1997 and 1999. Indeed, the triumph of the Dardennes' *Rosetta* and Dumont's *L'humanité* at the 1999 Cannes festival (notably including a controversial shared prize for best actress) could be taken as yet another key date in the international recognition of an important movement in French (or Franco-Belgian) cinema. As René Prédal recognizes, then, one key difference between the New Wave and the *jeune cinéma* is the relative concentration of the former and dilation of the latter: all of the key directors of the New Wave released their first features between the autumn of 1958 and the spring of 1961, whereas it took at least ten years, and maybe more, for all of the important directors associated with the *jeune cinéma* to make themselves known.[27] In this sense, it is not difficult to agree with Jeancolas when he asserts that the *jeune cinéma* was 'neither a wave nor a school'.[28]

If *Un monde sans pitié* cannot be seen as equivalent to *À bout de souffle* it is because, David Vasse suggests, it does not seek to constitute an 'epistemological break' within French cinema. Éric Rochant was not attempting, as Godard was, to 'defeat the conformism of the French film industry' with a single decisive gesture.[29] There is a notable difference in attitude between the New Wave and the *jeune cinéma* that must be largely attributed to the different cultural space occupied by cinema in France in the 1990s. On the one hand, as we have seen, cinema could no longer claim to be a mass entertainment medium, that mantle having definitively passed to television; but, on the other hand, with its transition from mass entertainment to a more niche lifestyle product, the high cultural status of the cinema in France was assured, supported by government subsidy, educational promotion and media discourse. In this sense, the discourse around the *jeune cinéma* lacks the urgency of the New Wave. Prédal complains that the mainstream press in France has lost any dynamism or polemical drive in its coverage of cinema: the *jeune cinéma* was simply 'the latest thing' and no longer 'a struggle, a cause to promote, an idea of cinema to be defended'.[30] Meanwhile, as Jeancolas notes, the value of the concept of 'auteur' has been transformed: in their criticism of the 1950s, the generation of the New Wave debated endlessly over sixty years' worth of film history in an effort to identify a select band of (around a dozen) directors worthy of the 'auteur' label.[31] Today, the concept of auteur has become so commonplace that, as *Cahiers du cinéma* mordantly quipped in 1993, 'one can no longer enter the cinema without being an auteur';[32] the category has become a marketing tool and lost its polemical value. Meanwhile, today's young directors are more likely to learn their craft in school than in the cinema,[33] which also implies a certain social homogeneity among the 1990s generation since the time commitment required of France's most prestigious film school, Fémis, does not allow students to work to support themselves at the same time.[34] It is difficult to imagine how a young cinephile from a modest background like François Truffaut would gain entry to the world of filmmaking today. There was an autodidact quality to the French New Wave which was perhaps partly responsible for the ferocity with which its ideas of cinema were defended: a sense of opinions hard won at personal expense and therefore invested with a kind of talismanic value. By comparison, the 1990s were marked by the relative professionalization of young filmmakers. This can be seen in the significance of the screenplay for both movements. Famously, several New Wave directors (Godard, Rivette, Varda) largely rejected the screenplay, improvising the direction of the narrative on the basis of day-to-day developments on the film set. But, as Prédal points out, a solid screenplay is indispensable to any bid for funding in contemporary French cinema, and scripts are likely to go through several rewrites in an effort to attract funding from a variety of different sources.[35] This may help to account for the quality of writing that gives us, for instance, the rich verbal sparring of Arnaud Desplechin's films, but arguably it means that few films of the *jeune cinéma* can match the sense of spontaneity and openness to incident that make the best New Wave films so fresh and surprising.

As we have seen repeatedly in previous chapters, the emergence of the New Wave is commonly related to a singular set of social and demographic circumstances. Can we identify elements of the social and political situation in the 1990s that explain the development of the *jeune cinéma* in a comparable manner? The *jeune cinéma* is sometimes identified as a political film movement, but this seems to be largely because of an appeal published in *Le Monde* in February 1997. Led by Arnaud Desplechin and Pascale Ferran and signed, initially, by fifty-nine filmmakers, the text called upon French citizens to disobey legislation criminalizing any attempt to shelter illegal immigrants (or 'sans papiers', as they were known).[36] As Joe Hardwick remarks, this episode affected the media portrayal of the *jeune cinéma*, notably in Trémois's book which was published later that same year, even though the tone and content of the declaration have little visible effect on the films of the signatories.[37] In fact, the political tenor of the *jeune cinéma*, certainly prior to 1997, might more accurately be situated somewhere between despair and apathy. While the characters are often marginal in some way, there is little move to defend their rights and status but rather a kind of post-political sense that further progress and emancipation are unlikely.[38] As Noël Herpe puts it, the generation of the *jeune cinéma* arrives 'after the battle, after the fading of the great ideological and aesthetic causes';[39] the early films of the *jeune cinéma* are marked by the sense of surrender that infected some on the left following the collapse of Soviet bloc communism and the hasty declaration of the 'end of history'. However, as Martin O'Shaughnessy has argued, the widespread strikes and social movements in France in 1995 can be seen to have created the conditions of possibility for a return to the political in French cinema of the late 1990s and beyond.[40] The fluid boundaries of the *jeune cinéma* therefore make it a hazardous business to try and pin down the movement's political character: on the basis of its early films, the movement can come across as apathetic and disillusioned, whereas if one allows the definition of *jeune cinéma* to embrace the late 1990s, including directors such as the Dardenne brothers and Laurent Cantet, it appears to be a very politically aware and even committed cinema. David Vasse suggests, furthermore, that this return to politics goes hand in hand with a rediscovery of cinema following what he sees as the 'closed' French cinema of the 1980s, the artificial worlds and 'cocooning' associated with Jean-Jacques Beineix and Luc Besson. Vasse also points to the 1980s trend for heritage cinema as a 'restauration of the tradition of quality', all of which allows him to position the *jeune cinéma* as a breath of fresh air in the industry comparable to the one represented by the New Wave in relation to the French cinema of the immediate post-war years.[41]

The *jeune cinéma français* is thus necessarily in a relationship with the cinema of the past and arguably this is a relationship of antagonism to the recent past (French cinema of the 1980s) and affection for a more distant past (the New Wave), effectively mirroring the New Wave's own complex set of relations to its forebears.

Some critics have suggested that the cinematic past may constitute an oppressive weight for the generation of the *jeune cinéma*: if the New Wave marks a 'year zero' for this movement, the filmmakers of the 1990s could not fail to be aware that they were the third or even fourth generation to inherit the legacy of this aesthetic revolution, even as the generation of the original New Wave continued, for the most part, to operate in innovative and critically acclaimed ways (Godard, Resnais, Rivette, Rohmer, Varda).[42] As Noël Herpe puts it, the *jeune cinéma* exists in an atmosphere of 'cinephilic saturation' with the young directors obsessively revisiting key aspects of their predecessors' work (thus Pascale Ferran borrows the complex interlocking narrative structures of Alain Resnais, while Arnaud Desplechin reinvests the autobiographical introspection of François Truffaut).[43] Other critics have suggested that questions of inheritance and coming to terms with the past feature as key thematic devices in the *jeune cinéma*, most especially in the work of Desplechin.[44] In places, this exploration of the past features explicitly in terms of grief, as in Ferran's *Petits Arrangements avec les morts* (1994) in which three separate characters cope differently with the death of someone close to them. Elsewhere, this sense of confronting the past and moving on is materialized in the narrative device of characters moving house, which, as David Vasse astutely observes, has become a recurring theme in contemporary French cinema whereby 'the crisis of the couple coincides with the housing crisis'.[45] As we discussed in the previous chapter, a different housing crisis was central to the urban environment of the New Wave: then, rent controls and an outdated Parisian housing stock drove characters to live out their lives and relationships in streets and cafes; in the 1990s a combination of the property boom of the 1980s plus the rising unemployment generated by a globalizing neoliberalism[46] meant that many young people could not afford their own place, especially in the capital, until well into their thirties. In two of the films we discuss in the remainder of this chapter (*Comment je me suis disputé* and *Oublie-moi*), the protagonist is effectively without fixed abode, staying with friends, relatives or sexual partners; in the other two films the protagonist lives with his mother, in the case of Pharaon (Emmanuel Schotté) in *L'humanité* until well into early middle age. One is reminded of New Wave films in which the protagonists are made temporarily homeless (*Les Quatre Cents Coups, Le Signe du Lion* [Rohmer, 1962], *Vivre sa vie* [Godard, 1962]) and others where they struggle to assert their autonomy despite living with parents or other older relatives (the early films of Claude Chabrol, notably).

As these examples might imply, adolescence is an important terrain in the *jeune cinéma français*. Adolescent protagonists are central to the work of Bruno Dumont and the Dardenne brothers, as they are to the early features of Olivier Assayas or to the memorable portrait of teenage girlhood in Noémie Lvovsky's *La Vie ne me fait pas peur* (1999). But, if youth is ultimately a state of mind for this 'young cinema',[47] it is perhaps partly because economic conditions increasingly oblige us to live in semi-dependence well into adulthood. As Dina Sherzer points out, the characters of the *jeune cinéma* often resemble adolescents, regardless of their physical age, because they 'have not yet entered real life'.[48] This is notably the case of Paul Dédalus (Mathieu Amalric) in *Comment je me suis disputé*, who has no home of his own, is struggling to finish a PhD thesis in which he has lost interest and is reluctant to commit to his girlfriend, despite having been with her for ten years, instead carrying on affairs with two other women who are already in relationships. David Vasse suggests that if French cinema is so fond of adolescent characters, it is doubtless because they are undergoing a physical transformation that allows the film to cast its existential interrogations in terms of a raw corporeal realism.[49] This is one of the key lessons the *jeune cinéma* has learned from Maurice Pialat (himself the author of memorable film portraits of adolescents): the demonstration of social and emotional tensions in their physical impact upon the body.[50] Jean-Pierre Jeancolas talks about a 'realism of proximity' in the *jeune cinéma français*, a concern for the way that political structures and social change affect the body and the local environment (family, community, neighbourhood).[51] In this sense, we might say that French cinema has incorporated one of the most important insights of feminism: the realization that the personal, the intimate and the local are not so much refuges from macroscopic political structures as further, and finer, iterations of them.

Indeed, as many critics have pointed out, one of the most positive developments in French cinema since the early 1990s has been the proliferation of women filmmakers who accounted for around one-third of all film production in France by the middle of the decade. As Claude-Marie Trémois puts it, the successful integration of women into the French film industry can be measured by the fact that female directors are no longer discussed primarily in terms of their gender (as was the case for pioneers like Varda and Akerman).[52] Dina Sherzer argues that men and women appear with equal frequency in the films of the *jeune cinéma*; that masculine domination, notably in terms of seduction, has largely disappeared; that women appear as independent, expecting nothing from men nor seeking security in marriage; and that they enjoy 'a dynamic control of their bodies'.[53] Female stars associated with the *jeune cinéma*, like Jeanne Balibar, Valeria Bruni Tedeschi and Emmanuelle Devos, have developed their personas around an image of intellectual maturity rather than on the basis of looks and sex appeal.[54] The prominence of women is just one aspect of the celebrated diversity of contemporary French cinema that also includes greater representation of the regions, the suburbs, the working classes and underclass (the unemployed and underemployed), migrants and children of migrants.[55] In what follows, we will look in detail at a handful of films from the *jeune cinéma français*, considering how far they reflect this greater equality and diversity of French culture and society while also assessing the nature and extent of their debt to the Nouvelle Vague.

Comment je me suis disputé (Ma vie sexuelle)

Among the most striking novelties of the French New Wave was the way these films depicted the everyday domestic intimacy of heterosexual couples. Naturally, the amorous relations between men and women have been central to cinematic representation since the earliest days of the medium, and French cinema has long been famous for its depiction of sex and romance. But the Nouvelle Vague brought a number of subtle adjustments to this classic formula, which heralded a certain modernization of the depiction of intimacy in cinema. This was rarely achieved through the explicit representation of sexual activity. Instead the novelty was found in the banality of the locations (cramped apartments, cheap hotel rooms, cafe tables); in the prominence and duration of the scenes (*Le Mépris*, 1963, with its half-hour domestic dispute, is iconic here); in the shifting tones of such scenes, between farcical comedy and tragic melancholy (especially in Truffaut); in the space allowed for the woman's point of view (in Varda, in Rohmer and, more than is usually recognized, in Godard); this undermining of the masculine point of view is often achieved (especially in Rohmer) through carefully written, ironic dialogue, while dialogue also showed a new frankness about the consequences of sexual relations with frequent references to pregnancy, contraception and abortion.

What, then, is the legacy of these characteristics in more recent French cinema and in particular in the *jeune cinéma français*? Like the filmmakers of the Nouvelle Vague, the *jeunes cinéastes* of the 1990s sought to ground their films in reality by writing about the world they knew. Arnaud Desplechin's *Comment je me suis disputé (Ma vie sexuelle)* (1996) is one of the most emblematic of these films, a three-hour exploration of the lives and loves of a group of Paris intellectuals. As with much of Desplechin's work, however, there is a self-consciousness about his appropriation of the domestic drama, which he sees as the most 'Franco-French' of genres.[56] Desplechin's aim, he claims, was to take the most decried of French film clichés – the sentimental adventures of a group of intellectuals 'situated between Saint-Michel and the Luxemburg Gardens'[57] – and attempt to 're-mythologize' it through aesthetic renewal.[58] The film is, then, in some ways, a deliberate 'provocation'[59] and one that was greeted with predictable impatience in some quarters of the French press. The satirical magazine *L'Organe* described the action as follows: 'opening and closing of doors in real time, lighting of cigarettes, scenes between friends, domestic scenes, soft bedroom scenes [...], scenes with the therapist, scenes in the café, more lighting of cigarettes' and concluded that the film was 'soporific, when its vacuity and pretention don't render it altogether grotesque'!ature[60]

As this description implies, there is little real action, as conventionally defined, in *Comment je me suis disputé* but instead a great deal of talking. Desplechin commented that one of his challenges in making the film was how to transform sentiment or psychology into action, or vice versa, by speeding up or slowing down the rhythm of a scene.[61] In this way, sentiment takes on a concrete reality[62] and this incarnating of ideas and feelings on screen is at the heart of the New Wave conception of mise en scène.[63] Desplechin has also repeatedly stressed his resistance to character psychology, offering the example of Rabier (Michel Vuillermoz), fellow philosophy professor and arch-rival of the film's main protagonist, Paul (Mathieu Amalric). The character is introduced not with a psychological backstory but with a simple name plate on a door accompanied by a dramatic chord on the soundtrack, the figure then fleshed out by the absurd accessory of Rabier's pet monkey, who is quickly dismissed when he gets trapped behind a radiator.[64] Despite the insistence on action, however, the film's principal character is distinguished by his apparent inability to act, replacing decisive gestures with words.[65] More precisely, Paul's verbosity is at once action – a means of seducing three different women – and procrastination – a drawn-out and often disingenuous analysis of his own behaviour that seemingly dispenses him from choosing between these different women.[66] But, as Vincent Remy suggested in *Télérama*, the bittersweet humour of the film stems from the way in which the stubbornness of this discourse is brought up short against 'the incandescent sensuality of a voice, of a pout, or of the movement of a body'.[67] For *Comment je me suis disputé* also contains several scenes of physical intimacy, although Desplechin has stated his desire to invert the traditional associations of mawkish sentiment and crude sex scenes by having his characters 'talk very coarsely about feelings and render sexuality almost evanescent'.[68] In practice, this results in three notable effects in the film. First, the violence demonstrated in lovers' discourse not just in actual threats of physical violence, as when Paul tells Esther (Emmanuelle Devos), 'As soon as you open your mouth, I want to strangle you', but in the subsequent juxtaposition of such sentiments with fantastically romantic declarations, as when Paul ends the same scene by telling Esther that 'our love is worth it and everyone else's is pitiful'. Second, while sex and nudity are generally filmed in carefully posed and artistically lit glimpses, sexuality is often discussed in the crudest of terms, as when Paul and Nathan (Emmanuel Salinger) openly admire the physical assets of Bob's (Thibault de Montalembert) new girlfriend or when Paul interrogates Bob regarding the detail of Valérie's (Jeanne Balibar) bedroom habits prior to seducing her himself. But, third, sex is often described in terms approaching that of a religious experience. Paul's brother Yvan (Fabrice Desplechin) decides to convert to Catholicism and become a priest after the sight of a young woman's nude dancing convinces him that he 'loves humanity', while Paul himself describes the act of reaching into a woman's underwear for the first time as one of the most humbling experiences life has to offer and one of the few that makes him feel alive.

As these descriptions make clear, *Comment je me suis disputé* features multiple characters and the narrative explores the evolving relations between them. Since Paul is a philosophy professor, much of the drama stems from the epistemological doubt occasioned by uncertainty over what other people may be thinking or feeling or, as Desplechin puts it, the difficulty of accepting that other people exist at all.[69] More precisely, the film seems to dramatize a Hegelian dialectics of recognition, that is the requirement for the other to recognize me in order for me to exert power over them. Paul's new colleague Rabier is a former friend from graduate school with whom he has lost touch under obscure circumstances. Paul feels humiliated by Rabier's failure, or refusal, to recognize him, even after he has retrieved his former friend's dead monkey from behind the radiator. Paul eventually forces Rabier to recognize him by inadvertently causing Rabier to slam a door shut on his own fingers and thus to lament, 'Paul Dédalus has seriously injured me!' The film never elucidates the backstory between these two men, instead playing out an almost abstract dialectic of recognition through their relationship, but one that is given concrete cinematic existence through the improbable episodes with the monkey and the fingers in the door. Numerous other relationships in the film can also be interpreted in terms of this dialectic. Jean-Jacques (Denis Podalydès) tells a story about how Valérie announced her intention to get an abortion, simply, he believed, in order that he would tell her not to, but, when he refused to intervene, in an attempt to reassert his own psychic authority, 'everything turned to absolute hatred between us'. When Paul first meets Jean-Jacques at the beginning of the film, Jean-Jacques shakes his hand, then refuses to let go while he is introduced to Paul's entourage. The gesture has an unsettling ambiguity: does it imply a kind of challenge from one man to the other, thereby pre-empting the narrative development in which Paul will embark on an affair with Valérie; or does it, on the contrary, imply Paul's humiliating invisibility to the other man (who has perhaps simply not noticed that he is still holding Paul's hand)? Paul begins his sexual relationship with Valérie in part because she recognizes his desire for another woman, Sylvia (Marianne Denicourt), an infatuation Paul has resisted telling anyone else about since Sylvia is going out with his friend Nathan. In an effort to secure more of Paul's attention, Valérie invents a story about being abused in childhood. Yvan's conversion to Catholicism stems, it transpires, not from some internal conviction but from a desire to have his external demonstrations of faith validated by the Church. The film gradually shows that this anxious compulsion to secure the recognition of the other is not just a neurosis of Paul's but is a generalized trait (even Rabier, the cocksure villain of the piece, worries that Paul will make fun of him when he learns the name of his monkey). In this way, Desplechin demonstrates his understanding and adoption of one of the most fundamental, if perhaps least remarked upon, characteristics of French New Wave filmmaking, that is a certain generosity extended towards the characters of a film, an acceptance of their humanity and refusal to judge that Claude-Marie Trémois has called 'the morality of the gaze'.[70]

Desplechin himself has suggested that when he started out as a film student, his models were less the New Wave than the subsequent generation of French filmmakers like Maurice Pialat, Jean Eustache and Philippe Garrel.[71] He claims that he would have felt crushed by the weight of precursors like Truffaut, Rivette or Resnais.[72] On the contrary, however, where the inimitable model of the Nouvelle Vague became a pale ghost haunting the sparse aesthetic of Eustache and Garrel, Thierry Jousse has suggested that Desplechin belongs to the first generation of filmmakers 'emancipated' from the New Wave as a kind of cinematic 'superego'.[73] This perhaps explains why New Wave influences are worn so lightly in *Comment je me suis disputé*. Desplechin notes that what he has inherited from the New Wave is what he calls its *'fantaisie'*, a word which, in French, does not have the strong connotation of 'fantasy', but something closer to 'make-believe' or 'whimsy'.[74] He adds that the New Wave is often misremembered as an aesthetic principally concerned with realism and improvisation whereas the movement also generated films as playful as *La Mariée était en noir* (Truffaut, 1968), *Céline et Julie vont en bateau* (Rivette, 1974) or *Die Marquise von O* (Rohmer, 1976).[75] This playfulness is to be found in such deliberately unrealistic elements of Desplechin's film as Paul's encounters with Rabier and the monkey; his improbably spectacular tumble down two flights of stairs after learning that his secret love, Sylvia, is moving in with his friend; or the character of Valérie who, with her compulsive lies, violent outbursts and idiosyncratic accessorizing (she wears a wedding ring on her index finger and attaches little horn-like appurtenances to her hair), recalls some of the eccentric but ultimately harmless femmes fatales of Truffaut's oeuvre. Truffaut is no doubt responsible for the most significant elements of New Wave influence in Desplechin's work. His interview with Anne Gillain and Dudley Andrew demonstrates a detailed and precise knowledge of Truffaut's films and he claims that a collection of Truffaut's own interviews constitutes one of the few books on film that are of practical use to directors: 'It's like the Bible to me.'[76] In interviews around *Comment je me suis disputé*, he talked affectionately of *Tirez sur le pianiste* (Truffaut, 1960), reading it as a kind of disguised autobiography,[77] which is also how Desplechin's own film has been interpreted.[78] David Vasse meanwhile has remarked on a technique Desplechin borrows from Truffaut that consists of 'an isolated gesture at the edge of a scene whose function is to betray some torment but without affecting the unity of the action'.[79] Like Truffaut was for the New Wave, Desplechin is sometimes identified as the 'leader' of the *jeune cinéma* of the 1990s[80] and *Comment je me suis disputé* as a 'generational' film somewhat in the manner of *Les Quatre Cents Coups*.[81] Jean-Michel Frodon suggests that this is the first time Desplechin's generation has been represented with such accuracy and dignity in the cinema.[82] With this in mind, the remainder of this section will seek first to examine the style of *Comment je me suis disputé*, with particular reference to the echoes of the New Wave therein, and second to scrutinize the film as a social portrait, paying particular attention to its treatment of gender.

While the Nouvelle Vague became famous for its often distinctive and irreverent style, the *jeune cinéma français*, largely associated with realism, is, for the most part, less conspicuous in its deployment of cinematic techniques. Indeed, those rare critics who reviewed *Comment je me suis disputé* negatively sometimes lamented the absence of style. Claude Baignères, writing in *Le Figaro*, sniffed, 'The direction is marked by an absence – no doubt voluntary – of imagination. The camera is there, captures what is being done, and above all what is being said, but without attempting the slightest stylistic effect.'[83] René Prédal, assessing Desplechin's style from greater distance, notes that while he directs his actors in a rather nervous, highly strung mode, reminiscent of Patrice Chéreau or Jacques Doillon, the excitement of the performance is not underlined by jarring or fragmentary edits, the director instead tending to favour medium and long shots over close-ups.[84] The most immediately striking formal choice of *Comment je me suis disputé* is its length – three hours – a duration highly unusual for all New Wave directors except Jacques Rivette. The film's duration instead recalls another 'generational' work based around interminable discussions of sex, Eustache's *La Maman et la Putain* (1973). But Desplechin replaces the narrow focus (essentially three characters) and lengthy monologues of Eustache's film with an ensemble cast and a large number of mostly very short scenes (I count a total of 69 scenes in 178 minutes, giving an average length of just two and half minutes per scene). The unusual length of ... *disputé* ... is also 'compensated', as Carole Le Berre points out, by the extreme mobility of the camera as well as by the seemingly constant motion – walking, pacing, gesticulating – of the characters.[85] The camera will not infrequently move independently of the characters, roaming around a space and sometimes connecting to another movement in the succeeding shot or scene, creating a curious rhythm that, in the words of Claude-Marie Trémois, is 'without transitions, but without breaks either'.[86] In fact, despite its superficial lightness, the film's montage and narrative structure have a daunting sophistication, boasting a time scheme worthy of early Resnais.[87] The film moves without warning between the present, the recent past (in which Paul's infatuation and affair with Sylvia are played out) and the distant past of childhood memories: the film even opens misleadingly with a series of images of Bruges, a glancing reference in one of Paul's memories recounted to his therapist, but without relevance to the remainder of the narrative. The playful montage operates on several levels at once, sometimes between shots linked by neat matches (Jean-Jacques's protracted handshake with Paul cuts to a more casual one with Sylvia) or sharp contrasts (a scene of Paul and Esther embracing eagerly in the street cuts to a tearful Esther telling Paul over the phone, 'You're dead to me'). Elsewhere, the juxtaposition of scenes illustrates Desplechin's principle of translating emotion into action, as in the aforementioned tumble down the stairs or Paul's sudden anxiety attack while out for a jog, immediately following the scene with Rabier's monkey. Finally, there are more distant visual and thematic rhymes within the narrative, as when Paul's snooping into Valérie's diary recalls his own mother's indiscretion with his first attempted novel, itself based around a cruel fictional portrait of his father. The much remarked novelistic quality of *Comment je me suis disputé* is also found in the film's use of voice-over narration, a technique sometimes dismissed as a sign of a director's incompetence[88] but praised by Desplechin as a means of 'restoring independence to the image'.[89] The New Wave's affection for voice-over, he claims, is to be related to their love of silent cinema: it is a way of liberating the image from sound.[90] Voice-over has a way of telling the spectator what to think, dispensing with the business of narrative exposition and leaving the filmmaker 'free to invent visual solutions'.[91] The film's first voice-over, coming in the opening minutes, introduces all the key elements of Paul's character – his profession, his inferiority complex, his living arrangements, his relationship with Esther and his clandestine infatuation with Sylvia – thereby freeing up the remaining three hours to show how these relationships are played out in gestures, physical confrontations and verbal sparring, but without the need for didactic expository scenes. Elsewhere, in a comic use of voice-over, Paul's break-up with Esther is recounted crisply over a short, silent scene, only to be followed by a lengthy, post-break-up fight between the couple, as though the voice-over represented Paul's cowardly fantasy of the simplicity with which the scene might play out.

As discussed in the introductory section of this chapter, one commonly noted quality of the *jeune cinéma français* is its progressive treatment of gender and sexuality. Within this encouraging panorama, *Comment je me suis disputé* can come across as rather regressive. Indeed, despite the film's large cast of characters, it is not even clear that it would pass the famous Bechdel test of female autonomy.[92] Where all the men of the film have conversations about various kinds of existential, epistemological and theological doubt, the women rarely join in such discussions, instead talking almost exclusively about sex and relationships, mostly with Paul.

Desplechin has demonstrated his awareness of this tendency, wondering whether it makes him misogynistic,[93] but claiming, provocatively, that he would be 'flattered' by such a label.[94] Desplechin has also claimed a desire to invert traditional gender stereotypes in his film, having 'men react like women, and vice versa'.[95] In classical cinema, he suggests, men care about their 'destiny' whereas women only care about their image;[96] in *Comment je me suis disputé*, on the other hand, men chatter idly while women come across as more solitary creatures absorbed by their own (somewhat obscure) plans.[97] Marie-Claire Ropars, however, has rejected such claims as disingenuous, arguing that ... *disputé* ... takes its place in a long line of films in which 'female figures [serve] as auxiliary to the identity realization of the hero and [are] effective because sexually other'.[98] This is most clearly the case in the film's treatment of nudity. The film's three principal female characters are all shown fully or partially naked during the narrative, which is, needless to say, not the case for any of the men and, indeed, when Paul and Nathan appear in swimming trunks, their mutual embarrassment is so acute that it accounts for the totality of the scene's dialogue. This is also the scene in which Paul first meets Sylvia, and the nature of their relationship is established when he walks in on her naked in a changing cubicle. He deliberately prolongs his gaze, which she appears almost to invite or welcome, as a result of which he conceives an ardent passion ('I don't think I'll ever get over meeting you', he tells her immediately afterwards). The film's final scene is a flashback to Paul and Sylvia's brief affair in which they play a (presumably post-coital) game of pick-up sticks during which she is completely naked and he fully dressed. Wareheime describes this image as 'doubly regressive, both in its quality as a flashback and in its fetishizing of the woman's body, the visual image substituting for the sexual possession that is no longer possible'.[99] Desplechin notes that even his own film crew protested at the sexism of this mise en scène, but, in his defence, he insists that the opposite (a naked man and a clothed woman) would be inconceivable, since a man's nudity acts as a mask concealing his identity whereas a woman's serves to reveal her true self: 'Presence is feminine in nature', he concludes.[100] While this statement, in some ways, condenses rather neatly several hundred years of art history, there is no sense of historical contextualization within Desplechin's discourse, leaving it thoroughly complicit with an essentializing hegemony whereby woman is rendered irrevocably mysterious purely on the basis of her anatomical gender, a tendency confirmed by Claude-Marie Trémois's description of the character of Sylvia as 'the sphinx'.[101]

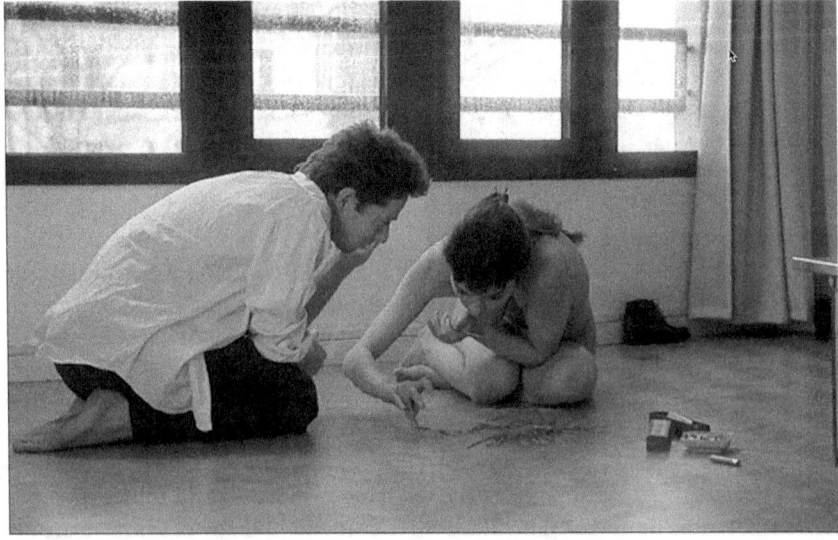

FIGURE 3.1 *Mathieu Amalric and Marianne Denicourt in* Comment je me suis disputé (Ma vie sexuelle) *(1996). Courtesy Cahiers du cinéma.*

Something similar occurs with the sexual relations depicted in ... *disputé* ... : Desplechin complains that whenever one man sleeps with two or more women in a film, spectators inevitably protest that he is insufficiently attractive to be credible, yet such protestations are never heard when the gender roles are reversed. Again, here, Desplechin hits upon an interesting point about the visibility of value in femininity under a patriarchal culture as opposed to the transparency of masculinity, yet any potential for analysis of this situation is evacuated by the essentializing quip: 'a man serves to disappoint; a woman, to magnify'.[102] However, before condemning entirely the gender representation of *Comment je me suis disputé*, we should note the lengthy scenes towards the end of the film devoted exclusively to Esther in the everyday environment of the hostel where she lives and the university where she attends advanced translation classes. At stake in these scenes is a possible pregnancy and we see Esther repeatedly checking her underwear and bed sheets for signs of menstrual blood and visiting a gynecologist. Marie-Claire Ropars dismisses these scenes, arguing that the favouring of Esther's point of view is undercut by the essentializing association of her with her potential maternity: 'Esther becomes autonomous only in order to recover the indubitable signs of her femininity.'[103] While it is true that, in this way, the shadow of Paul continues to hang over these scenes, such undiluted screen time is exceptional in what is otherwise such a populous movie: in total, these scenes account for some thirteen minutes of screen time, a privilege accorded to no other character apart from Paul.[104] And when having finally got her period again, Esther breaks down in the shower, first laughing in relief and then crying in apparent sadness, the complexity of her emotional response and the consequential gravity of her sexual relationship with Paul are rendered tangible for the spectator.

This remains, however, an isolated example of the film's openness to the real lived experience of women and, overall, it is perhaps cause for regret that the 'leader' of the *jeune cinéma français*, the 'most gifted of his generation',[105] should appropriate the dynamic mise en scène of the French New Wave without sharing so many of his peers' ability to question the regressive sexual politics and misogynist clichés of representation that unfortunately marred some of the best films of the Nouvelle Vague.

Oublie-moi

The immediately obvious feature linking Noémie Lvovsky's *Oublie-moi* (released in France in January 1995) to the New Wave is the proportion of the film that takes place on the streets of Paris. As in so many of the debut features of the Nouvelle Vague (*Les Quatre Cents Coups, À bout de souffle, Le Signe du Lion, Cléo de 5 à 7, Paris nous appartient*), the heroine of *Oublie-moi*, Nathalie (Valeria Bruni Tedeschi), spends the film pacing the streets, ducking into cafes and going back and forth between different friends' apartments. But Lvovsky's film seems deliberately to take this spatial disposition to extremes: only rarely is Nathalie indoors in *Oublie-moi*. Following a brief prologue in which Nathalie and her friend Christelle (Emmanuelle Devos) dance together, presumably in the latter's apartment, the film opens with a lengthy series of scenes on the Parisian transport network: first in the metro, then in her boyfriend Antoine's (Emmanuel Salinger) car, then in the metro again and finally at a bus stop awaiting a night bus. Twenty-five minutes of film time elapse before we see another interior space (the next morning in Antoine's apartment) and then, as though to stress the fragility of this temporary haven, no dialogue passes between the couple before Nathalie is back on the streets again. Repeatedly, when Nathalie goes to see the men in her life – Antoine or her ex Éric (Laurent Grévill) – they immediately lead her outside again so that their important conversations take place in a cafe, on the roof of the hospital where Éric works or in a Laundromat. Thus, as Julia Dobson remarks, interior spaces 'offer neither sanctuary nor structure' in Nathalie's life or in the narrative space of the film.[106] As several critics noted on the film's release, the mise en scène privileges in-between spaces like doorways, corridors and hallways, stairwells and telephone booths, Nathalie finding herself in a kind of 'spatial limbo'.[107] Stéphane Bouquet observes that these are so many spaces of communication and circulation, yet the transmission of meaning seems to be blocked in the film's many dialogues of the deaf:[108] Nathalie insistently declares her love for Éric, even though he has moved on from their relationship; Antoine's caring overtures to her are met mainly with spiteful and self-destructive responses; meanwhile, she gravitates towards a physical relationship with Fabrice (Philippe Torreton) despite not really being attracted to this young man who seems as lost as she is. Lvovsky has gone as far as to suggest that the film's visual landscape of doorways and landings is almost an expressionistic exteriorization of Nathalie's psychological state, at once *beside herself* (with love, anger, despair) and imprisoned within herself.[109] But Nathalie's precarious situation is not just psychological, it is also social: as Nathalie shuttles back and forth between different men's apartments, the spectator begins to doubt the very existence of the studio in which she claims to live.[110] In an age before mobile phones, Nathalie memorizes a series of addresses, telephone numbers and security codes like so many lifelines. If *Oublie-moi* is strongly marked by pedestrian movement through urban space, then, as in many New Wave films, Nathalie is hardly a flâneur, the archetypal French urban walker characterized by possibilities of economic and erotic consumption. The urban backdrops of the New Wave are spaces of wandering, since there always seems to be the time and opportunity to stop and contemplate passers-by or incidents unrelated to the main narrative thread. Even Michel Poiccard in *À bout de souffle*, on the run from police and wanted for murder, never seems in much of a hurry. (Indeed, it is one of the most striking qualities of Godard's film, and a key trait of the New Wave more generally, to be able to marry narrative drive with long, seemingly open-ended moments of relaxation.) In *Oublie-moi*, the only time the camera contemplates scenes outside the narrative proper it constitutes a troubling reminder of Nathalie's precariousness since we see a man searching through a public litter bin for items of use. There is an urgency to Lvovsky's film, in other words, that combines Nathalie's psychological distress with the suggestion of her social frailty.

This sense of urgency gives the film an impressive rhythmic drive. The film comes across as a headlong rush forward. As Trémois remarks, there are few temporal markers to orient the spectator within the narrative aside from changes in clothes and light conditions.[111] But the pace of the film tends to give the impression that its events happen over the course of a couple of days, even if they could just as plausibly occupy weeks or months. This pace is communicated by the seemingly constant motion, particularly in the early sequences of the film. Thus, Nathalie and Antoine have a conversation while striding hurriedly along a moving walkway in the underground, she talking to his back while he calls responses over his shoulder. Later, the couple have a serious discussion of their relationship while driving, the awkwardness of the conversation heightened by the music playing insistently on the car stereo.[112] Although the volume is low, the saxophone glissandi and belligerently barked chorus (ironically, given the situation, 'You speak my language') cannot help but add to the tension of the scene. Indeed, throughout the film, music seems to be used in a conflictual rather than complementary way. It has become commonplace to open a film soundtrack with a pop song, but when Lvovsky couples Patti Smith's 'Distant Fingers' with a scene of Nathalie and Christelle dancing, the effect is unsettling. The two women are concentrated and largely unsmiling in their movements and, if this is an instance of two friends pastiching the seriousness of professional dance routines, the lack of any contextualizing dialogue before or after leaves the tone of the scene uncertain. Nathalie, in particular, despite dancing with Christelle, comes across as inward-looking and rigid in her careful poses, while her gaze at the other woman appears more challenging than complicit. Similarly, when Fabrice, floundering in his conversation with Nathalie, puts on Lou Reed's 'There Is No Time', it is hardly possible to appreciate the music since Fabrice urgently translates all the lyrics into French. The effect is not a shared moment of harmonious communion, as in certain musical interludes of the New Wave, but instead a further demonstration of the young man's off-putting earnestness and inability to unwind.

Even when the characters are relatively still, the camera remains restless, combining shot/reverse-shot editing with nervous pans back and forth between speakers. As critics noted, this is a film rich in dialogue and in which characters cling desperately to their words and those of their interlocutors. Fabrice's speech seems inappropriately serious, existentially loaded from the first moment he meets Nathalie, multiplying questions and uncertainties ('I don't know why I'm going to this party. Are we going to go together? What about afterwards? Will we go home together?'). Later, noticing Nathalie's heavy smoking habit, he starts talking uncontrollably about cancer of the lips. Language builds a fortress around the characters; in Jean-Michel Frodon's evocative phrase, these 'torrents of words' are thrown out the way a besieged population might throw buckets of oil on their assailants.[113] Elsewhere, the rapid-fire combative dialogue between seemingly mis-matched couples is somewhat reminiscent of the screwball comedy of classic Hollywood cinema and indeed Lvovsky admits that she saw her film as a kind of 'remarriage comedy'[114] (in the playful final scene, Nathalie, having broken up with Antoine, calls him from a phone booth; he pretends to be a new tenant in Antoine's apartment, the couple flirt with each other and the film ends with a fragile promise of their reconciliation). The failure of communication in the film's dialogue is frequently marked by the collapse of simple question–answer formulations: questions are often rhetorical, unanswered or turned back on the speaker. When Fabrice asks Nathalie, late at night, 'Wouldn't you rather come and sleep at my place?' she replies, 'Are you mad? [*Ça va pas?*]' When he explains that he desires her company not for sex but for conversation, she asks, logically, 'Aren't we talking now?' Elsewhere, questions lose their interrogative value. When she does come to Fabrice's apartment, Nathalie asks, 'Shall we go to your room?' before losing the intonation of a question to continue, 'We'll take our clothes off. We'll get into bed.'[115] Jacques Morice has pointed to a curious quality of Valeria Bruni Tedeschi's voice which allows statements to resonate as questions and vice versa.[116] The tendency for characters to answer their own questions implies that some of the dialogues in the film are closer to monologues. Indeed, when Nathalie comes to see Éric at home, he takes her across the street to a cafe to talk only to find that she grins mutely at him as he speaks. Later, on the hospital roof, the situation is reversed when Nathalie puts words into Éric's mouth, forcing him to say the words she is most afraid to hear ('I don't love you. There is no chance that I will ever love you. You disgust me.'). As Julia Dobson astutely puts it, Nathalie is like 'a negative version of the unruly woman of screwball comedy displaying not opportunism but compulsion and replacing a spontaneous, unconventional *joie de vivre* with a performative *mal de vivre*'.[117]

The classic era of the Hollywood romantic comedy was also influential over the New Wave (especially Godard and Truffaut) but, if those films were self-conscious in their quotation of a more innocent age of screen romance, they nonetheless retained a sense of excitement and playfulness about the very possibility of sexual relations, as in the lengthy 'Hôtel de Suède' sequence in *À bout de souffle* which essentially consists of Michel Poiccard trying to talk Patricia into bed with him. In this sense, one of the most striking differences in *Oublie-moi* (and, by extension, perhaps in much of the *jeune cinéma*) is the seemingly irrevocable loss of this sexual innocence, replaced by a weighty sense of sexual exhaustion. This sombre mood is unimaginable in the original screwball comedies or even in the New Wave: it is only after several decades of relative sexual freedom that the prospect of sex with different partners can come to be experienced as an injunction or a chore rather than an opportunity. When, in the aforementioned hotel-room scene from *À bout de souffle*, Michel asks Patricia how many sexual partners she has had, the question is part of the game of seduction; Patricia replies coyly by holding up her fingers while Michel himself evades the question with bluster and improbable boasting. In *Oublie-moi*, on the other hand, Éric is able to proceed with a cold arithmetic deconstruction of Nathalie's love life, reasoning that, at the rate of two partners a year, she can expect to fall in love once every five years and to meet a real marriage prospect once a decade. Sex has here become a joyless calculation. Where Michel talks Patricia into sex, Nathalie and Fabrice talk each other out of it. Having undressed, they share the most hurtful comments they have ever received on their lovemaking (Fabrice is 'concentrated and laborious' in bed; Nathalie 'enthusiastic but disorganised') until they have thoroughly killed the mood.

This is indicative of the self-destructive patterns of behaviour that Nathalie displays throughout the film. This is most apparent in her reluctance to let go of her relationship to her ex-boyfriend Éric. In an early scene, Nathalie sees him on the metro and, even after he has told her, 'It's over. I don't want to see you any more', she runs after him asking, 'Can I call you tomorrow?' As Éric will tell her later, it is not actually him Nathalie loves so much as the dizzy sense of her own infatuation ('*Ce que tu aimes, c'est le vertige*'); anyone else would have served just as well. This sense that Nathalie is indiscriminately reaching out for connection is further demonstrated in the scene in which she has sex in a toilet with an anonymous stranger. She compounds the self-defeating humiliation of this perfunctory, joyless sex by telling the contemptuous man that she had hoped to be 'transformed' by the encounter. There is ultimately little difference between this unfortunate confrontation and the scene in which Nathalie, seemingly deliberately, crashes into another car, her attempts at human connection being conducted, as Claire Vassé remarks, with all the subtlety of a cannonball.[118] If Nathalie's behaviour is frequently unsubtle, however, the same is not true of Bruni Tedeschi's performance, which avoids the clichés of 'the hysterical woman' to produce a nuanced portrait of a vulnerable, if never exactly likeable young woman.[119] Throughout the film, Bruni Tedeschi appears pale and naturally made up, her hair frequently lank or dishevelled. Her performance is restless and fidgety. Nathalie walks fast, with short strides and her facial expressions are unpredictable, often sneering or laughing, just once, without apparent amusement, in exchanges with her boyfriends, yet elsewhere smiling openly at nothing and no one in particular while walking in the street. The performance moves quickly from the appearance of charm to develop elements of menace as in the scene where, believing she hears voices inside, she kicks in the door of Éric's apartment. It is largely Bruni Tedeschi's performance that gives the film its rhythm: as Jean Coutances remarks, the jerky, breathless pace to the scenes reflects Nathalie's loss of control.[120] Indeed, if we were to interpret Nathalie as a woman in the manic phase of a bipolar disorder, we could almost characterize the film's rhythm as manic-depressive: its breakneck pace occasionally collapsing into stillness, as when Nathalie falls asleep on the stairs outside Éric's apartment, or the scene, late in the film, where she rocks silently back and forth alone on a bed (this short scene, coming some eighty minutes into a ninety-two minute film, is the only one in the film that might plausibly take place in Nathalie's own home). The French New Wave produced a lot of memorable portraits of women – the Catherine of *Jules et Jim*, the Nana of *Vivre sa vie*, Camille in *Le Mépris* or Varda's Cléo – but perhaps none as extraordinary as Lvovsky and Bruni Tedeschi's creation in this film. For all her frustratingly objectionable behaviour, Nathalie imposes herself by virtue of what Dobson calls 'her persistently obstinate physical presence',[121] a presence that Vassé finds 'staggering'.[122] In this, Nathalie is comparable to another great female portrait from the *jeune cinéma français* (broadly defined), Émilie Dequenne's Rosetta from the Dardenne brothers' 1999 film of the same name. It perhaps required the gradual incorporation of several decades of feminist ideas for two such claustrophobically uncompromising portrayals of inchoate feminine resistance to be represented in the cinema without judgement on the part of the filmmakers.

A character like Nathalie could no doubt not have been imagined by the New Wave, although Varda's 1985 *Sans toit ni loi* is an important precursor in terms of the nomadism of the protagonist, the circularity of the narrative and the dispassionate gaze at the central character's antisocial behaviour. But the most important lesson that Lvovsky has learned from the New Wave, aside from the urban staging of her narrative, is doubtless the deceptively simple combination of the naturalistic with the non-naturalistic. In interview, Lvovsky has admitted that she finds her work torn between competing influences: the raw emotion of Pialat (whom she admires) and the more carefully constructed entertainment of Truffaut (whom she loves).[123] But, in *Oublie-moi*, Lvovsky succeeds in combining the appearance of naturalism with a deliberately designed structure that is reminiscent of some of the best work of Truffaut, Varda or Rivette. The film, as we have seen, uses real Parisian locations and is shot mostly using natural light and costumes provided by the cast and crew.[124] Yet basic elements of verisimilitude are missing from the narrative: we never learn what, if anything, Nathalie does for a living or whether she really has a flat of her own. In Lvovsky's own assessment, this is because the characters, or at least Nathalie and Fabrice, are trapped in the prisons they have created for themselves, obsessively rehearsing improbable questions such as, 'Do I just love him like crazy or do I love him like this because I'm actually crazy?'[125] The result is a film of a determined intimacy, far from sociological realism.[126] There are even elements of melodrama, as Dobson notes, in the film's 'attempt to define relationships through serial, compulsive confrontations'.[127] Far from documentary realism, the film's aesthetic is closer to the sensation of a bad dream, going around in maddening circles.[128] As Stéphane Bouquet puts it, this is the film as spinning top, turning around itself until it runs out of energy and collapses.[129]

La Vie de Jésus and *L'humanité*

With his first films, Bruno Dumont was initially aligned with other filmmakers from the *jeune cinéma français* engaged in making broadly defined 'social cinema', in particular directors based, like Dumont, in northern France such as Érick Zonca, Xavier Beauvois, Thomas Vincent and, across the border in Belgium, the Dardenne brothers. Dumont's first feature, *La Vie de Jésus* (1997), depicted the lives of a group of mostly unemployed young people in the northern town of Bailleul, where the director grew up. The climax of the narrative in a racially motivated murder seemed to confirm this taste for socially significant subjects. *Libération* described the film as 'a documentary about survival in the ordinary provinces'.[130] However, as Maryline Alligier points out, in *La Vie de Jésus* and, increasingly so in all of Dumont's subsequent films, the focus of the narrative rapidly narrows to a central couple or triangle of characters: here, the young 'hero' Freddy (David Douche), his girlfriend Marie (Marjorie Cottreel) and Freddy's Arab rival Kader (Kader Chaatouf).[131] Dumont himself claimed he was less interested in talking about the 'social context' of these characters than about 'human nature'.[132] David Vasse adds that Dumont is less concerned about unemployment as a social problem than he is about inactivity as an idea for mise en scène, the largely goalless trajectories of these young men on their mopeds giving the shape and rhythm to the film.[133]

Dumont's second film, *L'humanité* (1999), set in the same town as *La Vie de Jésus*, continues the tendency for deceptively social filmmaking. The film presents itself as a police-procedural drama, following the investigation into a brutal child murder in this depressed northern town where, at one point, the employees of a factory go on strike. Where elements of the film come across as brutally realistic, however (in particular, as we shall see, the depiction of sexual activity), the verisimilitude is fatally undercut by the performance of Emmanuel Schotté as detective superintendent Pharaon de Winter. With his wide-eyed gaze, effeminate voice and hunched shoulders, Pharaon is inarticulate to the point of autism and never credible as a police detective. As Didier Rochet remarked, the film is 'light years away from realism',[134] and the effect is clearly deliberate on the part of Dumont, who states simply, 'I am not a filmmaker of the real [...] I needed someone completely apart, completely 'other' in order to rethink humanity.'[135]

One area in which Dumont's cinema engages enthusiastically with realism is in the focus on bodies, and indeed Dumont's work, alongside that of Claire Denis, has been central in the theorization, within Film Studies, of a certain 'bodily turn' in art cinema privileging an intense, and sometimes abject, appeal to the viewer's senses.

Both *La Vie de Jésus* and *L'humanité* are set at least partly in the summer months and feature multiple scenes of characters standing and sitting outside, sweating and sunburned and complaining about the heat. The films also include images of characters in fields, pressing themselves into the earth, and graphic scenes of sexual intercourse (the latter sometimes overlapping with the former). As Maryline Alligier remarks, largely through his choice of actors, Dumont offers no aestheticizing filter between the body and its presentation on screen.[136] Dumont's non-professional actors have imperfect bodies and his camera captures them in unflattering postures, notably during sex scenes. Critics and scholars comment repeatedly on sexual representation in Dumont, with a consensus rapidly developing that the intercourse in these films appears, in the words of Antony Fiant, 'savage, mechanical, bereft of pleasure or orgasm, and with no apparent aspiration to anything other than release'.[137] The animalistic aspect to these scenes is heightened by the fact that they often take place outdoors (especially in *Twentynine Palms* (2003) and *Flandres* (2006), but already in *La Vie de Jésus*). In short, Dumont's cinema has been seen as particularly responsible for the trend in millennial French cinema that Tim Palmer labels 'brutal intimacy' and that is characterized by 'disaffected and emotionless sex, ambiguously consensual sexual encounters, arbitrary sex stripped of conventional or even nominal gestures of romance'.[138] *La Vie de Jésus* sets the tone for this sexual representation when, in practically its second scene, Freddy and Marie are presented naked after sex and we watch her cleaning herself on the bidet while Freddy is gripped by an epileptic seizure. Later, the pair have sex in a field and a hardcore insert shows Marie guiding Freddy's penis inside her in close-up (body doubles were used). *L'humanité* features three explicit sex scenes between Pharaon's neighbour, Domino (Séverine Caneele), with whom he is mildly obsessed, and her taciturn boyfriend Joseph (Philippe Tullier). Most French reviewers commented on these scenes, describing the sex as 'desperate', without feeling or thought, 'bestial and brutal' or, in one memorable phrase, 'as indecipherable as a hieroglyph'![139] Dumont's films, then, with their explicit sex and violence, have been at the centre of a debate about the representational ethics of recent French cinema. Some critics, like James Quandt, have seen this material as representative of a cynical 'shock tactics', betraying the 'desperate measures' of a national cinema that has lost its traditional identity basis.[140] Hampus Hagman has also suggested that films like Dumont's exploit representational taboos as a kind of marketing strategy on a festival circuit where a degree of 'transgression' is expected: 'sensationalism is put to work in order to facilitate media exposure and break through the competitive noise of the world cinema market'.[141]

Arguably, inarticulate characters who express themselves mostly through sex and violence increasingly constitute a kind of 'international language' of art cinema.

But Dumont, like so many young French directors, is an articulate and knowledgeable subject who is only too happy to reflect upon the theory and practice of his filmmaking. What is striking in interviews with Dumont is the extent to which his approach to direction is couched in terms of an ethics of mise en scène that often recalls the rhetoric of the 1950s generation of French critics who effectively invented modern mise en scène criticism, some of whom would go on to create the films of the Nouvelle Vague (this is despite the fact that Dumont's films superficially bear little resemblance to the New Wave, whose canonical directors are not points of reference in his interviews). A key word recurring in discussions of Dumont's debut feature is 'humility'. In his working notes on the film, subsequently published in *Positif*, Dumont expressed his wish to film 'the inside' of things by focusing scrupulously on external details of landscape and faces: 'By dint of this humility – of its perseverance, its extension in time – there would be an overflowing.'[142] Elsewhere, Dumont explained this humility by suggesting that the 'immobility of the mise-en-scène' allowed him to erase his own point of view.[143] This recalls, then, the rhetoric of the 1950s French critics, whose complex, demanding, and sometimes paradoxical, notion of mise en scène has been usefully summarized by Jacques Aumont. As Aumont points out, in the classical conception of mise en scène, artistic creation and expression must constitute a 'recreation of the world' that can be shared with the viewer in complete clarity.[144] Given its ability to capture the affective potential of every gesture, gaze and movement, mise en scène is less a technique, in this view, than a kind of force or energy. Better still, mise en scène is a virtue, from the Latin *virtus* (force), but preserving an apt ethical dimension: a mise en scène worthy of the name should be 'pure', in the sense that it is stripped of the artifices of 'style' and sheltered from the egotism and narcissism of the director's personality: 'there is no mise-en-scène but melded with, and made from, the world', writes Aumont.[145] The artist is thus constrained in the type of representation he can produce since his role is paradoxically to efface himself before the world, to let the world, as it were, speak for itself.

How, then, does Dumont's controversial imagery sit with the self-proclaimed humility of this approach to mise en scène? *La Vie de Jésus* is at least consistent in its aesthetic approach and remains, arguably, one of the most successful exercises in mise en scène in Dumont's erratic career. The film offers a scrupulously materialist mise en scène throughout, presenting the life of the physical body as central to its dramatic arc and narrative meaning. In the film's setting of Bailleul it is demonstrated that there is little else for young people to do than to ride around on their mopeds and to have sex. These depersonalized sensual pleasures are stressed by the long shots and largely static frames in which the boys on their bikes appear typically as distant, fast-moving figures and, conversely, by the unambiguous close-ups that stress the sweaty friction of sex. There appear to be few employment prospects in this town aside from the supermarket in which Marie works and almost no culture other than the television constantly playing in the cafe run by Freddy's mother. The film places constant stress on the physical experience of boredom and entrapment in this town through its long shots of often immobile and taciturn characters, the discomfort (of protagonists and spectators) exacerbated by the summer heatwave. This is brilliantly achieved in the lengthy scene in *La Vie de Jésus* where Freddy and his friends lounge idly on the steps of the town hall, the camera roaming restlessly over their faces and bodies. As Marine Landrot argues, Dumont has a knack for filming boredom without becoming boring.[146] This is one of the key moments in the film that arguably makes a meaningful social point through mise en scène alone: the sense of fidgety adolescent energy deprived of an outlet makes the scene, in Brett Bowles's words, 'almost unbearable' and sufficient in itself to explain the violence that erupts at the end of the narrative.[147] Freddy's own frustration and alienation are rendered more acute by his living with epilepsy; we witness two seizures and his routine hospital visits. Freddy expresses his hatred of this defective body through dramatic (though always solitary) instances of self-harm, repeatedly kicking the wall of the hospital and deliberately throwing himself from his moped; for much of the film he carries an angry road-rash scar on his shoulder.

Sex does, then, play a crucial role of physical escapism in this universe, and its almost purely physical significance motivates the graphic representation. The reigning emotional illiteracy around sex is demonstrated by the boys' half-admiring, half-bashful exclamations at Freddy's perceived prowess and stamina ('He never stops!'), but also by Michou's (Samuel Boidin) earnest but rather confused announcement that he won't have sex so long as he is mourning his brother's death. This older brother has died of AIDS, a circumstance that is never explained and barely evoked, as though in sympathy with the boys' fear and embarrassment around the topic (only a grown-up neighbour asks, with surprise, whether Cloclo was gay, receiving a vague, non-committal response from Freddy's mother). Narrative development in *La Vie de Jésus* is unquestionably motivated by sex. Since Freddy and Marie's relationship is based almost exclusively around fornication, it is understandable that she grows distanced from him when the sex ceases to satisfy. First, she complains that he has hurt her: the narrative placement of this exchange implies that it was the hardcore outdoor session that was to blame; Freddy's response is insensitive to say that least ('Next time I'll take you up the arse', he jokes). Marie breaks up with Freddy after learning that he has sexually assaulted a girl in his marching band, an unthinking moment of asserted dominance from Freddy that results in physical revulsion for Marie. If she gravitates subsequently towards Kader, it is simply because he is better looking and better mannered than Freddy. Her rough come-on to Kader, aggressively stuffing his hand into her underwear, repels him and is later cause for regret by her, a sign that her sexual behaviour has been shaped by Freddy's blunt, masculine world and needs to be leavened with tenderness before she can enjoy more satisfying relationships. This physical narrative is, then, entirely sufficient to motivate Freddy's final murder of Kader. It is clear that this crime is inspired by sexual jealousy rather than racial hatred. The scene in which the boys hesitantly proffer racist insults between giggles demonstrates that this is more a mischievous quotation of a language they half understand than an expression of sincere ethnic enmity. *La Vie de Jésus* can thus be seen to have an 'ethical' mise en scène in the sense that it adequately demonstrates, without resorting to psychology, the physical pressures that lead to murder. The brutal physicality of the mise en scène explains Freddy's evolution into a killer, without ever excusing it.

In a very approving review of *La Vie de Jésus*, Jean-Michel Frodon claimed that Dumont had 'invented for himself a position from which he can show everything', as demonstrated by the shot of Freddy's ageing and obese mother rising naked from the bathtub (though the mother, too, is presumably granted the dignity of a body double), a shot which Frodon asserts is 'born from a necessity of mise en scène rather than a narrative obligation'.[148] We

FIGURE 3.2 *David Douche and Marjorie Cottreel in* La Vie de Jésus *(1997). Courtesy Blaq Out.*

can perhaps accept this argument in relation to *La Vie de Jésus*, since the mother's slow, heavy body, her evident struggle with the heat and the sense of moral exhaustion expressed by her parenting style contribute to the film's wider portrait of oppressed bodies in a claustrophobic community. Does this same all-encompassing materialist aesthetic apply to Dumont's next film, *L'humanité*? As mentioned, the film's narrative is based around the police investigation of the rape and murder of a schoolgirl, and Dumont 'announces' this generic plot with a shocking close-up of the girl's bloodied genitals. Much later, towards the end of the film, this shot is 'matched' by a frontal close-up of Domino's genitals as she lies sobbing on the bed, the shot staged and framed in an unmistakable allusion to Gustave Courbet's *L'Origine du monde* (1866). Dumont himself referred to the second shot as 'the exact counterpoint' of the first, adding, 'I would never have dared film the sex of the raped little girl if I didn't have the shot of Domino [...] The unrepresentable only interests me if I can find a way around it.'[149] Here, though, Dumont's rhetoric is much less convincing. The graphic close-up of the murder victim could be justified by an extreme naturalism of the mise en scène, yet this is fatally undercut by the bizarre, seemingly autistic performance of Emmanuel Schotté as the police inspector (his 'catatonic evanescence', as *Les Inrockuptibles* put it[150]). This gormless performance tends to drain all urgency away from the police investigation thus also nullifying the shocking image as a spur to moral outrage and narrative action (indeed forty-seven minutes of sedate weekend activities intervene before the film returns to the criminal investigation). The shot of Domino's pubis is, in turn, unmotivated, since she is alone in her room after rejection by Pharaon, so the implied post-coital diegetic observer of Courbet's painting has no place here. There is, then, a rather sterile, circular logic at work in the mise en scène of *L'humanité*: according to Dumont, the shot of the murder victim's naked body is only justified by the later, redemptive shot of Domino, and yet this latter shot contains no intrinsic motivation, its appearance ultimately only explicable in relation to the earlier image.

One might argue that in keeping with his declared humility, Dumont is seeking to develop a contemplative and thereby de-sensationalizing aesthetic in his treatment of sex. Certainly, the sex scenes between Domino and Joseph in *L'humanité* are lengthy and mostly filmed in full-shot long takes, avoiding the fragmentation and fetishization of body parts familiar from the grammar of video pornography. But these scenes do not ultimately suggest much beside the fact that young lovers have little else to do in Bailleul except have sex. The fact that Joseph is identified, at the end of the narrative, as the murderer of the little girl might imply a connection between his sexual appetite and his criminal tendencies. Yet, despite the excessive rhetoric of critics, there is nothing in the scenes with Domino to indicate anything other than a healthy enjoyment of adult heterosexual relations. In keeping with Dumont's offhand treatment of the crime narrative, Joseph's motivation remains entirely opaque, neither attributable to social alienation (since, as we have seen, any concessions to social realism in the film are half-hearted) nor to individual pathology (since Joseph's psychology is sketchily drawn at best). In short, Dumont's focus on sex is neither sufficiently sustained to have a distancing effect nor sufficiently pointed to imply that it has a key stake in the narrative development. Once again, then, one struggles to find an explanation for it beyond that of empty provocation.

In his early films, Dumont's recurring aesthetic strategy, as Antony Fiant notes, is to make systematic use of widescreen while emptying out the image as much as possible.[151] Extreme long shots are often used to show characters isolated in the landscape, as though confronted with their own solitude. At the opposite end of the scale, extreme close-ups (such as those on the sweaty neck of the police chief in *L'humanité*) create an oppressive atmosphere with little sense of a properly human scale in between these two extremes.[152] Maryline Alligier suggests that the figures in landscapes in Dumont's work imply not so much the encounter between characters and the immensity of nature but rather their confrontation with the enormity of their *own* nature.[153] As this suggests, and as James Williams confirms, the depiction of the natural world in Dumont is inclined more towards pictorialism than naturalism, symbolizing the psychological condition of the characters.[154] In a brilliant close reading of the director's films, Williams persuasively demonstrates that Dumont's is an 'entirely anthropocentric universe', since the natural world is invariably linked to a human gaze and allowed no kind of ontological autonomy.[155] Far from implying the 'dispersal of the self's structural integrity', Dumont's wide shots of landscape are almost always revealed as point-of-view shots, thereby reinforcing that very integrity.[156] Ultimately, argues Williams, Dumont's 'aesthetic mission' can be seen as 'to transform meaningless and pitiless nature into a compliant, hospitable space and refuge for human reflection and salvation'.[157]

But, if the natural world is constantly reduced to the parameters of the human and refused any alterity, then it is difficult to see how it can also be invested with spiritual significance, as seems to be the intention at the end of *La Vie de Jésus*, when Freddy lies in a meadow and weeps, seemingly learning his own lesson in humility after hearing of the death of Kader from the consequences of Freddy's beating. There is an apparently spiritual impulse in much of Dumont's cinema and early critics were quick to label it 'mystical', albeit finding the sacred in the most profane material.[158] Observers like Tina Kendall and Catherine Wheatley have grouped Dumont together with other 'post-theological' European filmmakers such as Ulrich Seidl, Jessica Hausner and Alice Rohrwacher interested in the possible manifestations of the sacred in a largely secular society.[159] Dumont himself has called the cinema 'a mystical art'[160] and insisted – as per his comments above about persevering in an attitude of humility – that the sacred can be attained by filming the ordinary world.[161] A number of critics have interpreted *La Vie de*

Jésus as representing the 'redemption' or even the 'ascension' of Freddy,[162] although this interpretation relies almost exclusively on the shot of the sun's rays illuminating Freddy's tearful face in the meadow and on the film's overdetermined title. As Dumont admits, without this title, the film would be 'too raw, too desperate'.[163] In a similar way, the auspicious title of *L'humanité* has also facilitated spiritual interpretations, permitting critics to interpret Pharaon as a kind of holy innocent or Christ-like figure whose uncommon sensitivity allows him to take the sins of the world upon himself.[164] At the end of the film, upon learning that Joseph is responsible for the murder of the child, Pharaon kisses him at length upon the mouth, as though absorbing the other man's sin, an action that recurs twice in Dumont's *Hors Satan* (2011) where it appears as a kind of folk remedy for demonic possession. In the end, though, Dumont's claim to make a 'humble' cinema is belied by these examples. Despite claims to the contrary, Dumont is far from the model of Robert Bresson who sought, through the sheer persistence of a neutral, impassive gaze, to show the operation of grace in the lives of, for instance, the eponymous protagonists of *Pickpocket* (1959) and *Mouchette* (1967). Instead, Dumont seeks to impose the sacred upon his films, through his unwieldy titles; through otherwise inexplicable, non-naturalistic behaviour such as Pharaon's kiss; and through the portentousness of a prolonged (but always anthropocentric) gaze. As Catherine Wheatley has argued, a kind of lazy association has developed between slow cinema and the spiritual, even in the absence of any manifest content. 'We are nostalgic for the sacred so we collect examples of cinematic seriousness and call it spirituality.'[165]

Conclusion

The concept of 'generations' is notoriously difficult to circumscribe with any certainty. Still, the generation of the *jeune cinéma français* are effectively the 'children' of the Nouvelle Vague in the sense that a child born between the late 1950s and the mid-1960s would be of an age to enter the film industry by the early-to-mid 1990s (few people make a mark on cinema before about thirty, following higher education and apprenticeship). And, in terms of sheer numbers, one can assert that more significant auteur directors came to prominence in France during the 1990s than in any other decade since the New Wave. What remains in question is the extent to which this flowering of young talent can be seen as, in any sense, the result of a coherent 'movement' as opposed to simply the long-term, and ongoing, consequence of France's well-established institutional and cultural support for cinema. What is clear is that the names associated with the *jeune cinéma*, and whatever significant aesthetic shifts they brought with them, emerged much more gradually, over a decade and a half, as compared to the dramatic appearance and cultural impact of the New Wave. The amorphous profile of the *jeune cinéma* is well demonstrated by the films discussed in this chapter: where *Comment je me suis disputé* and *Oublie-moi* are in many ways very similar – to the extent of being almost gendered mirror images in places – the films of Bruno Dumont are very different. Where Desplechin and Lvovsky set their films in the city, Dumont chooses the country; Desplechin and Lvovsky favour fast rhythms where Dumont's films are deliberately slow; ... *disputé* ... and *Oublie-moi* are driven by dialogue whereas *La Vie de Jésus* and *L'humanité* focus on inarticulate subjects and resistant bodies. Yet *La Vie de Jésus* clearly deserves to be included within the developing 'canon' of the *jeune cinéma*, at least in terms of the criteria given by critics like Trémois, Prédal and Jeancolas: it chronicles a year in the lives of marginalized and disaffected young people, characterized by aimless wandering (albeit on mopeds rather than on foot); it favours long takes and it develops open spaces and unanswered questions in its narrative.

Of course, the films of the New Wave, too, at least in retrospect, are a lot more different from each other than early accounts may have allowed. But the Nouvelle Vague was at least united by the cinema that it was reacting against: the so-called *cinéma de papa* or *tradition de qualité* of 1950s France. In the *jeune cinéma* of the 1990s, there is less evidence of a concerted effort at changing the fundamental forms and functions of cinema. Some critics have suggested that the *jeune cinéma* is a corrective response to trends in 1980s French film that turned away from contemporary realities (*cinéma du look* and heritage drama), yet it is not easy to find statements to this effect from the 1990s directors themselves; there is no equivalent in the *jeune cinéma* of the polemical texts François Truffaut published in the 1950s condemning the state of mainstream French filmmaking. Part of the difference between the two movements perhaps lies in the changing meaning of 'youth' in the late twentieth century. The understanding of youth underwent a first transformation in the 1950s and 1960s when rapid economic growth was compounded by the development of consumer culture and an expansion of higher education. Young people were under less immediate pressure to take up a profession and start a family and had more time, space and disposable income to explore ideas, identities and relationships. It is this sense of youth as a time of discovery and opportunity, and a conscious rejection of the older generation's culture of austerity (allied, in France, to suspicion over the generation's ethical record during the Second World War), that lends the New Wave much of its freshness and irreverent energy. By the end of the century, however, the growth in unemployment and the rise in housing costs had extended further the period during which young people sought their identity, in many cases turning a protracted youth from a luxury into a precarious limbo. This sense is perhaps responsible for the rather darker mood that many films of the *jeune cinéma* display in comparison to their New Wave forebears. While the city in the Nouvelle Vague often appeared as a playground of possible seductions and unexpected encounters, in the *jeune cinéma* Paris frequently comes across as a space of anxiety to which the protagonists have insecure access. Indeed, one of the most famous and successful French films of the period, *La Haine* (Mathieu Kassovitz, 1995), depicts the nocturnal odyssey through Paris of three young men who simply can't afford to be there and are consequently made to feel that they do not belong.

Related to this uncomfortably prolonged adolescence is a recurring sense, in the *jeune cinéma français*, of a certain inability to act. Where the New Wave, and other modernist cinemas, often chose to depict idleness over action, the *jeune cinéma* tends to favour characters who are paralysed into inaction by some form of neurosis: Paul Dédalus in *Comment je me suis disputé* seems unable to decide upon a direction, a career or a lover; Nathalie in *Oublie-moi* uses her constant motion to conceal her inability to take herself in hand and move on from her self-destructive patterns of behaviour; Pharaon in *L'humanité* seems so overwhelmed by his compassion for humanity that he appears unable to work up any urgency in his criminal investigation or to respond to Domino's sexual overtures. In the absence of meaningful action, the *jeune cinéma français* is often a cinema of talking and, as such, places more importance on the screenplay than did the New Wave. In some ways, it might even be seen to reach back to an older tradition in French cinema that held a particularly significant role for *dialoguistes*, part of a privileging of the verbal in French culture that affects all areas of society. Yet the *jeune cinéma* is also, as critics have noted, a cinema of the body, often requiring a strikingly physical performance from its actors.

It is noteworthy that all of the films discussed in this chapter deal unblushingly with sex as though the challenge of finding new ways to approach its representation was central to the mission of any filmmaker at the end of the twentieth century: How to avoid at once coy allusiveness, romanticization and the titillations of pornography? Desplechin chooses to idealize the naked body while displacing the crudity of the act into dialogue; Lvovsky shows how a casual promiscuity can be coupled to acute anxiety around sex, while Dumont opts for confrontation with the material reality of the act itself yet stripped of either emotional context or seductive visual rhetoric.

More broadly, two overriding principles might be seen to unite these diverse films. First, a conscious attempt to blend realism and artifice: Desplechin's broadly realistic aesthetic rendered strange by deliberately two-dimensional characters appearing almost as generic hand-me-downs (the cartoonish villain, the femme fatale); Lvovsky's physical proximity to the action taking the place of conventions of social and temporal verisimilitude; and Dumont's realistic milieu and crude materialism married to a persistent spiritual aspiration. Second, all of these directors seek, in different ways, to translate emotion and psychology into the mise en scène: thus Desplechin offers short-hand definitions of character through costume and accessories and concretizes psychological conflict in precise physical confrontations; Lvovsky presents Nathalie's spatial limbo as a metaphorization of her psychological fragility; and Dumont uses landscape to underline his characters' existential isolation. Both of these fundamental ideas about cinema are very familiar from the New Wave yet they are no doubt not, in themselves, sufficient to deduce an unequivocal and unilateral influence of one movement upon the other. Although the writers and directors of the New Wave helped to formulate and illustrate these ideas more clearly than most, they are ultimately among the most basic responses to the practical problems of filmmaking: a live-action fiction film necessarily bears the indexical imprint of the real while also making choices, which in the last instance have to be seen as arbitrary, about the shaping of that real into around two hours of screen time.

Meanwhile, the enforced externality of the film camera and microphone means that thoughts, feelings and personalities can only ever be expressed in concrete visual and auditory terms; mise en scène *is* this process of translating emotion and intention into spatially organized action. In short, while the filmmakers of the *jeune cinéma français* may have found some particularly innovative responses to these creative questions, the questions themselves are part of the basic grammar of cinema of the kind that any student would learn in film school or any cinephile from reading books and journals. In the end, rather than an isolated film movement responding directly to the New Wave, the *jeune cinéma* can perhaps best be seen as an effective demonstration of how far the love, appreciation and study of cinema have become embedded in French culture in the decades since the end of the Nouvelle Vague.

Notes

1   Another important film movement that emerged in France in the 1990s is the overlapping terrain of so-called *beur* and *banlieue* cinema, which fall beyond the scope of this book. While some of these films – and notably one of the most famous examples, *La Haine* (Mathieu Kassovitz, 1995) – may have drawn occasional inspiration from New Wave models, the movement as a whole can be seen to respond to a rather different set of social and aesthetic conditions and criteria. For an overview of the terrain, the reader is invited to consult Carrie Tarr, *Reframing Difference: Beur and Banlieue Filmmaking in France* (Manchester: Manchester University Press, 2005), Sylvie Durmelat and Vinay Swamy (eds), *Screening Integration: Recasting Maghrebi Integration in Contemporary France* (Lincoln: University of Nebraska Press, 2012) and Will Higbee, *Post-beur Cinema: North-African Emigré and Maghrebi French Filmmaking in France since 2000* (Edinburgh: Edinburgh University Press, 2013).

2. See Claude-Marie Trémois, *Les Enfants de la liberté: Le jeune cinéma français des années 90* (Paris: Seuil, 1997), 30–1, and René Prédal, *Le Jeune Cinéma français* (Paris: Armand Colin, 2005 [first published 2002]), 2.
3. René Prédal, 'La déferlante', in *Le Jeune Cinéma français*, ed. Michel Marie (Paris: Nathan, 1998), 11.
4. Jean-Pierre Jeancolas, 'Un cinéma de la responsabilité: Esquisse de cartographie du cinéma français vivant en 1998', *Australian Journal of French Studies* 36: 1 (1999), 12, and Jean-Pierre Jeancolas, 'The Confused Image of *le jeune cinéma*', *Studies in French Cinema* 5: 3 (2005), 157–8.
5. Thierry Jousse, Nicolas Saada, Frédéric Strauss, Camille Taboulay and Vincent Vatrican, 'Dix places pour le jeune cinéma', *Cahiers du cinéma* 473 (November 1993), 29.
6. Trémois, *Les Enfants de la liberté*, 63.
7. Prédal, 'La déferlante', 12.
8. Prédal, *Le Jeune Cinéma français*, 52.
9. Ibid., 2.
10. Jeancolas, 'Un cinéma de la responsabilité', 13.
11. Jacqueline Nacache, 'Group Portrait with a Star: Jeanne Balibar and French "jeune" Cinema', *Studies in French Cinema* 5: 1 (2005), 50.
12. See David Vasse, *Le Nouvel Âge du cinéma d'auteur français* (Paris: Klincksieck, 2008), 100, 107. On the influence of Pialat, see also Olivier Assayas, Claire Denis, Cédric Kahn and Noémie Lvovsky, 'Quelques vagues plus tard', *Cahiers du cinéma* special issue *Nouvelle Vague: Une légende en question* (1998), 72–3.
13. Michel Marie, '"Une famille avec des goûts communs mais des démarches personnelles … ": Entretien avec Nicolas Boukhrief', in *Le Jeune Cinéma français*, ed. Michel Marie (Paris: Nathan, 1998), 42–3.
14. Trémois, *Les Enfants de la liberté*, 47–55. Other lists are offered by Prédal and Jeancolas. Prédal notes the liveliness of performers; disruption of rhythm and of expected reactions; polyphonic composition; confusion of relationships; a refusal of psychology. *Le Jeune Cinéma français*, 42. Jeancolas points to the significance of actors; the importance of family; a sense that these films are 'generational'; the blurring of genres; the presence of 'the people'; an interest in redemption; an exploration of the regions; and a certain aspiration towards utopia. 'Un cinéma de la responsabilité', 22–5.
15. Prédal, *Le Jeune Cinéma français*, 74, 95–6. Jacqueline Nacache points out this tendency is reflected in the titles of many of these films with their preference for first- and second-person singular pronouns: in addition to *Comment je me suis disputé (Ma vie sexuelle)* (Arnaud Desplechin, 1996) and *Oublie-moi* (Noémie Lvovsky, 1994), Nacache cites *Personne ne m'aime* (Marion Vernoux, 1994), *N'oublie pas que tu vas mourir* (Xavier Beauvois, 1995), *J'ai horreur de l'amour* (Laurence Ferreira Barbosa, 1997) and *La Vie ne me fait pas peur* (Lvovsky, 1999). Nacache, 'Was There a Young French Cinema?' in *A Companion to Contemporary French Cinema*, ed. Alistair Fox, Michel Marie, Raphaëlle Moine and Hilary Radner (Chichester: Wiley-Blackwell, 2015), 194.

16 Prédal, 'La déferlante', 8.
17 Olivier de Bruyn, 'Une incertaine tendance du jeune cinéma français', *Positif* 399 (May 1994), 48–50.
18 Jousse et al., 'Dix places pour le jeune cinéma', 28.
19 Trémois, *Les Enfants de la liberté*, 20.
20 Cited in Trémois, *Les Enfants de la liberté*, 232.
21 Claire Vassé, 'Transgression des liens du sang', in *Le Jeune Cinéma français*, ed. Michel Marie (Paris: Nathan, 1998), 64–5.
22 Noël Herpe, 'Y aura-t-il un jeune cinéma français?' in *Le Jeune Cinéma français*, ed. Michel Marie (Paris: Nathan, 1998), 30–1.
23 David Vasse makes these comparisons but names *Adieu Philippine* (Jacques Rozier, 1962) as the closest New Wave model for *Un monde sans pitié*. See *Le Nouvel Âge du cinéma d'auteur français*, 25–6.
24 Prédal, *Le Jeune Cinéma français*, 8.
25 On this series, see Judith Mayne, 'Tous les garçons et toutes les filles', *Studies in French Cinema* 5: 3 (2005), 207–18.
26 See Joe Hardwick, 'The *vague nouvelle* and the *Nouvelle Vague*: The Critical Construction of *le jeune cinéma français*', *Modern & Contemporary France* 16: 1 (2008), 53.
27 Prédal, *Le Jeune Cinéma français*, 10–11.
28 Jeancolas, 'Un cinéma de la responsabilité', 21.
29 Vasse, *Le Nouvel Âge du cinéma d'auteur français*, 26.
30 Prédal, *Le Jeune Cinéma français*, 35.
31 Jeancolas, 'Un cinéma de la responsabilité', 13.
32 Jousse et al., 'Dix places pour le jeune cinéma', 30.
33 Prédal, *Le Jeune Cinéma français*, 37–8.
34 Nacache, 'Was There a Young French Cinema?', 193–4.
35 Prédal, *Le Jeune Cinéma français*, 68–9.
36 For an account of this episode, see Jeancolas, 'Un cinéma de la responsabilité', 16–17.
37 Hardwick, 'The *vague nouvelle* and the *Nouvelle Vague*', 55.
38 Trémois writes of Hippo (Hippolyte Girardot) in *Un monde sans pitié*: 'Marginalized in a world that has given up hope in another May '68, Hippo knows that he is condemned to solitude.' *Les Enfants de la liberté*, 21.
39 Herpe, 'Y aura-t-il un jeune cinéma français?', 32.
40 Martin O'Shaughnessy, 'Post-1995 French Cinema: Return of the Social, Return of the Political?', *Modern & Contemporary France* 11: 2 (2003), 189.
41 See Vasse, *Le Nouvel Âge du cinéma d'auteur français*, 16–18.
42 On this point, see Jacqueline Nacache, quoted in Vasse, *Le Nouvel Âge du cinéma d'auteur français*, 32.

43 Herpe, 'Y aura-t-il un jeune cinéma français?', 32.
44 Vasse, *Le Nouvel Âge du cinéma d'auteur français*, 12–13. See also Vassé, 'Transgression des liens du sang'.
45 Vasse, *Le Nouvel Âge du cinéma d'auteur français*, 174.
46 According to Insee, unemployment in France rose from 6 per cent of the population at the beginning of the 1980s to 10 per cent by the mid-1990s.
47 As Jousse et al., point out, 'Dix places pour le jeune cinéma', 28.
48 Dina Sherzer, 'Gender and Sexuality in New New Wave Cinema', in *Gender and French Cinema*, ed. Alex Hughes and James S. Williams (Oxford: Berg, 2001), 229.
49 Vasse, *Le Nouvel Âge du cinéma d'auteur français*, 99.
50 Ibid., 95.
51 Jeancolas, 'Un cinéma de la responsabilité', 22.
52 Trémois, *Les Enfants de la liberté*, 32–3.
53 Sherzer, 'Gender and Sexuality in New New Wave Cinema', 230.
54 Nacache, 'Group Portrait with a Star', 54. That said, it is perhaps worth pointing out that all of these women come from privileged backgrounds that no doubt facilitated their entry into the world of cinema: Balibar is the daughter of the public intellectual and distinguished philosophy professor Étienne Balibar; Bruni Tedeschi is the child of wealthy Italian industrialists and sister of the former model Carla Bruni-Sarkozy; Devos's mother was the actress Marie Henriau. For all France's visible equality, access to positions of power and influence continues to be determined largely by social capital and networks of acquaintances.
55 See Hardwick, 'The *vague nouvelle* and the *Nouvelle Vague*', 61.
56 Pierre Murat, 'Arnaud ou le paradoxe', *Télérama*, 12 June 1996.
57 Ibid.
58 Arnaud Desplechin and Emmanuel Salinger, 'Interview', *Cahiers du cinéma* 503 (June 1996), 34.
59 Jean-Michel Frodon, 'Comment ils ont travaillé … (avec Arnaud Desplechin)', *Le Monde*, 13 June 1996.
60 René Gatif, 'Comment je me suis emmerdé (au film de Desplechin)', *L'Organe*, 15 December 2004 (first published 2001), http://www.lorgane.com/COMMENT-JE-ME-SUIS-EMMERDE-au-film-de-Desplechin_a239.html
61 Carole Le Berre, 'Comment Desplechin a tourné *Comment je me suis disputé*', *Cahiers du cinéma* 149 (May 1995), 43.
62 Emmanuèle Frois, 'Arnaud Desplechin: "Misogyne? Tant mieux"', *Le Figaro*, 11–12 May 1996.
63 See, for instance, Desplechin's comments on Truffaut's *Les Quatre Cents Coups* (1959): 'The sequence is between ideas and feelings, and that is something which exists only in films. I don't know exactly if it's emotion or thinking. It's ideas on screen, it's mise-en-scène.' Anne Gillain and Dudley Andrew, 'Interview

with Arnaud Desplechin', in *A Companion to François Truffaut*, ed. Dudley Andrew and Anne Gillain (Chichester: Wiley-Blackwell, 2013), 12.

64 This approach to characterization based less in psychology than in elementary symbolism is something Desplechin also admires in Truffaut. See Gillain and Andrew, 'Interview', 10.

65 As Michel Guilloux notes, 'Quand le sujet entre dans le vif de lui-même', *L'Humanité*, 13 May 1996. See also Antoine de Baecque, 'Le livre ouvert', *Cahiers du cinéma* 503 (June 1996), 28.

66 On this point, see Vasse, *Le Nouvel Âge du cinéma d'auteur français*, 63.

67 Vincent Remy, '*Comment je me suis disputé (ma vie sexuelle)*', *Télérama*, 12 June 1996.

68 Murat, 'Arnaud ou le paradoxe'.

69 Desplechin and Salinger, 'Interview', 30. See also Didier Péron and Olivier Seguret, 'Interview with Arnaud Desplechin', *Libération*, 12 June 1996.

70 Trémois, *Les Enfants de la liberté*, 55.

71 Gillain and Andrew, 'Interview', 3.

72 Frois, 'Arnaud Desplechin'.

73 Cited in Vasse, *Le Nouvel Âge du cinéma d'auteur français*, 28.

74 Philippe Royer, 'Arnaud Desplechin chorégraphie les états d'âme de trentenaires', *La Croix*, 12 June 1996.

75 Murat, 'Arnaud ou le paradoxe'.

76 Gillain and Andrew, 'Interview', 4. The book in question is *Le Cinéma selon François Truffaut*, ed. Anne Gillain (Paris: Flammarion, 1988).

77 Péron and Seguret, 'Interview'.

78 Marja Warehime, 'Politics, Sex, and French Cinema in the 1990s: The Place of Arnaud Desplechin', *French Studies* 56: 1 (2002), 64.

79 Vasse, *Le Nouvel Âge du cinéma d'auteur français*, 30.

80 Warehime, 'Politics, Sex, and French Cinema', 61.

81 See, for instance, Péron and Seguret, 'Interview', and Remy, '*Comment je me suis disputé*'.

82 Frodon, 'Comment ils ont travaillé … '

83 Claude Baignères, 'Tu causes, tu causes!', *Le Figaro*, 13 May 1996.

84 Prédal, *Le Jeune Cinéma français*, 40.

85 Le Berre, 'Comment Desplechin a tourné', 43.

86 Trémois, *Les Enfants de la liberté*, 113.

87 Warehime, 'Politics, Sex, and French Cinema', 72.

88 Baignères makes this accusation, 'Tu causes, tu causes!'

89 Jean-Michel Frodon, 'Comment je me suis raconté', *Le Monde*, 14 May 1996.

90 Desplechin and Salinger, 'Interview', 32.

91 Gillain and Andrew, 'Interview', 117.
92 The simple test asks whether a film, or other work of fiction, features a scene in which two women talk to each other about something other than a man. In the most prominent women-only scenes of *Comment je me suis disputé* (Esther, Sylvia and Valérie jump-starting Esther's car during the party early in the film; a later scene in which Sylvia confronts Valérie), the main topic of conversation is Paul.
93 Péron and Seguret, 'Interview'.
94 Frois, 'Arnaud Desplechin'.
95 Royer, 'Arnaud Desplechin chorégraphie les états d'âme'.
96 Péron and Seguret, 'Interview'.
97 Murat, 'Arnaud ou le paradoxe'.
98 Marie-Claire Ropars, 'The Search for the Neuter: Sexual Difference and the Status of the Subject in Contemporary Films, Masculine and Feminine', *L'Esprit Créateur* 42: 1 (2002), 123.
99 Warehime, 'Politics, Sex, and French Cinema', 77.
100 'La présence est de nature féminine,' Murat, 'Arnaud ou le paradoxe'.
101 Trémois, *Les Enfants de la liberté*, 226.
102 'un garçon est là pour décevoir, une fille, pour magnifier', Murat, 'Arnaud ou le paradoxe'. Desplechin notes that the same criticism was made, for instance, about Truffaut's *Deux Anglaises et le continent* (1971) (but, by implication, not about *Jules et Jim*, 1962). Gillain and Andrew, 'Interview', 17.
103 Ropars, 'The Search for the Neuter', 132.
104 This point is also made by de Baecque, 'Le livre ouvert', 29.
105 Murat, 'Arnaud ou le paradoxe'.
106 Julia Dobson, *Negotiating the Auteur: Dominique Cabrera, Noémie Lvovsky, Laetitia Masson and Marion Vernoux* (Manchester: Manchester University Press, 2012), 69.
107 Ibid., 70.
108 Stéphane Bouquet, 'Attache-moi', *Cahiers du cinéma* 488 (February 1995), 25.
109 See Lvovsky, quoted in Trémois, *Les Enfants de la liberté*, 167.
110 As Claire Vassé remarks, '*Oublie-moi*: Le boulet qui trace son chemin', *Positif* 408 (February 1995), 37.
111 Trémois, *Les Enfants de la liberté*, 165.
112 'You Speak My Language' by Morphine, from the *Good* album (Rykodisc, 1993).
113 Jean-Michel Frodon, 'Tour de force, tour de grâce', *Le Monde*, 26 January 1995.
114 See Michèle Levieux, 'La Mostra découvre une jeune réalisatrice', *L'Humanité*, 15 September 1994.
115 'On va aller dans ta chambre? On va se déshabiller. On va se coucher.'

116 Jacques Morice, 'Valéria Bruni-Tedeschi (sic)', *Cahiers du cinéma* 473 (November 1993), 40.
117 Dobson, *Negotiating the Auteur*, 68.
118 Vassé, '*Oublie-moi*', 38.
119 Jacques Morice notes this subtlety in relation to a different role that many critics saw as a companion piece to *Oublie-moi*, Martine in *Les Gens normaux n'ont rien d'exceptionnel* (Laurence Ferreira-Barbosa, 1993). See Morice, 'Valéria Bruni-Tedeschi'.
120 Jean Coutances, 'Une ronde vertigineuse', *Télérama*, 25 January 1995.
121 Dobson, *Negotiating the Auteur*, 70–1.
122 Vassé, '*Oublie-moi*', 37.
123 Levieux, 'La Mostra découvre une jeune réalisatrice'. See also Dobson, *Negotiating the Auteur*, 81–2.
124 Noémie Lvovsky, 'Je ne suis pas partie d'une histoire mais de l'idée de rébellion', *Le Monde*, 26 January 1995.
125 Françoise Audé, 'Entretien avec Noémie Lvovsky: Une belle personne', *Positif* 408 (February 1995), 40.
126 Vasse, *Le Nouvel Âge du cinéma d'auteur français*, 75.
127 Dobson, *Negotiating the Auteur*, 68.
128 Coutances, 'Une ronde vertigineuse'.
129 Bouquet, 'Attache-moi', 25.
130 Gérard Lefort, 'Les pieds dans le cru', *Libération*, 4 June 1997.
131 Maryline Alligier, *Bruno Dumont: L'animalité et la grâce* (Pertuis: Rouge Profond, 2012), 53.
132 'B.B.', 'Bruno Dumont, l'ennui et la rédemption', *Le Figaro*, 9 May 1997.
133 Vasse, *Le Nouvel Âge du cinéma d'auteur français*, 157.
134 Didier Rochet, 'Pharaon simple flic', *L'Humanité*, 19 May 1999.
135 Anne Boulay, 'Le pire pour moi, ce serait l'indifférence', *Libération*, 18 May 1999.
136 Alligier, *Bruno Dumont*, 30.
137 Antony Fiant, 'Les bêtes humaines: Notes sur le cinéma de Bruno Dumont', *Positif* 554 (April 2007), 52.
138 Tim Palmer, 'Style and Sensation in the Contemporary French Cinema of the Body', *Journal of Film and Video* 58: 3 (2006), 22.
139 'Desperate', Michel Guilloux, 'Il voit le nord en peinture', *Libération*, 27 October 1999; 'without the slightest feeling', Claude Baignères, 'Constat de néant', *Le Figaro*, 19 May 1999; 'she gives herself to Joseph like she lights her cigarettes: without thinking', Carlos Gomez, '*L'Humanité*, le film poil à gratter qui a scandalisé Cannes', *Le Journal du Dimanche*, 24 October 1999; 'bestial and brutal', Serge Kaganski, 'Dumont de piété', *Les Inrockuptibles*, 27 October 1999; 'as indecipherable as a hieroglyph', Louis Guichard, 'Radical et captivant', *Télérama*, 27 October 1999.

140 James Quandt, 'Flesh and Blood: Sex and Violence in Recent French Cinema', in *The New Extremism in Cinema: From France to Europe*, ed. Tanya Horeck and Tina Kendall (Edinburgh: Edinburgh University Press, 2011), 19.
141 Hampus Hagman, '"Every Cannes Needs Its Scandal": Between Art and Exploitation in Contemporary French Film', *Film International* 9: 5 (2007), 33.
142 'Qu'à force de cette humilité – de sa persévérance, de celle du temps – il y aurait un débordement.' Bruno Dumont, 'Notes de travail sur *La Vie de Jésus*', *Positif* 440 (October 1997), 58.
143 Anne Boulay, 'Au fond de la nature humaine', *Libération*, 12 May 1997.
144 Jacques Aumont, *Le Cinéma et la mise en scène* (Paris: Armand Colin, 2010), 81.
145 'Il n'est de mise en scène que fondue (et fondée) dans le monde', ibid., 89.
146 Marine Landrot, '*La Vie de Jesus*', *Télérama*, 4 June 1997.
147 Brett Bowles, '*The Life of Jesus (La Vie de Jésus)*', *Film Quarterly* 57: 3 (2004), 49.
148 Jean-Michel Frodon, 'À bras le corps dans l'enfer du Nord', *Le Monde*, 5 June 1997.
149 'L'irreprésentable ne m'intéresse que si j'y trouve une issue.' Boulay, 'Le pire pour moi'.
150 Kaganski, 'Dumont de piété'.
151 Fiant, 'Les bêtes humaines', 48.
152 Ibid., 49–50.
153 Alligier, *Bruno Dumont*, 48.
154 James S. Williams, *Space and Being in Contemporary French Cinema* (Manchester: Manchester University Press, 2013), 43.
155 Ibid., 78.
156 Ibid., 50.
157 Ibid., 63.
158 Pascal Richou called *La Vie de Jésus* a 'mystical, Christian film', '*La Vie de Jésus* de Bruno Dumont', *Cahiers du cinéma* 513 (May 1997), 75. Danièle Heymann, meanwhile, identified a 'mysticism without God' in *L'humanité*, 'La mort, le sexe, la vie, bref, "l'Humanité" selon Dumont', *Marianne*, 25 October 1999.
159 See Tina Kendall, '"No God But Cinema": Bruno Dumont's *Hadewijch*', *Contemporary French and Francophone Studies* 17: 4 (2013), 405–13, and Catherine Wheatley, 'Holy Motors', *Sight & Sound* 24: 12 (December 2014), 44–8.
160 Boulay, 'Au fond de la nature humaine.'
161 Marie-Noëlle Tranchant, 'Bruno Dumont et les larmes de Pharaon', *Le Figaro*, 24 May 1999.

162 The word 'redemption' is used by B.B., 'Bruno Dumont', Noël Tinazzi, 'La rédemption de Freddy, jeune paumé', *La Tribune*, 4 June 1996, and Bowles, *'The Life of Jesus'*, 50. Dumont describes Freddy's trajectory as an 'ascension' in Boulay, 'Au fond de la nature humaine' and Philippe Royer, 'Les Flandres servent de cadre à une "Vie de Jésus" assez particulière', *La Croix*, 4 June 1997.

163 Isabelle Daniel, 'C'est au spectateur de devenir humain', *Télérama*, 4 June 1997.

164 See, for instance, Philippe Royer, '*L'Humanité*, un film qui laisse à désirer', *La Croix*, 19 May 1999, Didier Rochet, 'Humain, trop humain, le cinéma de Bruno Dumont', *L'Humanité*, 26 May 1999, and François-Guillaume Lorrain, '*L'humanité*', *Le Point*, 22 October 1999.

165 Wheatley, 'Holy Motors', 47.

4

The Old New Wave

Introduction

In the mid-1990s, both Agnès Varda and Jean-Luc Godard released films to commemorate the centenary of cinema that was celebrated in France in 1995. Coincidentally, both films starred Michel Piccoli, who had also worked with each director in the 1960s: in Godard's *Le Mépris* (1963) and in Varda's *Les Créatures* (1965). In Godard's *2 x 50 ans de cinéma français* (1995), Piccoli is interviewed in his role as President of the Association for the First Century of Cinema. In Varda's *Les Cent et une nuits* (1995), Piccoli plays an incarnation of cinema called Simon Cinéma. Both films are played in a more or less comic mode, yet the implication in each is that the history of cinema has already been largely forgotten. In his interview with Piccoli, Godard suggests that people are only keen to commemorate the cinema because they are aware that it is already dying. This is subsequently demonstrated in Piccoli's staged encounters with actors playing hotel staff who show no recognition when he evokes the names of classic French films, actors and directors. In Varda's film, a young student (played by Julie Gayet) is hired to 'perform aerobics on Mr Cinéma's memory'. Their discussions of film history are illustrated by numerous clips and invited guests (including many associated with the New Wave – Jeanne Moreau, Jean-Claude Brialy, Jean-Paul Belmondo, Catherine Deneuve – as well as various international figures: Marcello Mastroianni, Hanna Schygulla, Robert De Niro). The suggestion of both films is that cinema is effectively mortal and that its lifespan may not be much longer than that of the average human. With these films, then, two surviving directors of the French New Wave set themselves up as something like the guardians of the memory of cinema. But this work is inevitably also tied to their own ageing process and reflection on their own lives and careers. In subsequent works released around the turn of the twenty-first century, this preoccupation with memory and cultural history is confirmed. Godard completed his epic *Histoire(s) du cinéma* project in 1998 while Varda's surprise hit *Les Glaneurs et la Glaneuse* (2000) combines a self-portrait as a seventy-year-old with a peripatetic reflection on both the history of the visual arts and the history of economic inequality in France. Shortly afterward, Éric Rohmer released the controversial *L'Anglaise et le Duc* (2001), a film set during the French Revolution. All three films provoked significant commentary and debate in France and further afield, confirming the capacity of the New Wave generation, even when relatively advanced in age, to set the cultural agenda in France and largely to dictate the terms in which film history and, more broadly, the audiovisual representation of history were discussed.

Histoire(s) du cinéma (Jean-Luc Godard, 1998)

Regarding Jean-Luc Godard's work in and around *Histoire(s) du cinéma*, Georges Didi-Huberman has written that 'Godard seems to represent, by himself, all the authority of cinema'.[1] Among the late works by New Wave filmmakers, *Histoire(s) du cinéma* is particularly daunting for the spectator. It impresses by its length, running for a total of around four and a half hours, and by its complex production history: the video essays were ten years in the making, but the project for an idiosyncratic history of cinema dates back to the 1970s.[2] *Histoire(s) du cinéma* risks further alienating the spectator of modest means through its proliferation of formats and deluxe editions: the films were initially released on VHS by Gaumont in 1998 and have since seen several DVD versions. They were accompanied by a boxed set of the complete CD soundtrack, together with expansive liner notes, produced by ECM Records in 1999.

But, perhaps most significantly, the initial release of *Histoire(s) du cinéma* also took the form of four lavishly illustrated art books published in Gallimard's *collection blanche*,[3] thereby realizing an old dream of Godard's.[4] Once the spectator has gained access to *Histoire(s) du cinéma*, moreover, the work remains daunting, thanks to the famous density of its image and sound montage and to the authoritative rhetoric with which Godard delivers pronouncements on film history (and which we will discuss in more detail below). In addition, to further discourage students and scholars, a vast bibliography of secondary literature has grown up around *Histoire(s) du cinéma*, such that it has become, in under two decades, probably the most discussed film in all of Godard studies, more so even than early classics like *À bout de souffle* (1960) or *Le Mépris* (1963).[5]

The intimidating labyrinth of *Histoire(s) du cinéma* is guarded by none other than Godard himself. The first (of many) words we see written on the screen in *Histoire(s)* are 'Hoc opus hic labor est', a quotation from Virgil's *Aeneid* in which the Sibyl warns Aeneas of the difficult labour involved in retracing one's steps back up from the underworld.⁶ As Jean-Louis Leutrat has remarked, this incipit implies that the plunge into film history is like descending into hell and that Godard is our guide, or indeed that he is the Sibyl, guiding us only through riddles and paradox.⁷ Other critics have taken this mythological imagery further: for the historian François Furet, Godard speaks with the voice of a prophet, announcing 'a new religion of images' and seeking to save an elect few from this iniquitous history, while condemning many more.⁸ Youssef Ishaghpour takes up the same theme, telling Godard that he is the guardian of the museum of cinema while also coming across as a eulogist, an orchestra conductor or a great priest orating from his pulpit.⁹ Michael Witt suggests that Godard's self-portrait as 'the keeper of the New Wave museum' in chapter 3B of *Histoire(s)* is 'humorous',¹⁰ but one could see how viewers agnostic about Godard's legendary status might find it presumptuous or pompous.

In other words, as Daniel Morgan has correctly remarked, 'How we see [*Histoire(s) du cinéma*] is caught up in our relation to the figure of Godard, at least as he presents himself on screen.'¹¹ Now Godard has a very long history of self-portraiture on screen and self-mythologizing in the cinema. As early as *Bande à part* (1964), he famously referred to himself as 'Jean-Luc Cinéma Godard' in the credits (a title that today stubbornly persists in the search bar of IMDb); and, just half a decade into his filmmaking career, in *Pierrot le fou* (1965), he had already begun the process of quoting himself.¹² *Histoire(s) du cinéma*, as Jacques Aumont notes, is less of an historical enterprise than an autobiographical one, or perhaps somewhat akin to the private diary that an author might update in the evening, alongside more polished works.¹³ To some extent, Godard's self-representation in *Histoire(s)* is inevitable: as a filmmaker himself, he necessarily 'positions himself as both author of the inquiry and part of its subject'.¹⁴ And since, as has become well known, Godard's history condemns the cinema for its moral failings, he must stand as both accuser and accused. Didi-Huberman suggests that this international, political history of cinema can also be seen as a very personal family history for Jean-Luc Godard: cinema's culpable negligence in failing to testify to the horrors of the Second World War, the willful blindness to history that is tantamount to collaboration, is precisely that for which the director disowned his birth family in the post-war period.¹⁵

Godard's investment in film history, then, is deeply personal and profoundly emotional and to suggest, as he did in *Le Monde* on the film's release, that he appears in *Histoire(s)* 'in the same way as other directors' is another example of Godard's frequent disingenuousness.¹⁶ One striking point about *Histoire(s) du cinéma*, at least on initial viewings, is the impression that while Godard quotes widely from the first half-century of cinema, he quotes few films from the period after 1960 other than his own. Close scrutiny of Godard's sources reveals that this impression is not entirely fair: by my count, there are some 28 of Godard's own films cited in *Histoire(s) du cinéma* compared to 102 films by other directors dating from after 1960. However, this is to reckon without the fact that several of Godard's films are cited repeatedly while many of the other films may not be recognized by the spectator as important examples of cinematic art due to their usage within *Histoire(s)*: some films appear merely as resonant titles, without citation of either image or sound (*Cries and Whispers* [Bergman, 1972], *Marie pour mémoire* [Garrel, 1968], *India Song* [Duras, 1975]); some are from the very early 1960s, the period when Godard was still publishing film criticism (*Splendor in the Grass* [Kazan, 1961], *The Rise and Fall of Legs Diamond* [Boetticher, 1960]); some are by directors whose careers in cinema had been long established before the 1960s (Cocteau, Hitchcock, Bresson, Rossellini); some are period dramas and, as such, not easy to date at a glance (*The Leopard* [Visconti, 1963], *The Merchant of Venice* [Welles, 1969], *Hamlet* [Kozintsev, 1964]); some are chosen in order to represent the Shoah (*Lili Marleen* [Fassbinder, 1980], *Shoah* [Lanzmann, 1985], *Pasazerka* [Munk, 1963]) or to encapsulate an abstract notion (war: *Apocalypse Now* [Coppola, 1979]; blindness: *The Miracle Worker* [Penn, 1962]). In short, *Histoire(s) du cinéma* tends to suggest that the only director of the post-1960 period who can be considered an artist of the calibre of Renoir, Lang, Hitchcock, Ford, etc., is Godard himself. The only other director who receives noteworthy treatment (nine citations of four different films) is Pier Paolo Pasolini.

Michael Witt has stated that Godard's historical project needs to be understood as 'a re-engagement with his own films, but also with his early critical texts' (since many of the films, and indeed individual sequences, Godard cites are ones he addressed in his writing for *Cahiers du cinéma* and *Arts*).[17] Indeed, the lectures at the Montreal Cinémathèque that marked the beginning of this project took as their starting point a comparison of one of Godard's films with another from film history with which it was placed in meaningful dialogue.[18] It is important to note, however, that Godard's placing of himself within film history is not articulated in an analytical mode, but rather an incantatory one. In an astute early assessment of *Histoire(s) du cinéma*, Jean-Marc Lalanne noted that there is always an effect of conjuration in the drawing up of a list, an effect deliberately exploited by Godard in *Histoire(s)* through his sonorous enunciation of titles.[19] Godard's argument in *Histoire(s)* is less an empirical demonstration than a kind of hypnotic persuasion.[20] As James Williams notes, the declamation and repetition of titles and key phrases encourage 'slippage from the semantic level to the phonetic'.[21] Jacques Aumont, too, has remarked that Godard features, first and foremost in *Histoire(s) du cinéma*, as a voice 'that colours the entire image with its inimitable grain'.[22] Since this voice is often disembodied and treated with reverb or other alienating effects, it takes on connotations of the ghostly or memorial.[23] Cecilia Sayad has also proposed that Godard's tendency to whisper on film (as he frequently does in *Histoire(s)*) 'suggests at once intimacy and elusiveness'.[24] There is, in short, a kind of self-sacralizing quality to Godard's performance in *Histoire(s) du cinéma* that presents him as an unquestionable authority on film history while also erecting a kind of mausoleum around himself and around cinema (Jean-Marc Lalanne remarked that his 'wall of books already resembles a tomb'[25]).

Let us see how Godard's history of cinema tends also to become a personal reminiscence by looking in more detail at the first episode, 1A, of *Histoire(s) du cinéma*.[26] The opening minutes of *Histoire(s)* show clips and stills of Charlie Chaplin from *Modern Times* (1936) and *The Cure* (1915), Ida Lupino in *While the City Sleeps* (Fritz Lang, 1956) and Nicholas Ray in Wim Wenders's documentary homage *Lightning over Water* (1980). In this introductory montage, then, three eras of filmmaking – the burlesque comedy of silent cinema, the sophistication of classical Hollywood genre film and postmodern art cinema – are mapped on to the ages of man: Chaplin's childlike innocence, Lupino's adult sexuality and Ray's old age. Reigning over all of this is the recurring image of Godard at his typewriter, intoning a series of enigmatic titles.[27] The imagery implies that cinema is a kind of family and indeed images of children and childhood proliferate throughout *Histoire(s)*. Also early in 1A we see a photograph of Roberto Rossellini appearing to strangle his daughter Isabella, overwritten with a quotation from Freud's *Interpretation of Dreams*. The Oedipal implications of the image are all the more significant when one knows the paternalistic role that Rossellini played in the early careers of the New Wave filmmakers; this suggests that Godard, in *Histoire(s)*, is measuring himself against his symbolic fathers in this imaginary House of Cinema.

The comparison to forefathers is further implied in a later montage which evokes a number of filmmakers named 'Jean' who were pioneers of French cinema: Cocteau, Epstein and Vigo (Jean Renoir has also been present since the beginning of 1A since the first title Godard speaks is *La Règle du jeu* [1939], and the soundtrack includes excerpts from this film as well as from *Boudu sauvé des eaux* [1932]). Meanwhile, the imagery of fathers and sons recurs in the portrait of the producer Irving Thalberg, who is identified in Godard's commentary as both 'the founding father' and 'the only son', while his enunciation of titles coincidentally arrives at *Les Enfants terribles* (novel by Cocteau, 1929; film by Melville, 1950). A running strategy throughout *Histoire(s) du cinéma* is the concern to link the public history of successful films and political events to private stories of desire,[28] and this is very evident in the evocations of the classical Hollywood producers Thalberg and Howard Hughes. Godard insinuates that Thalberg's extraordinary productivity was a kind of overcompensation for his congenital heart disease that turned his career into a race against time (the commentary insists upon Thalberg's 'young body, fragile and beautiful').[29] The portrait of Howard Hughes, meanwhile, stresses, alongside the producer's famous aviation exploits and government connections, his predatory relations with young actresses (enumerated in text and image) and his late reclusiveness (evoked through an engraving of Robinson Crusoe).[30] Yet spectators familiar with Godard's own biography are likely to see in this another, perhaps less flattering, comparison: for Godard, too, has developed a reputation for reclusiveness in recent decades, and has his own history of erotic obsession with his leading ladies, both those he married (Anna Karina, Anne Wiazemsky) and those who were more resistant to his advances (Marina Vlady, Myriem Roussel, Bérangère Allaux).[31] Indeed, when Godard remarks that Thalberg was, 'what's more, married to one of the most beautiful women on earth', it is tempting to read this as a reference to his own marriage to Karina. This supposition is encouraged by the willful disconnect between image and sound across 1A: a portrait of Thalberg's wife, Norma Shearer, does appear in the chapter, but at 00:09:08,[32] before the M-G-M producer has even been evoked (in a sense, Shearer announces this sequence). When Godard pronounces the line about Thalberg's wife, much later at 00:17:51, the photo that irises out from a still of Thalberg is actually of Rita Hayworth. Later still (00:26:48), we see Anna Karina, in the scene from *Bande à part* in which she recites Aragon's 'Les Poètes'. As Roland-François Lack has noted, Godard's enumeration of titles across this sequence can clearly be interpreted as a commentary on the development and decline of Godard and Karina's relationship.[33] The titles are as follows: *L'École des femmes* (as Karina's recitation begins in voice-over), *Les Liaisons dangereuses, On ne badine pas avec l'amour* (these latter two barely audible in the background of the shot of Karina), then *Adieu ma jolie* (*Farewell, My Lovely*, as the image cuts from Karina to a clip from a silent porn reel, implying the degradation of love into smut); as Karina's voice continues, off, we hear *Bonjour tristesse* and then, to close the sequence, following the end of Karina's recitation, *L'Éducation sentimentale*. The sequence is given further autobiographical resonance through the inclusion of the on-screen title *Le Mépris* (Godard's 1963 film can be read as a fictional representation of his own marital troubles on and around the film set) and the fact that Otto Preminger's 1958 film of *Bonjour tristesse* inspired Godard to cast Jean Seberg in *À bout de souffle*, another film about a fatal attraction to a beautiful woman.

This sad litany of titles implies a sense of regret at Godard's failed marriage to Karina and indeed melancholy and remorse give much of the emotional tone to 1A and, arguably, the whole of *Histoire(s) du cinéma*. This is appropriate since Godard's central argument suggests that the cinema failed to fulfill its potential (by neglecting to record the true horrors of the Second World War). 1A is full of references that suggest things incomplete or unfulfilled, such as the repeated use of Schubert's 'Unfinished' symphony (begun 1822) or the title *Chemins qui ne mènent nulle part*.[34] The Karina sequence described above interrupts a commentary by Godard about 'all the films that were never made'. This includes famous examples like Orson Welles's aborted *Don Quixote* and André Malraux's novel *La Condition humaine* (1933), whose adaptation was envisaged by directors as diverse as Sergei Eisenstein, Fred Zinnerman, Costa-Gavras and Michael Cimino.[35] But the sequence also includes a brief glimpse of Molly Ringwald in Godard's *King Lear* (1987), a film that, although it was eventually completed, had a notoriously cursed existence, with various personnel walking off set or disowning the film, and which has only ever known the most cursory distribution.[36] In short, much of *Histoire(s) du cinéma*, and especially 1A, is coloured by a sense of loss and unrealized ambition that probably belongs more properly to Godard himself than to cinema in general. Another film featured in 1A is Renoir's *La Grande Illusion* (1937), from which Godard cites the scene in which the ageing and injured Captain von Rauffenstein (Erich von Stroheim) laments to his French counterpart (Pierre Fresnay), 'I was a warrior; now I'm just a civil servant.'[37] Should we interpret this, too, as an image of Godard's own trajectory? From the audacious young Turk filming in the streets of Paris, marrying his actresses and propounding a revolutionary aesthetics of cinema, he has become something like a reclusive cultural historian, sighing over missed opportunities.

In this context, we might usefully ask how Godard represents the New Wave – the movement that launched his career and brought him to international prominence – in *Histoire(s) du cinéma*. While chapter 3B of *Histoire(s)*, entitled 'Une vague nouvelle',[38] explicitly addresses the New Wave, it is striking how few canonical films and directors of the movement are cited by Godard. There is no equivalent here to the stirring tribute to the golden age of post-war Italian cinema that ends 3A, editing together easily identifiable clips from famous films by Fellini, De Sica, Visconti, Pasolini, Antonioni, De Santis and Rossellini to Riccardo Cocciante's lachrymose song 'La nostra lingua italiana' and thereby becoming the only section of *Histoire(s) du cinéma* that arguably resembles the facile aesthetics of music video or televisual montage. In fact, Godard's New Wave peers are given short shrift in *Histoire(s)*: Claude Chabrol and Jacques Rivette are absent; Éric Rohmer is present through briefly glimpsed stills of *Le Rayon vert* (1986) and *Nadja à Paris* (1964; both in 4B); the end of 3B includes a brief clip from Agnès Varda's documentary *Les Demoiselles ont eu 25 ans* (1993) in which Jacques Demy is seen talking to Catherine Deneuve.[39] One can therefore understand why Youssef Ishaghpour asserted that *Les Quatre Cents Coups* (Truffaut, 1959) is 'the only emblematic film of the New Wave in [Godard's] film',[40] although he fails to spot the presence of *Adieu Philippine* (Jacques Rozier, 1962), also in 3B.

By contrast, 3B cites, more or less in extenso, the opening sequence of *Alphaville* (1965), including image, music, voice-over and dialogue, in which Lemmy Caution (Eddie Constantine) arrives in Alphaville, checks into his hotel and is shown to his room by the 'third-order seductress' Béatrice (Christa Lang). Although superimposed with other images and sounds, the sequence lasts nearly two and a half minutes, one of the longest continuous sequences quoted in all of *Histoire(s) du cinéma*. The *Alphaville* sequence is superimposed, most notably, with scenes from Fritz Lang's expressionist melodrama *Der müde Tod* (1921). The point of this montage is surely to demonstrate, through the visual twinning of the two films' lugubrious monochrome designs, the way in which the films and filmmakers of the French New Wave self-consciously entered into a dialogue with film history. Historians have long demonstrated how the European expressionist cinema of the late-silent and early-sound era exerted an influence over classical Hollywood genre filmmaking via the emigration of key personnel before impacting back upon the French New Wave through the *politique des auteurs*. The *Alphaville* montage of 3B shows this influence in action while also working to suggest that Godard was already producing an audiovisual historiography of the New Wave as early as 1965.[41]

3B also includes, as does so much of *Histoire(s) du cinéma*, recurring archival footage from the Second World War and the Holocaust. This is perhaps more surprising in a chapter ostensibly 'about' the New Wave, since the Nouvelle Vague is explicitly associated with a generation of young people born during or shortly after the war (or at least too young to have fought in it) and who were often accused, as we saw in the Introduction to this book, as being rather dismissive of politics, in particular the broadly communist tradition of intellectual thought that developed out of the Resistance movement in post-war France. Tellingly, in 3B, Godard juxtaposes some of the harrowing images filmed at the liberation of the Nazi death camps with scenes of drinking and partying from films like *Summer with Monika* (Bergman, 1952), *Gigi* (Minnelli, 1957) and *The Beautiful Blonde from Bashful Bend* (Sturges, 1949).[42] The implication here is that the frivolous antics of the Nouvelle Vague have as their unspoken backdrop the horrors of the Second World War; that a willful process of forgetting needed to happen in Europe in order to allow for cultural renewal. But the image of Jerry Lewis's sad-faced clown from *Hardly Working* (1980) – oddly reminiscent of the melancholy Ferdinand (Jean-Paul Belmondo) at the end of *Pierrot le fou* (1965) – suggests an acknowledgement that the carefree lifestyle of this newly affluent generation was actually built upon the devastation of Europe and the buried trauma of their parents. In the same way, a juxtaposition of archival footage of Hitler with the image of Jefferies (James Stewart) wielding his telephoto lens in *Rear Window* (Hitchcock, 1954) invites us to reinterpret the saga of post-war cinephilia as an oblique way of coming to terms with the past: the generation of the New Wave, in other words, were not only seeking their place within film history but within 'la grande histoire', as Serge Daney puts it in his filmed interview with Godard in chapter 2A.

Another striking opposition in 3B is that between, to put it bluntly, God and money. The chapter quotes the scene of the Sermon on the Mount from *Il Vangelo secundo Matteo* (Pasolini, 1964), in which Jesus (Enrique

Irazoqui) insists that one cannot serve both God and Mammon (Matthew 6:24). This is intercut with the scene from the climax of *Touchez pas au grisbi* (Becker, 1954) in which Gabin's loot goes up in smoke. The chapter also evokes that most French model of piety, Joan of Arc, through the filmic depictions by Dreyer, Bresson and Rossellini and includes Christian iconography from Gozzoli, Botticelli and Fra Angelico while the soundtrack features Gesualdo's *Tenebrae responsories for Holy Saturday* (1611). All this sacred material introduces a section of the chapter devoted to Henri Langlois as one of the godfathers of the New Wave. The suggestion, then, is that the God/Mammon dichotomy maps on to the gulf separating the elusive object of cinephilic obsession from the commercial cinema of what Godard calls 'Saturday films' (hence the significance of the specific choice of Gesualdo). 'True cinema', says Godard, for the children of the Cinémathèque Française, 'was that which could not be seen'. And, as critics have noted, this devotion to an object that remains stubbornly inaccessible has all the hallmarks of religious faith with the *politique des auteurs* becoming a kind of liturgy.[43] As Richard Neer suggests, picking up on Jean-Marc Lalanne's point about incantation, noted above: 'It is not the names that are sacred but the enumeration of them.'[44]

For Godard, then, in *Histoire(s) du cinéma*, the French New Wave appears as a movement that was resolutely turned towards the past rather than, as has often been assumed in the popular reception of the Nouvelle Vague, a movement acutely tuned in to the present moment or indeed an opening up of new beginnings for the cinema. For, as Godard laments near the end of 3B, 'our only error then was in mistaking this for a beginning'. Hence the symbolic resonance of the one truly iconic moment that Godard quotes from a New Wave film: the end of *Les Quatre Cents Coups*. Antoine Doinel's (Jean-Pierre Léaud) arrival at the seashore, having run away from the juvenile detention centre, is only superficially an image of liberation; Doinel has systematically closed off all avenues during the course of the film and is left with nowhere to run, alone and hunted, as Truffaut's final freeze frame implies. It is significant that *Histoire(s) du cinéma* contains no mention of the subsequent important developments in world cinema inspired by the Nouvelle Vague: the eastern European new waves of the late 1960s, Brazilian Cinema Novo, New Hollywood cinema or the new cinemas of China and Taiwan,[45] let alone the rich vein of post-New Wave French cinema discussed in this book. For Godard, the Nouvelle Vague marked the final flowering of an already moribund cinema that subsequently surrendered its territory to television.

It is clear, then, that the history of cinema presented in *Histoire(s) du cinéma* is a very partial one, and it is understandable that some commentators might conclude that this 'work that is explicitly about history is in fact profoundly unhistorical'.[46] Morgan suggests that with a kind of Kantian subjective universality, Godard is presenting his personal experience of cinema as a more general one.⁴⁷ But Godard's constitution of film history also needs to be seen as a self-conscious gesture of film criticism, one that Morgan situates within a 'modernist lineage', comparing it to Leavis's identification of 'the great English novelists' at the outset of *The Great Tradition* (1960).⁴⁸ In other words, as we saw with Michael Witt's remarks above, *Histoire(s) du cinéma* in many ways restates or pursues Godard's film criticism of the 1950s and early 1960s in another form. This probably explains the narrow geographical reach of *Histoire(s)*, what Jacques Aumont has identified as a 'Europe of three' (France, Germany, Italy), with a deep documentary tradition in filmmaking, balanced between the diametrically opposed fictionalizing tendencies of Hollywood and the Soviet Union.⁴⁹ As Jacques Rancière has insisted, this is '*one* history of cinema and one only'.⁵⁰ The almost complete absence of Asian and African filmmaking from *Histoire(s) du cinéma* can thus be seen as partly historical – the culture of film festivals that has provided a showcase for world cinema in recent decades was still in its infancy when Godard was a critic – but also partly ideological: for Rancière these traditions are excluded because they simply don't fit into Godard's narrative of a 'Judeo-Christian quarrel over images'.⁵¹

As this remark suggests, *Histoire(s) du cinéma* really needs to be understood as a lyrical approach to film history, what Didi-Huberman sees as an essay that also aspires to be a poem.⁵² A number of critics have pointed out that Godard's models for his *Histoire(s)* are not professional historians but a peculiarly French tradition of what Didi-Huberman calls 'scholar-prophets':⁵³ most notably André Malraux and Élie Faure, but also figures like Victor Hugo, Jules Michelet, Charles Péguy and Paul Valéry, writers with a tendency to make dramatic historical judgements in an aphoristic style.⁵⁴ To these French precursors, we must add Walter Benjamin, whose *Arcades Project* (1927–40) can be seen as 'almost entirely a montage of quotations'.⁵⁵ There is a mutual mistrust between figures like these and professional historians, so much so that, in Michael Temple's assessment, 'the very act of historicizing' is treated with distrust by Godard.⁵⁶ The danger of this approach is that it encourages short cuts that lead to unilateral simplifications of the complexity of history.⁵⁷ In the words of Richard Neer, '*Histoire(s)* makes many assertions but few real arguments'⁵⁸ while Jean-Marc Lalanne opines that Godard 'subtracts meaning as much as he produces it'.⁵⁹ The risk, then, is that Godard's assertions become 'totalising interpretations',⁶⁰ which, ironically, is precisely the kind of dubious 'control of the universe' that *Histoire(s)* criticizes in the ideological projects of Hollywood and Soviet cinema.⁶¹

If *Histoire(s)* has a tendency towards simplification, it is because its governing formal principle of montage means that it makes its argument largely through processes of juxtaposition, however complex, such that, in the words of Daniel Morgan, 'analogy becomes equation, comparison turns into identity'.⁶² And this methodology clearly appeals more to the heart than to the intellect: Jacques Aumont notes, in particular, that the rapidly alternating juxtapositions frequently used in *Histoire(s)* generate 'pure emotion' because they are 'pure rhythm'.[63] More precisely, what Godard's montage does, in the analysis of Jacques Rancière, is to 'organize a clash and construct a continuum':[64] a brutal contrast or, on the contrary, a striking formal similarity creates a shock of recognition thereby implying an historical connection or continuity between the two poles (as in the example of *Alphaville* and *Der müde Tod*, for instance). In retrospect, these comparisons can often seem rather obvious (again, the Godard/Lang superimposition in 3B is a good example); as Richard Neer comments, 'The affinities are astonishing, but they are astonishing exactly because they are self-evident.'[65] Again, however, this may be related to Godard's past as a film critic since the criticism of *Cahiers du cinéma* was often concerned with a form of *stating the obvious*. A key tenet of *Cahiers* criticism was that a film could only have a 'hidden meaning' to the extent that it was hidden in plain sight, in the immediately observable evidence of the mise en scène that was intuitively grasped by any spectator.[66]

Once again, then, it is important to trace the methodology of *Histoire(s) du cinéma* back to Godard's own apprenticeship in cinema in 1950s France. *Histoire(s) du cinéma* is a cinephile's history, both in terms of its content (it is a history of the films valued by Western cinephiles in the 1950s) and in its form. As Christian Keathley has argued, cinephilia tends to be obsessed by the fetishization of minor details from films, details that are subsequently detached from their context (in the process of critical writing, notably) in an attempt 'to maintain the pleasure of the original encounter'.[67] The entire aesthetic of *Histoire(s) du cinéma* is built around this process of detachment, showing how images, sounds and sequences can be removed from their original context and yet still made to signify through their combination with other images, thanks to the embedded narrative charge they carry.[68] This is the point of the celebrated sequence in 4A in which Godard enumerates the banal everyday objects we may remember from Hitchcock's films (a glass of milk from *Suspicion* [1941], a hairbrush from *The Wrong Man* [1956], a lighter from *Strangers on a Train* [1951], etc.). Rancière has taken issue with this sequence, arguing that, if these objects are memorable, it is only because of their importance to the narrative.[69] But Godard's point is rather that we might remember moments, or at best individual scenes, involving these objects but still have lost all sense of how they connect to a broader narrative. Furthermore, Godard's montage demonstrates the ease with which these images and episodes can be confused and recombined by deliberately disconnecting the enumeration of objects on the soundtrack from their appearance in the image and thereby creating new sets of virtual relations between objects and sequences that in reality are drawn from quite different films (thus a key dropped down a drain in *Marnie* [1964] rhymes with the key dropped by Alicia Hubermann [Ingrid Bergman] in *Notorious*

[1946], but also with the hand reaching into the drain for the lighter in *Strangers on a Train*).[70]

The Hitchcock sequence in 4A suggests something important, therefore, about the interplay between the indexical power of the image and the combinatory logic of montage that is central to the understanding of *Histoire(s) du cinéma*. This can perhaps best be illustrated by reviewing Godard's argument about the cinema's historical responsibility. Godard suggests in *Histoire(s) du cinéma*, and principally in the first episode 1A, that the cinema somehow anticipated the horrors of the Second World War through the accumulation of ominous imagery built up over the 1920s and 1930s,[71] but also that cinema failed in its historical mission to testify to this horror by neglecting to show us, until it was too late, what was happening in the Nazi death camps. Jacques Rancière has argued that this position is fundamentally illogical because it is self-contradictory. Rancière paraphrases Godard's historical narrative thus: 'Cinema is guilty of not having filmed the camps at the time; it is great for having filmed them ahead of time; it is guilty of not having recognized them.'[72] But this does indeed capture something of the twofold operation of cinema examined by Godard. In 1A of *Histoire(s)*, Godard talks of cinema's 'humble and formidable power of transfiguration'.[73] The cinema is humble in the sense that it always records more of the real than anticipated in the image, yet the true significance of that reality is only uncovered when the image is brought into contact with others through montage.

Something similar is perhaps implied by the quotation from Robert Bresson's *Notes sur le cinématographe* that provides the first words heard in *Histoire(s) du cinéma*: 'Change nothing so that everything may be different.'[74] The cinematic image may provide a faithful representation of the real, and it may allow us to see reality anew, but it only does so through the combination of images. The other most prominent line quoted from Bresson's text in *Histoire(s) du cinéma* is: 'An image must be transformed through contact with other images like a colour through contact with other colours.'[75]

Godard's argument in *Histoire(s) du cinéma* undoubtedly owes a great deal to André Bazin. Dudley Andrew has made the case that Bazin 'was the first to intuit that World War II had brought a modern cinema into existence, responsive and responsible to a descriptive mission that the customary (classical) style was incapable of fulfilling'.[76] This is essentially Godard's position, too, although, with the exceptions of 'the astonishing harvest of the great Italian cinema'[77] and the late blooming of the French New Wave, he suggests that this mission went largely unfulfilled. Bazin has had a reputation, within film studies, for being an evangelical proponent of the photographic image's indexical connection to reality but, as recent research has shown, this is based on a very partial reading of the French critic's work. As Andrew has argued, Bazin always displayed an awareness of the strange spectral quality of the image which tends to mean that 'the reality attained by a film is what precisely is not visible in its images'.[78] Andrew suggests that Bazin's conception of the image could be more properly conveyed using terms like 'trace', 'fissure' and 'deferral', thereby implying that he was a kind of Derridean *avant la lettre*.[79] Derridean film theory has stressed that 'as reality imprints itself upon the image, it must also necessarily imprint itself as different from itself'.[80] At the same time, just as language always says more than we intend, thanks to the remainder of sense that allows words and phrases to combine with each other in unanticipated ways, so too the film image always records more of the real than the filmmaker may appreciate. As Jacques Aumont comments: 'The image resists, in all its obtuseness, obstinately saying more or saying differently, escaping us in unpredictable and uncontrollable ways.'[81] And it is this supplement to intended meaning that tends to produce those images and moments valued by cinephilia, an encounter that Keathley calls 'an excess of exchange between a film's makers and its viewers'.[82]

This conception of the image can therefore help to explain Godard's apparently almost metaphysical claim that the cinema anticipated, in its images, something of the reality of the Second World War. But this leaves us with two questions: first, what is the role of montage? And second, what becomes of the reality imprinted on the image when that image ceases to be an analogue apprehension of the light of the world and becomes, instead, a digital construct, as in *Histoire(s) du cinéma*? Jacques Rancière argues that Godard's rhetoric of the image in *Histoire(s)* is contradictory: the director seems to insist that the image is at once 'an incommensurable singularity' and, at the same time, 'an operation of communalization', that is to say that the image acts upon us both as a unique rendering of the real and through combination with other images, in montage.[83] But, in his refusal to accept this duality, Rancière risks renewing ties with the tired dichotomy between mise en scène and montage that for so long drew up artificial distinctions within film history, notably pitting Bazin against montage theorists like Eisenstein. In reality, as all film practitioners know instinctively, both are necessary to cinema. In his famous critical essay 'Montage, mon beau souci', Godard memorably wrote that 'mise en scène is a gaze, but montage is a heartbeat';[84] there is no cinema without the image, but montage is the heartbeat that gives it life.

From this point of view, video can be seen as a technique that facilitates montage. Godard was an early adopter of video technology and has used it regularly since the 1970s as a means of systematically deconstructing and interrogating images.[85] As Alan Wright notes, following Philippe Dubois, video 'bestows a tactile dimension upon the image' such that it 'appears to possess the properties of a material object' and can be manipulated as such.[86] Jacques Aumont has further suggested that the pause button was responsible for one of the most significant shifts in audiovisual art in the late twentieth century, since it allowed spectators to see not still images so much as moving images frozen but with their kinetic energy somehow virtually present, even as they broke, undermined or interrogated the spectator's fascination with the on-rushing flow of images.[87] Youssef Ishaghpour points out that video was the condition of possibility for *Histoire(s) du cinéma*, since it facilitated the endless editing and recombination of film clips in a way that would have been much more laborious on film[88] (and, as suggested by Aumont's comparison of *Histoire(s)* to a private diary, Godard was able to make most of the video series in his home studio[89]). Ishaghpour goes on to suggest that video is to cinema what photography was to painting in the practice of art history in the sense that the new technology permitted a thorough archiving of the earlier medium and new possibilities for comparative study of its works.[90] The video image's distance from the indexical reality perhaps allows the spectator-historian to take a more analytical – less spellbound – relation to the depicted world. Daniel Morgan has proposed that it is precisely this distance from photographic indexicality that has allowed cinema to become properly historical.[91] After all, being present to the event is no guarantee of historical thought, as Godard's constant criticism of news media makes clear.[92] In Morgan's words, 'Cinema, then, can learn how to think about history by learning how to think about itself, not just as a physical medium but as an art with its own *histoires*.'[93]

If cinema needs video to make its own history, however, then this does tend to imply that cinema is finished, as an art form, or that its project remains somehow incomplete, because of its inability to historicize itself ('One can do everything except the history of what one is doing', says Anne-Marie Miéville, quoting Péguy in episode 4B of *Histoire(s) du cinéma*[94]). This is why Godard talks of a sense of impossibility underlying his project. As he stated in one of the Montreal lectures that marked the beginning of this historical thinking, 'In the end, the history of cinema you make will be a trace, like a regret that it isn't even possible to make the history of cinema. But you'll see traces of that history.'[95] This sense of impossibility, coupled to a feeling of regret and the observation that cinema may now be a thing of the past, means that the dominant tone of *Histoire(s) du cinéma*, and indeed of all of Godard's work in this period (broadly, the 1990s), is one of a persistent melancholy, expressed through Godard's mournful voice-overs, the frequent citation of works from or about the end of life (Broch's *Death of Virgil* [1945], Woolf's *The Waves* [1931]) and the use of many minor-key musical works.[96] This melancholy is perhaps problematic since it tends to mean that *Histoire(s) du cinéma* and other works of the period are split between properly analytical motives on the one hand – exploring hitherto unidentified relationships within film history and stressing the complexity of the image's relation to the real – and, on the other hand, an occasionally indulgent nostalgia that consigns the cinema to the past and focuses regretfully on what it failed to achieve. It is no doubt Godard's personal reminiscences – inextricable as they are from his film historical project – that impinge upon the objectivity of the more analytical strand of *Histoire(s)* and make it difficult to accept the director's sharpest insights without also indulging his sometimes facile shortcuts and hasty conclusions.

L'Anglaise et le Duc (Éric Rohmer, 2001)

L'Anglaise et le Duc attracted considerable attention among film critics and scholars in part because it was apparently so different from Éric Rohmer's previous work. It is often remarked that of all the New Wave directors, Rohmer has remained the most faithful to the principles that animated the movement. Rohmer's career developed slowly, without the sudden success enjoyed by Truffaut, Godard or Chabrol. The first feature he directed, *Les Petites Filles modèles* (1952), was never released[97] and the second, *Le Signe du Lion* (filmed 1959, released 1962), was a commercial failure. Rohmer made his name through his film criticism and his short and medium-length works, and it would be 1967 before he released another feature. Subsequent to that, however, his career has been remarkably consistent, with a new film every couple of years, the majority of them following a similar production model, shot on location using a small budget and minimal crew, often with unknown actors, and based on scripts written by Rohmer himself, typically turning around gentle domestic or sentimental dramas usually with an ironic twist. This sense almost of uniformity to Rohmer's work is exacerbated by his tendency to work in deliberately designed series: the *Six Moral Tales* (1962–72), the *Tales of the Four Seasons* (1989–97) and the *Comedies and Proverbs* (six features between 1980 and 1986). By contrast, *L'Anglaise et le Duc* was based on one of the most significant and sensitive subjects in all of French history: the Revolution of 1789 and subsequent Terror, as recounted in the memoirs of the Scottish aristocrat Grace Elliott. It had, 'by far', the biggest budget of any of Rohmer's films,[98] with a crew of hundreds and an audacious visual design: for exterior scenes, the actors were digitally inserted into painted backdrops modelled on representations of Paris and its surroundings from the era of the Revolution.

Thus, where other New Wave directors like Godard and Varda explored the history of their own medium through film historical works, Rohmer turned to one of the most important episodes of French history. This was not, however, Rohmer's first or his last historical work. In the 1970s, he had made two period adaptations, *Die Marquise von O …* (1976), based on the 1808 novella by Heinrich von Kleist, and *Perceval le Gallois* (1979), after the medieval romance by Chrétien de Troyes. Following the success of *L'Anglaise et le Duc*, Rohmer's final two features before his death would also be set in the past: *Triple Agent* (2004) is based on real events that took place in Paris in the 1930s while *Les Amours d'Astrée et de Céladon* (2007), based on an early seventeenth-century text by Honoré d'Urfé, is set in a mythical fifth-century Gaul. It would no doubt be misleading to place too much stress on the coincidence of these last three period films in Rohmer's career; they were not planned as a trilogy in the same way that the director's earlier series were conceived. Nevertheless, it seems clear that at the end of Éric Rohmer's working life, the director turned away from the present and sought inspiration in a more or less distant past, perhaps in some sense returning to his roots: Rohmer had worked as a teacher of classics prior to his career in film, and his first, unreleased, feature was an adaptation of a nineteenth-century novel by the comtesse de Ségur. What is indisputable is that the release of a film about (or at least set during) the French Revolution by a director associated with the Nouvelle Vague, the austerity of whose subsequent career had commanded the respect of the critical establishment, was greeted as a major cultural event in France. As Rohmer's biographers note, the press attention devoted to the film was 'exceptional' with a number of very lengthy articles and interviews published and a real debate taking place regarding the historical value of this representation.[99] (Anecdotally, we might note that the *dossier de presse* for this film, consultable at the Bibliothèque du Film in Paris, is probably more voluminous than that of any other film discussed in this book.) While opinions differed regarding the success and accuracy of Rohmer's representation, there was, it seemed, no real questioning of the legitimacy of his right to make a film on such a sensitive subject. The respect afforded to Rohmer on the basis of his New Wave credentials effectively rendered him a public intellectual whose standing was comparable to that of any famous philosopher, historian or novelist.

L'Anglaise et le Duc is, then, a kind of composite film, using live action, but digitally inserting actors over painted backdrops for exterior scenes. Rohmer engaged the painter Jean-Baptiste Marot to create images of Parisian scenery, some with recognizable landmarks like Notre Dame and the Pont Neuf, others of Grace Elliott's house on the rue de Miromesnil, which no longer exists, and still others around Elliott's country residence in Meudon. There were some thirty-six paintings in total, and their use in the film accounts for just under eighteen minutes of film time in this 129-minute feature[100] (although, perhaps unsurprisingly, they generated a disproportionate amount of discussion in the press). As mentioned above, this seems a curious aesthetic choice for a director apparently wedded to naturalism and to the strange magic of cinema's indexical relationship to the real. Even in interviews around *L'Anglaise et le Duc*, Rohmer maintains this basic position. He states, for instance, that an entirely 'virtual' film, without actors, would hold little appeal because 'the interest of cinema resides in its objective nature, in its mechanical reproduction of reality'.[101] Rohmer also claims not to be attracted to the superior manipulability of lightweight digital cameras,[102] of the kind used by Varda in *Les Glaneurs et la Glaneuse*, and he complains that the majority of camera movements in contemporary films are unnecessary.[103] The director's age may also have been a factor in the stylistic choices of *L'Anglaise et le Duc* (he was 81 when the film was made): he has admitted that his failing physical strength made it easier for him to film in studios than on location.[104]

While there are undoubtedly a number of justifications for Rohmer's aesthetic approach in *L'Anglaise et le Duc* – artistic, economic, technical, personal – the key question of the representation of the real deserves to be more fully explored given the vociferousness with which Rohmer defended a certain view of cinema, against all others, in his criticism. Rohmer was a disciple of André Bazin and, indeed, as Tom Gunning puts it, 'few theorists have been as willing to acknowledge continuing a previous theorist's legacy as Rohmer has'.[105] Like Bazin, Rohmer believed in the fundamental objectivity of the film camera, indeed suggesting that objectivity is as central to Bazin's theory as the straight line is to geometry.[106] As Gunning suggests, there is something intriguingly non-anthropocentric about this theory,[107] since the cinema is able to present to us the objects and phenomena of the world 'as they are, in spite of us'.[108] As we saw briefly in the section on *Histoire(s) du cinéma* above, it has become fashionable in recent years to downplay the idea of cinema's indexical relationship to the real in Bazin's theory or at least to suggest that this is a facile and partial reading of Bazin.[109] Without wishing to discredit this argument, which is based on a careful and extensive rereading of Bazin, it is difficult to ignore, in the critical writing of Éric Rohmer, the future director's faith in the real as the basis of all true cinema. Rohmer states quite unequivocally that the real in all its contingency is the very material of cinema.[110] He writes: 'The auteur-director of tomorrow will know the exultant joy of finding his style in the very texture of the real.'[111] Elsewhere, Rohmer defines the material of cinema as 'movement',[112] as life itself,[113] or as 'pure event'.[114] Cinema, for Rohmer, does not invent beautiful forms but rather discovers them,[115] and this is why he advocates a style of filmmaking that, in the words of Gunning, 'eschews the rhetorical [...] in favour of a direct embrace of the world'.[116] This style is most emblematically represented by Roberto Rossellini, before whose *Stromboli* (1950) Rohmer claims to have experienced a 'Damascene' moment of clarity that changed his view of cinema.[117]

How, then, are we to reconcile this seemingly uncompromising support for a cinema of the real with the digital trickery of *L'Anglaise et le Duc* which, as various commentators noted, is arguably more reminiscent of the visual illusionism of early cinema pioneers like Georges Méliès?[118] The first and most obvious point to make is that, in a story like *L'Anglaise et le Duc* set hundreds of years in the past, 'the real' cannot be directly represented because it no longer exists. There is sometimes a hasty assumption made that period dramas were anathema to the French New Wave. This conclusion is no doubt based on the association of the Nouvelle Vague with contemporary subjects, on the equally persistent linking of the preceding *cinéma de qualité* with period adaptations and on Truffaut's denigration of certain of these in 'Une certaine tendance du cinéma français'.[119] In reality, however, many of the New Wave directors went on to make important period films. In fact, Godard and Varda are the only two of the prominent New Wave auteurs to have avoided this trend. Six of Truffaut's twenty-one features are set in the past, as are five of Rohmer's (out of twenty-three) and five of Rivette's twenty (including the limit-case of *Noroît* [1976] and counting the two parts of *Jeanne la Pucelle* [1994] as a single film). As a proportion of his prolific output, Claude Chabrol made fewer period films, but they include some of his most celebrated works, notably *Violette Nozière* (1978) and *Madame Bovary* (1991).[120] This suggests that these filmmakers – who all had a hand in the theorization of cinema as the mise en scène of the real – viewed the adaptation of period subjects as a particularly intriguing challenge in this regard; but perhaps also that, as they moved further into their respective careers, they felt that broadly realist films about contemporary reality had exhausted their potential. Indeed, Rohmer said exactly that at the time of *Perceval le Gallois*: he described his medieval film as 'a means of getting off certain well-trodden paths, of avoiding the trap of naturalism, which I feel has completely exhausted its possibilities',[121] a question to which we will return below.

In his historical films, Rohmer seeks, in his own words, to 'attain the past without prejudice',[122] that is to resist the temptation to project any contemporary concerns on to the subject and instead to see the past as it might have been seen by those living at the time. This is a subtle but significant difference that can have major implications for aesthetic choices. The medieval world of *Perceval le Gallois*, for instance, does not reflect the way the world of the time may actually have looked but rather the way that artists of the time might have chosen to represent it. The result in that particular film is profoundly unrealistic, resembling a schematic stage set rather than anything from the natural world. In other words, Rohmer attempts to film the past not as it might have looked if movie cameras had been available at the time, but rather as the pre-cinematic imagination of the era's inhabitants might have conceived it.[123] This is why Rohmer chooses to model the mise en scène of *L'Anglaise et le Duc* on period paintings, and commentators have suggested that the effect for the spectator (as indeed in *Perceval*) is of a curious distanciation. Charles Tesson remarked that in *L'Anglaise*, Rohmer 'distances things in order to bring us closer to them'[124] while Jerry Carlson described the effect as one of being 'inside and outside of the past at the same time'.[125] To put it another way, Rohmer resists the approach of most so-called heritage cinema which assumes that the past is knowable; instead, Rohmer takes the problem of that knowability as the spur for the formal design of his films.[126] For Florence Bernard de Courville, in *L'Anglaise et le Duc* cinema interrogates its own image-making function and thereby lays bare its illusions.[127] She argues that, in this way, the film issues a strong challenge to the realist theory of cinema. *L'Anglaise et le Duc* suggests that revolutionary Paris can only be present to us as 'grotesque double, deceptive resemblance, derisory imitation' and that this challenges the cinema's apparent power to be 'the immediate expression of that which is represented, the close union between the film and its object'.[128] This may seem heretical from the point of view of a traditionally conceived Bazinian film theory; but Bernard de Courville offers it instead as a paradoxical accomplishment of Bazin since it is, so to speak, authentic in its artifice.[129] Rohmer made a similar point in interview, saying, 'I don't like cheating. I like to take reality the way it is, even if it's a reality I created through painting, like here. Truth comes from the painting, not the editing.'[130] Or, as he put it elsewhere, 'I preferred to find the true through the false rather than making something fake using pieces of the real.'[131]

Although it does not seek to conceal the 'fakeness' of its exteriors, it remains one of the undoubted achievements of *L'Anglaise et le Duc* that the film successfully integrates this painted scenery with live action. This is accomplished, despite Rohmer's claim to the contrary, partly through the editing, as an analysis of the film's opening images may demonstrate. The film begins with paintings of different Parisian street scenes from the period as a voice-over briefly recounts the life and amorous adventures of Grace Elliott up to that point, before directing our attention to her home on the rue de Miromesnil. Dissolves between different paintings here give the impression of gradually focusing in on more and more specific details of a scene, although, in this case, we are presumably moving between separate paintings rather than details of the same image. A further dissolve brings us into the interior of Lady Elliott's house, a studio set which is matched to the painted exteriors through its pale colour palette yet clearly equipped with 'real' props (chairs and tables, etc.). The smooth continuity between painted exterior and 'real' interior is further established by dissolving to the portraits of Grace and the Duke d'Orléans that hang on the Lady's wall before we meet the characters as portrayed by the actors Lucy Russell and Jean-Claude Dreyfus. The opening minutes of *L'Anglaise et le Duc* have therefore described, with a perfectly classical film grammar, a typical sequence of establishing shots, with the gradation of shots moving from long shots of the city, then the street, then the house, to interior long-shots of a room followed by medium-close and finally close-up shots of the key characters. By mixing together paintings and 'live' shots in this gradation of images, the film immediately sutures the spectator into its composite, hybrid space, such that the use of painted exteriors rapidly loses its shock value.

One of the effects of the film's composite image is to suggest – somewhat as Godard does through the inclusion of numerous other artworks of different media in *Histoire(s) du cinéma* – the cinema's place within an art historical lineage. Cinema thus confidently lays claim to its right, alongside eighteenth-century painting, to represent reality, whether contemporary or historical. Indeed, the relationship of cinema to the other arts was a constant preoccupation of Rohmer's critical writing and the central exploration of the series of essays collectively entitled *Le Celluloïd et le marbre*. Rohmer insisted on the importance of maintaining contact with older art forms in order to help younger arts like the cinema progress.[132] Writing in the 1950s he also suggested that the cinema alone was now capable of expressing noble classical ideas like destiny or the sublime, since the other arts had effectively exhausted themselves.[133] Expounding on his ideas in interview in 1984, Rohmer explained that he believed art history moved in cycles with periodic returns to forms or patterns that were prevalent in the past. Thus, following the Renaissance, artistic Romanticism could be seen to return to the values of the Middle Ages.[134] This suggests, as Rohmer makes clear, that artistic modernity can only ever be temporary. In other words, film forms that appeared inescapably modern in the 1950s or 1960s, such as those of Roberto Rossellini or the French New Wave, may now appear dated or naïve. Meanwhile, extrapolating from Rohmer's argument, and on the evidence of *L'Anglaise et le Duc* and much of the commentary around it, we might suggest that postmodern digital cinema reconnects with the taste for spectacle and trickery in much early film, the so-called cinema of attractions.[135] This is an argument that is sometimes made about contemporary Hollywood action cinema and, despite Rohmer's protests that his film is 'authentic' because it films 'real' paintings, it is ultimately a little difficult to see how this is any different, ontologically speaking, from a Hollywood film that would have live-action stars fighting fantasy monsters or giant robots created in a computer. After all, Rohmer does not just show us Jean-Baptiste Marot's paintings nor does he show us the actors performing against a green screen; instead, much like his contemporaries in Hollywood, he incorporates the two into a largely seamless fictional world.

Indeed, not all critics admired Rohmer's stylistic choices, even though the consensus was that they were daring, provocative and even – appropriately for the topic of the film – revolutionary. A handful of critics (albeit not in organs best known for their film coverage) found *L'Anglaise et le Duc* to be a disappointingly stilted and artificial film. Annie Coppermann in *Les Échos* called it 'as cold as a museum exhibit'[136] whereas, for *Charlie Hebdo*, it resembled 'a little puppet theatre, distanced and haughty'.[137] *Marianne* drew a rather more serious consequence from the film's arguably somewhat stiff mise en scène: Philippe Petit complained that Rohmer's representation of the past was 'idealised, out-dated and predictable' with the result that history, in the film, appeared as though played out in advance.[138] The discussion of the apparent political stance of *L'Anglaise et le Duc* was central to the film's reception. This may be partly because previous French films about the Revolution by auteur directors have tended to have an explicitly political inspiration. The most famous examples are *La Marseillaise* (1938), directed by Jean Renoir at the time of his support for the left-wing Popular Front, and *Danton* (1983) by the Polish director Andrzej Wajda, which was widely interpreted as an allegorical reflection on the Solidarity movement in his home country. Presenting the point of view of a British aristocrat with ties to the royal family (Grace Elliott's former lover, the Duke d'Orléans, was the cousin of Louis XVI), Rohmer's film can be seen as the 'anti-*Marseillaise*'.[139] It was rumoured that *L'Anglaise et le Duc* had not been chosen for the Cannes Film Festival because it was 'politically incorrect'.[140] Rohmer avoids the mythologizing that tends to present the Revolution as a mass popular uprising, instead focusing on individuals, the eponymous Lady and the Duke.[141] Grace Elliott, as presented in the film, is not opposed in principle to the Revolution, and indeed is close to the liberal Charles Fox, a supporter of the revolutions in France and America, but she cannot accept the violent eradication of the monarchy, presumably envisaging instead a constitutional monarchy along the lines of the British model.[142]

Certain critics saw *L'Anglaise et le Duc* as a thoroughly reactionary film. Jean-François Kahn in *Marianne* called it 'counter-revolutionary' and 'revisionist', seeing in it a 'ferocious, implacable, terrible hatred of the people'.[143] *France-Soir* agreed that the working classes in the film were systematically presented as 'ugly, narrow-minded, blood-thirsty and terrifying'.[144] Jean-Pierre Jeancolas accused Rohmer of stereotyping the working classes through their physiognomy: 'the representatives of the Parisian municipality are ugly little men with sly faces, the *sans-culottes* of the Committees are hideous gnomes with menacing faces and lubricious gazes'. He concluded damningly that this type of argumentation was worthy of 'propaganda films of the 1940s'.[145] Indeed, the most decisive scene in the film in terms of this depiction of the terrifying populace – in which an angry mob besieges Lady Elliott in her carriage, brandishing on the end of a pike the head of Madame de Lamballe – was not lifted directly from Elliott's memoir, but added by Rohmer himself.[146]

In interviews around *L'Anglaise et le Duc*, Rohmer rejected these accusations that his film was reactionary and contemptuous of the people. In his defence, he pointed out that Grace Elliott's servants are sympathetic characters in the film[147] but this hardly helped his cause since critics saw the implied message to be that 'the only good poor are servants who remain faithful to their masters'.[148] Rohmer insisted further that the revolutionaries seen in the film should not necessarily be taken as representatives of the people, but are rather 'the hooligans [*les "casseurs"*] of their era'.[149] Arguably, however, this comment serves only to demonstrate that Rohmer has no more respect for the working classes of today than for those of 1792. Finally, it was pointed out that Rohmer showed revolutionaries as coming from the aristocracy and not just the working classes.[150] But this could also be interpreted as a rather patronizing suggestion that 'the real democratic sentiment stems from the nobility'.[151] While Rohmer's films set in the present day tend to avoid explicitly political issues and confine themselves to personal, often sexual, moral questions, close observers of the New Wave saw the counter-revolutionary, and seemingly pro-monarchist, stance of *L'Anglaise et le Duc* as a confirmation of positions long suspected to be held by the director. Rohmer is typically seen as the most conservative of the New Wave critic-directors, regularly making reference in his writing to the cinema's inheritance of the classical tradition of art and literature. In one passage of *Le Celluloïd et le marbre* which now seems altogether shocking, Rohmer insists that cinema is 'western in its origins' and 'remains so in its spirit': he suggests that successful cinema can only come from nations with a long cultural heritage, in particular one that equates nature with beauty (the implication, presumably, is that American cinema draws on European cultural heritage). In language that recalls the self-justifying rhetoric of colonizing powers, Rohmer argues that European civilization has attained 'an unquestionable universality' and it is for this reason that it, alone, can aspire to make great cinematic art.[152] It is known that Rohmer, during the 1950s, was a subscriber to the weekly royalist publication *La Nation française*.[153] The Romanian writer and critic Jean Parvulesco, a self-professed fascist who was exiled in Franco's Spain, frequented the New Wave critics during the 1950s and later claimed that, with the exception of Jacques Rivette, they were all on the extreme right politically. Parvulesco suggested that all of them subsequently dropped these views following the dictates of fashion, but that, in the case of Rohmer, they were more deeply held and that the director's 'aching nostalgia for the monarchy [...] only emerged in *L'Anglaise et le Duc*'.[154]

Rohmer claimed in interview that he 'wasn't especially intent on making a film about the Revolution' and added that he didn't do so for 'political reasons' but rather 'to help cultivate a taste for history in audiences'.[155] But it was surely inevitable that a French film about the Revolution would have sparked political interest and risked provoking a political controversy. Rohmer himself admitted, 'I was feeling a bit limited by love stories and was nostalgic for big subjects.'[156] The director's recognition of the Revolution as a *grand sujet* suggests he was well aware that his film would be taken as a significant statement on an important topic of national interest. Indeed, as Derek Schilling rightly remarks, 'to film the French Revolution is to perform a historiographical act'.[157] Since the very division of French politics into 'left' and 'right' wings dates from the Revolution, the means of conceiving, remembering and representing the event and its aftermath remain profoundly political in France.[158] Rohmer admitted that he wanted to redress the balance of representation following the bicentennial commemorations of 1989 which he saw as having been overwhelmingly pro-Revolution and focused on the 'good people' while ignoring the reality of the Terror that followed.[159] The director added that he thought the Terror anticipated all of the totalitarian regimes that were to come[160] and stressed the relevance to the present day by noting that people today are far more afraid of the possibility of terrorism than they are of revolution.[161] In one particularly striking comment, Rohmer remarked that one could identify with Grace Elliott's account of the Revolution and Terror if one had lived through the Occupation,[162] and Francis Vanoye notes that this is the closest Rohmer ever came to evoking on-screen the France he experienced in his early twenties, characterized by 'collaboration and betrayal, curfews and the hiding of wanted persons, denunciation, searches, interrogation and resistance'.[163] But, however similar these episodes may be in terms of the elements that allow them to be treated as 'historical thrillers' on film, it remains provocative to compare the founding events of the French Republic to that same Republic's darkest hour when it was occupied by a belligerent foreign power.

Rohmer's ultimate defence of his film is that it is not intended to be an objective historical account but rather presents the subjective point of view of an eyewitness, Lady Elliott. Marc Fumaroli, who accepts this position wholeheartedly, suggests that the subjective point of view allows the spectator to relive something of the 'density' of what Elliott experienced and avoid the traps of melodrama on the one hand or the *film à thèse* on the other.[164] Rohmer's film follows Elliott's journal very closely to the extent that, in the words of Jacob Leigh, 'reading the journal while listening to the film is like following a script'.[165] In some ways, this allows Rohmer to shelter behind the journal when challenged on the film's ideological position since he is able to state, for instance: 'If anyone wants to pass judgment on historical grounds, they should judge the book on which the film was based, not the film itself.'[166] At no point does the film part company with Grace Elliott such that it is effectively entirely focalized through her point of view. Rohmer has stated that he doesn't like the contemporary trend for films that switch between different characters suggesting that in too many cases it is only done 'because people are incapable of filming a long scene'.[167] Now Rohmer has, for much of his career, based his films around the dominant point of view of a single character, but typically that character's perspective is ironically undermined, often by discrepancies between what they say and what we see them do, a distance that reveals what Jean-Paul Sartre might have called their 'bad faith'. Strikingly, however, and in contrast to the director's other films, '*L'Anglaise et le Duc* does nothing to undermine Grace's viewpoint; it treats her experiences of the Revolution without irony'.[168] Lady Grace Elliott is effectively used as a transparent channel through which to represent the direct experience of the Revolution and the Terror, but this is all the more surprising when one knows a little about her life. Elliott was a scandalous figure in her time, having enjoyed liaisons not only with the Duke d'Orléans but also with the Prince of Wales, by whom she had a child. Close to both the English and French royal families, but also to British liberals, it seems that Elliott may have been involved in a kind of espionage and indeed Rohmer describes her as a 'double agent'.[169] The journal itself is a text of uncertain status: supposedly written in the first years of the nineteenth century at the behest of the King of England, yet not published until 1859, it seems plausible that it underwent some rewriting and a degree of fictionalization.[170] Rohmer notes that the style of the memoir is almost reminiscent of English novelists like Dickens and Stevenson.[171] Antoine de Baecque and Noël Herpe suggest that in the light of these enigmas surrounding Elliott, she can be seen as a 'typically Rohmerian heroine', marked by 'the contradiction between what she says and what she is'.[172] Yet the film does almost nothing to make visible this discrepancy, such that most critics, on the contrary, seemed struck by Elliott's constancy and heroism, calling her 'admirable in her gracious determination'[173] or 'on the side of life, defending those she sees in peril'.[174]

I would like, finally, to look in some detail at the use of space in *L'Anglaise et le Duc* in order to see how it may illuminate these questions of the political stance and point of view of the film and, again, to consider the proximity or distance of this film from Rohmer's critical philosophy and from his other cinematic works. Space is a central preoccupation in Rohmer's work. Indeed, Marie-Laure Guétin has argued that 'the whole of Rohmer's oeuvre as a theorist and critic, as well as his work as a filmmaker, demonstrates a recurring interrogation of place'.[175] Rohmer's first published article was entitled 'Le cinéma, art de l'espace',[176] and his biographers note that, in it, his critical and theoretical system is 'already entirely constituted'.[177] He also wrote a doctoral thesis on the organization of space in Murnau's *Faust* (1926).[178] For Rohmer, the art of mise en scène consists simply in recording the relationships between bodies in space, and any formal effects beyond the rigorous organization of bodies in space must be considered as empty rhetoric that rapidly risks falling into cliché, what Rohmer calls 'the beauty of the image sought for its own sake'.[179] The project of *L'Anglaise et le Duc* also has spatial questions at its origin. Rohmer notes how, having read an article in a historical magazine about Lady Elliott, his interest was piqued by the suggestion – erroneous, as it turned out – that her Parisian home was still visible on the rue de Miromesnil today.[180] Rohmer has also remarked, comparing *L'Anglaise et le Duc* to his other period adaptations, 'I enjoy the practice of pure mise en scène on the basis of pre-existing texts', adding, 'often, one is more attached to the mise en scène when the subject is not one's own'.[181] But he also noted the practical difficulties of reconstructing the spaces of the past, especially in a city like Paris where so much of the physical environment is marked by contemporary trappings that it cannot be used to represent the eighteenth century without obvious anachronism. This is why, rather than restrict himself to tightly framed street corners, Rohmer quickly chose to use painted exteriors in an effort to show historical spaces that cannot normally be shown on screen.[182]

In his original conception for the film, Rohmer stressed the idea of a contrast between Grace Elliott's 'peaceful apartment' and 'the rest of the city in the throes of revolutionary turmoil'.[183] *L'Anglaise et le Duc* is thus built around an opposition between interior and exterior space, which, as earlier chapters of this book have demonstrated, was a key structuring division and element of rhythmic design in the films of the original New Wave. Inside and outside of course map on to the distinction between private and public spaces but also, in this film, on to the division between 'live' cinema and digital recomposition.[184] The establishment of this clear opposition allows Rohmer to present the Revolution, as experienced by Grace Elliott, as the invasion of her private, interior space by the public, and indeed the most dramatic scenes in the film clearly stage this trespass. Grace is presented as vulnerable in her carriage – a kind of hybrid space, an inside–outside – when rioting revolutionaries leer through the window or present her with the head of Madame de Lamballe. She also suffers the indignity of repeated searches of her bedroom by Republican patrols. Jean-Michel Frodon, who has noted this spatial transgression as key to the design of Rohmer's film, suggests that the establishment of distance is essential to mise en scène, since a distance between figures, between bodies, is necessary in order to bring them subsequently into meaningful relation. Frodon argues that the abolition of this distance is the scourge of contemporary (visual) culture and seems to imply that Rohmer, with *L'Anglaise et le Duc*, is locating its origins in the discourteous infringement of private space that characterized the French Revolution.[185]

This reading of the film suggests the kind of monarchist stance for which Rohmer was criticized in some quarters. It implies that the film invites us to share Grace Elliott's point of view and thereby to experience the Revolution as an unjust invasion of sacrosanct private property. From this perspective, any interrogation of the inequitable division of this property, or of the historical conditions of its establishment, appears illegitimate. A closer look at the film's mise en scène, however, suggests that this reading may be too simplistic. For, while the dialogue may imply that the nobility's domestic space is, or should be, a safe haven from the tumult of the rabble outside, the mise en scène tends rather to suggest that these aristocrats are trapped within their luxurious homes. Restriction of movement is, of course, central to the film's plot. Since the municipality controls the movements of anyone into or out of Paris, Grace must seek written permission to move between her Paris residence and her home in Meudon or else sneak out under cover of darkness. Meanwhile, figures wanted by the Republican authorities, such as the marquis de Champcenetz, are literally trapped indoors, hiding out in an attic or between the mattresses of Grace's bed. More than this, though, the homes of the nobility, when shown in the film, come across, for all their presumed grandeur, as profoundly claustrophobic and this is for reasons of mise en scène. When interiors are filmed in *L'Anglaise et le Duc*, we are never provided with establishing shots of grand rooms nor with tracking shots showing the passage of characters through houses from the front door to the inner sanctum. Such shots may be common in high-budget heritage cinema, but are entirely absent from Rohmer's film. Instead, interiors tend to be filmed in mostly static shots showing only one narrow corner of a room. These shots may be busy with antique props and decor (fireplaces, mirrors, candelabra, pictures, wallpaper and drapes, busts, tables and chairs, tea sets, etc.), yet the narrow framing tends only to make them seem crowded. At the same time, while deep space is often used, it tends not to create a sense of life in the off-screen space, but rather to emphasize the impression of enclosure. Thus, servants may come and go through a door, but little is visible beyond the door beside a near-identical room perhaps with another closed door. In addition, there are no reverse shots to connect these interior spaces to the world outside. The windows are either filmed at oblique angles that prevent any view through them or else are covered with a clearly painted backdrop of an indistinct green garden. The noble characters' irreparable enclosure within these spaces is further emphasized by the striking harmony between their clothes and the décor: Grace's pale and pastel-coloured dresses match her tastefully decorated walls, while both she and Orléans at different points wear stripes that seem to mirror the wallpaper. It is notable, too, that there is little really to distinguish one interior from another, since all tend to be filmed with the same tight framing and reflect a similar class-specific taste. Thus, it is not immediately easy to tell Grace's Parisian house from her property in Meudon (at least one critic appears not to have noticed that there are two different bed chambers in the film[186]) or from the homes of her friends.

FIGURE 4.1 *Lucy Russell in* L'Anglaise et le Duc *(2001). Courtesy Potemkine.*

While interior spaces are cramped and seemingly interchangeable, the use of painted scenery in exteriors allows for wide open views. One of the most striking aspects of these paintings, for viewers who know contemporary Paris, is the amount of open space between the buildings in *faubourgs* that have as yet not been extensively built up. There is, then, a greater sense of freedom in the exteriors or at least of what Derek Schilling calls 'monumentality and openness, combining deep corridor-streets and broad panoramic vistas'.[187] In one of the few moments of *L'Anglaise et le Duc* that makes its irony plain, Grace is heckled by drunken men as she is led through the streets from prison to her tribunal: 'What's your hurry?' they shout, 'It's nicer outside than in!' In interview, Rohmer recognized that despite what many saw as the 'Hitchcockian' suspense of *L'Anglaise et le Duc*,[188] the film's use of space is closer to the work of Fritz Lang,[189] in particular in its almost abstract design around straight lines, curves and planes.[190] Lang is known, especially in his American films noirs, for a spatial design that makes use of surfaces, lines, light and shade to create a sense almost of characters trapped in a glass cage. The implication tends to be that Lang's characters are ensnared in the playing out of a destiny that they don't fully understand, the extent and parameters of which they cannot see. If *L'Anglaise et le Duc* is 'Langian', then, in its use of space, it perhaps suggests, against the widespread assumption of the film's monarchist ideology, that the noble characters are trapped in an outdated worldview that leaves them little room to manoeuvre, while the Revolution, for all its trespasses and excesses, denotes an inevitable social progress whose achievement cannot be forestalled. In other words, and in common with the subtle ironies of many of Rohmer's other films, while the dialogue and the direction of sympathy through point of view may suggest one ideological stance in *L'Anglaise et le Duc*, the rigour of the mise en scène tends to propose an alternative reading.

The restricted physical space in *L'Anglaise et le Duc* – the confined interiors and artificial exteriors – tends to place less emphasis on the spectacle of properties and locations and more on bodies. This is notably the case in the extraordinary physicality of Jean-Claude Dreyfus's performance as the Duke d'Orléans who seems almost fit to burst out of his constraining costumes. Orléans crowds Grace's personal space with his urgent kissing of her hands, and yet there appears a kind of extreme nervousness about his eyes and about his bearing, as though he were carrying the weight of a terrible burden upon his shoulders. There is tremendous melodrama to the hunch of his shoulders and to grandiloquent roll of his R's at the end of sentences. Jean Roy has noted that *L'Anglaise et le Duc* is unusual in Rohmer's career in that the protagonists are not tempted to sleep together; instead, this sexual activity is in their past and, as such, no longer on the agenda.[191] That said, there remain undeniable sexual undertones to much of the action in the film. The dramatic searches of Grace's bedchambers are a clear violation of her intimacy, and the comments of some of the soldiers make explicit the assumption that it would take very little for this symbolic rape to become an actual physical assault. Similarly, when a patrol comes to search for letters in Grace's possession, their defiling of her private writing desk appears all the more shocking, perhaps, since the presumed use for these hidden compartments is to conceal a lady's correspondence from her lover. Ultimately, when Grace is arrested, it seems almost as an excuse for the soldier to place his hand on her person (and notably on her shoulder, one of the Duke's favourite places to touch the lady) in a kind of dramatic performative gesture that seems to claim ownership of this woman's previously inaccessible body.

There are repeated suggestions in the film, then, that the political is bound up with, and perhaps inextricable from, the sexual. Indeed, close attention to the use of space in the film reveals that the majority of Elliott's interviews on political matters, mostly, but not exclusively, with Orléans, take place in her boudoir. Various critics, but most notably Charles Tesson in *Cahiers du cinéma*, have also remarked upon the eroticism that the film generates, in particular around Grace/Lucy Russell's neck and throat.[192] Respecting the vestimentary modesty of the era, *L'Anglaise et le Duc* avoids any representation of nudity, yet plays repeatedly on the exposure of Grace's shoulders, neck, throat and cleavage, both in her night shirts and in her more public gowns. The film's costume designer, Pierre-Jean Larroque, admits that particular attention was paid to Grace's *décolleté* in order to highlight the lady's 'fragile and sensual side'.[193] Indeed, the image of a white shift slipping from a lady's shoulder to reveal a suggestion of breast is a motif that recurs with the persistence of fantasy in Rohmer's historical films: it can also be found in *Die Marquise von O …*, in *Perceval le Gallois* and in *Les Amours d'Astrée et de Céladon*. Here, however, as Tesson notes, the eroticism of the throat is always linked, unconsciously or otherwise, to the threat of the Guillotine, a menacing absent presence in the film, never seen on screen but evoked through the cruel jibes of the crowd and imagined in the memorable scene of the King's execution where Grace listens to the roll of drums and the shouts of the onlookers from a distant position in the heights of Meudon. When Grace is imprisoned, her faithful servant Nanon brings her a posey which she conceals in her breast and the gesture seems to seal the film's unconscious network of imagery connecting sex to death through the displacement of bosom to throat. Finally, in the film's last scene, a close-up of Grace in prison, dressed in black against a black background, emphasizes the pallor of her throat to stress the immediate threat of the Guillotine, until an intertitle reveals that the death of Robespierre gave her back her freedom. The film's treatment of bodies, then, suggests that Rohmer does, despite first appearances, seek subtly to remind the viewer of Elliott's reputation as 'royal courtesan' and that, in so doing, he conspires to undermine somewhat her dignified and aristocratic rhetoric. At the same time, however, the film seeks to uncover some of the hidden, libidinal impulses underlying the Revolution, a covetousness that may have been more than simply material.

In conclusion, *L'Anglaise et le Duc* appears, in the image of its director, as a film of contradictions. Rohmer is apparently a shy and retiring individual, deliberately refusing television appearances for fear of being subsequently identified in public and able, even after four decades of filmmaking, to travel every day to the film studio on the RER.[194] Yet this same bashful gent, at over eighty years of age, chooses to make the dramatic public statement of a controversial film about the French Revolution. All of Rohmer's writing about cinema betrays a very classical view of the arts, and in interviews around *L'Anglaise et le Duc* he comes across as largely dismissive of contemporary cinema, and yet he makes a 'revolutionary' film using cutting-edge digital technology. That said, however novel the film's aesthetic approach may seem and however striking the initial distanciation caused by the use of painted backdrops, the film works quickly and efficiently to suture the spectator into a classical film grammar that allays any discomfort. The film appears, on first viewing, to take up a position of sympathy for the persecuted monarchists during the Revolution, yet, on closer inspection, its mise en scène of space suggests a social class trapped in a narrow view of the world that cannot be sustained. Rohmer seems, from his writings and his biography, to have been a rather old-fashioned, not to say puritanical man, yet we find that bodies, and indeed erotics, are central to the mise en scène of *L'Anglaise et le Duc*, as I suspect they would appear given a thorough reassessment of the director's oeuvre.

Les Glaneurs et la Glaneuse (Agnès Varda, 2000)

Les Glaneurs et la Glaneuse was made in the wake of the commercially unsuccessful *Les Cent et une nuits*. As Melissa Anderson suggests, it is possible to see the later, very successful documentary as prolonging the theme of memory in Varda's work (her two preceding works – *Les Demoiselles ont eu 25 ans*, 1993, and *Jacquot de Nantes*, 1991 – were both films revisiting moments and memories from the life of Varda's husband Jacques Demy, following his death in 1990). Varda admits to having a poor memory and suggests that her recollection of cinema is patchy, often marked more by her own emotional states than by remembrance of facts or aesthetic details of films. As Anderson suggests, the process of sorting through memories can itself be regarded as a kind of gleaning, the central practice in *Les Glaneurs et la Glaneuse* that becomes a wide-ranging metaphor both in the film and in the surrounding criticism.[195] As with a lot of her previous films, Varda prepared for *Les Glaneurs* by travelling around France and interviewing people, gradually tracking down a set of twenty-first-century gleaners who were willing to appear on film.[196] Varda has recognized in interview that the unobtrusive, hand-held digital video camera she used facilitated these initial interviews and indeed its cheapness, and ease of use with minimal assistance, effectively made the film possible when producers showed little interest in funding what appeared at first glance as an abstruse and unenticing topic.[197] The film was eventually made for only €300,000 and Varda estimates that she filmed twenty minutes of its eighty-minute runtime herself.[198] *Les Glaneurs et la Glaneuse* was first broadcast on Canal Plus in France the day before its theatrical release and, following a modest debut, the film went on to have a lengthy run, notably with demand for copies coming from small provincial towns and villages as well as from international festivals.[199] Varda was very active in the promotion of the film: she and various of the individuals featured in the film made public appearances at screenings, presentations and debates and spectators responded with notable warmth. Varda herself remarked, 'I've never in my entire career felt that people have loved a film of mine as much as this one.'[200] As a gesture of gratitude for this enthusiastic welcome, Varda made a follow-up, 63-minute film, *Les Glaneurs et la Glaneuse: Deux ans après* (2002), for inclusion on the DVD, in which she shows some of the letters and gifts received in response to *Les Glaneurs* and re-interviews some of the figures from the first film in order to satisfy spectators' curiosity as to their subsequent trajectory. In 2003, Varda curated an exhibition at the Venice Biennale, and subsequently in Paris, entitled *Paratutopia*, taking as its starting point the heart-shaped potatoes celebrated in *Les Glaneurs*.[201]

This very successful film appears, at first glance, to be less about history and memory than about the present. Having said that, *Les Glaneurs et la Glaneuse* does begin with an appeal to the past by turning to the Larousse dictionary, the pages of which Varda films in extreme close-up, in order to define the key terms *glaner* and *glanage* that generate the film. The need for a definition implies that the very concept (collecting leftover crops after a field has been harvested) is one that belongs to another era, and Varda's dictionary contains reproductions of the two most famous images of gleaning that recur throughout the film: Jean-François Millet's *Des Glaneuses* (1857) and Jules Breton's *La Glaneuse* (1877). But Varda quickly demonstrates, through a montage of images, that far from having disappeared from our societies, gleaning has spread from the rural environment (where it continues) to urban centres where the poor pick up discarded produce from market stalls or rummage through bins outside supermarkets. Varda's film thus renders very visible a certain kind of poverty: individuals in both town and country living on the margins of society, minimally employed, precariously housed and relying on scavenging for at least a part of their nourishment. The film suggests, then, the widening of the gulf between rich and poor in France (and, by extension, in other modern capitalist economies) while also implying a critique of the culture of waste in food production and distribution and in the wider consumer economy. Varda visits a potato-sorting factory in the Beauce region south-west of Paris and discovers that potatoes bigger or smaller than a standard 45–75 cm diameter are rejected as 'unsellable' and dumped back into the fields. There is, however, no official notice of this dumping for the benefit of local residents so the potatoes will simply rot and go to waste unless news of their availability gets around by word-of-mouth.

In many ways, then, *Les Glaneurs et la Glaneuse* can be seen as a political documentary exposing key concerns of the moment: economic precariousness and the culture of obsolescence and waste encouraged by overconsumption. As such, the film to a degree returns to the interest in social and political ferment displayed by Varda in the late 1960s and 1970s in documentaries such as *Black Panthers* (1969), *Salut les Cubains* (filmed 1962, released 1971) and *Réponse de femmes* (1975). But *Les Glaneurs* avoids didacticism – as Frédéric Bonnaud remarks, Varda makes her points 'without raising her voice or crying scandal'[202] – and leaves the spectators to draw their own connections between the economic inequality on display and the politics of environmentalism. In this sense, *Les Glaneurs* might be labelled a post-political film. As Jake Wilson comments: 'Without specifically referring to political movements or events, the film embodies a quasi-anarchist ethos now in the air in all sorts of ways – a resistance to consumerism, a suspicion of authority, and a desire to reconnect politics with everyday life.'[203] Martin O'Shaughnessy goes further, suggesting that 'although the film lacks a clear and overarching political discourse, what it shows seems to cry out for one'.[204] One reason for this lack of organized political response may well be the solitude of the gleaners depicted in the film. Varda herself remarks in her voice-over that whereas nineteenth-century paintings show gleaning as a communal activity, today 'everyone gleans alone'. An old woman interviewed for the film recalls episodes in her youth when, after a day of back-breaking work gleaning in the fields, the community would gather in the evening to laugh and sing over wine and coffee. By contrast, the majority of the contemporary gleaners interviewed demonstrate the limited articulacy and awkward gaze of individuals deprived of regular and varied social contact. Through these juxtapositions, then, and through the implied contrast of past and present, *Les Glaneurs et la Glaneuse* suggests that the resurgence of gleaning at the end of the twentieth century, and its changing forms, is partly a consequence of the breakdown of community through social atomization.

Another way of interpreting *Les Glaneurs*, however, is to see the focus on gleaning as more of a formal exercise than a political statement. As Varda notes in the film, gleaning is, first and foremost, a physical gesture of bending down to pick something up and, in places, particularly the montage sequence mentioned above, Varda's film seems almost to be working through a series of visual rhymes. But, beyond the literal gesture of picking up waste material, gleaning becomes a powerful symbolic activity in the film. Serge Kaganski suggests that Varda herself can be seen as 'gleaning images' since she is interested in seeing and showing precisely those people and practices that are typically regarded as society's outcasts.[205] Just as Varda shows artists, such as Louis Pons and Sarah Sze, who create – sometimes very expensive and highly regarded – visual works from scavenged detritus, her film demonstrates that the status of images and objects depends on their context and framing. For instance, Varda films a large damp patch on the ceiling of her Paris apartment but, placing artificial picture frames around sections of the mould, she suggests it resembles abstract-expressionist artworks by painters like Antoni Tàpies, Cai Guo-Qiang or Clément Borderie. Elsewhere, Varda includes a footage she accidentally filmed when she left the lens cap off her video camera and turns it into a 'dance' by adding, on the soundtrack, a jazz accompaniment.

Les Glaneurs et la Glaneuse also resembles the practice of gleaning in its eccentric, digressive structure. As Jake Wilson notes, the film offers a 'narrative not as progress towards a goal but as an open-ended gathering of disparate elements'.[206] Just as a life dependent on scavenging would make planning difficult and require adaptability and spontaneity, Varda's film stresses the role of chance, as in the moment when she and her crew happen across a second-hand shop named Trouvailles (roughly 'Rare Finds') in which they discover an amateur painting of gleaners that combines the famous works by Millet and Breton. There is an element of surrealism to this interest in the chance encounter: Bohdan Litnianski's *Jardin des Merveilles*, visited in the film, an eerie collection of pillars constructed by a former mason and built out of discarded dolls and other rubbish, is notably reminiscent of Ferdinand Cheval's *Palais idéal* that was much admired by André Breton, and Varda's voice-over commentary makes the connection explicit. Indeed, Varda's delight in flea markets is itself in the lineage of Breton and other French surrealists who found that objects often took on a poetic aura when divested of their original function.[207] Like the surrealists, too, Varda shows some interest in psychoanalysis as a model. One of her interviewees is the psychoanalyst Jean Laplanche who also owns a vineyard in Burgundy. Varda claims not to have realized Laplanche's celebrity as a psychoanalytic theorist when she made *Les Glaneurs*, and she visits him again in the follow-up, *Deux ans après*, whereupon Laplanche muses that psychotherapy, too, could be understood as a form of gleaning. As Homay King glosses, 'Like the filmmaker's look, the analyst's listening is a kind of gleaning, an attunement to the under-remarked and to what at first glance seems insignificant or without value.'[208] The structure of *Les Glaneurs et la Glaneuse* often seems to follow a kind of free associative chain. For instance, Varda cuts from Laplanche, whose wife has just revealed that they are approaching their fiftieth wedding anniversary, to another married couple, seen earlier in the film and based in the south of France, who are asked to recount the story of how they met. Elsewhere, a discussion of self-portraits (Rembrandt's and Varda's own) moves, via Maurice Utrillo's self-portrait and the museum where it is held in Sannois, outside Paris, to an interview with a contemporary scavenger-artist, who lives nearby. But perhaps the film's most audacious sequence of associations moves from a sculpture of a reclaimed fridge populated with Playmobil figures enacting a political demonstration, via footage of a real demonstration on the place Denfert-Rochereau in Paris, through the connection of statues of lions on that square and in the southern town of Arles, to a report from an apple orchard in that region.

The comparison of the artist, and artistic practice, to gleaning, scavenging and what we might today refer to as 'dumpster-diving' may suggest a kind of *nostalgie de la boue* in Varda's film. S. D. Chrostowska comments:

> As Baudelaire the poet and Benjamin the materialist historian were drawn to the figure of the chiffonnier, so Varda the filmmaker is drawn to that of the glaneuse. Both 'paradigms' involve members of the French artistic milieu being drawn lower, to the destitute, disturbing and dangerous, as models and modi operandi for their work.[209]

Varda herself admits that, in the last analysis, the comparison between artist and scavenger is 'too heavy an analogy' to be meaningfully sustained.[210] Still, we might ask again what are the political implications of Varda's formal gleaning. Martin O'Shaughnessy suggests that the sheer variety of practices shown in the film under the inclusive umbrella of gleaning means that the work resists any totalizing political discourse. However, its stress on 'creative bricolage' arguably implies that 'some assemblage of minor alternatives could produce a more substantial oppositional project'.[211] Occasional commentators, though, have offered a more critical interpretation of the digressive structure of *Les Glaneurs*: Nathalie Rachlin provided a rare voice of dissent in the chorus of approval with which Varda's film was greeted. She suggests that Varda's formal choices in *Les Glaneurs* represent a 'diversion' that allows spectators to 'master the emotions' provoked by the vision of poverty and distress.[212] In one particularly striking montage in the film, following an interview with an unemployed alcoholic man, living in a caravan on a patch of wasteland after losing his job and his family, and surviving by scavenging food from bins, Varda cuts to the kitchen of a gourmet restaurant. What we learn in this scene is that the top end of food production in France also has its practices of gleaning: the restaurant kitchen abhors waste, using leftovers to make sauces and stocks, while the chef, Édouard Loubet, prefers to use herbs that he has picked locally. Still, the initial juxtaposition is brutal. Virginia Bonner remarks that in her experience of screenings of *Les Glaneurs*, 'middle-class audiences always laugh at this comparison'.[213] While Bonner charitably interprets this laughter as 'a gesture of inclusivity',[214] it would be easy to see it instead as the nervous laughter of spectators relieved to be placed back in more familiar territory after the uncomfortable spectacle of Claude in his caravan. Rachlin, discussing this very montage, suggests that 'Varda's camera is complicit in our shame' and she adds that the film's success implies that we spectators have been grateful for this complicity.[215] Bonner reports that, in public discussions around the film, Varda has vociferously refused accusations that 'the more light-hearted' aspects of gleaning tend to dominate the film to the detriment of serious questions about social exclusion.[216] In a statement on her website, Varda stresses that she believes in 'personal commitment', adding: 'Through my work as a filmmaker, I am personally committed.'[217]

We shall return to this problematic question of the politics of *Les Glaneurs et la Glaneuse* at the end of this chapter. Varda's reference to the 'personal', however, reminds us that the film is also a kind of self-portrait and that gleaning is also related to memory. As Florence Assouline notes, if by throwing away we forget, then by picking up, reclaiming or gleaning we 'nourish memories'.[218] Indeed, several of the figures in the film glean not in order to survive but to collect, to create, or to accumulate a kind of personal archive. Varda herself, claiming a poor memory, says that she 'gleans images in order to see where she's been' and films herself unpacking a suitcase of souvenirs on returning from a trip to Japan. But, if gleaning can be seen as a kind of archiving, it is, suggests Domietta Torlasco, a 'heterodox, subversive' kind since apparently following little order.[219] In this sort of chaotic archiving, argues Torlasco, 'there is no stable archival object or archiving subject that we can hold, or by which we can be held, in a time that is simply present or past'.[220] Torlasco adds that, since gleaning involves recuperating materials that have already had at least one useful life in another context, gleaning is 'a gesture that has no original, that constitutes and undoes its own original through repetition'.[221] As such, gleaning is arguably a particularly 'subversive' practice to employ in the arts since it challenges such fundamental concepts as originality and authorship.

All the same, commentators have tended to discuss Varda's film in explicitly auteurist terms. Ben Tyrer affirms that '*Les Glaneurs* is foremost an Agnès Varda film, and should be understood as a part of her ongoing auteurist project'.[222] As Frédéric Bonnaud remarks, for all her wanderings around France and the wider world, Varda, in this film, 'always comes back to herself'.[223] Both journalistic reviewers and academic scholars have seen echoes of numerous other works by Varda in *Les Glaneurs*, so much so that Agnès Calatayud calls it 'a career-summarizing film, a kind of "auto-film festival"'.[224] Jacques Mandelbaum suggested that *Les Glaneurs* could be seen as a prolongation of the liberty and lightness, and of the willful subversion of genres found in *Cléo de 5 à 7* (1961).[225] Varda herself remarked that the mixture of objective and subjective approaches in *Les Glaneurs* recalls her interest in both the subjective experience and objective passage of time in *Cléo*.[226] *Les Glaneurs* clearly evokes the memory of *Sans toit ni loi* (1985) not only through its depiction of the marginal and the homeless but also through its digressive structure.[227] More generally, *Les Glaneurs* appears as an extension of Varda's long engagement with documentary form, mixing social issues with intimate portraits as she does in films like *Mur murs* (1981) and, in the process, also creating a self-portrait, as in works like *Opéra-Mouffe* (1958), *Daguerréotypes* (1976) or *Documenteur* (1981), and as she would do again in *Les Plages d'Agnès* (2008) and *Visages villages* (2017). It might be tempting to ask whether there is something indulgent or narcissistic about Varda's constant reversion to her own person over the course of *Les Glaneurs* and indeed the course of her career. It is striking, for instance, that one of the most memorable individuals in *Les Glaneurs* – Alain, the formidably austere and committed young man who makes a living selling a homeless newspaper, survives on foraged food and teaches nightly classes in literacy on a voluntary basis – when asked for his views on the film in *Deux ans après*, calls it 'well done' but says he finds the scenes of self-portraiture 'unnecessary'. Yet, if we read Varda's film as being a politically engaged hymn to all that is needlessly discarded by our society, then Varda's self-portrait must take its place within that same logic. As she herself observes, 'As one gets older, one becomes waste material oneself.'[228] For Lucy Fischer, *Les Glaneurs et la Glaneuse* is a film exploring the abject and, following Julia Kristeva, she notes that 'abjection selectively attaches to the female – especially as she ages'.[229] The scenes in which, in the terms of Varda's own voice-over, she 'enters into the horror' of her ageing body, filming in extreme close-up the grey roots of her hair and her wrinkled, liver-spotted hands, can thus be seen as a deliberate refusal of what Rosello calls 'the cultural imperative that makes beauty mandatory in our representational universe'.[230]

Despite this unflinching gaze on her ageing body, there is often a childlike quality to the perspective of *Les Glaneurs et la Glaneuse*. This is seen, for instance, in the pleasure Varda takes at observing trucks on the motorway, what she calls 'the kind of beautiful trucks we loved when we were little'. Overtaking them is like 'a children's game' and later, in a scene that has become famous, Varda films her hand in the foreground closing in a sort of makeshift iris around the trucks seen through the windscreen. The fun with trucks is just one sign of Varda's very evident curiosity and enjoyment of life: we might compare her excitement at discovering heart-shaped potatoes or the visible sensual pleasure she takes in eating ripe figs straight from the tree. This same warmth and openness to experience is brought to Varda's human encounters in the film. She gives the impression of genuinely liking the people she interviews, from the most impoverished vagrants to the most bourgeois landowners. She herself states simply, 'I like this film because I like the people who are in it.'[231] She is also modest enough to suggest that the spectators like it for the same reason: 'When you applaud, you're applauding what they say, not me.'[232] Varda repeatedly demonstrates respect and attention for the people she films. Claude, the alcoholic caravan-dweller, is given time to explain his situation and how he arrived at it. Varda describes her meeting with Alain, the volunteer literacy tutor, as 'the thing that most impressed me during the filming' and, as a mark of respect, she places the portrait of him at the end of the film so that his inspirational example is likely to be remembered by spectators leaving the screening. It is no doubt Varda's long association with feminist discourse and movements that also leads her to question those who might have been left out of a more traditional documentary, in particular the wives of well-known figures like Jean Laplanche and Bohdan Litnianski. These brief insights into the domestic lives of semi-public figures work to deflate their own slightly pompous intellectual rhetoric and thereby to humanize them.

Commentators on the film have responded to this overriding sense of warmth and humanity. Anne de Gasperi in *Le Figaro* praised Varda's 'curiosity for places, humour for situations, gravity and joy in encounters and talent for capturing moments'.[233] *Les Inrockuptibles* noted her 'social generosity',[234] while Virginia Bonner has highlighted the 'sincerity and sensitivity' of her approach.[235] Another quality admired in Varda's work is modesty. The director herself has asserted that 'documentary film is a discipline that teaches modesty', and she adds that the hand-held digital video camera facilitates this since it obliges the filmmaker to look her

FIGURE 4.2 *Bohdan Litnianski and his wife in* Les Glaneurs et la Glaneuse *(2000). Courtesy Artificial Eye.*

subjects in the eye.²³⁶ Varda resists taking up an authoritative – and arguably even an authorial – voice in the film, stressing the collaboration of her interviewees. This is notable, for instance, in the case of François, the eccentric, wellington-booted denizen of Aix-en-Provence. Varda points out that François agreed to appear in the film on condition that it mention the oil spill caused by the sinking of the *Erika* off the coast of Brittany in 1999. As Varda admits, 'François was the first one who made the connection' between cultures of gleaning, an economy based on over-consumption and environmental damage.²³⁷ In recognition of François's key creative role in the film, Varda invited him to participate in a public debate after a screening in Aix, at which he denounced the tyranny of expiration dates by bringing cakes retrieved from the trash and offering them to audience members.²³⁸ Far from the imposing, self-important auteur, then, Varda sometimes seems to adopt a role closer to that of a facilitator. Sandy Flitterman-Lewis suggests that the director can be seen as an 'intermediary who gives voice to those who have none',²³⁹ while Virginia Bonner talks about 'a complex but direct circle of communication among filmmaker, filmed subjects, and viewing audience'.²⁴⁰ Finally, we might suggest that if gleaning is a result of the breakdown of community, as the film implies, then Varda's openness and generosity, both within the film and in the extra-textual circuits in which the film is disseminated, functions as a kind of virtual and actual community building.

In conclusion, then, *Les Glaneurs et la Glaneuse* can be seen as related to the other films discussed in this chapter since gleaning is a practice and a process connected to memory (the hoarding of souvenirs and relics, the sifting through images and impressions), but the investigation of gleaning also allows Varda to conduct a historical investigation. The gestures of gleaning tie France's rural past to its urban present and, in doing so, they raise important political questions: about the failure of economic growth to eradicate poverty and about the role of community breakdown in social exclusion. The politics of *Les Glaneurs* are somewhat inchoate and intuitive: it is, in the words of Jacques Mandelbaum, a 'discreetly anarchist' film.²⁴¹ It suggests that resistance to the culture of overproduction and consumption must be local, personal, intimate, creative. As such, the film also betrays its connection to a lineage of particularly Parisian artistic and cultural movements: Varda's interest in ragpickers and the urban poor evokes the distant inheritance of Baudelaire, while the film's haphazard structure and acquisition of evidence recall Walter Benjamin's open-ended historical work. At the same time, the taste for playful free association and unforeseeable encounters revives the lessons of surrealism that resonate through Varda's work as far back as *Opéra-Mouffe*. All of this might have given rise to a dry and worthy formal exercise were it not for Varda's combination of generosity and gratitude towards the participants in her film. It would no doubt be reductive to ascribe the warm tone of *Les Glaneurs* to a simple question of the gender of the director. Rebecca DeRoo has recently suggested that we need to see a certain strategic naïveté at work in much of Varda's production. She suggests that the director sometimes feigns ignorance as a way of pre-empting or deflecting the condescending commentary of misogynist male critics.[242] In addition, we must recognize that this kind of self-effacing behaviour has been a traditional aspect of women's largely unacknowledged emotional labour for many generations, and it continues to be disproportionately expected of women in the service industries today.[243] Still, from her close involvement with the feminist movement in the 1970s, Varda has clearly retained the lesson that politics is as much a question of everyday interactions as it is of theory and principles. The attentive and fruitful exchanges of *Les Glaneurs et la Glaneuse* demonstrate this lesson in action.

Conclusion

There are no doubt as many differences as there are similarities between *Histoire(s) du cinéma*, *L'Anglaise et le Duc* and *Les Glaneurs et la Glaneuse*. Any attempt to draw meaningful comparisons between the three is likely to find that one film refuses to fit into a neat argument. Perhaps first and foremost, it is differences in tone that strike the viewer: stentorian and prophetic from Godard, sober and serious in Rohmer, playful and effusive in Varda. All the same, these three films by veteran New Wave directors, released within four years of each other, deliberately combine the old and the new in productive and thought-provoking ways, relying variously on video editing, on compositing and on portable digital cameras either to evoke the past or to undertake historical enquiries linking past to present. The status of these New Wave directors as 'cultural mandarins' in France has no doubt given the seal of legitimacy to these historical interrogations and shaped the reception of the films.[244] Each of these films has generated a vast commentary both in the press and in academic scholarship, such that they have rapidly come to be discussed more than any other work in each director's oeuvre.

There are several reasons why the French New Wave might be regarded as a particularly appropriate training ground for asking historical questions on film. First, the New Wave, as has been widely documented, is a movement that grew out of the love and voracious study of film history and many New Wave films, in particular those of Godard and Truffaut, can almost be seen as self-contained lessons in film history. Second, the critics of the New Wave, and most especially Éric Rohmer, additionally sought to situate the cinema within a wider history of the arts, a process extended in the films of the movement through the inclusion and citation of countless works of literature, painting and music. Third, several of the New Wave directors, with Rohmer again chief among them, were attracted to period dramas in their later careers and, in directing them, experimented with innovative ways of representing the past on film. At the same time, though, the film theory developed in the genesis of the New Wave can be seen as crucial in the question of representing the past and also in the notion of using the cinema as a historiographical tool. The notion of the film image's indexical relationship to the real, central to the theory of André Bazin and seminal in the writings of all the New Wave critics but particularly Rohmer, stresses that the cinema retains a trace of the past and, as such, holds an almost tangible relationship to history. When this indexicality is allied to the critical power of montage to generate historical thinking by drawing unexpected connections – a power most thoroughly theorized by Jean-Luc Godard – the cinema appears as a formidable historiographical machine.

The importance of the New Wave in this regard may help to explain why there is so much self-reference in these late, memorializing films from Nouvelle Vague directors. *Histoire(s) du cinéma* and *Les Glaneurs et la Glaneuse* can effectively be seen as self-portraits as much as they are about their ostensible subjects (the history of cinema, gleaning). Rohmer does not appear directly in *L'Anglaise et le Duc* but, as we have seen, his film is in dialogue with others from his filmography not just over the question of historical representation but more generally over the issues of self-representation and self-preservation through speech that are central to Rohmer's oeuvre. Indeed, Charles Tesson suggests that the French Revolution represents the 'primal scene' of the contemporary bourgeoisie who populate the majority of the director's films.[245] Noël Herpe expands on this point, suggesting that in *L'Anglaise et le Duc*, Rohmer seeks 'the exact moment when classical discourse sank into deceit, happenstance, and betrayal'.[246] At the same time as all three directors evoke and explore their own back catalogue in these works, they also place themselves within a lineage of art history. Godard takes up his place in a spectral and forbidding House of Cinema; Rohmer inscribes his film within a tradition of classical painting; and Varda situates herself within a legacy of plastic arts that runs from nineteenth-century realism, through the ludic encounters of surrealism, to contemporary gallery installations and non-figurative painting.

While these intertextual references may serve, in part, to place the New Wave directors within an 'official' history of the arts, the filmmakers also show an interest in the necessary interpenetration of public and private histories. Godard recounts not just the narrative of cinema found in history books but also the hidden stories of desire driving key filmmakers and the private tragedies of unrealized works. Rohmer relates one of the most famous and significant episodes in all of French history from the exclusive perspective of one woman, herself an outsider to the extent that she is not even French. Varda points to historical continuities in the everyday practices of the poor in France, but she does so through warm personal encounters with ordinary people. The mixture of 'public' and 'private' histories, however, gives the impression that, even in films like *Histoire(s) du cinéma* and *L'Anglaise et le Duc* that appear to have serious historiographical aspirations, there is always something much more personal at stake.

These films are unlikely to be taken seriously as works of history by professional historians because of the type of historiography they present. Both Godard and Rohmer favour historiographical narratives that, in giving a recognizable shape to events, tend to simplify the process of historical causality. *Histoire(s) du cinéma*, for all the complexity of its granular detail, ultimately presents a rise-and-fall narrative of film history. Meanwhile, Rohmer, a self-confessed believer in the theory of historical cycles, offers a vision of the Revolution as the end of an era of classical civilization and the beginning of an implied new barbarism. While it would do a disservice to the intricacy and sophistication of their films to do so, both directors could arguably be labelled as reactionary in these historical works: Godard for his Eurocentric account of cinema and Rohmer for his apparent monarchism. The political and countercultural ferment of the late 1960s and 1970s may have had a long hangover in French film culture, but, by the end of the century, there were some signs that Godard and Rohmer, at least, may have been drifting back to the right-wing anarchism that various observers identified in the work of the early New Wave. A key reference point here is the contested legacy of the Second World War that continues to make its presence felt in this late work. The war, and in particular the Holocaust, is the pivotal point around which Godard's history of cinema turns, while Rohmer's evocation of the Revolution has been seen by some as a sort of displacement of another time of terror during the Occupation. This traumatic episode of France's past, during which the New Wave filmmakers came of age as teenagers or young men, tends to be the unsurpassable horizon of all their historical enquiry.

It may be partly this darkness in the past that is responsible for a certain mood of melancholy that is persistent throughout Godard's late work but perceptible too in *L'Anglaise et le Duc*. If it would be excessive to call these films nostalgic, there is sometimes a sense of regret for vanished cultural contexts and a heightened attunement to missed opportunities. We must inevitably relate these sentiments to the directors' own ageing: Godard turned seventy in the year 2000 and Rohmer eighty, with Varda passing her seventieth birthday a couple of years earlier. While Godard's impending mortality is implicit throughout *Histoire(s) du cinéma*, with its obsessive focus on endings and late works, it is only Varda who addresses her ageing directly on screen and it is perhaps significant that, of the three, she comes across as by far the most open, optimistic and engaged with the contemporary world. Both Godard and Varda display an interest in archiving and its more pathological form of hoarding. A project like Litnianski's *Jardin des merveilles* marks the grey area where artistic ambition shades into unhealthy obsession or even mental illness; and, for all the wondrous architecture of its completed form, there is perhaps something of the mad compulsion about *Histoire(s) du cinéma*, Godard's massive collection of cinematic memories built up over two decades. The already mentioned tendency of all three directors to cite or evoke their own works in more or less explicit ways also suggests a preoccupation with the shape of their oeuvre as it nears its completion, a concern, in other words, for legacy.

It is intriguing, finally, to reflect on the nature of this legacy for these three directors by considering the changing shape and perception of their careers over their decades in filmmaking. Éric Rohmer, having taken the longest to establish himself unequivocally as a full-time filmmaker, ironically ended up with perhaps the most stable and traditional career. For four decades, from the late 1960s until 2007, he reliably released a feature film every couple of years, the majority of them produced on the same model and following a broadly similar aesthetic and narrative formula attracting a loyal if modest following. Jean-Luc Godard, on the other hand, having been one of the world's most prolific and controversial filmmakers in the early and mid-1960s, a director whose work was eagerly awaited by critics and cinephiles for news not just of the future of film form but of French society itself, never fully recovered his high profile after abandoning mainstream filmmaking in 1968. Godard's films have become increasingly abstruse and recondite, and casual observers can be forgiven for seeing him as a cantankerous old hermit who is effectively talking to himself in his work. In this context, the multiple formats of *Histoire(s) du cinéma*, and especially the expensive art books published by Gallimard, risk coming across as a particularly self-conscious and anxious concern for legacy.

This seems unfortunately inconsistent given Godard's frequently radical rhetoric over intellectual property in the arts and is anyway unnecessary in light of the singular richness of his film. By contrast, it is Agnès Varda who seems to have made the most successful transition to a post-cinematic world (i.e. to a world in which theatrical distribution no longer dominates the culture of audiovisual production). Writing in 1991, René Prédal described Varda as a marginal figure in French cinema, suggesting that she was 'rediscovered' by the viewing public approximately once per decade (to wit: *Cléo de 5 à 7*, *L'Une chante, l'autre pas*, *Sans toit ni loi*, *Jacquot de Nantes* ...) while the rest of her work, much of it in short- and medium-length formats, remained largely invisible.[247] On the contrary, however, Varda must now be seen as one of the most central figures in French cinema since the Second World War. Indeed, Phil Powrie, when preparing his four-volume anthology of scholarship on French cinema, noted that Varda and Godard were the two most ubiquitous objects of enquiry over four decades of academic research.[248] As a pioneer of women's filmmaking in France, Varda's work has obviously benefited in terms of exposure from the generalized uptake of a feminist agenda and discourse across the academic study of the humanities. At the same time, however, Varda's preference for unconventional formats has been well suited to successive revolutions in film distribution. Her many short films, documentaries and diaristic asides were ideally suited as DVD extras before they became uploadable to YouTube. Her company Ciné Tamaris has taken advantage of this context by releasing a compendium of shorts, *Varda tous courts* (Ciné Tamaris, 2007), and, more recently, a career retrospective, *Tout Varda* (Ciné Tamaris/ARTE, 2012). Lastly, the kind of openness and curiosity we found in *Les Glaneurs et la Glaneuse* – the willingness to engage more or less directly with her audience – can only have been beneficial for Varda's profile in a media-saturated era in which promotion and public relations have never been more important.

Notes

1 Georges Didi-Huberman, *Passés cités par JLG: L'oeil de l'histoire*, 5 (Paris: Minuit, 2015), 123.
2 For a thorough account of this production history, see Michael Witt, *Jean-Luc Godard, Cinema Historian* (Bloomington: Indiana University Press, 2013), in particular chapter 1, '*Histoire(s) du cinéma*: A History', 10–44.
3 Jean-Luc Godard, *Histoire(s) du cinéma*, 4 vols (Paris: Gallimard, 1998).
4 Didi-Huberman, *Passés cités par JLG*, 149. Godard has suggested that the books will 'last longer' than the films, although this strikes me as disingenuous or misguided: despite the best efforts of critics to present Godard as a multimedia artist, he remains best known as a filmmaker, and, with the rapidly expanding digitization of film history's archives, the video version of *Histoire(s) du cinéma* is likely to be more accessible over the coming years than an out-of-print art book whose value relies heavily on the quality of its paper and the resolution of its images. Godard makes the comment about the longevity of the book in Jean-Luc Godard and Youssef Ishaghpour, *Archéologie du cinéma et mémoire du siècle: Dialogue* (Tours: Farrago, 2000), 39.
5 It is beyond the scope of this chapter to provide a survey of this literature. The most authoritative work, by some distance, is Witt's *Jean-Luc Godard, Cinema Historian*, which also contains the most thorough bibliography of books and articles related to *Histoire(s) du cinéma*.
6 'But to retrace your steps to heaven's air / There is the trouble, there is the toil.' Virgil, *The Aeneid*, trans. by Robert Fitzgerald (London: Harvill, 1993), 164.
7 Jean-Louis Leutrat, 'Retour sur *Histoire(s)*, 4', *Trafic* 73 (Spring 2010), 78–9. The idea of a descent into hell is also implied through recurring references to the Orpheus legend. On this cluster of imagery in *Histoire(s)*, see Jacques Aumont, *Amnésies: Fictions du cinéma d'après Jean-Luc Godard* (Paris: P.O.L., 1999), 33–66.

8   Antoine de Baecque, 'Entretien avec François Furet à propos des *Histoire(s)* de Godard', in *Feu sur le quartier général! Le cinéma traversé: Textes, entretiens, récits* (Paris: Cahiers du cinéma, 2008), 164.
9   Godard and Ishaghpour, *Archéologie du cinéma et mémoire du siècle*, 23.
10 Witt, *Jean-Luc Godard, Cinema Historian*, 156.
11 Daniel Morgan, *Late Godard and the Possibilities of Cinema* (Berkeley: University of California Press, 2013), 227.
12 On this point, see Douglas Morrey, *Jean-Luc Godard* (Manchester: Manchester University Press, 2005), 23–4.
13 Aumont, *Amnésies*, 151 and 34.
14 Morgan, *Late Godard*, 5.
15 Didi-Huberman, *Passés cités par JLG*, 57–8.
16 Jean-Luc Godard, 'C'est le cinéma qui raconte l'histoire: Lui seul le pouvait', *Le Monde*, 8 October 1998.
17 Michael Witt, 'Archaeology of *Histoire(s) du cinéma*', in Jean-Luc Godard, *Introduction to a True History of Cinema and Television*, trans. by Timothy Barnard (Montreal: Caboose, 2014), xxxiii.
18 Godard's *Introduction to a True History of Cinema and Television* is a transcription of these lectures. It was originally published in French as *Introduction à une véritable histoire du cinéma* (Paris: Albatros, 1980).
19 Jean-Marc Lalanne, 'Toutes les histoires. 1A', *Cahiers du cinéma*, Special issue *Histoire(s) du cinéma*, supplement to no. 537 (July–August 1999), 6.
20 Jonathan Rosenbaum notes that an important early montage in *Histoire(s)* 1A combines 'three very different versions of [...] hypnotic persuasion': the image track intercuts the diabolical temptation from *Faust* (Murnau, 1926) with a seductive dance from *The Band Wagon* (Minnelli, 1953), while, on the soundtrack, the male protagonist of *L'Année dernière à Marienbad* (Resnais, 1961) seeks to remind his female interlocutor of events that may or may not have happened the previous year. See Rosenbaum, 'Trailer for Godard's *Histoire(s) du cinéma*', *Vertigo* 1: 7 (1997), available at: https://www.closeupfilmcentre.com/vertigo_magazine/volume-1-issue-7-autumn-1997/trailer-for-godard-s-histoire-s-du-cinema/, accessed May 2018.
21 James S. Williams, 'The Signs amongst Us: Jean-Luc Godard's *Histoire(s) du cinéma*', *Screen* 40: 3 (1999), 312.
22 Aumont, *Amnésies*, 11.
23 Ibid., 35.
24 Cecilia Sayad, *Performing Authorship: Self-Inscription and Corporeality in the Cinema* (London: I. B. Tauris, 2013), 19.
25 Lalanne, 'Toutes les histoires', 6.
26 For more extensive commentaries on chapter 1A, 'Toutes les histoires', consult Leutrat, 'Retour sur *Histoire(s)*, 4', and Douglas Morrey, *Jean-Luc Godard and the Other History of Cinema*, unpublished PhD thesis, University of

Warwick, 2002, 16–60, available at: http://wrap.warwick.ac.uk/1303/ accessed August 2016.

27 On the use of titles as a kind of running commentary throughout the early chapters of *Histoire(s) du cinéma*, see Roland-François Lack, 'Sa voix', in *For Ever Godard*, ed. Michael Temple, James S. Williams and Michael Witt (London: Black Dog, 2004), 320–2.

28 The 's' on *Histoire(s)* of course implies this sense of both (official) history and (private or personal) stories. Another good example from 1A is the evocation of Max Ophuls's abandoned film adaptation of *L'École des femmes* in 1940, stymied both by the Nazi invasion of France and by star Louis Jouvet's indignation when he learned of an affair between his wife and co-star Madeleine Ozeray and Ophuls.

29 For an account of the life and career of Irving Thalberg, see Roland Flamini, *Thalberg: The Last Tycoon and the World of M-G-M* (London: André Deutsch, 1994).

30 On the more sordid aspects of Hughes's reputation, see Charles Higham, *Howard Hughes: The Secret Life* (London: Sidgwick and Jackson, 1993).

31 The most detailed and authoritative biography of Godard, for more information on all of these points, is Antoine de Baecque, *Godard: Biographie* (Paris: Grasset, 2010).

32 Timings relate to the 2007 Gaumont DVD edition.

33 Lack, 'Sa voix', 325.

34 Literally 'Paths that lead nowhere', *Chemins qui ne mènent nulle part* is the French title given to a translation of Martin Heidegger's essays originally entitled *Holzwege* (1950). The translation, by Wolfgang Brokmeier, was published by Gallimard in 1962.

35 See Jean-Louis Jeannelle, *Films sans images: Une histoire des scénarios non réalisés de La Condition humaine* (Paris: Seuil, 2015).

36 For an account of the troubled production and post-production of *King Lear*, see de Baecque, *Godard*, 661–72.

37 'J'étais un combattant; maintenant je suis un fonctionnaire.'

38 The punning title translates as 'A new wave', but also as 'A vague piece of news', appropriately given Godard's somewhat indirect evocation of the French film movement.

39 Demy is also present on the soundtrack of 1B via the song 'Je souviendrai' from *Les Parapluies de Cherbourg* (1964). Among other filmmakers associated with the French New Wave, Alain Resnais appears via a prominent citation of the soundtrack of *L'Année dernière à Marienbad* (1961) in 1A and again in 4A plus a textual evocation of *Hiroshima mon amour* (1959) in 4B and various archival images of the Holocaust borrowed from *Nuit et brouillard* (1956); the director's illustrious later career is not mentioned. There are also a couple of clips from political documentaries by Chris Marker: *Le Fond de l'air est rouge* (1977, in 4A) and *Le Tombeau d'Alexandre* (1993, in 3B and 4A). Jean-Pierre Mocky sees his little known

1983 film, *La Machine à découdre*, cited in 3B; this seems to be another example where a scene is used for its content (here, violent sexual assault) more than its mise en scène or its provenance.

40 Godard and Ishaghpour, *Archéologie du cinéma et mémoire du siècle*, 28.
41 Chris Darke's monograph, *Alphaville* (London: I. B. Tauris, 2005), is good on this sense of Godard's film as a kind of living history lesson.
42 Note, again, that Godard chooses to illustrate the New Wave's allegedly dissolute lifestyle with images not from their own films but from those of directors admired by the generation of critics who launched the Nouvelle Vague.
43 See, for instance, Aumont, *Amnésies*, 200.
44 Richard Neer, 'Godard Counts', *Critical Inquiry* 34: 1 (2007), 161.
45 James Tweedie reads these latter two examples as new waves on the model of the Nouvelle Vague in *The Age of New Waves: Art Cinema and the Staging of Globalization* (Oxford: Oxford University Press, 2013).
46 Morgan, *Late Godard*, 171–2.
47 Ibid., 228.
48 Ibid., 196 and see F. R. Leavis, *The Great Tradition: George Eliot, Henry James, Joseph Conrad* (London: Chatto and Windus, 1979), 1.
49 Aumont, *Amnésies*, 115.
50 Jacques Rancière, 'The Saint and the Heiress: A Propos of Godard's *Histoire(s) du cinéma*', trans. by T. S. Murphy, *Discourse* 24: 1 (2002), 114. Originally published as 'La Sainte et l'héritière: À propos des *Histoire(s) du cinéma*', *Cahiers du cinéma* 536 (July–August 1999), 58.
51 Rancière, 'The Saint and the Heiress', 115 ('La Sainte et l'héritière', 59).
52 Didi-Huberman, *Passés cités par JLG*, 75.
53 Ibid., 76. For a detailed discussion of this point, see Witt's chapter on 'Models and guides', *Jean-Luc Godard, Cinema Historian*, 69–111.
54 Didi-Huberman, *Passés cités par JLG*, 151. Michael Temple, who develops a detailed comparison between *Histoire(s) du cinéma* and Malraux's *Les Voix du silence* (1947–65), quotes Maurice Blanchot's criticism of Malraux implying its pertinence for Godard: 'It is true that the ideas he develops have their whims: they are peremptory, sudden, they remain unresolved. They disappear and return. And since they often affirm themselves in formulas they find pleasing, they seem to think themselves thereby defined, and this achievement satisfies them.' See Michael Temple, 'Big Rhythm and the Power of Metamorphosis: Some Models and Precursors for *Histoire(s) du cinéma*', in *The Cinema Alone: Essays on the Work of Jean-Luc Godard 1985–2000*, ed. Michael Temple and James S. Williams (Amsterdam: Amsterdam University Press, 2000), 77.
55 Monica Dall'Asta, 'The (Im)possible History', in *For Ever Godard*, ed. Michael Temple, James S. Williams and Michael Witt (London: Black Dog, 2004), 354.

56 Temple, 'Big Rhythm and the Power of Metamorphosis', 81. Temple also points out that another of Godard's key influences, Élie Faure, whose *Histoire de l'art* (1919–21) is borrowed at length in *Histoire(s)* 4A, is 'virtually non-existent as far as professional art historians are concerned', ibid., 86.
57 Didi-Huberman, *Passés cités par JLG*, 84.
58 Neer, 'Godard Counts', 136.
59 Lalanne, 'Toutes les histoires', 6.
60 James S. Williams, 'European Culture and Artistic Resistance in *Histoire(s) du cinéma* chapter 3A, *La Monnaie de l'absolu*', in *The Cinema Alone: Essays on the Work of Jean-Luc Godard 1985–2000*, ed. Michael Temple and James S. Williams (Amsterdam: Amsterdam University Press, 2000), 113–139 (136).
61 'Le Contrôle de l'univers' is the title of chapter 4A of *Histoire(s)*. On Godard's use of the Universal Pictures logo as a symbol for the totalizing ambitions of Hollywood, see Morrey, *Jean-Luc Godard and the Other History of Cinema*, 115–20.
62 Morgan, *Late Godard*, 215.
63 Aumont, *Amnésies*, 98.
64 Jacques Rancière, *The Future of the Image*, trans.by Gregory Elliott (London: Verso, 2009), 60. Originally published as *Le Destin des images* (Paris: La Fabrique, 2003), 70.
65 Neer, 'Godard Counts', 148.
66 Aumont makes this point in *Amnésies*, 125–6. The notion of obviousness is probably best developed in the critical writing of Jacques Rivette, notably 'Génie de Howard Hawks', *Cahiers du cinéma* 23 (May 1953), 16–23, translated as 'The Genius of Howard Hawks', in *Cahiers du cinéma, Vol 1: The 1950s: Neo-Realism, Hollywood, New Wave*, ed. Jim Hillier (London: Routledge and Kegan Paul, 1985), 126–31. For an analysis of this idea, see Douglas Morrey and Alison Smith, *Jacques Rivette* (Manchester: Manchester University Press, 2009), 11–13. and Douglas Morrey, 'The Lost Art of Keeping a Secret: Jacques Rivette's Film Criticism for *Arts*', *Film Criticism* 39: 1 (2014), 56–8.
67 Christian Keathley, *Cinephilia and History, or The Wind in the Trees* (Bloomington: Indiana University Press, 2006), 129.
68 See Aumont, *Amnésies*, 96.
69 Jacques Rancière, *La Fable cinématographique* (Paris: Seuil, 2001), 218–19. Translated as *Film Fables*, trans. by Emiliano Battista (Oxford: Berg, 2006), 172.
70 For a detailed analysis of this sequence, see Morrey, *Jean-Luc Godard and the Other History of Cinema*, 185–94.
71 In this, Godard is close to the well-known argument put forward by Siegfried Kracauer in *From Caligari to Hitler: A Psychological History of the German Film* (London: Dennis Dobson, 1947).
72 Rancière, 'The Saint and the Heiress', 116 ('La Sainte et l'héritière', 59).
73 Godard, *Histoire(s) du cinéma*, vol. 1, 90.

74 Robert Bresson, *Notes sur le cinématographe* (Paris: Gallimard Folio, 1975), 136.
75 Ibid., 22.
76 Dudley Andrew, *What Cinema Is! Bazin's Quest and Its Charge* (Chichester: Wiley-Blackwell, 2010), 38.
77 Godard, *Histoire(s) du cinéma*, vol. 3, 86.
78 Andrew, *What Cinema Is!*, 8.
79 Ibid., 9. See also Louis-Geogres Schwartz, 'Deconstruction *avant la lettre*: Derrida before André Bazin', in *Opening Bazin: Postwar Film Theory and Its Afterlife*, ed. Dudley Andrew (Oxford: Oxford University Press, 2010), 95–103.
80 Peter Brunette and David Wills, *Screen/Play: Derrida and Film Theory* (Princeton: Princeton University Press, 1989), 68.
81 Aumont, *Amnésies*, 125.
82 Keathley, *Cinephilia and History*, 53.
83 Rancière, *The Future of the Image*, 34; *Le Destin des images*, 44.
84 Jean-Luc Godard, 'Montage, mon beau souci', in *Jean-Luc Godard par Jean-Luc Godard, tome 1, 1950–1984* (Paris: Cahiers du cinéma, 1998), 92, my translation.
85 For a detailed history of Godard's engagement with video, see Witt, *Jean-Luc Godard, Cinema Historian*, 51–8.
86 Alan Wright, 'Elizabeth Taylor at Auschwitz: JLG and the Real Object of Montage', in *The Cinema Alone: Essays on the Work of Jean-Luc Godard 1985–2000*, ed. Michael Temple and James S. Williams (Amsterdam: Amsterdam University Press, 2000), 58.
87 Jacques Aumont, *Que reste-t-il du cinéma?* (Paris: Vrin, 2012), 41–2.
88 Godard and Ishaghpour, *Archéologie du cinéma et mémoire du siècle*, 28.
89 See de Baecque, *Godard*, 676–7.
90 Godard and Ishaghpour, *Archéologie du cinéma et mémoire du siècle*, 31.
91 Morgan, *Late Godard*, 166.
92 This criticism is included, somewhat obliquely, in *Histoire(s) du cinéma* episode 3A, in which Godard makes a remark about 'the story of the battle of Baghdad as told by CNN' before adding the comment: 'The triumph of American television, and its groupies' as a list of onscreen titles identifies these "groupies" as CBS, TF1, RTL, ZDF, NBC, FR3 and RAI, the latter ultimately transforming into "REICH."' See Godard, *Histoire(s) du cinéma*, vol. 3, 36–7.
93 Morgan, *Late Godard*, 166.
94 Godard, *Histoire(s) du cinéma*, vol. 4, 276. The reference is to Charles Péguy, *Clio: Dialogue de l'histoire et de l'âme païenne*, in *Œuvres en prose 1909–1914* (Paris: Gallimard Pléiade, 1961), 240.
95 Godard, *Introduction to a True History of Cinema*, 135.

96 On the role of melancholy in *Histoire(s) du cinéma*, see Aumont, *Amnésies*, 175–208.
97 For an account of this troubled production, see Antoine de Baecque and Noël Herpe, *Éric Rohmer: Biographie* (Paris: Stock, 2014), 71–9.
98 Ibid., 430.
99 Ibid., 443.
100 Ibid., 434.
101 Éric Rohmer, 'J'ai voulu faire mieux que les Américains', *Le Nouvel Observateur*, 30 August 2001.
102 Éric Rohmer, 'La Révolution numérique', *Les Inrockuptibles*, 4 September 2001.
103 Éric Rohmer, 'Le Large et le haut', *Cahiers du cinéma* 559 (July–August 2001), 59.
104 Noël Herpe and Cyril Neyrat, 'Interview with Éric Rohmer: Video Is Becoming Increasingly Important', in *Éric Rohmer: Interviews*, ed. Fiona Handyside (Jackson: University of Mississippi Press, 2013), 169.
105 Tom Gunning, 'Éric Rohmer and the Legacy of Cinematic Realism', in *The Films of Éric Rohmer: French New Wave to Old Master*, ed. Leah Anderst (New York: Palgrave Macmillan, 2014), 23.
106 Éric Rohmer, 'La "Somme" d'André Bazin', in *Le Goût de la beauté* (Paris: Cahiers du cinéma/Éditions de l'Étoile, 1984), 104.
107 Gunning, 'Éric Rohmer and the Legacy of Cinematic Realism', 25–6.
108 Éric Rohmer, 'Vanité que la peinture', in *Le Goût de la beauté*, 54.
109 Gunning's article cited above is a good example of this trend. Andrew's *What Cinema Is!* is another.
110 Rohmer, 'Vanité que la peinture', 55–6.
111 Éric Rohmer, 'Nous n'aimons plus le cinéma', in *Le Goût de la beauté*, 46.
112 Éric Rohmer, 'Réflexions sur la couleur', in *Le Goût de la beauté*, 48.
113 Éric Rohmer, *Le Celluloïd et le marbre, suivi d'un entretien inédit avec Noël Herpe et Philippe Fauvel* (Paris: Éditions Léo Scheer, 2010), 21.
114 Éric Rohmer, 'De trois films et d'une certaine école', in *Le Goût de la beauté*, 70.
115 Éric Rohmer, 'Le Goût de la beauté', in *Le Goût de la beauté*, 84.
116 Gunning, 'Éric Rohmer and the Legacy of Cinematic Realism', 24–5.
117 Éric Rohmer, 'Le Temps de la critique', in *Le Goût de la beauté*, 15.
118 See, for instance, Serge Kaganski, 'L'Anglaise et le continent', *Les Inrockuptibles*, 4 September 2001.
119 François Truffaut, 'A Certain Tendency of the French Cinema', in *Movies and Methods: An Anthology*, ed. Bill Nicholls (Berkeley: University of California Press, 1976), 224–37. First published as 'Une certaine tendance du cinéma français', *Cahiers du cinéma* 31 (January 1954), 15–29.

120 For one detailed study of the New Wave directors' engagement with period adaptation, see Zahra T. Zea, *La Bande des quatre: Late Nineteenth-Century Literary and Artistic Sources in Late Nouvelle Vague Filmmaking*, unpublished PhD thesis, University of Kent, 2016.

121 Gilbert Adair, 'Rohmer's *Perceval*', in *Éric Rohmer: Interviews*, ed. Fiona Handyside (Jackson: University of Mississippi Press, 2013), 44.

122 Éric Rohmer, 'Je voulais que la réalité devienne tableau', *Cahiers du cinéma* 559 (July–August 2001), 54.

123 See François Amy de la Brétèque, 'Éric Rohmer et son rapport à l'Histoire en particulier dans ses "tragédies de l'histoire"', in *Rohmer en perspectives*, ed. Sylvie Robic and Laurence Schifano (Paris: Presses Universitaires de Paris Ouest, 2013), 59. See also Marc Fumaroli, 'Cinéma et Terreur', *Cahiers du cinéma* 559 (July–August 2001), 44.

124 Charles Tesson, 'La Révolution selon Rohmer', *Cahiers du cinéma* 559 (July–August 2001), 41.

125 Jerry W. Carlson, 'Éric Rohmer, Historiographer', in *The Films of Éric Rohmer: French New Wave to Old Master*, ed. Leah Anderst (New York: Palgrave Macmillan, 2014), 210.

126 Ibid., 208.

127 Florence Bernard de Courville, '*L'Anglaise et le Duc*: Le réel et le tableau', in *Rohmer et les autres*, ed. Noël Herpe (Rennes: Presses Universitaires de Rennes, 2007), 170.

128 Ibid., 176.

129 Ibid., 175.

130 Aurélien Ferenzi (sic), 'Interview with Éric Rohmer', in *Éric Rohmer: Interviews*, ed. Fiona Handyside (Jackson: University Press of Mississippi, 2013), 143.

131 Éric Rohmer, 'Éric Rohmer sous le signe du Lion', *Le Figaro*, 7 September 2001.

132 Rohmer, 'Le Temps de la critique', 14–15.

133 See Rohmer, 'Nous n'aimons plus le cinéma', 41–2, and Rohmer, 'Roberto Rossellini: *Stromboli*', in *Le Goût de la beauté*, 135–6.

134 Rohmer, 'Le Temps de la critique', 14.

135 Tom Gunning, 'The Cinema of Attraction: Early Film, Its Spectator, and the Avant-Garde', *Wide Angle* 8: 3–4 (1986), 63–70.

136 Annie Coppermann, 'La Terreur dans le boudoir', *Les Échos*, 6 September 2001.

137 Michel Boujut, 'Le boudoir de Rohmer', *Charlie Hebdo*, 12 September 2001.

138 Philippe Petit, 'Le film qui enterre 1789', *Marianne*, 3 September 2001.

139 Rohmer, 'Je voulais que la réalité devienne tableau', 53.

140 François Gorin and Marc Cerisuelo, 'Conte de la Terreur ordinaire', *Télérama*, 5 September 2001.

141 Jean Tulard, 'Une cruauté extraordinaire', *Le Figaro*, 12 September 2001.
142 See Fumaroli, 'Cinéma et Terreur', 43.
143 Jean-François Kahn, 'L'aveu de la haine du peuple', *Marianne*, 3 September 2001.
144 Sophie Guichard, 'Je l'aime, moi non plus', *France-Soir*, 11 September 2001.
145 Jean-Pierre Jeancolas, quoted in de Baecque and Herpe, *Éric Rohmer*, 445. First published in *Politis*, 6 September 2001.
146 Gorin and Cerisuelo, 'Conte de la Terreur ordinaire'.
147 Rohmer, 'La Révolution numérique'.
148 Jean-Michel Frodon, 'Dans le regard d'une belle étrangère, un monde s'effondre', *Le Monde*, 5 September 2001. Michel Boujut makes the same point in 'Le boudoir de Rohmer'.
149 Gorin and Cerisuelo, 'Conte de la Terreur ordinaire'.
150 Jacques de Saint Victor, 'Ce sang était-il donc si impur?' *Le Figaro*, 12 September 2001.
151 Gorin and Cerisuelo, 'Conte de la Terreur ordinaire'.
152 Rohmer, *Le Celluloïd et le marbre*, 61.
153 de Baecque and Herpe, *Éric Rohmer*, 85.
154 Jean Parvulesco, quoted in Antoine de Baecque, 'Rohmer/Politics: From Royalism to Ecology', in *The Films of Éric Rohmer: French New Wave to Old Master*, ed. Leah Anderst (New York: Palgrave Macmillan, 2014), 126.
155 Ferenzi, 'Interview with Éric Rohmer', 141–2.
156 Rohmer, 'Je voulais que la réalité devienne tableau', 58.
157 Derek Schilling, *Éric Rohmer* (Manchester: Manchester University Press, 2007), 173.
158 Tulard, 'Une cruauté extraordinaire'.
159 Rohmer, 'Je voulais que la réalité devienne tableau', 53.
160 Rohmer, 'Éric Rohmer sous le signe du Lion'.
161 Rohmer, 'Je voulais que la réalité devienne tableau', 53.
162 Rohmer, 'Éric Rohmer sous le signe du Lion'.
163 Francis Vanoye, *L'Emprise du cinéma* (Lyon: Aléas, 2005), 232.
164 Fumaroli, 'Cinéma et Terreur', 43.
165 Jacob Leigh, *The Cinema of Éric Rohmer: Irony, Imagination, and the Social World* (New York: Continuum, 2012), 227.
166 Ferenzi, 'Interview with Éric Rohmer', 144.
167 Rohmer, 'Je voulais que la réalité devienne tableau', 54.
168 Leigh, *The Cinema of Éric Rohmer*, 229.
169 Rohmer, 'Je voulais que la réalité devienne tableau', 53.
170 Ibid.

171 Ibid.
172 de Baecque and Herpe, *Éric Rohmer*, 427.
173 Danièle Heymann, 'La Révolution sur le visage d'une femme', *Marianne*, 3 September 2001.
174 Marie-Noëlle Tranchant, 'Révolution sans convention', *Le Figaro*, 10 September 2001.
175 Marie-Laure Guétin, 'Des décors révolutionnés: Le Pari(s) historique d'Éric Rohmer', in *Rohmer en perspectives*, ed. Sylvie Robic and Laurence Schifano (Paris: Presses Universitaires de Paris Ouest, 2013), 71.
176 Éric Rohmer, 'Le Cinéma, art de l'espace', in *Le Goût de la beauté*, 27–35, first published in *La Revue du cinéma* 14 (June 1948).
177 de Baecque and Herpe, *Éric Rohmer*, 45.
178 Published as Éric Rohmer, *L'Organisation de l'espace dans le Faust de Murnau* (Paris: Cahiers du cinéma/Éditions de l'Étoile, 2000).
179 Rohmer, 'Le Cinéma, art de l'espace', 29.
180 Rohmer, 'Je voulais que la réalité devienne tableau', 50.
181 Rohmer, 'J'ai voulu faire mieux que les Américains'.
182 Rohmer, 'Je voulais que la réalité devienne tableau', 52.
183 Ferenzi, 'Interview with Éric Rohmer', 140.
184 See also, on this point, Charles Tesson, 'Sueurs froides', *Cahiers du cinéma* 559 (July–August 2001), 48.
185 Frodon, 'Dans le regard d'une belle étrangère, un monde s'effondre'.
186 Keith Tester, *Éric Rohmer: Film as Theology* (Basingstoke: Palgrave Macmillan, 2008), 38. Tester talks about a change of angle revealing a crucifix above Grace's bed in the latter part of the film. In fact, this is a different bed in a different house (in Meudon, rather than Paris).
187 Schilling, *Éric Rohmer*, 176.
188 Charles Tesson stresses this aspect of the film in 'Sueurs froides'.
189 Gorin and Cerisuelo, 'Conte de la Terreur ordinaire'.
190 Éric Rohmer, 'J'aurais pu être beaucoup plus violent', *Libération*, 7 September 2001.
191 Jean Roy, 'Votons pour la grâce d'Éric Rohmer', *L'Humanité*, 7 September 2001.
192 Charles Tesson, 'Le cou de Grace', *Cahiers du cinéma* 559 (July–August 2001), 48.
193 Pierre-Jean Larroque, 'Le tissu déchiré de l'Histoire', in *Rohmer et les autres*, ed. Noël Herpe (Rennes: Presses Universitaires de Rennes, 2007), 214.
194 de Baecque and Herpe, *Éric Rohmer*, 454.
195 Melissa Anderson, 'The Modest Gesture of the Filmmaker: An Interview with Agnès Varda', *Cineaste* 26: 4 (2001), 26.
196 Ibid., 25–6.

197 Agnès Varda, 'Agnès Varda, glaneuse sachant glaner', *Le Monde/Aden*, 5 July 2000.
198 Kelley Conway, *Agnès Varda* (Urbana: University of Illinois Press, 2015), 85–6.
199 Élisabeth Lequeret, 'Le bel été de la Glaneuse', *Cahiers du cinéma* 550 (October 2000), 32–3.
200 Chris Darke, 'Refuseniks', *Sight & Sound* 11: 1 (January 2001), 32.
201 Agnès Calatayud, 'The Self-Portrait in French Cinema: Reflections on Theory and on Agnès Varda's *Les Glaneurs et la Glaneuse*', in *Textual and Visual Selves: Photography, Film and Comic Art in French Autobiography*, ed. Natalie Edwards, Amy Hubbell and Ann Miller (Lincoln, NE: University of Nebraska Press, 2011), 217.
202 Frédéric Bonnaud, '*Les Glaneurs et la Glaneuse*', *Les Inrockuptibles*, 23 May 2000.
203 Jake Wilson, 'Trash and Treasure: *The Gleaners and I*', *Senses of Cinema* 23 (2002).
204 Martin O'Shaughnessy, 'Post-1995 French Cinema: Return of the Social, Return of the Political', *Modern and Contemporary France* 11: 2 (2003), 193.
205 Serge Kaganski, 'Ciné brocante', *Les Inrockuptibles*, 4 July 2000.
206 Wilson, 'Trash and Treasure'.
207 Surrealism has had a very long resonance in French culture, the parameters of which are far beyond the scope of this chapter. The interested reader might begin by consulting Krzysztof Fijalkowski and Michael Richardson (eds), *Surrealism: Key Concepts* (London: Routledge, 2016).
208 Homay King, 'Matter, Time, and the Digital: Varda's *The Gleaners and I*', *Quarterly Review of Film and Video* 24: 5 (2007), 427.
209 S. D. Chrostowska, 'Vis-à-vis the glaneuse', *Angelaki: Journal of the Theoretical Humanities* 12: 2 (2007), 123.
210 Ibid., 128.
211 O'Shaughnessy, 'Post-1995 French Cinema', 193.
212 Nathalie Rachlin, 'L'exclusion au cinéma: Le cas d'Agnès Varda', *Women in French Studies*, special issue (2006), 94.
213 Virginia Bonner, 'The Gleaners and "Us": The Radical Modesty of Agnès Varda's *Les Glaneurs et la Glaneuse*', in *There She Goes: Feminist Filmmaking and Beyond*, ed. Corinn Columpar and Sophie Mayer (Detroit: Wayne State University Press, 2009), 126.
214 Ibid.
215 Rachlin, 'L'exclusion au cinéma', 97.
216 Virginia Bonner, 'Beautiful Trash: Agnès Varda's *Les Glaneurs et la Glaneuse*', *Senses of Cinema* 45 (2007).
217 Varda quoted in Ruth Cruickshank, 'The Work of Art in the Age of Global Consumption: Agnès Varda's *Les Glaneurs et la Glaneuse*', *L'Esprit créateur* 47: 3 (2007), 130.

218 Florence Assouline, 'Agnès Varda ne filme que les restes', *L'Événement*, 6 July 2000.
219 Domietta Torlasco, 'Digital Impressions: Writing Memory after Agnès Varda', *Discourse* 33: 3 (2011), 393.
220 Domietta Torlasco, 'Against House Arrest: Digital Memory and the Impossible Archive', *Camera Obscura* 26: 1 [76] (2011), 52.
221 Ibid., 53.
222 Ben Tyrer, 'Digression and Return: Aesthetics and Politics in Agnès Varda's *Les Glaneurs et la Glaneuse*', *Studies in French Cinema* 9: 2 (2009), 174.
223 Bonnaud, '*Les Glaneurs et la Glaneuse*'.
224 Calatayud, 'The Self-Portrait in French Cinema', 223.
225 Jacques Mandelbaum, 'Biens sans maître glanés par maîtres sans bien', *Le Monde*, 5 July 2000.
226 Varda, in Anderson, 'The Modest Gesture of the Filmmaker', 24.
227 See Mireille Rosello, 'Agnès Varda's *Les Glaneurs et la Glaneuse*: Portrait of the Artist as an Old Lady', *Studies in French Cinema* 1: 1 (2001), 33.
228 'Quand on est dans son vieillissement, on va vers son propre déchet.' Agnès Varda, 'Interview', *Les Inrockuptibles*, 4 July 2000.
229 Lucy Fischer, 'Generic Gleaning: Agnès Varda, Documentary, and the Art of Salvage', in *Gender Meets Genre in Postwar Cinema*, ed. Christine Gledhill (Urbana: University of Illinois Press, 2012), 115.
230 Rosello, 'Agnès Varda's *Les Glaneurs et la Glaneuse*', 34.
231 Varda, 'Interview'.
232 Varda, quoted in Lequeret, 'Le bel été de la Glaneuse', 32.
233 Anne de Gasperi, 'La patate d'Agnès Varda', *Le Figaro*, 16 May 2000.
234 Kaganski, 'Ciné brocante'.
235 Bonner, 'The Gleaners and "Us"', 126.
236 Ibid., 127–8.
237 Anderson, 'The Modest Gesture of the Filmmaker', 25.
238 Ibid.
239 Sandy Flitterman-Lewis, 'Varda: The Gleaner and the Just', in *Situating the Feminist Gaze and Spectatorship in Postwar Cinema*, ed. Marcelline Block (Newcastle-upon-Tyne: Cambridge Scholars Press, 2008), 219.
240 Bonner, 'The Gleaners and "Us"', 120.
241 Mandelbaum, 'Biens sans maître glanés par maîtres sans bien'.
242 Rebecca J. DeRoo, *Agnès Varda: Between Film, Photography, and Art* (Berkeley: University of California Press, 2018), 17.
243 On this point, see the pioneering work of Arlie Russell Hochschild, *The Managed Heart: Commercialization of Human Feeling* (Berkeley: University of California Press, 1983).
244 Morgan, *Late Godard*, 12.

245 Tesson, 'Sueurs froides', 49.
246 Noël Herpe, 'The Fall into Words: From *Contes des quatre saisons* to *L'Anglaise et le Duc*', in *The Films of Éric Rohmer: French New Wave to Old Master*, ed. Leah Anderst (New York: Palgrave Macmillan, 2014), 67.
247 René Prédal, 'Agnès Varda: Une oeuvre en marge du cinéma français', *Études cinématographiques* 179–186 (1991), 13–39.
248 Phil Powrie, 'General Introduction', in *French Cinema*, 4 vols, ed. Phil Powrie (London/New York: Routledge, 2014), vol. 1, 10, 12.

5

Contemporary Auteur Directors in France

Despite various recent developments – notably a growth in popular generic filmmaking following the broad model of Hollywood (action, horror, science fiction, romantic comedy) – 'French cinema' as a national body of production and as a critical concept no doubt remains most associated, in the minds of global film enthusiasts, with auteur cinema. The model of auteur cinema that shapes our thinking about film today stems, in large part, as this book has sought to demonstrate, from discourses and practices popularized by the generation of the New Wave. But what characterizes auteur cinema in France today? This final chapter considers the work of three of the most prolific and successful French directors currently recognized on the global stage. Both François Ozon and Christophe Honoré began their filmmaking careers around the turn of the twenty-first century, releasing their first features in 1998 (Ozon's *Sitcom*) and 2002 (Honoré's *Dix-sept fois Cécile Cassard*). Olivier Assayas has had a longer trajectory, directing films since the mid-1980s (*Désordre*, 1986, was his first feature), but only came to international prominence in the mid-to-late 1990s following *Irma Vep* (1996). Assayas is a difficult director to situate within the trends and movements of recent decades in French cinema. He was routinely included in accounts of the *jeune cinéma français* of the 1990s (discussed in Chapter 3), despite beginning his career a decade earlier than most of those filmmakers. His first features are contemporaries of the *cinéma du look*, yet he had no obvious affinities with that development. Indeed, Assayas told Rosanna Maule that he 'feels [...] he has no true interlocutors among his generation of film directors'.[1] It is for this reason that we have chosen, instead, to consider Assayas alongside Ozon and Honoré. This chapter suggests that what the three directors have in common is a tendency towards a highly referential (at times almost parodic) style in their early films, that is more or less clearly indebted to the New Wave depending on the individual director.

In each case, however, this intertextual flurry gives way to a more mature style with a distinctly international outlook.

Olivier Assayas

Irma Vep (1996), Olivier Assayas's sixth feature, was his first to find significant international success, perhaps because it appears more 'transnational' than French: much of the dialogue is in English and the film's star, Maggie Cheung, is Hong Kong Chinese, best known at the time from martial arts franchises. Assayas himself has commented that the (precarious) financial conditions in which the film was produced are familiar to independent filmmakers around the world except, ironically, in France.[2] *Irma Vep* reflects the fragmentation of cinema at the end of the twentieth century, its division into multiple special-interest genres, periods and national cinemas. The film includes clips from sources as diverse as *The Heroic Trio* (1993) by Johnnie To and *Classe de lutte* (1969) by the radical French filmmaking collective Groupe Medvedkine and ends with an homage to the scratched celluloid of experimental filmmakers like Stan Brakhage and Isidore Isou. However, in its central reflection on the silent serial *Les Vampires* (Louis Feuillade, 1915), the film suggests a kind of nostalgia for an era (no doubt fantasized) of unity in cinema, when a film star could serve as the vector for a whole population's desire.[3] In *Irma Vep*, Maggie Cheung, playing herself, dressed in a skintight catsuit like the heroine of *Les Vampires*, and the object of fantasy projections of characters and spectators alike, is thus, in the words of Brett Farmer, 'required to function [...] as nothing less than a figural representation of cinema itself'.[4] But, if she is able to do so at the end of the twentieth century, it is because she herself, as a Hong Kong Chinese, has 'a hybrid, complex and fragmented identity'.[5]

Taking its cue from Cheung, the film borrows from Hong Kong action cinema a taste for movement and acceleration – what *Cahiers du cinéma* called 'agitation, excitation, trépidation':[6] scenes often begin disorientingly in media res,[7] and Assayas has a taste also for scenes of arrival and departure (Maggie's arrival in Paris; the departure of the crew at the end of a day's shooting; Maggie and Zoé's [Nathalie Richard] arrival at a rave, followed by Maggie's immediate re-departure) that adds to the film's unsettled feel. *Cahiers du cinéma* went as far as to see in *Irma Vep* a 'genealogy of movement in the cinema'[8] or perhaps more properly, following Deleuze and Guattari[9] (an evident influence on Bouquet's article), a *geology*, since the film seems to present the history of film form as so many sedimented layers that can be scraped away, the restless movement of experimental film appearing as the unexpected missing link between the rhythms of silent cinema and the onward rush of contemporary action movies.[10]

For all its internationalism, however, *Irma Vep* is also determinedly in dialogue with French cinema and notably with the Nouvelle Vague. Indeed, the very fact of seeking to combine diverse cinematic traditions on screen in order to provide a kind of archaeological meta-commentary on the film's form is a practice thoroughly familiar from the New Wave work of, especially, Truffaut and Godard.

As Howard Hampton comments, however broad the intertextual references in *Irma Vep*, they are combined with 'a highly specific French sensibility/sensitivity'.[11] The film was made in the context of the French celebrations of cinema's centenary in 1995, and the central idea derives from an offer Assayas received to remake *Les Vampires* for television. The theme of the film can thus be summarized as 'how to (re)make images out of ones that already exist?'[12] This was already a key concern for the generation of the New Wave, but Assayas has been critical of that generation for positing themselves as already post-cinematic – arriving after the end of cinema – thereby disqualifying in advance the inevitable subsequent evolutions of film form.[13] For Assayas, the concern is with 'how to take a step beyond' cinematic forebears, 'albeit modest'.[14]

Still, commentators have seen plenty of evidence of the influence of the New Wave over *Irma Vep*. The production model of the film – a cheap and quite spontaneously made film (it was written in nine days and filmed in twenty-four [days]), made while trying to assemble funding for a longer, prestige production (*Les Destinées sentimentales*, 2000)[15] – is reminiscent of the New Wave and particularly the most prolific Godard of the mid-1960s. Like Godard but also Rivette and Varda, Assayas in interview claimed to have a 'literal phobia of writing, re-writing, of the finished screenplay [...] I feel like I'm stifling the impulse'.[16] Some critics saw Jean-Pierre Léaud's portrayal of René Vidal, the capricious, pretentious, somewhat autistic director of *Irma Vep*'s film-within-the-film, as a cruel nod to Godard ('He used to be very good', sneers Zoé, confirming what Maggie has heard). Vidal's unexplained disappearance from the film set, however, is more reminiscent of a famous story about Jacques Rivette in the 1970s,[17] a reference also evoked through the presence of Nathalie Richard and, in a supporting role, that of Bulle Ogier. Meanwhile, Assayas, like Godard, ended up marrying his leading lady, the film appearing in retrospect, like *Le Petit Soldat* (1961), as a kind of aggressive seduction tactic. The use of Léaud of course also evokes the spectre of François Truffaut, and Assayas has spoken of his trepidation at filming this actor uniquely impregnated by the spirit of cinematic modernity.[18] The film most commonly alluded to in reviews of *Irma Vep* was Truffaut's own paean to filmmaking, *La Nuit américaine* (1973).

In interview Assayas notes that the directors and critics of the New Wave were the bearers of a certain idea – or ideal – of cinema, but that they found it difficult to maintain this ideal in the face of the industry's exigencies.[19]

The problem with a dogmatic idea of cinema is that it can lead to either exhausted capitulation to the market or petrification into an unchanging style, stubbornly maintained with a contempt for the interests of the spectator.[20] It is certainly the case, in the fictional world of *Irma Vep*, that the male auteurs of the New Wave generation (both Vidal and his eventual replacement José Murano [Lou Castel]) are depicted as self-indulgent and out of touch. In the colourful words of Howard Hampton: 'They're a couple of slobbery mammals flailing miserably at the ends of their worn-out tethers.'[21] Something of this critique is perhaps also intended in the scene in which a young French journalist interviews Maggie Cheung, singing the praises of John Woo and dismissing French cinema as 'nombrilistic, you know? Cinema about your *nombril*'. He adds that French cinema can be defined as 'friends giving money to friends to make films nobody sees'. *Cahiers du cinéma* called this scene 'predictable and a little silly',[22] and Assayas has admitted that the satire is directed at himself as much as at other directors.[23] But it is perhaps ironic that the film's criticism of French cinema ends up reproducing some of what many might see as its worst faults: *Les Échos* noted that the film was full of 'knowing winks and private jokes' and found the whole thing 'rather gratuitous'.[24]

The suspicion among some critics that *Irma Vep* was little more than a superficial in-joke may have been sparked by Assayas's disregard for traditional character psychology. *Cahiers du cinéma* argued that the characters of *Irma Vep* were not the kind of psychological constructions we are used to seeing in the cinema. Assayas is no more interested in character psychology than he is in storytelling: what interests him, instead, is filming 'varied agitations, opposed intensities', in other words bodies moving according to different rhythms.[25] What the modish Deleuzian vocabulary of flows and intensities conceals here is a conception of mise en scène that is actually very familiar from the *Cahiers du cinéma* of the 1950s, in which mise en scène was already described (for instance by Rivette[26]) as the disposition and movement of bodies in space. Kent Jones, who has repeatedly stressed Assayas's skill as a rhythmic filmmaker, suggests that there is 'an overriding perception of people *as* action, beings who can be seen fully only when they're in motion'.[27] This raises the question, however, as to whether the continuity in French cinema is at the level of film style and filmmaking practices or simply of the discourse operative in *Cahiers du cinéma* and its imitators.[28]

The most striking and representative example of this 'non-psychological' style is the dreamlike scene in which Maggie dons her catsuit while in her hotel room then skulks around the hotel corridors, entering another guest's room and stealing a necklace that she proceeds to throw off the roof in a rainstorm. But, although the scene drew much critical approval, and merited a five-page commentary in *Cahiers du cinéma* itself, Assayas admits that it was 'boring' to film, that he finds it a 'mechanical' piece of 'filmed cinema' and that Maggie Cheung appears 'frigid' (*'frigorifiée'*) in it.[29] Indeed, characters in the film themselves observe this artificial quality to Cheung's Irma Vep: Zoé compares her to a plastic toy while Vidal, in his halting English, admits 'Irma's no flesh, no blood, she's just an *idee*'. Brett Farmer, meanwhile, suggests that the scene has 'the feel of an MTV video'.[30] The scene is the consequence of combined fetishistic – scopophilic and auditory – desires: the desire to film Maggie Cheung in a skintight catsuit; the desire to film the same on a rooftop in the rain, a noirish location par excellence; and the desire to construct a scene according to the spiraling art-rock architecture of Sonic Youth's 'Tunic (Song for Karen)'.[31] Vicki Callahan concurs that Maggie's function in the film seems 'to be the projection screen of every possible desire' such that she comes to be a kind of 'screen within a screen'.[32] But the result, if it gives spectatorial pleasure, affords little directorial satisfaction since it is oddly solipsistic: affording no real agency to the actress, it offers no chance for the development of a relationship on set.

Elsewhere in *Irma Vep*, by contrast, Assayas shows himself to be particularly open to the work of actors. Assayas only gives technical (as opposed to psychological) direction to actors, taking care not to 'spoil with words the intimate truth of what they might express'. He describes the director's role as creating the conditions – as he puts it 'the showcase' – in which an actor can take risks, give something truly intimate of herself to the role.[33] This is how Assayas sought to achieve the 'fusion' between Maggie Cheung the actress and Maggie Cheung the character in the film, a process rendered possible only through the use of long takes and mobile camerawork that can allow for improvisation on the part of the performers.[34] Cheung confirms that it was the lack of rehearsal or advance learning of her lines that allowed her to perform naturally, helped by the constant on-set improvisation of Léaud.[35]

Sils Maria (2014), made nearly twenty years later and one of Assayas's most critically acclaimed films, also a film about actors and acting, allows us to see the distance travelled by the director across his career. This film, even more explicitly than *Irma Vep*, is about different generations of artists and filmmakers. The successful actress Maria Enders (Juliette Binoche) came to fame twenty years previously playing the character Sigrid in a play in which she seduces and rejects an older woman, Helena. Now middle-aged, Enders is asked to take on the role of the older woman while an up-and-coming starlet (Chloe Grace Moretz) will play Sigrid. The majority of the film shows Maria discussing and rehearsing the new role with her personal assistant Valentine (Kristen Stewart). This plot, about the ceding of power and influence from one generation to another, is thus reflected in the casting. Assayas is clear that he wanted an American actress of the young generation who could incarnate 'a certain toughness' and who had the capacity to 'put [Binoche] at risk, to shake her up'.[36] At the same time, the increasingly tense and intimate relationship between Sigrid and Helena is reflected in the rapport between Maria and Valentine, such that their readings from the play can often come across as natural conversations pertaining to their own situation. At certain key moments, as when Binoche/Maria complains, 'Nothing gets to you – you radiate self-confidence!' and Stewart/Valentine scoffs, *sotto voce*, 'And you don't?', the telescoping of actor, character and character-within-character is complete: the exchange is equally meaningful between Helena and Sigrid, between Maria and Valentine or between Binoche and Stewart.

From a director whose career contains a long reflection on film history and lineage, *Sils Maria* is a mature work whose precise focus is the question of generational change, artistic legacy and the humility or humiliation involved in making way for successive exponents of one's own cherished *métier*. While never avoiding the pain of Maria's ageing process, the film seeks to present a broadly positive portrayal of this inevitable transition. Binoche, interviewed about her role, stated: 'You have to accept that you'll lose a step or two. That way, you open up to life, you're freer, calmer, more grown up, you gain in humility and grace, with a new truthfulness and lightness.'[37] Assayas confirmed that he was not interested in depicting age in terms of nostalgia for lost youth: 'Rather as active maturity, with an experience, an awareness and a knowledge of the world. And more of a critical distance to the times.'[38] And indeed critics praised a director 'at the peak of his maturity'.[39] At the same time, *Sils Maria* can be seen as the latest in a long line of films by Assayas depicting characters on the threshold of adulthood and who are, in the words of Kent Jones, 'looking for one last, elusive element that will allow them access to real adulthood'.[40] This is Valentine's situation in the film, struggling to assert her own identity and autonomy from within the confines of a role (Maria's personal assistant) that necessarily makes her subordinate to another personality. Jones has also argued that if Assayas often depicts the process of change in adolescent lives, this tends to mean 'capitulation and compromise in consumer society, as the energies of youth are drawn, quartered, and channelled into the endless march of usefulness'.[41] *Sils Maria* depicts Valentine's efforts of resistance to this process, but her unexplained disappearance at the end of the film, while it leaves open the possibility of the character's uncompromising self-reinvention, tends to suggest that this can only be achieved at the cost of permanent exile from the milieus of success and influence. Valentine's disappearance leaves the viewer with a set of uneasy questions and the film's epilogue provides no reassuring answers.

The film's central relationship between Maria/Binoche and Valentine/Stewart can also be read as an allegorical reflection on the relations between European and American culture by a director whose career in cinema, ever since *Irma Vep*, has been determinedly international (of his ten major works since *Irma Vep*, more than half have been filmed predominantly in English). As commentators pointed out, the setting in Sils Maria, a location favoured by cultural giants like Friedrich Nietzsche and Thomas Mann, and latterly the site of mountain films (*Bergfilme*) made by Nazi collaborators like Arnold Fanck, evokes a slowly waning European cultural tradition, ably represented by the precious eighteenth-century quintet who play in the rarefied surrounds of the Waldhaus Vulpera. The responses of Maria and Valentine to this culture – accepting a position in an indefinite cultural reproduction or refusing it by fleeing altogether – reflect Assayas's own wavering role as sometime French auteur (period films, family dramas, stories of Parisian intellectuals) but frequent international maverick (action movies, ghost stories, peripatetic road movies).

The mirroring that goes on in *Sils Maria* between Binoche and Stewart and Maria and Valentine is further complicated by the film's very deliberate engagement with the twenty-first-century culture of celebrity. As Jean-Marc Lalanne notes, the film is playful in its relationship to celebrity, with Binoche's character closely resembling the actress's real-life fame and experience while there is a deliberate disjunction between Stewart's global stardom and her downbeat, casually dressed role as an assistant intended to fade into the background.[42] As much as the relationship between actress and role, or celebrity and personal assistant, the film thus also explores the coexistence of human being and media icon. As Assayas notes, actors today effectively have not two, but three lives: their private life, the character they play and the persona cultivated on social media.[43] This is most strikingly represented in the character of the starlet Jo-ann (Moretz), who is first introduced to us through an array of Google Images and a set of YouTube videos of her attacking paparazzi and appearing drunk on a television interview or belligerent in a press conference.

The celebrity culture surrounding actors thus gives rise to several paradoxes. Juliette Binoche is articulate on the subject:

> It's difficult for an actor to go from self-effacement – from the humility necessary in the service of a role – to the great circus of the celebrity industry. It's often painful. You leave behind this feeling of communal creation that acts as an elixir and enter into a domain of isolation and fragility.[44]

The acting profession is thus presented as a kind of dialectic between self abandonment and self-obsession, between creative collaboration in small groups and painful isolation in the public spotlight. *Sils Maria* replays this dialectic of isolation and exposure through its choice of location. In the words of Lalanne: 'The deep dive down into the self that comes with a mountain retreat is constantly disrupted in the film by the planetary noise.'[45] This is neatly represented in the film's opening sequence where Valentine and Maria, switching back and forth between two, or even three, mobile phones, seek to plan their business and social schedules, and negotiate Maria's high-stakes divorce, while repeatedly losing the signal on the rickety old train that winds through the Alps. Again, an astute comment by Kent Jones on Assayas's early work rings true when applied to the relationship between Maria and Valentine in *Sils Maria*: 'They don't hate each other, but they don't have enough mental time to sort out the knot of emotions in their heads.'[46]

But it is also this combination of public renown and social isolation that creates the need for the personal assistant, hence Stewart's role in the film. The celebrity is in high demand yet almost unable to appear in public. Stewart reprises the role in Assayas's subsequent film, *Personal Shopper* (2016), in which she performs menial tasks (shopping, software updates) for a fashion icon who appears to divide her time exclusively between glamorous public events and the solitude of her dark apartment. In interview, Stewart has noted, from her own experience, actresses' 'dependence' on their personal assistants and the slightly odd or inexplicable nature of this relationship, somewhere between work and play, 'neither exactly friendly nor entirely professional'.[47] In *Sils Maria*, Valentine speaks for Maria without asking her advice (for instance on entering a hotel room: 'Can we turn this [television screen] off? And remove the fruit.') and rolls her eyes at the questions of acolytes who know the star less well than she does. Yet she also wolf-whistles her employer from the wings of a theatre stage in a gesture that is part sisterly encouragement, part butch possessiveness and part ingenuous fandom.

Assayas has stated that in directing Kristen Stewart, he was inclined to treat her somewhat as a beginner since, despite her global superstardom, she actually had little experience beyond the lucrative *Twilight* franchise (2008–12). He added that in Stewart's role as Joan Jett in *The Runaways* (2010), 'we find in her quite a hard, tense quality. I was hoping to locate a kind of humour behind this wall, something human, close to us, that might allow for identification'.[48] Like a number of other female performers in Assayas's work, Stewart seems to combine contradictory qualities. Kent Jones's description of Sophie Aubry's character in *Une nouvelle vie* (1993) would apply equally well to Valentine: 'she's fiercely self-protective and maintains a wall of silence, yet she's also an open book'.[49] Stewart's turn in *Sils Maria* (and in *Personal Shopper*) is also reminiscent of the performance of Asia Argento in Assayas's *Boarding Gate* (2007) as described by Steven Shaviro: it is at once 'unself-conscious' yet 'deeply *knowing*', intensely committed but ironically off-hand.[50] As such, Stewart arguably becomes the kind of twenty-first-century superstar fantasized but not quite attained in *Irma Vep*: a vector of desire yet at the same time a self-deconstructing performer.

Stewart admits in interview that she does not rehearse for her film roles, that, as soon as rehearsal is involved, all she can see is the 'grotesque' spectacle of 'actors at work' and that she fears being unable to find the same spontaneous emotions from rehearsal once the cameras are rolling.[51] Stewart herself notes the contrast with Binoche who 'rehearses non-stop'.[52]

As in *Irma Vep*, Assayas's direction remained technical, without seeking to impose a psychology upon the characters or to get too close to the actors. As he puts it, 'There is an element of fantasy in my choice of actors which would lose some of its force if I got to know them better.'[53] This light-touch direction allowed for a degree of spontaneity in Binoche's performance, which was important for developing on set between the lead actresses the productive friction that exists in the narrative between Maria and Valentine. In Assayas's words, Binoche has 'an ability to live within the shot, to take risks, even if it might end up being all wrong. As a result, Juliette wanted to shock [Kristen], to provoke her'.[54] Stewart, on the other hand, displays 'a total – almost diabolical – control of her body and her movements'.[55] In a scene in which the two women bathe together in a mountain lake, Assayas allowed them to decide their own degree of undress, stating only that Stewart should enter the water first. But Binoche took the younger actress by surprise by stripping naked and running into the lake without waiting.[56]

There is thus a further layer to the paradoxes of acting in this central screen relationship between Binoche and Stewart. Kristen Stewart takes an unrehearsed, spontaneous approach to acting, yet her performance appears tightly controlled, her speech and body language guarded and grudging in the image of young people of her generation. Binoche, on the other hand, despite a detailed classical preparation for her role, gives the more spontaneous performance – it is typically she who defines the space of the mise en scène through her unpredictable movements. Yet Stewart, for all her self-conscious mumbling and slouching, appears the more 'natural' in the role, as though 'acting herself', while Binoche, despite the unplanned gestures, appears, without ever quite breaking the fictional illusion, to be *inhabiting a role*.

Assayas has inherited a number of characteristics from the French New Wave, in particular the desire for spontaneity in his production models and a propulsive mixture of cerebral mise-en-abyme with kinetic genre cinema.

Assayas's work, like that of the New Wave directors, demonstrates a clear awareness of film history, and of his own place within it, yet he rejects the earlier generation's arrogant presumption of arriving after the end of cinema (discussed in detail in Chapter 4). Assayas insists that our very conception of what cinema is must remain fluid and flexible if the medium is to avoid becoming reified into outdated forms of inevitably limited appeal. As a result, too, Assayas's depiction of ageing, and relationship to younger generations of creators, is free from the melancholy and anxiety that sometimes colours the later work of Jean-Luc Godard in particular. This can partly be seen through the nuance and sophistication of Assayas's work with actors that demonstrates a keen awareness of the crystalline complexity of their persona built through multiple resonances between actor, character and previous roles, yet that also captures a precious sense of spontaneity and immediacy in the performances. In *Sils Maria*, in particular, this mysterious dialectic of spontaneity and preparation – a central tension in filmmaking that the New Wave helped to make plain – is the foundation on which the whole film is built and the constant spark kindling the relationship between Maria and Valentine.

François Ozon

François Ozon is surely one of the most successful and widely recognized auteur directors in contemporary French cinema, thanks in part to his prolific output and his often controversial subject matter which means he is rarely away from the art-cinema circuit for long. *Swimming Pool* (2003) can be seen as one of the films that consolidated Ozon's international reputation. Coming at the end of a loose trilogy of films about older women – following *Sous le sable* (2000) and *8 femmes* (2002) – *Swimming Pool* took over 10 million dollars at the US box office where it played for three and a half months.[57] Writing at a time just before Ozon's status was confirmed, Adam Bingham complained at the director's apparent marginalization within French film criticism and scholarship, suggesting that this may be because 'it is impossible to put any kind of label on him or to place him with confidence in any aspect of French filmmaking. He has self-consciously flirted around several genres and trends'.[58] If we were to return to the original positions of the *politique des auteurs*, however, we might recall that it was precisely a director's ability to sustain a personal signature across different genres and production contexts that was the most unequivocal sign of the auteur. Thus it is those aspects of Ozon's work that remain most consistent across his playful appropriation of comedy, drama, thrillers, musicals, melodrama and magic realism that facilitate his consideration as an auteur and, as we shall see, in the time since Bingham's article, film scholars have not been slow to venture interpretations and commentaries of these authorial motifs.

Indeed, Alistair Fox has recently been able to suggest that it is precisely the blending of genres and styles that has become the hallmark of Ozon's oeuvre.[59] Critics noted that *Swimming Pool*'s narrative – about an ageing British crime writer who has an unexpected criminal encounter with the highly sexed young daughter of her publisher at his house in the south of France – combines 'noble' references (Hitchcock, Buñuel, Chabrol) with 'popular' ones (in places resembling an erotic TV movie for the French cable channel M6).[60] *Swimming Pool* followed immediately on from *8 femmes*, which has been described as 'the most deliberately "meta" film in French cinema'[61] with its generic mash-up of the musical, the melodrama and the country-house whodunnit plus its knowing deployment of the career trajectories of its female stars. Ozon himself makes no apology for this generic hybridity, declaring himself to be part of a generation that is at ease referencing a variety of cinema traditions and has no misplaced guilt about it.[62] Once again, though, this is not so different from the film critics and directors of the New Wave generation who would readily cite the high-minded art of an Ingmar Bergman, a Jean Renoir or a Max Ophuls alongside the generic thrillers of an Allan Dwan, a Raoul Walsh or a Robert Aldrich. In the wake of Bingham, other scholars have wondered whether Ozon's generic playfulness makes him resistant to the critical establishment in France. Kate Ince has suggested that a fundamental misunderstanding, or refusal, of the thematics of queer desire in Ozon's work has led to 'some damagingly judgmental dismissals' and 'inadequate appreciation' of his films.[63] I am not persuaded, however, that a close study of the reception bears this out; film criticism must retain the ability to judge some films more aesthetically successful than others, if it is to remain criticism at all. In the following comparative analysis of *Swimming Pool* and *Dans la maison* (2012), I suggest that it is neither queer desire nor generic hybridity that most clearly separates these films but narrative control and mise en scène.

If Ozon marshals a broad range of influences in his films, however, what evidence is there of the direct influence of the French New Wave? Certainly, as compared to Assayas or Honoré, Ozon rarely mentions New Wave directors as significant inspiration, instead stressing the importance of queer cinema icons like Fassbinder and Douglas Sirk. Indeed, Honoré has gone so far as to say of Ozon: 'I don't think he likes the New Wave. In fact, I think he hates it.'[64] If any New Wave director could be seen as an influence over Ozon, it is doubtless the most 'commercial' and 'generic' of them all: Claude Chabrol. In interview, Ozon recalls a childhood fascination with a still from Chabrol's *Les Biches* (1968), in which Stéphane Audran kneels at the feet of Jacqueline Sassard, apparently about to undress her.[65] Critics noted certain 'Chabrolian turns' in the murder narrative of *Swimming Pool*.[66] Ozon shares with the veteran New Wave director an interest in exploring the mechanisms and consequences of bourgeois repression, its seemingly inevitable corollaries of murder, perversion and madness.[67] *Swimming Pool* also plays with the trope of doubling common to the thriller or *noir* genres and frequently deployed by Chabrol, particularly in the splitting of his protagonist into two complementary characters.[68] Ozon, too, likes to project different aspects of a single personality into paired characters of opposite genders or different ages.[69] Thus Julie (Ludivine Sagnier) in *Swimming Pool* is the mirror image of Sarah (Charlotte Rampling), a trope underlined through the repeated use of literal mirrors in the mise en scène, through the deliberate reprise of certain scenes or through the offset rhythm of the non-diegetic piano music.[70]

This interest in doubling among the characters in the films can also be seen in Ozon's effective doubling of himself in the character of Sarah Morton. As Ozon suggests, the fact of choosing a female character to represent the creative artist allows him to talk about himself in the film but 'with more lucidity and more cruelty'.[71] Indeed, if Ozon's work, and *Swimming Pool* in particular, bears the influence of the New Wave, it is perhaps most clearly in the film's acute self-consciousness, the pointed way in which it addresses the accursed vocation of the auteur. *Swimming Pool* is, in short, a 'self-portrait of the filmmaker as writer'.[72] Ozon pointed out in interview that he is frequently asked to justify his prolific productivity in which each new film follows closely on the heels of the last. The character of Sarah Morton – a successful author of a multivolume series of detective novels – thus becomes a way of reflecting on this process since she too is seeking to 'find herself' through the ongoing sequence of her works.[73] Ozon adds that the relationship of publisher to novelist – represented in the film as a rather manipulative and bullying bond, although not without the potential for dramatic reversals in the balance of power – has certain similarities to the alliance between producer and director in the cinema.[74]

The problem with self-consciousness is that it can easily tip the balance into self-obsession, at which point it becomes less interesting for viewers. By this stage in cultural history, the theme of the writer's inspiration can be regarded, in the words of *Cahiers du cinéma*, as 'a cliché with a rather leaden inflection'.[75] It is true that the reception of *Swimming Pool* was mixed, to say the least, with many critics finding the imagery of the pool somewhat hackneyed and obvious, given its unmistakable avatars in French cinema such as Jacques Deray's *La Piscine* (1969, another film about intergenerational tension and desire) and Henri-Georges Clouzot's *Les Diaboliques* (1955, another film where two women apparently conspire to murder a man). As in the latter work, the pool in Ozon's films seems to represent the troubling desires of the unconscious mind. Thus commentaries on the role of the pool in the film range from the obvious – the covered pool at the beginning of the narrative symbolizes Sarah's repression, whereas when she finally decides to swim in it, this marks her 'newfound emotional and sexual liberation'[76] – to the tiredly psychoanalytic: the water of the pool becomes an 'amniotic fluid' that 'connects the two women'.[77] At the same time, in an 'obligatory mise-en-abyme, the blue rectangle of the pool refers back to the cinema screen and marks the frontier between reality and fiction'.[78] In short, in the judgement of *Les Inrockuptibles*, there is nothing to *Swimming Pool* apart from 'a few cine-literary fantasies, some plot twists and meta-fictional tricks, all of them largely predictable'.[79]

For all its cleverness, then, *Swimming Pool* ultimately gives the impression of being insubstantial. As *Le Monde* put it, the spectator seeking conviction in the treatment of the characters will find only 'speculation and smokescreen'.[80] Many saw the uncertainty generated by the narrative not as carefully crafted ambiguity but as evidence of Ozon's incompetence as a screenwriter. For some, Ozon was 'not entirely in control of his idea' and the resulting film was 'half-baked, even confused'.[81] Because of this, when the murder finally arrives in the narrative, 'we don't care',[82] indeed we are 'bored'.[83] Ozon has stated that he wanted to try and recreate, in the film, the rhythm of artistic creation, beginning slowly with the tentative exploration of possibilities and then, once the idea takes hold, 'everything speeds up, I go faster and faster'.[84] One explanation of *Swimming Pool* might then be that Ozon got carried away by his own accelerating rhythm, such that the film, towards its climax, loses all sense of proportion. Thus, we have such incongruous scenes as the prematurely aged woman melodramatically declaring 'Julie's mother is dead!' before slamming the door in Sarah's face (there is no narrative justification for this indignation) and Sarah returning home to find Julie in an altered state, mistaking the Englishwoman for her mother and then screaming hysterically when corrected. In the film's denouement, we glimpse the English daughter, Julia, of Sarah's publisher and are invited to wonder whether the character of the French Julie (and thus also the murder she committed) is a pure invention of Sarah's, fantasized on the basis of this more prosaic reality. For some critics, this 'final pirouette' was 'rather lumbering and rather vain in its insolence',[85] leaving the spectator with a disappointing impression of mediocrity.[86]

Swimming Pool is a good example of a film that has been more charitably interpreted in the academic literature than in its initial critical reception. Certain authors, for instance, have sought to offer a feminist reading of the film. Fiona Handyside suggests that *Swimming Pool* challenges the traditional triangular structure of the family and, in particular, the role of the patriarch within it (the problematizing of father figures in Ozon's work has been widely observed from the beginning of his career and throughout). Julie's father and, it is implied, Sarah's (ex-)lover, John (Charles Dance), remain peripheral to the narrative, in London, while Julie's (absent, or dead) mother becomes an increasingly important ghostly presence. Thus the film 're-imagine[s] the family triangle as a wholly female space'.[87] At the end of the film, in a kind of feminist pact, Julie gives Sarah her mother's manuscript of a romance novel that had been cruelly rejected by John. Back in London, Sarah presents John with her new novel but, anticipating his rejection, has already had it published elsewhere. Further narrative ambiguities are in play here: Are we supposed to understand that Sarah simply shows John a translation of Julie's mother's novel (a shot that pans back and forth between the typewritten manuscript and Sarah working at her laptop might imply as much)? Or is she publishing a version of the narrative we have just seen on screen, based on the folder she provisionally entitled 'Julie' (and which, when published, is called *Swimming Pool*)? But, here again, there is some suggestion that Sarah simply copied out chunks of Julie's diary (the aforementioned panning shot reprises an earlier one between the handwritten diary and Sarah's laptop), such that the implied authorship of this new novel is multiple, a combined revenge on John by the three women.

Ozon, like Assayas and Honoré, is a director who clearly likes working with women performers. Can we therefore say that, in his films, he takes an interest in women's experience, and notably in the experience of ageing women, as does Assayas in *Sils Maria* or Honoré in *Les Bien-Aimés*? Unfortunately, on the contrary, Sarah in *Swimming Pool* appears as a narrow-minded stereotype of a repressed middle-aged Englishwoman. Her wardrobe is all in shades of beige (at least until she tries on a red robe, under the dangerous influence of Julie ...); she is clearly prone to alcoholism (drinking whisky in the morning in London and her abstinence upon arrival in France is short-lived once Julie turns up); her consumption of food is equally neurotic (nothing but yoghurt and fresh fruit until she is irritated by Julie, after which she raids the fridge for the younger woman's *foie gras* and sausage); she is, finally, presented as meekly beholden to her ex-lover, plaintively telling John, without eye contact, 'You don't look after me any more.' In the analysis of Andrew Asibong, Sarah in *Swimming Pool* is consistent with other characters from Ozon's films of the 2000s, 'presided over by compulsive, lonely subjects who stuff themselves with empty desires, vomiting, running from the world, preferring the solidity of their own moribund fantasies to the stimulation of living others'.[88] Meanwhile, the contrast between Sarah and Julie is reductive to the point of caricature.[89] As Olivier Bonnard suggested, Julie is 'less a character than an idea'[90] and this despite the fact that the film was shot in sequence in an effort to 'let the characters live'.[91] Ozon has admitted that Sarah's character was based on real-life British crime writers like Patricia Highsmith, Ruth Rendell and P. D. James, but the language he uses to describe these women betrays an extremely judgemental and outdated binary view of gender. Hence they are portrayed as 'rather masculine'[92] or even as 'unpleasant and foul-mouthed old maids'.[93] This prejudice is reflected in writing about the film: thus, Britt-Marie Schiller calls Sarah 'a woman who plays at being a man'.[94] Sarah is then understood to 'blossom' through contact with the younger and sexually undiscerning Julie.[95] Commentators on the film further imply that Sarah 'compensates' for her childlessness through her literary creation.[96] The gender stereotypes deployed in *Swimming Pool* may well be deliberate and 'self-conscious' in much the same manner as the film's symbolism; they may, in the words of Defne Tüzün, 'verge on the absurd',[97] but that does not make them any less offensive.

Also highly problematic, from a perspective informed by the politics of gender, is the treatment of the gaze in *Swimming Pool*. Ozon's camera repeatedly ogles Ludivine Sagnier's near-naked body to the extent that, in the words of Charles Tesson, 'her breasts eclipse her face in several close shots'.[98] It is revealing to see how Julie/Sagnier is described in the French press reception of the film: she is a 'ripe fruit with generous breasts' (*Le Nouvel Observateur*[99]); she has 'the voice of an adolescent in a fully-developed man-eater's body' (also *Le Nouvel Observateur*[100]); she is 'a wild thing with an excessively free spirit' (*Le Journal du Dimanche*[101]) or a 'sexually obsessed nymphette tease' (*Le Figaro*[102]); *Le Monde* called Julie 'a juicy young girl with an unfettered sexuality'[103] and *Libération* 'a brainless young nymphomaniac'[104] or, better yet, 'tornado-girl'.[105] Even Ludivine Sagnier herself, commenting on her role as Julie, remarked that 'I became a perfect slut'.[106] Such comments certainly form a pretty damning account of the sexual politics of contemporary French film journalism: the overwhelmingly masculinist perspective, the unremitting focus on the physical attributes of female performers and the hypocritically puritanical condemnation of women's sexual agency and activity.

But we must also recognize that this dismissive reaction to Julie is in large part determined by the way the character is written and, above all, the way she is filmed in *Swimming Pool*. Julie is constantly presented as a figure to be looked at: Sarah repeatedly watches her swim, sunbathe and have sex and the camera regularly travels up and down her near-naked body in close-up. Indeed, the formal system of *Swimming Pool*, and much of its fantasy narrative, is based around the recurring trope of a panning shot that moves from the feet to the head of a naked or near-naked woman and reveals another figure standing over her with a desiring gaze. In practically all cases, however, the ownership of the gaze is intended to be somewhat ambiguous, as set out in the table below.

Despite the ambiguity of these scenes, which allows for them to be interpreted as a woman's fantasy about herself or about another woman, the clearest diegetic gaze, in three out of four cases, is that of a man at a woman. In addition, the lingering pan up the body is a cliché of exploitation cinema, and the scenarios involved (a young woman in a bathtub; sex by the pool; a bourgeois woman who invites the working-class gardener into the house for sex) are all overly familiar from the world of pornography. As with the stereotypes of older and younger women, then, the sexualized gaze in *Swimming Pool* presents itself as a deliberate citation of cliché yet never does enough to distance itself from the gendered implications of that cliché.

A common defence of François Ozon is that he is a filmmaker who works, above all, in the realms of fantasy. Fantasy being, of necessity, sexual more often than not, such work is bound to include sexual representation, reference to sexual desire and even pornographic scenarios, all of which constitute the raw material of so much fantasy. As Ozon himself has put it, 'Fantasy is part of creation. As soon as we imagine a story, we are already drawing on our fantasies [...] A person is defined as much by her fantasies as by her actions.'[107] Alistair Fox has recently argued that Ozon's work can best be understood in terms of what he calls 'an authorial fantasmatic' which determines certain fundamental narrative structures and motifs that recur obsessively across the director's films.[108] The central fantasy narrative present in practically all of Ozon's work ever since his very first short film, *Photo de famille* (1988), evokes murderous violence against family members

Example No.	Mise en scène	Diegetic onlooker	Implied point of view	Camera movement and cuts
1. [22mins]	Julie/Sagnier in the bath	None	Sarah's imagination	CU in bathtub, movement left to right
2. [29mins]	Julie/Sagnier by the pool in white one-piece swimsuit	Franck	Sarah's dream	Right to left, pan up to Franck's face, back down to Julie as both start to masturbate; cut to Franck's pov on Julie's hands in crotch and pan up to her face
3. [48mins]	Sarah/Rampling by the pool	Marcel	Unclear: another dream of Sarah's? (in the following shots she appears to be asleep by the pool)	Right to left and up to Marcel's face
4. [86mins]	Sarah/Rampling, naked in bedroom	Marcel	Also ambiguous: Marcel's pov on Sarah's body, but cut to Julie with eyes closed implies possible dream of hers. Scene also rendered retrospectively more ambiguous by film's denouement	Right to left. Marcel starts to caress Sarah, camera cuts to Sarah's face (eyes closed) then to Julie's face (eyes closed by the pool)

as a means of enabling a kind of creative self-reinvention.[109] While there is no actual murder of family members in *Swimming Pool*, it is possible to see how this basic fantasy structure nonetheless shapes the narrative. Thus, in conspiring over the killing of Franck, Julie and Sarah effectively eliminate a substitute father figure as a way of liberating themselves from the *real* father figure (John). In addition, Fox identifies a recurring 'cinegram' in Ozon's work of a younger protagonist having sexual encounters with an older one, often expressing a kind of search for the missing or absent father.[110] As a whole, Ozon's films suggest an 'instability of sexual identification resulting from grief at neglect by paternal figures, and fear of the untrustworthy investment of maternal ones'.[111] In *Swimming Pool*, Julie's lovers are all older than her and it is not difficult to interpret her promiscuous sexual behaviour as a distressed search for comfort and stability resulting from her mother's death and her father's neglect. Sarah becomes a substitute mother figure whom Julie slowly learns to trust and respect over the course of the narrative.

On the one hand, then, the film provides us with enough narrative evidence to construct a 'realistic' psychological explanation for Julie's character and her behaviour. But, on the other hand, the film implies that Julie is not a 'realistic' character at all, that she is, herself, a fantasy of Sarah's. As has already been suggested, the film's denouement invites us to wonder whether all of the narrative events occurring in France, indeed perhaps the trip to France itself, occur only in Sarah's imagination. As Defne Tüzün writes: 'There is no single initiatory moment in the film that can be asserted as the beginning of Sarah's fiction; instead, the demarcation line between reality and Sarah's fiction, or Sarah's fantasy, is gradually erased.'[112] After her initial meeting with her publisher in London, when John suggests the trip to France, Sarah returns home, finds her father asleep in a chair, finishes his whisky, sits in a window seat and gazes at her laptop. A sound bridge then announces a cut to Sarah on the train to France but the context implies that this could be either a whisky-fuelled reverie or an act of novelistic imagination, or both. Furthermore, few commentators appear to have noted that, upon Sarah's arrival home, it is not immediately clear whether her father is asleep or dead (we don't see him wake up). Thus, recalling Fox's 'authorial fantasmatic', it would be possible to interpret the narrative of *Swimming Pool* as Sarah's fantasy of the newly liberated life she could lead if relieved of the burden of care for her elderly father. After she arrives in France, numerous shots and scenes of Sarah going to bed, closing her eyes or working at her writing desk further imply that various scenes of Julie (including the iconic shots of her sunbathing in a black-and-white two-piece bikini and, indeed, the murder of Franck) are either (day)dream or fictional invention. As Fiona Handyside notes, 'the film films fantasy as if it is reality, and reality as if it is fantasy, until we are unable to differentiate the two'.[113] This is clearly demonstrated in the panning shots of women's bodies discussed in the table above. But we also need to remember that these gazes, which are presented as possible dreams or imaginings of the characters, are, within the logic of the film, already part of the wider fantasy of the trip to France. In other words, when we admire Julie's body by the pool, what we are looking at is a dream of a character who isn't real, on a holiday that never took place.

Ozon has stated openly, in interview, that the refusal to distinguish clearly in a film between scenes that are 'real' and those that are 'fantasy' is a trick he learned from Luis Buñuel.[114] As is well known, Buñuel came from a background in the surrealist movement that deliberately sought to challenge the traditional ontological hierarchy between 'objective' reality on the one hand and dream, fantasy and imagination on the other. But, if the Spanish director chose film as the medium of his artistic expression, it is surely because, better than any other art form, cinema is able to *show* the equivalence between these different modes of perception. In a live-action film made with real human actors and recognizable spaces, *everything* – reality, memory, dream, fantasy – has the same ontological status. Or, to put it another way: Julie in *Swimming Pool* may be a fantasy; the entire trip to France may be a fantasy; but *Sarah is a fantasy too* since she is only a character in a fiction film. But, if this realization can be liberating for a director, it also necessitates a degree of rigour on the part of the critic because, if nothing in a film is 'more real' than anything else, then 'fantasy' becomes a weak excuse for exploitative gendered representation. Furthermore, if none of the characters or fictional scenarios in the film are real, the actors clearly are and Ludivine Sagnier's descriptions of her experience on set imply some rather regressive gendered relations in the filmmaking process. Describing her experience, Sagnier says, 'I'm very easy to mould [...] It's both pleasant and exhausting to be the tool of someone else's fantasies.'[115] Evoking Ozon, she says, 'You feel powerless before his gaze, and it's a feeling that makes you tremble because you can feel yourself dominated for his gain.'[116] Having subsequently worked with Christophe Honoré on *Les Chansons d'amour* (2007) and *Les Bien-Aimés* (2011), Sagnier reflected back on her 'cinematic education' with Ozon, describing his directing style as one of 'total domination, absolute possession'. She added that as she has matured (Sagnier was still only twenty-three during the filming of *Swimming Pool*), she has learned that this is not the only type of professional relationship possible on set and is more inclined to favour egalitarian working relationships.[117]

Another consequence of the universal reality status of film images is that cinema becomes a necessarily 'superficial' form, in the sense that everything important happens on the surface (because, if it didn't, how would we know about it?). As a result, the desire to evoke 'depth' (psychological, philosophical, etc.) on film can often come across as pretentious or simply clumsy. *Swimming Pool* seems to want, in the image of its central aquatic motif, to play on the tension between reflective surfaces and hidden depths, but it is precisely in these terms that Jacques Morice criticizes the film:

> This parade of psychology, the communicating vessels of the bimbo who gradually cracks up and the brittle old maid who grows more feminine, all this seems to obey the requirement for a minimum of 'depth', as though there were something wrong with staying on the surface of things, which is where Ozon is at his most inspired.[118]

Indeed, in *8 femmes*, Ozon succeeded in suggesting psychological depth through the use of 'superficial' pop songs and exaggerated costumes. Ozon clearly understands the principle when he recalls the famous scene from Buñuel's *Belle de Jour* (1967) in which a client presents a prostitute with a small box whose mysterious contents emit a high-pitched whine and make the woman smile. 'Everyone has always asked what was in the box, whereas Buñuel just laughed.'[119] It is ultimately rather disappointing, then, that the fantasy figure of Julie in *Swimming Pool* has to be explained away by a depressed, deceased mother and a neglectful father, as though a young woman's enjoyment of sex and pleasure in her own body could only ever be the result of family trauma.

In the end, this film about fantasy has been criticized for the poverty of its fantasies: Samuel Blumenfeld in *Le Monde* suggested that they were 'too reasonable to be unsettling'.[120] Yet François Ozon is not wrong when he points out that 'a fantasy necessarily leads to disappointment'[121] because of the inevitable discrepancy between the fantasy and lived experience. A fantasy, after all, can be seen as 'the staging [*la mise en scène*] of a frustrated pleasure'.[122] In addition, Mark Hain has suggested that although Ozon's characters may enjoy 'transgressive' pleasures during the course of the narrative, by the end of his films, 'all that remains is a heightened awareness of the oppression of such behaviours'.[123] This might suggest that Ozon is, after all, a more Chabrolian than Buñuelian director. The oppression at the end of *Swimming Pool* may not be completely clear but it is true that the characters' 'liberation' is limited: Julie leaves for a new job in St.-Tropez and it is implied that she may be putting her promiscuous ways behind her; Sarah returns to her London existence with a new publisher but still little sign of sensual pleasure in her life (her only real sexual act in the film is a desperate attempt to distract the gardener from discovering Franck's freshly dug grave). In *Dans la maison*, however, the next film we will consider, the relationship between fantasy and oppression is more fully elaborated.

In *Dans la maison*, a jaded high-school teacher, Germain (Fabrice Luchini), becomes fascinated by one of his pupils, Claude (Ernst Umhauer), who hands in creatively written stories apparently based on his observations of the family of fellow pupil Rapha (Bastien Ughetto). Adrien Gombeaud, reviewing the film, suggested that with *Dans la maison*, 'Ozon is ploughing the same poisonous furrow as *Swimming Pool*'.[124] *Dans la maison* is another film that takes writing as emblematic of the creative process and so can be seen as a further disguised self-portrait, the more so since Ozon's own parents were school teachers.[125] The film takes a similar Chabrolian pleasure in its gentle mocking of bourgeois manners, as in Rapha's father's (also called Rapha – hence revisiting Ozon's equally Chabrolian taste for doubling) frequent references to Chinese culture and wisdom. In the words of Claude's narration: 'He spent a week in China ten years ago and the Chinese hold no secrets for him.' Above all, *Dans la maison* is another film about fantasy. It reactivates key aspects of the 'authorial fantasmatic' identified by Alistair Fox: thus, Claude's mother is absent and his disabled father is only briefly glimpsed in a single scene towards the end of the film; Claude increasingly seeks to inveigle himself into the Artole family home, enjoying a kind of surrogate family while also hoping to instigate a sexual relationship with Rapha's mother, Esther (Emmanuelle Seigner), thereby reviving the intergenerational sex also common to Ozon's fantasmatic cinema. Ozon has once again cited the influence of Buñuel over this film[126] in which, as we shall see, it becomes increasingly difficult to distinguish Claude's fictional imagination from the reality of what may be taking place in the Artole family home, the narrative ultimately coming to resemble 'a hall of mirrors'.[127]

Like *Swimming Pool*, and indeed most of Ozon's films, *Dans la maison* is marked by diverse cultural influences and meta-cinematic references. In one climactic scene, Germain's wife Jeanne (Kristin Scott Thomas) knocks him out by hitting him over the head with a heavy hardback copy of Céline's *Voyage au bout de la nuit*, in a playful reference to the theatrical readings of the French author that Luchini had recently been touring.[128] Given the voyeuristic spying into another's private residence, Hitchcock's *Rear Window* (1954) is a constant point of reference,[129] and one that becomes very explicit in the film's final scene, to be discussed in more detail below. This Hitchcockian flavour is confirmed by echoes of Bernard Herrmann on the minimalist soundtrack, a style that Herrmann associated particularly with scenes of voyeurism.[130] Another American director present in the film is Woody Allen. Jean-François Julliard suggests that Germain resembles a character from the film-world of the veteran New York director[131] and, at one point, a poster for Allen's *Match Point* (2005) is prominently displayed, another film about the dangers of giving in to the temptations of fantasy. It was also pointed out that the film resembled an American sitcom (the model willfully perverted in Ozon's first feature, *Sitcom* [1998]), with its focus around a couple of domestic settings.[132] Ozon deliberately nurtured this impression by choosing to film in the suburban new town of Serris designed around the automobile and the shopping centre.[133] Adrien Gombeaud suggests that the tastefully neutral décor of the Artoles's home and the father and son's passion for basketball evoke 'the familiar yet totally preposterous world of American TV series dubbed into French'.[134] Aside from these American points of reference, several critics saw a comparison between *Dans la maison* and Pasolini's *Teorema* (1968), a film focused around a charming and beautiful young man who serves as a catalyst in the libidinal life of a whole family.[135] This comparison is rather misleading, however, since, in Ozon's film, Claude ultimately has little lasting effect over the Artole family; it is rather Germain's life that is transformed by his influence. In any case, *Dans la maison* is self-aware enough to evoke and dismiss the reference to Pasolini more or less in the same gesture. In one of his narrations, Claude claims that Rapha planted a passionate and confused kiss upon his lips. On hearing this, Germain scoffs, 'What is this, Pasolini?'

The reference to Pasolini, however, evokes the spectre of queer desire in *Dans la maison*. For it is true that Claude is not just an active protagonist but also an object of disconcerting desire, for characters and spectators alike, given his high-boned beauty. Adrien Gombeaud comments that the actor Ernst Umhauer 'looks like he was found on one of Visconti's beaches'.[136] Early in the film, the actor's taut young body is deliberately fragmented by Ozon's camera in a scene of him dressing for school. It has also been suggested that Ozon's decision to dress his characters in school uniforms – practically unheard of in real French *lycées* – is a deliberate attempt to 'excite the kind of erotic disturbance found in British school dramas'[137] (the fetishistic use of school uniforms is common in British cinema, such as the remake of *St. Trinian's* [Parker and Thompson, 2007]). The developing relationship between Claude and his teacher plays out something like a romance. When Germain wonders idly whether he should show Claude's troubling text to the school principal, Claude replies, 'I didn't write it for the principal, I wrote it for you.' The close-up shot/reverse-shots here, with Claude framed against a blue wall that brings out the colour of his eyes and Germain looking the boy up and down before dropping his gaze, seem to imply a sexual flirtation. Rapha warns Claude that rumours have begun to circulate in school about his relationship with Germain and eventually Jeanne asks her husband directly if he desires his pupil, noting that he has not made love to her since he began helping the boy. Germain seems genuinely shocked by such suggestions. There is no indication in the film that he consciously desires Claude and to suggest that he desires the boy unconsciously would be an inappropriate reification of the fluid subject positions in Ozon's fantasy. As Kate Ince reminds us, we need to think of Ozon as a queer and not a gay director.[138] The protagonists of his films are only rarely out gay (although there are often gay characters in supporting roles), and nor is Ozon interested in depicting the process of emerging from the closet or confirming a sexual orientation which, as Ince puts it, 'is only ever "fixed" in the most provisional manner'.[139] Instead, Ozon repeatedly demonstrates the power of desire to challenge and disrupt heteronormative social structures: Germain and Jeanne's bourgeois marriage, the Artoles's 'normal' family, the paternalistic relationship of teacher to pupil.

For a film about desire and fantasy, *Dans la maison* is determined more by what *doesn't* happen than by what does. But it is not the case, as in *Swimming Pool*, that we witness outrageous acts only to be asked subsequently to disbelieve our eyes; instead, in *Dans la maison*, we envisage possibilities but we never see them actualized. Thus Claude does not have sex with Esther, or with Germain, and, *contra* Fox's 'authorial fantasmatic', nobody is murdered in this film. *Cahiers du cinéma* complained that, as a result, 'the film goes nowhere'.[140] But I am more inclined to agree with

FIGURE 5.1 *Ernst Umhauer in* Dans la maison *(2012). Courtesy eOne.*

Alexis Campion who argued that Ozon creates 'an atmosphere that is at once parodic and tense, maintaining the sense that everything could, at any moment, tip over into another, forbidden, register'.[141] This atmospheric strength of *Dans la maison* stems from the fact that what is at stake in the film is not so much the desire for people, or bodies, as the desire for narrative. Alongside Hitchcock and Pasolini, the film also cites the *Ur*-narrative of Ulysses and the meta-narrative of Scheherazade. Germain begins the film by complaining about the lack of imagination of his pupils whose accounts of their weekend consist exclusively of pizza and television. It is the ability to create and sustain narrative tension (with the habitual closing refrain of 'To be continued … ') that intrigues Germain about Claude. It is his compulsive desire for narrative, and not his desire for the young man, that brings about Germain's downfall. He deliberately humiliates Rapha in class by having him read aloud a story entitled 'My Best Friend' purely in order to check the veracity of Claude's stories about the two boys' relationship. Then, when Claude complains that Rapha's probable failure on a maths test will put an end to his visits (Claude is supposed to be tutoring the other boy), Germain jumps to a surprising conclusion: 'Are you asking me to steal the maths test?' he enquires, hastily shutting the classroom door. This is perhaps the most revealing line in the whole film since, first, Claude had made no such request (this is entirely Germain's initiative) and, second, if Claude's stories are fiction, as Germain has been implying through his references to Flaubert and Dostoevsky, then why would it matter if he could no longer actually visit the house? Here, Germain reveals his fatal conflation of narrative and reality that will ultimately lead to his expulsion from the school. *Dans la maison* suggests that narrative is nothing short of addictive and that, as such, it can lead to irrational and self-destructive behaviour. In the film's epilogue, Claude finds a dishevelled Germain sitting on a park bench, having lost his job and his wife. Claude says that he has 'abandoned' his writing following the affair with the Artoles but, as they sit overlooking an apartment block, they are unable to resist the temptation to imagine the lives unfolding behind the windows.

There remains the question, however, as to how far any of this might be seen to relate to the influence of the French New Wave. Ozon gives a clue when he mentions that he had considered dedicating the film to three of his teachers at Fémis, the French national film school: Jean Douchet, Joseph Morder and Éric Rohmer.[142] Thus, despite Ozon's supposed aversion to the New Wave, two of his most influential teachers (Douchet and Rohmer) have an undisputed New Wave pedigree. Ozon sees the mark of Rohmer in particular over *Dans la maison*, in its use of a suburban new-town setting, but also in the casting of Luchini, familiar from six of the veteran director's films. Ozon suggests that the character of Germain can be seen as altogether Rohmerian 'in the way in which his theories, however finely articulated they may be, are constantly undermined by the facts'.[143]

But there is perhaps another, more unexpected film by a New Wave director whose subterranean influence can be felt over *Dans la maison*. In interview Ozon has been clear that '*In the House*, of course, means "in the fiction"',[144] in other words, that the Artoles's house in the film is both a fictional space and a meta-fictional space, a space that demonstrates the workings of fiction through the constant process of rewriting. This idea of a 'house of fiction' recalls the title of an article by Jonathan Rosenbaum about Jacques Rivette's *Céline et Julie vont en bateau* (1974).[145] In this film, the two eponymous heroines discover a mysterious old house that, after visiting, they are unable to remember until they suck on strange, hallucinogenic sweets they find in their mouths. Upon doing so, they view scenes from what resembles a nineteenth-century melodrama, seemingly taking place inside the house. Indeed, Stéphane Delorme suggested that Ozon was entering 'the territory of Henry James' with this film,[146] and it was two texts by James that provided the inspiration for the narrative-within-the-narrative of *Céline et Julie*. Ozon has also compared the house of *Dans la maison* to a dolls' house,[147] a comparison equally pertinent to *Céline et Julie* since, on the one hand, the characters seem fixed in pre-established roles (as the film goes on, they come more and more to resemble waxworks), yet, on the other hand, they are like toys in the hands of Céline and Julie who, it turns out, are free to alter their story and intervene within it. This interpretive freedom and meta-fictional mischief allow for frequent shifts of register in Rivette's film between austere melodrama and burlesque comedy, a playfulness also accomplished in *Dans la maison*.

At stake in *Céline et Julie vont en bateau* turns out to be the life of a young girl threatened with murder by two women competing for the hand of her widowed father. The film can thus be read as a feminist attack on a social system in which the lives of women are literally or metaphorically sacrificed to a patriarchal matrimonial order.[148] While it would perhaps be an exaggeration to call *Dans la maison* a 'feminist film', its gender politics are considerably more interesting than those of the only superficially progressive *Swimming Pool*. As we have seen, Claude first enters the Artoles's house because he is attracted to Rapha's mother, Esther, drawn to what he calls, in his first composition for Germain, 'the singular fragrance of women from the middle classes'. The somewhat patronizing tone of this line encapsulates Claude's view of Esther, at once desiring and condescending. His writing gently mocks her interest in tastefully neutral home decoration even as he invents schemes to find himself alone with her. Emmanuelle Seigner's performance as Esther occasionally has a wooden quality as though to emphasize that she is not so much a real woman as the projection of a teenage boy: some of her gestures, such as the way she bites thoughtfully on the end of her pen, are close to soft-erotica clichés of a housewife's disingenuous seduction. The film even includes a slow foot-to-head pan up Esther's body as she lies on the sofa, to a hackneyed saxophone accompaniment, a shot that recalls the fetishizing pans of *Swimming Pool* but is here more clearly presented (and so implicitly critiqued or ridiculed) as the perspective of a teenage boy (Claude recites in voice-over during the pan and then is shown sitting across from Esther, busily writing in his notebook as he gazes at her).[149] As in *Céline et Julie vont en bateau*, Claude announces to Germain that his ultimate goal is to 'rescue' Esther from this house; he describes her as 'the most bored woman in the world' and intends to take her away from her husband and son. The difference, however, in *Dans la maison*, is that Esther's suffering is never clearly established outside Claude's imagination. He imagines her making love to her husband 'mimicking a desire that had long since vanished', yet nothing in her physical or vocal performance of sex clearly signals a lack of enjoyment. Likewise, when Claude stays in the Artoles's spare room, he describes Esther's childhood dolls on the shelves as 'mutilated', a word that implies a secret life of trauma and violent acting-out on the part of Esther when, in fact, the mise en scène shows dolls that are simply old and broken, rather than deliberately deformed. Claude thus seems to want to rescue a woman who probably doesn't need rescuing. When he gives her a poem, Esther's response is sufficiently cautious and ambiguous to permit a variety of interpretations: is she subtly mocking Claude, is she carefully trying to spare his feelings without giving him any encouragement or might she actually reciprocate Claude's attraction? It is a testament to Seigner's nuanced performance that all of these possibilities remain in play: Danièle Heymann is right to note that she has 'a marvelous presence in what is a rather hollow role'.[150]

In his review in *Télérama*, Pierre Murat calls *Dans la maison* Ozon's best film, 'a troubling little masterpiece'.[151] Murat suggests that in his early films, Ozon was sometimes too fond of acting like a puppet-master in the cruel manipulation of his characters but that, over the course of his career, he has learned 'tenderness' and 'gentleness'.[152] This is, as academic scholars of Ozon have noted, a frequent narrative about his work: that his earlier work was obsessed with transgression and the desire to shock but that he has matured with age.[153] Ince and Asibong are rather dismissive of this view, implying that it betrays a fundamental discomfort with the more explicitly queer subject matter of Ozon's early films and a bourgeois satisfaction with the more 'grown-up' (i.e. tamer) narratives of his later work. Schilt also notes that *Sous le sable*, often identified as Ozon's first 'mature' work, is also his first film to be made without explicitly queer characters.[154] While these authors are not wrong to be wary of a latent homophobic prejudice within French film criticism, it is surely legitimate to recognize that a director can grow more accomplished, and his work more subtle, with practice. To insist on the equal value of a director's entire catalogue because of its perceived thematic consistency is an example of the worst kind of uncritical auteurism. As Ince remarks, Ozon at his best makes 'emotionally rich films while simultaneously working at a metacinematic level'.[155] But, if this combination may be the goal of all his films, we must acknowledge that some are more successful than others at one or other of these aspects. *Swimming Pool* works so hard at its deceptive meta-cinematic narrative that the characters become hollow caricatures about whom it is hard to care; *Dans la maison*'s meta-fictional structure is more subtly embedded in the lives and investments of its characters and, as such, becomes both more involving and more thought-provoking.

Christophe Honoré

Christophe Honoré may be more explicitly and obviously in thrall to the model of the French New Wave than any other director discussed in this book, with the possible exception of Leos Carax. Although he acknowledges the influence of other filmmaking traditions (notably the queer legacy of Fassbinder and Pasolini), Honoré has admitted that, in terms of the influences perceptible in his films, he is 'a bit Franco-French'.[156] At least in the cycle of films that runs from *Dans Paris* (2006) to *Les Bien-Aimés* (2011), Honoré seems to be systematically working through a kind of extended tribute to the New Wave (Honoré's most recent films – *Métamorphoses* [2014] and *Les Malheurs de Sophie* [2016], adaptations, respectively, of Ovid and the Comtesse de Ségur – suggest a rather different direction of travel, implying that the homage to the New Wave may have been a necessary phase for Honoré's cinema, but that his still-young career may take very different directions in the future). Even the opening titles of these films from the late 2000s reference the New Wave, in particular Jean-Luc Godard, with their big bold capitals and their minimalist reduction to names without functions.[157] Honoré's close focus on domestic arguments also betrays the influence of Godard, with *Dans Paris* referencing in particular *Le Mépris* (1963) and *Pierrot le fou* (1965).[158]

The other key New Wave figure whose influence over Honoré's work is most plain is Jacques Demy, whose almost single-handed importation of the Hollywood-style musical into France is lovingly referenced, indeed prolonged, in Honoré's *Chansons d'amour* (2007) and *Les Bien-Aimés*. Aside from the use of songs, to be discussed in more detail below, Demy's influence can be felt over the deliberate design of the colour scheme in the mise en scène of Honoré's films that tends to overemphasize certain combinations of bright colour to expressive effect. In *Les Bien-Aimés*, the colour blue is used repeatedly in the early scenes set during the 1960s and 1970s: in their first musical number together, both Madeleine (Ludivine Sagnier) and Jaromil (Rasha Bukvic) are wearing blue, and the window grills, road signs and a stationary Citroën 2CV all match their outfits. When they meet again a decade later and rekindle their passion, their duet takes place in a billiards hall where the blue baize of the tables complements Jaromil's blue and orange outfit, itself harmonizing with Madeleine's warm red and brown ensemble. Of course, Honoré's casting in *Les Bien-Aimés* also represents a nod to Demy, since he employs Catherine Deneuve to play the ageing Madeleine in the twenty-first century, the actress first made famous in Demy's *Parapluies de Cherbourg* (1964) and deployed again in *Les Demoiselles de Rochefort* (1967). The meta-cinematic edge to the casting is confirmed through the use of Deneuve's real-life daughter, Chiara Mastroianni, to play her on-screen daughter Véra and through the casting of Milos Forman, the director associated with the Czech New Wave, in the role of the older Jaromil. Through his focus on families, to be discussed in more detail below, Honoré offers a reflection on generations in French social and cultural life, in particular inviting us to think about the legacies – not just artistic or political but also emotional and sexual – of the 1960s in today's France.[159] In interview, Honoré has gone so far as to say, 'French cinema has never been so ambitious and widespread and desperate as it was in the 1960s. It's our golden age, our empire, our lost paradise.'[160] The comment, with its rather hyperbolic language, suggests *both* a naïve nostalgia for an irrecoverable era of cinematic and social possibility *and* an ironic awareness of the way in which the reality of the New Wave – and more broadly the era of economic prosperity and social mobility that nurtured it – has become lost behind a very partial legend. This dual awareness, I suggest, encapsulates neatly the tenor of Honoré's New Wave references in his films.

The directness with which Honoré appropriates his French cinematic models is certainly audacious. *Les Bien-Aimés* opens in a Demy-esque shoe store in 1964 with a musical montage of women's feet, legs and shoes that recalls the lower-limb fetishism of François Truffaut,[161] all set to a French cover of 'These Boots Are Made for Walkin'.[162] The confidence required of a young director to take on such cultural clichés is, however, the same confidence that was required of the untutored and untested directors of the New Wave when they arrogantly sought to measure themselves against Alfred Hitchcock, Fritz Lang or Jean Cocteau. Indeed, Honoré's career trajectory followed fairly closely the model of these Nouvelle Vague directors: resisting his family's desire for him to undertake a vocational degree, Honoré moved from his native Brittany to Paris with the explicit intention of becoming a filmmaker; he began writing criticism for *Cahiers du cinéma* and made an initial living writing children's books before being invited, first, to write a screenplay and, subsequently, to direct it himself.[163] With such a bold approach to filmmaking, there is no doubt a danger, as Lee Hill observes, that sometimes Honoré's 'reach exceeds his grasp'[164] and indeed some viewers clearly find the self-conscious arrogance of his style insufferable.[165] It is also in Honoré's cinema that Louis Garrel has been given freest rein to develop his free-wheeling, self-satisfied performance style that makes him, in the words of Peter Bradshaw, 'the most irritating actor in the world'.[166] But Honoré's self-conscious deployment of his references is evidently so deliberate that at times he sees himself as almost baiting the spectator with his chutzpah. He has said of the opening of *Dans Paris*, and in particular the scene in which Garrel directly addresses the camera, assuming

FIGURE 5.2 *Ludivine Sagnier and Rasha Bukvic in* Les Bien-Aimés *(2011). Courtesy New Wave Films.*

the position of omniscient narrator of the film, that 'what mattered was to really annoy the spectator'.[167] Gerstner and Nahmias suggest that the reception of Honoré has been 'uneven'.[168] However, if confined to France and to the most influential cultural papers and journals, particularly in the domain of cinema (*Cahiers du cinéma, Les Inrockuptibles, Libération, Le Monde, Télérama*), the response to Honoré's revival of the New Wave has been almost uniformly positive.

Honoré's critical success is further evidence of the ongoing relevance of the *Cahiers du cinéma* conception of mise en scène in French film culture. As Louis Guichard commented in *Télérama*, Honoré 'believes only in mise-en-scène, at a time when many French directors no longer know what the word means'.[169] Honoré himself confirms: 'I chose the camp of those for whom cinema is above all the art of mise en scène, and not the art of the subject.'[170] Like the critics of the New Wave generation, Honoré rejects a cinema whose cultural value would be determined by its subject matter, even though he suggests that the latter view has made a distinct comeback in recent French film culture.[171] One of Honoré's own most pointed critical articles, 'Triste moralité du cinéma français', written for *Cahiers du cinéma* in 1998, is a lament at the increasing trend for 'social cinema' in France.[172] Honoré admits that he is simply bored by this cinema and compares it unfavourably to the formal invention of international auteurs like Wong Kar-Wai, Tsai Ming-Liang and David Lynch. Gerstner and Nahmias explicitly compare this article to Truffaut's 'Une certaine tendance du cinéma français' in its wholesale rejection of the perceived dominant strain of current French cinema in favour of a personal filmmaking practice deemed incompatible with it.[173] Honoré insists: 'A filmmaker today can no longer pretend simply to bear witness to the world.'[174] While Honoré's position might be explained in terms of the sheer proliferation of image-making media technologies in operation in the world today, in fact this view has been prevalent in modern film theory and film practice since at least the Second World War – one thinks of the title of Jacques Rivette's first published article in 1950: 'We are no longer innocent.'[175] The apparatus and the deployment of cinema have simply been too sophisticated for too long to pretend that it can still be used naively as a window on the world, hence the illegitimacy of a cinema that claims to put the subject first. As Honoré argues, what we are left with, therefore, is an inevitably personal cinema: 'my vision of something', not so much 'the subject but how I saw it'.[176]

As in the work of Olivier Assayas, however, this very personal vision of cinema is often combined, in discourse by and around Honoré, with rather abstract definitions of mise en scène in terms of 'the precision of spacing'[177] or 'the assemblage of forms'.[178] But, again like Assayas, this finds its concrete personal expression most particularly in the director's work with actors, his exploration of their individual styles and rhythms. Honoré has described the way he likes to confront actors with very different styles, such as the 'airy'

Louis Garrel and the 'earthy' Romain Duris in *Dans Paris*.[179] In addition, although he may use the same performers repeatedly, he seeks to change the nature of their characters between roles in order to elicit a different performance. In *Les Bien-Aimés*, following several films with Louis Garrel as the protagonist, Honoré deliberately gave him a rather unsympathetic minor role. Likewise Chiara Mastroianni, having played a closed, resistant character in *Non ma fille, tu n'iras pas danser* (2009), is given a much more open, outgoing role in the later film.

Indeed, the mise en scène of the latter sections of *Les Bien-Aimés* seems to be largely built around Mastroianni's physical performance, her gangly but fluid movements and her gawkily confident face and demeanour. If the 'period' sequences of *Les Bien-Aimés* (set in 1964 and 1978) are, as described above, very carefully but artificially designed, as though to imply that they constitute only a *cinematic* memory of the past,[180] the scenes set in the recent past and present (1997–98, 2001, 2007) and therefore drawing on Honoré's personal experience are much more 'realistic', which is to say they are darker, there is more hand-held camera and the costumes are chosen with less fanatical care in the matching of colour schemes. The musical numbers in *Les Bien-Aimés*, most of which are performed on the streets, showcase both the bodies of the performers and the (typically unglamorous) Parisian locations thus becoming a pure distillation of the 'arrangement of bodies in space' conception of mise en scène.

At the same time, however, Honoré's use of songs is crucial to the emotional impact of his films. He admits that, with *Les Chansons d'amour*, he employed the musical format precisely because he was embarrassed about approaching the terrain of romantic love, afraid of falling into mawkishness.[181] In both *Les Chansons d'amour* and *Les Bien-Aimés*, the songs allow characters to express their feelings within a dynamic mise en scène that prevents the films from becoming bogged down in predictable or self-indulgent sentiment. The sincerity and emotional intensity of Honoré's films have been noted by critics.[182] His films are not just cerebral exercises in intertextual reference. Rather, they tend to confirm Richard Dyer's observation about pastiche that it 'recognizes its own difference from past forms while acknowledging their emotional truth'.[183] I have suggested previously that the perceived emotional truth of the New Wave films stems from the apparent spontaneity of their form, itself a function of their haphazard and sometimes precarious conditions of production.[184] These somewhat casual or improvised methods of production can be seen, in turn, as a deliberate attempt to shrug off the calcified practices, personnel and forms of the *cinéma de qualité*. Much like Assayas and Ozon, Honoré seeks to mimic this New Wave model by working quickly – at the time of the release of *Les Bien-Aimés*, he had made nine films in ten years – often with a limited shooting schedule and budget: *Dans Paris* was filmed in thirty days for the paltry sum of €1.5 million.[185] *Les Bien-Aimés*, with its high-profile cast, its musical numbers and its locations in Paris, London and Montreal (plus a confected Prague), was a more ambitious undertaking, yet here too one of Honoré's principal concerns was how to bring lightness and rapidity to the naturally slow and cumbersome medium of cinema.[186]

This taste for lightness (*légèreté*), which echoes that expressed by Assayas, is to be found in the playfulness of Honoré's narratives and mise en scène, and explains his loyalty to Louis Garrel's often clownish, grandstanding performances. Recalling the director's parallel life as a children's author, Gerstner and Nahmias propose that 'for Honoré, film finds its most rewarding aspect when it is conceived *as if through and for* the eyes of a child'.[187] In *Les Bien-Aimés*, the songs and the mise en scène give a lightness and playfulness to the film despite the gravity of its material. For the film is essentially a melodrama – a family saga with recurring themes of loss and unequally reciprocated love, illness and death. In the film's climactic scenes, Véra is stranded in Montreal in the immediate aftermath of the terrorist attacks of September 2001 on the way to meet the object of her affections, Henderson (Paul Schneider). In love with a gay man who can never fully return her passion, and who refuses her plea to conceive a child with her because he is HIV-positive, Véra sleeps with Henderson, and his boyfriend, before taking a fatal overdose of his medication. But a sequence that might have been absurdly histrionic is downplayed through the light touch of its mise en scène: the detail of Véra's suicide is related in voice-over by her mother, Madeleine, while, on screen, we see only her groggy swaying to a dance track playing on the TV in the hotel bar in the muffled atmosphere of the aftermath of atrocity where the sparse patrons of the bar look away in awkward embarrassment. It is the fact of having constructed the mise en scène of the film around Mastroianni's body and particularly her dancing and rhythmic movements (she first meets Henderson after dancing effusively to his band in a London club) that renders this muted climax both plausible and poignant.

It would be easy to see Véra's taking of her own life at the end of *Les Bien-Aimés* as an extremely selfish and short-sighted act, and indeed the film's lengthy coda that documents the grieving of Madeleine and Clément (Garrel) implies as much. As Louis Guichard has commented, 'There is something almost scandalous in the egotism of Honoré's characters since *Dans Paris*: obsessed with someone they have lost or can't have, they don't want to hear about anything else.'[188] Indeed, Garrel's character Clément in *Les Bien-Aimés* is similarly self-obsessed and often disagreeable. At one point, he turns up to the hospital in which Véra's father has just died, having written another woman's name on his neck in the hope of provoking a jealous scene, and then is angry when Véra doesn't recognize his own handwriting. Even in the immediacy of Véra's loss, Clément seeks to make the scene all about his own feelings. But, if Honoré is nonetheless able to prevent his characters from being simply repugnant, it is perhaps because he repeatedly demonstrates the possibility of what he calls 'the simultaneity of feelings'.[189] It is, after all, rare that our feelings are completely unilateral and unequivocal. Clément can feel compassion and loyalty for Véra while also feeling aggrieved at her lack of reciprocal feeling; Véra can feel suicidal despair over her intractable love for Henderson but it doesn't negate her love for her mother (as demonstrated by her tender telephone call to the latter immediately before she enters the Montreal hotel room for her final *ménage-à- trois*). This simultaneity of feelings is also explored in Honoré's other films.

Regarding *Dans Paris*, Gerstner and Nahmias evoke Jonathan's (Garrel) 'complicated but generous self-interest'.[190] In an effort to cheer up, or distract, his suicidally depressed brother Paul (Romain Duris), Jonathan wagers that he can travel on foot from their home in the sixteenth arrondissement to the Bon Marché department store (in the seventh) in under half an hour. In fact, after stopping to have sex with three different women he picks up on the way, it ends up taking over seven hours! Back at home later, however, Jonathan tries to explain to Paul that these conquests were his perverse, misguided attempt to commune with his brother. Or, at least, they served as a distraction from his terror that Paul might kill himself. As Gerstner and Nahmias further explain: 'what may be perceived as arrogant self-gratification [...] paradoxically sustains intimate relations'.[191] Similarly complex sexual-emotional behaviour is explored in *Les Chansons d'amour*. Thus, it is fairly clear that when Ismaël (Garrel) sleeps with Erwann (Grégoire Leprince-Ringuet), it is above all an expression of his grief following the sudden death of his girlfriend Julie (Sagnier). When Julie's sister, Jeanne (Mastroianni), surprises the two young men in bed together, the subsequent exchange on the street between Ismaël and Jeanne is particularly rich in its emotional complexity: sarcastically expressing what he takes to be Jeanne's attitude, Ismaël scoffs, 'I'm thoughtless, I'm stupid and – oh! – I'm a fag.' In Ismaël's defensive manner here is a mixture of guilt at his disloyalty to Julie's memory, indignation at the notion that Julie's family would police his behaviour, embarrassment at having been caught in what is, we presume, his first gay sexual encounter, plus a self-righteous defence of his right, nonetheless, to experiment sexually.

The example of *Les Chansons d'amour* raises the important question of how queer Christophe Honoré's cinema is. In their book, Gerstner and Nahmias make a strong case for Honoré as a queer auteur and it would be difficult to deny that 'his rewriting of New Wave concepts involves queer interference'.[192] Like Ozon, Honoré is a gay director for whom homosexuality is not the principal subject of his films but for whom queer desire is taken for granted as an unremarkable fact of daily life. These directors present sexual orientation as a spectrum such that it is considered perfectly natural when the basically straight Ismaël embarks on a relationship with another man or when a self-identifying gay man like Henderson falls in love with a woman. It is not the apparent shift in orientation itself that provides material for drama so much as the singular confrontation of individual personalities. Also refreshing in Honoré's films (notably *Les Bien-Aimés*) is the gaze of a gay male director that overturns the conventional gender hierarchy in straight sex scenes such that often the male partner is naked while the woman remains almost fully clothed. It is not clear, however, how subversive Honoré's approach really is. Gerstner and Nahmias describe his films as 'riddled by an unsettlingly queer seduction'.[193] But it is worth noting the success of Honoré's cinema, and particularly *Les Chansons d'amour*, among French high school students, the group responsible, according to Simon Daniellou, for turning it into a 'cult' film.[194] This popularity would suggest that, in fact, relative sexual fluidity is now widely accepted, at least in the bourgeois French milieu in which Honoré's films are set and to whom they are marketed. If a film like *Les Chansons d'amour* is so popular with high school students, it is surely not because it is 'subversive', but because it presents an aspirational portrait of metropolitan lifestyles in which glamorous young people enjoy multiple and varied sexual experiences (and in which the real-life pressures of work have almost no place).

These considerations return us to the question of 'lightness' in Honoré's work since the term is often used, in French, to designate an attitude towards sexual morality (*'une femme légère'* might be variously translated into English as a 'fast', 'loose' or 'easy' woman). Jean-Baptiste Morain, who praised the lightness of touch of Honoré's form, suggested that this is also a central ethical question in his films: 'How to live "lightly" [*vivre léger* ...] in a society whose morals condemn those who love to live fast?'[195] *Les Bien-Aimés* does not presume to judge relationships that are sometimes platonic-sometimes sexual (such as Véra and Clément's) or the tendency to use sex as an emotional comfort in the absence of a true beloved. Thus, we see a strange man in Véra's bed even as she sings of her longing for Henderson; and Henderson admits to Véra that he took a French boyfriend because 'I'm obsessed with everything French ever since I met you'.

This free sexual morality is also displayed in the older generation. Véra accepts matter-of-factly that her mother was an 'occasional' prostitute in younger days in order to pay for luxuries; indeed, that was how Madeleine met Véra's father. Madeleine continues to have regular sexual assignations with Jaromil to the full knowledge of her husband, François, who asks only that she keep the details to herself. The film then recounts the difficulty for the younger generation to live up to this 'lightness', as expressed in the duet between Deneuve and Mastroianni in which Véra laments the 'weight' of sentiment that prevents her from becoming 'une fille légère'. The difficulty of this lightness is demonstrated in the failure of Véra and Clément's open relationship/sexual friendship: he reacts furiously when she has sex with Henderson, punching the American in the face. *Les Bien-Aimés* portrays a confused sexual arena in which the younger generation are excessively careful not to restrict each other's sexual freedom and attempt to be sexually responsible yet, in their emotional desperation, end up taking crazy risks. Thus, Henderson believes he became infected with HIV on a night of drunken sex when seeking to stifle thoughts of Véra; Véra is willing to overlook the risk of infection in her love for Henderson, and even asks him to make her pregnant, then rashly takes her own life when he refuses. Meanwhile, the older generation are casually imprudent in their infidelities yet their settled little arrangement actually appears very comfortable and bourgeois compared to the chaotic love lives of their children.

As these examples suggest, questions of sexuality in Honoré's films are never very far from questions of family. Indeed, the director has remarked that he is interested in depicting sensuality in a different domain to that normally encountered in the cinema, that is to say within the family.[196] In the end, as Véra observes in *Les Bien-Aimés*, 'I am the sex life of my parents. That's all I am.' Speaking in 2011, after the completion of *Les Bien-Aimés*, Honoré observed: 'All my films, apart from *La Belle Personne*, are films about family.'[197] The director has also been very honest about the pragmatic family concerns underlying his filmmaking choices. His first features were shot in Toulouse and the Canary Islands but, following the birth of his daughter, he wanted to remain closer to home, which is what gave rise to *Dans Paris*.[198] As we have seen in the examples discussed above, the family relationships in Honoré's films are complex, and sometimes give rise to conflict, but above all are warm, loving and supportive.

This is perhaps one of the most striking differences between Honoré and his New Wave models since, in the films of the Nouvelle Vague, families tend either to be absent (Godard, the early Rivette) or to be the focus of a quite classically Oedipal overcoming (Truffaut, Chabrol). Yet the family in Honoré's work is also, by his own admission, a *cinematic* family. In *Dans Paris*, says Honoré, he cast Louis Garrel and Romain Duris in full knowledge of their different star personae (associated more with auteur or popular cinema, respectively), then, in casting their parents, he looked not for actors physically resembling the younger performers, but rather for roughly equivalent career trajectories (hence Guy Marchand from popular cinema and Marie-France Pisier from the auteur cinema of Truffaut, Rivette, Buñuel or Alain Robbe-Grillet).[199] The director also notes that two of his favourite actors, Louis Garrel and Chiara Mastroianni, inevitably bring their impeccable French cinematic pedigree to their roles.[200] Casting Deneuve and Mastroianni as mother and daughter of course acknowledges their real-life relationship, yet it also references the generations of French cinema since, for Honoré, Deneuve evokes François Ozon as much as François Truffaut, while Mastroianni brings memories of the French auteur cinema of the 1990s, in particular Arnaud Desplechin, another disciple of Truffaut.[201]

It is possible, finally, to see Christophe Honoré's films, and his film families, as a series of hauntings.[202] Honoré's father was killed in an automobile accident when the future director was only fifteen years old and he has acknowledged the formative influence of this loss in his artistic vocation. The 'scandal' of choosing a different path in the small Breton town where Honoré grew up no longer seemed so insurmountable after the death of his father had already singled him out as unusual.[203] A sudden death is also at the origin of *Les Chansons d'amour*, since the songwriter Alex Beaupain's partner, who was also Honoré's close friend, died in similar circumstances, and at a similar age, to Julie in the film.[204] The families in Honoré's films thus tend to be preoccupied by grief and loss (the suicide of a younger sister in *Dans Paris*, the deaths of Julie in *Les Chansons d'amour* and of Véra in *Les Bien-Aimés*) just as his cinematic family evokes absent friends and inspirations, some of them having disappeared too soon (Jacques Demy, François Truffaut, Françoise Dorléac ...). At the same time, Honoré's tendency to surround himself with a cinematic family suggests a nostalgia for an era when artistic work could be collectively conceived. He laments the fact that, today, 'artists emerge in a solitary way', whereas his preferred models – the New Wave in cinema and the *nouveau roman* in literature – were both created as movements in which 'the work could be thought through as a group'.[205] On a broader social scale, the need for cultural and personal liberty was collectively expressed in the revolts of May 1968, but had to be interpreted and lived out individually in the subsequent generation. As Lee Hill remarks, 'Both Jonathan and Paul [in *Dans Paris*] are clearly the children of the children of 1968 – clued into the need for individual happiness and self-expression, but also overwhelmed by how such values make it difficult to make others happy or to simply communicate without complicating life further.'[206] The spectre of AIDS, dramatized in *Les Bien-Aimés*, is also central to this paralysis that makes it impossible to live as openly and optimistically as the models of the 1960s seem to do. As Honoré notes, all of the queer 'totems' of his adolescence (Serge Daney, Jacques Demy, Hervé Guibert, Bernard-Marie Koltès) were dead from AIDS by the time he arrived in Paris as a young man to pursue his artistic dream.[207]

Christophe Honoré's films are very clearly indebted to the French New Wave: in their mise en scène, in their use of stars and in their appropriation of the musical genre. But, in this appeal to the past, there is both a real nostalgic affection and an acute awareness of the risk of cliché, which no doubt explain the distinction between the self-conscious mise en scène of the period scenes in *Les Bien-Aimés* and the more naturalistic style of the scenes in the present and recent past. There is inevitably a kind of arrogance for a young director to measure himself in this way against the model of the New Wave, but this arrogance is itself, in a sense, second-hand: it is the same audacity with which the New Wave critics, in their time, launched themselves, untested, into the adventure of directing. There is almost a taunting of the spectator at certain points in Honoré's cinema, a readiness to come across as insufferably smug and self-satisfied, that recalls the most daring conceits of the early Godard and Truffaut. But for Honoré, as was already the case for the New Wave generation, this very personal framing of the filmmaking experience is the only way to avoid a disingenuous naïveté in a cinema that has long since lost its innocence. It is the personal quality to these films, their idiosyncratic touches over and above their value as documentary evidence, that lends them a sincerity and an emotional truth. All the same, *Les Bien-Aimés* deliberately dramatizes the struggle to live up to the perceived lightness and openness of the earlier generation at a time when the distant optimism of the *Trente Glorieuses* has diffracted and hardened into a complicated set of social, economic and sexual conditions with a global reach. For this reason, Honoré's films are persistently haunted by grief and loss even among their vibrancy and playfulness.

Conclusion

The early films of Olivier Assayas, François Ozon and Christophe Honoré tend to be highly self-aware meta-cinematic works, often deliberate pastiches of other filmmaking traditions, including the New Wave, or analogies for the filmmaking process itself. These are directors who make films self-consciously about acting and the direction of actors (Assayas) or about narrative and storytelling (Ozon). What is perhaps striking about this generation, however, is that the breadth of audiovisual reference includes traditions that might often be considered lowbrow or tacky: the erotic thriller and the sitcom (Ozon), Hong Kong action cinema (Assayas), even gay pornography (Honoré). This implies, as some of Ozon's comments quoted above suggest, that evaluative hierarchies may be a thing of the past in film criticism. The current generation are not so much deliberately overturning hierarchies (as did, for instance, Beineix and Besson in the 1980s) but embracing an open and inclusive audiovisual field of influence.

The increasing fragmentation and specialization of film production and consumption are sometimes accompanied, on the part of these directors, by a nostalgia for an era in which group identities and collective creative endeavours were more feasible. The difference between the directors discussed here, as compared to every other chapter in this book, is that there is no sense of a 'movement' cohering across their work. This may be partly because of a willingness on the part of these filmmakers to cross genres between projects.

The maintenance of a personal signature across genres was a key tenet of the *politique des auteurs* but, as Rosanna Maule suggests, authorship for many directors today is associated more 'with reflexive tactics of re-appropriation and re-inscription of cinema's formulaic and commercial characteristics'.[208] There is, in the end, little real continuity between, say,

Ozon's *Potiche* (2010), *Jeune et jolie* (2013) and *Frantz* (2016). But these directors demonstrate little patience with the figure of the filmmaker as outsider artist, so enthusiastically embraced by the likes of Philippe Garrel and Leos Carax. They seem to recognize that, in the profession of cinema, either you compromise or you disappear, like Valentine at the end of *Sils Maria*. Assayas, Ozon and Honoré are prolific because they are pragmatic, willing to use more 'commercial' films to fund their personal projects.

Another of the most striking points of connection between these three directors is the clear value they attribute to their work with actors, and in particular with women who feature as central protagonists of several – indeed, arguably, of most – of their films. Unlike the generation of the 1960s or the 1990s, these directors have not given rise to a circumscribed troupe of actors (only isolated individual stars like Ludivine Sagnier and Louis Garrel). Instead they work cannily with existing celebrities, part of the pleasure of the casting, the characterization and the viewing of these roles thus becomes the intertextual play of echoes between films. The directors' methods of working with actors vary: Assayas married his leading lady, after the manner of Godard and Truffaut, and Ozon establishes a relation of domination (again like Godard) as opposed to Honoré's more Rivettian collaboration and generosity. All three directors, however, display a persistent concern with the question of how to bring lightness and spontaneity to a medium that is almost inherently cumbersome (in its finance, its machinery, its large teams of personnel), and it is through their work with actors and performance that this lightness of touch is most often and most clearly conveyed.

Each of these male directors has shown a laudable interest in creating rich and rewarding roles on screen for women in middle age or older. Indeed, every film discussed in this chapter could be interpreted as a work about the relationship between generations, yet practically all of them demonstrate more respect, understanding and sympathy with regard to the older generation than do most films of the New Wave. In terms of their gender and sexual politics, these films, for the most part, take a non-judgemental attitude towards 'open' or multiple sexualities (*Swimming Pool* is an exception here, which is why it comes across as flawed and mean in places): the little orgy at the end of *Les Bien-Aimés* may be melancholic in its context, but it is by no means presented for condemnation. No doubt because two of these directors are openly gay men, the ordinariness of queer desire is taken as read in these films. Suggestions of queer desire are everywhere: between Maggie and Zoé in *Irma Vep*; between Maria and Valentine in *Sils Maria*; between Sarah and Julie in *Swimming Pool*; between Germain and Claude in *Dans la maison*. What is striking, however, is that this desire is neither the subject of the film nor a shamefully buried subtext but an everyday reality that can be acknowledged and incorporated, adding richness to the films without weighing them down. Indeed, in many of these films (*Irma Vep, Sils Maria, Dans la maison*), sexuality is not at all, or at least not directly, at issue, in the sense that significant intimate couples are not formed, and yet the films display a constant awareness of the subterranean workings of desire. One is reminded of the moment in *Sils Maria* when Valentine suggests that the young Maria had been in love with Wilhelm. Maria's correction is illuminating: 'Stop over-simplifying. It was less than that; it was better.'

Notes

1. Rosanna Maule, *Beyond Auteurism: New Directions in Authorial Film Practices in France, Italy and Spain since the 1980s* (Bristol: Intellect, 2008), 91.
2. Olivier Assayas and Jean-Michel Frodon, *Assayas par Assayas* (Paris: Stock, 2014), 250.
3. See Marie-Noëlle Tranchant, 'Olivier Assayas joue avec le chat', *Le Figaro*, 14 November 1996, and Jean-Michel Frodon, 'Le gai parfum de la dame en noir', *Le Monde*, 14 November 1996.
4. Brett Farmer, 'Tracking the Vamp: *Irma Vep* and Postclassical Cinematic Anxiety', *Postcolonial Studies* 3: 1 (2000), 46.
5. Dale Hudson, '"Just Play Yourself, 'Maggie Cheung'"': *Irma Vep*, Rethinking Transnational Stardom and Unthinking National Cinemas', *Screen* 47: 2 (2006), 224.
6. Stéphane Bouquet, '*Irma Vep* d'Olivier Assayas', *Cahiers du cinéma* 502 (May 1996), 56.
7. An observation made more generally about Assayas's cinema by Kent Jones, 'Tangled up in Blue', *Film Comment*, 32: 1 (1996), 51.
8. Bouquet, '*Irma Vep* d'Olivier Assayas'.
9. Gilles Deleuze and Félix Guattari, *Mille plateaux* (Paris: Minuit, 1980), 53–94.
10. Indeed, Louise Shea suggests that Hong Kong action cinema rejoins to some extent the aesthetics of silent cinema in its taste for movement and its expressionistic performance style, 'From Louis Feuillade to Johnny To: Olivier Assayas on the Future of French Cinema', *French Forum* 34: 3 (2009), 128.
11. Howard Hampton, 'The Strange Case of Irma Vep', in *Olivier Assayas*, ed. Kent Jones (Vienna: Österreichisches Filmmuseum/SYNEMA, 2012), 101.
12. Didier Péron, '*Irma Vep*, vampire dans le désordre', *Libération*, 17 May 1996.
13. See Assayas quoted in Paul Sutton, 'Olivier Assayas and the Cinema of Catastrophe', in *Five Directors: Auteurism from Assayas to Ozon*, ed. Kate Ince (Manchester: Manchester University Press, 2008), 17–37 (28).
14. Éric Gautier and Olivier Assayas, 'Le vol des bijoux', *Cahiers du cinéma* 507 (November 1996), 40.
15. Emmanuèle Frois, 'Olivier Assayas: du cinéma dans le cinéma', *Le Figaro*, 17 May 1996.

16 Gautier and Assayas, 'Le vol des bijoux', 37.
17 In the mid-1970s, Rivette took on the Herculean task of shooting four films back-to-back. After completing two of them (*Duelle* and *Noroît*, both 1976), Rivette abandoned the set of the third in a state of nervous exhaustion, and it was never finished. See Hélène Frappat, *Jacques Rivette, secret compris* (Paris: Cahiers du cinéma, 2001), 150, and Mary M. Wiles, *Jacques Rivette* (Urbana: University of Illinois Press, 2012), 62–3.
18 Assayas and Frodon, *Assayas par Assayas*, 245.
19 Olivier Assayas and Maggie Cheung, 'Dialogue entre un auteur français et une star chinoise', *Le Monde*, 14 November 1996.
20 Rosanna Maule traces this critique of the French model of auteur cinema through Assayas's early critical writings. See *Beyond Auteurism*, 88–90.
21 Hampton, 'The Strange Case of Irma Vep', 107.
22 Bouquet, '*Irma Vep* d'Olivier Assayas'.
23 Assayas and Cheung, 'Dialogue'.
24 Annie Coppermann, 'Feuillade revisité', *Les Échos*, 14 November 1996.
25 Bouquet, '*Irma Vep* d'Olivier Assayas'.
26 See, for one example of this kind of mise en scène criticism, Jacques Rivette, 'Génie de Howard Hawks', *Cahiers du cinéma* 23 (May 1953), 16–23.
27 Kent Jones, 'Westway to the World', in *Olivier Assayas*, ed. Kent Jones (Vienna: Österreichisches Filmmuseum/SYNEMA, 2012), 28.
28 *Télérama* described the film in very similar terms. See Jacques Morice, '*Irma Vep*', *Télérama*, 13 November 1996.
29 Gautier and Assayas, 'Le vol des bijoux', 41.
30 Farmer, 'Tracking the Vamp', 50.
31 Assayas and Frodon, *Assayas par Assayas*, 248–9.
32 Vicki Callahan, *Zones of Anxiety: Movement, Musidora, and the Crime Serials of Louis Feuillade* (Detroit: Wayne State University Press, 2005), 151–2.
33 Gautier and Assayas, 'Le vol des bijoux', 41.
34 Assayas and Cheung, 'Dialogue'.
35 Barbara Théate, '*Irma Vep*, la vampire chinoise', *Le Journal du Dimanche*, 10 November 1996.
36 Olivier Assayas, 'Interview', *Les Inrockuptibles*, 14 May 2014.
37 Stéphanie Belpêche, 'L'émouvante mise à nu de Binoche', *Le Journal du Dimanche*, 25 May 2014.
38 Marie-Noëlle Tranchant, 'Olivier Assayas, phénomène nuageux', *Le Figaro*, 19 August 2014.
39 S. G., '*Sils Maria*', *Le Nouvel Observateur*, 14 August 2014.
40 Jones, 'Westway to the World', 22.
41 Jones, 'Tangled up in Blue', 56.

42 Jean-Marc Lalanne, 'Sils Maria d'Olivier Assayas', Les Inrockuptibles, 20 August 2014.
43 Tranchant, 'Olivier Assayas, phénomène nuageux'.
44 Juliette Binoche, 'Juliette Binoche ou l'âge d'or d'une comédienne', Le Nouvel Observateur, 14 August 2014.
45 Lalanne, 'Sils Maria d'Olivier Assayas'.
46 Jones, 'Tangled up in Blue', 51.
47 Laurent Rigoulet, 'Interview with Kristen Stewart', Télérama, 30 July 2014.
48 Assayas, 'Interview'.
49 Jones, 'Tangled up in Blue', 51.
50 Steven Shaviro, Post-cinematic Affect (Winchester: Zero Books, 2010), 54.
51 Rigoulet, 'Interview with Stewart'.
52 Kristen Stewart, 'J'adore les films qui parlent de la fabrication des films', Le Monde, 25 May 2014.
53 Rigoulet, 'Interview with Stewart'.
54 Assayas, 'Interview'.
55 Rigoulet, 'Interview with Stewart'.
56 Assayas, 'Interview'.
57 Thibaut Schilt, François Ozon (Urbana: University of Illinois Press, 2011), 103.
58 Adam Bingham, 'Identity and Love: The Not-So-Discreet Charm of François Ozon', Kinoeye 3: 13 (2003).
59 Alistair Fox, 'Auteurism, Personal Cinema, and the Fémis Generation: The Case of François Ozon', in A Companion to Contemporary French Cinema, ed. Alistair Fox, Michel Marie, Raphaëlle Moine, and Hilary Radner (Chichester: Wiley-Blackwell, 2015), 216–17.
60 Serge Kaganski, 'Eaux troubles', Les Inrockuptibles, 21 May 2003.
61 Jean-Marc Lalanne, 'Les actrices', Cahiers du cinéma 565 (February 2002), 82.
62 Philippe Piazzo, 'François Ozon: "On se définit aussi par ses fantasmes"', Le Monde (Aden), 21 May 2003.
63 Kate Ince, 'François Ozon's Cinema of Desire', in Five Directors: Auteurism from Assays to Ozon (Manchester: Manchester University Press, 2008), 112, 132.
64 Christophe Honoré, quoted in David A. Gerstner and Julien Nahmias, Christophe Honoré: A Critical Introduction (Detroit: Wayne State University Press, 2015), 184.
65 Pierre Murat, 'Plongeons avec Ozon', Télérama, 21 May 2003.
66 Noël Tinazzi, 'Les hésitations d'Ozon', La Tribune, 21 May 2003.
67 On this point, see Mark Hain, 'Explicit Ambiguity: Sexual Identity, Hitchcockian Criticism, and the Films of François Ozon', Quarterly Review of Film and Video 24: 3 (2007), 278.

68 See Guy Austin, *Claude Chabrol* (Manchester: Manchester University Press, 1999), 7.
69 See Alistair Fox, *Speaking Pictures: Neuropsychoanalysis and Authorship in Film and Literature* (Bloomington: Indiana University Press, 2016), 224.
70 On the latter point, see Cécile Carayol, *Une musique pour l'image: Vers un symphonisme intimiste dans le cinéma français* (Rennes: Presses Universitaires de Rennes, 2012), 196.
71 François Ozon, 'Je voulais réaliser un film sur l'écriture', *Synopsis* 25 (May–June 2003), 21.
72 Charles Tesson, 'Eau plate', *Cahiers du cinéma* 579 (May 2003), 49.
73 Alain Riou, 'Ozon du côté de Highsmith', *Le Nouvel Observateur*, 15 May 2003.
74 Piazzo, 'François Ozon'.
75 'un propos cliché à la résonance bien terne', Tesson, 'Eau plate', 48.
76 Fox, *Speaking Pictures*, 220.
77 Britt-Marie Schiller, 'On the Threshold of the Creative Imagination: *Swimming Pool* (2003)', *International Journal of Psychoanalysis* 86 (2005), 558.
78 Olivier Bonnard, 'Duel au soleil', *Télé Obs Cinéma*, 20 May 2003.
79 Kaganski, 'Eaux troubles'.
80 Samuel Blumenfeld, 'Vagues fantasmes au bord de la piscine', *Le Monde*, 20 May 2003.
81 See Annie Coppermann, 'Deux femmes et un roman', *Les Échos*, 21 May 2003 and Tinazzi, 'Les hésitations d'Ozon'.
82 Kaganski, 'Eaux troubles'.
83 Philippe Piazzo, '*Swimming Pool* de François Ozon', *Le Monde (Aden)*, 21 May 2003.
84 Ozon, 'Je voulais réaliser un film sur l'écriture', 16.
85 Danièle Heymann, 'Avec *Swimming Pool*, Ozon risque la noyade', *Marianne*, 19 May 2003.
86 Éric Libiot, '*Swimming Pool* de François Ozon', *L'Express*, 22 May 2003.
87 Fiona Handyside, 'Girls on Film: Mothers, Sisters and Daughters in Contemporary French Cinema', in *Affaires de famille: The Family in Contemporary French Culture and Theory*, ed. Marie-Claire Barnet and Edward Welch (Amsterdam: Rodopi, 2007), 221–37 (225).
88 Andrew Asibong, *François Ozon* (Manchester: Manchester University Press, 2008), 83.
89 Tesson, 'Eau plate', 49.
90 Bonnard, 'Duel au soleil'.
91 Charlotte Rampling, 'Retrouver ce chemin initiatique', *L'Humanité*, 21 May 2003.
92 Riou, 'Ozon du côté de Highsmith'.

93 Ozon, 'Je voulais réaliser un film sur l'écriture', 15.
94 Schiller, 'On the Threshold of the Creative Imagination', 558.
95 Riou, 'Ozon du côté de Highsmith'.
96 Carlos Gomez, 'Charlotte Rampling en eau trouble', *Le Journal du Dimanche*, 18 May 2003. Thibaut Schilt also suggests that childlessness underlies the suffering of Charlotte Rampling's characters in both *Sous le sable* and *Swimming Pool*, see *François Ozon*, 79.
97 Defne Tüzün, 'Abject's "Ideal" Kin: The Sublime', in *The Sublime Today: Contemporary Readings in the Aesthetic*, ed. Gillian B. Pierce (Newcastle-upon-Tyne: Cambridge Scholars Press, 2012), 119.
98 Tesson, 'Eau plate', 49.
99 Christian Brincourt, 'Grand reporter', *Le Nouvel Observateur*, 3 July 2003.
100 Riou, 'Ozon du côté de Highsmith'.
101 Gomez, 'Charlotte Rampling en eau trouble'.
102 Dominique Borde, 'L'écrivain et la nymphette', *Le Figaro*, 19 May 2003.
103 Blumenfeld, 'Vagues fantasmes au bord de la piscine'.
104 Philippe Azoury, 'Ozon boit la tasse', *Libération*, 19 May 2003.
105 Samuel Douhaire, 'Dans le bain', *Libération*, 20 May 2003.
106 Emmanuèle Frois, 'La petite grande', *Le Figaro*, 20 May 2003.
107 Ozon, in Piazzo, 'François Ozon'.
108 Fox, 'Auteurism, Personal Cinema, and the Fémis Generation', 216.
109 Ibid., 218.
110 Fox, *Speaking Pictures*, 226, 230.
111 Fox, 'Auteurism, Personal Cinema, and the Fémis Generation', 224.
112 Tüzün, 'Abject's "Ideal" Kin', 129.
113 Handyside, 'Girls on Film', 234.
114 Murat, 'Plongeons avec Ozon'.
115 Frois, 'La petite grande'.
116 Alain Riou, 'L'effrontée de Cannes', *Le Nouvel Observateur*, 22 May 2003.
117 Jean Cléder and Laura Le Cleac'h, 'Aimer les acteurs', in *Christophe Honoré: Le cinéma nous inachève*, ed. Jean Cléder and Timothée Picard (Lormont: Le Bord de l'eau, 2014), 197–8.
118 Jacques Morice, 'Contre: étalage psy', *Télérama*, 14 May 2003.
119 Murat, 'Plongeons avec Ozon'.
120 Blumenfeld, 'Vagues fantasmes au bord de la piscine'.
121 Piazzo, 'François Ozon'.
122 Murat, 'Plongeons avec Ozon'.
123 Hain, 'Explicit Ambiguity', 281.
124 Adrien Gombeaud, 'Ozon, nouvelle saison', *Les Échos*, 10 October 2012.

125 Florence Colombani, 'Ozon, le prof et le petit démon', *Le Point*, 4 October 2012.
126 Aureliano Tonet, 'Comment François Ozon s'est sauvé de chez lui', *Le Monde*, 10 October 2012.
127 Aureliano Tonet, '*Dans la maison* intime de François Ozon', *Le Monde*, 10 October 2012.
128 Colombani, 'Ozon, le prof et le petit démon'.
129 Olivier Delcroix, 'François Ozon jusqu'à l'obsession', *Le Figaro*, 10 October 2012.
130 Cécile Carayol, 'Phénomène du minimalisme répétitif dans le cinéma français contemporain: Philippe Rombi, *Dans la maison* de François Ozon', in *Musiques de films: Nouveaux enjeux*, ed. N. T. Binh, Séverine Abhervé and José Moure (Paris: Les Impressions Nouvelles, 2014), 44.
131 Jean-François Julliard, '*Dans la maison* (Hôte-toi de là…)', *Le Canard enchaîné*, 10 October 2012.
132 Alexis Campion, '*Dans la maison*', *Le Journal du Dimanche*, 7 October 2012.
133 Tonet, 'Comment François Ozon s'est sauvé de chez lui'.
134 Gombeaud, 'Ozon, nouvelle saison'.
135 See Colombani, 'Ozon, le prof et le petit démon' and Éric Libiot, 'Le coup de la panne', *L'Express*, 10 October 2012.
136 Gombeaud, 'Ozon, nouvelle saison'. Olivier Delcroix also references Visconti's *Death in Venice* (1971) in 'François Ozon jusqu'à l'obsession'.
137 Tonet, '*Dans la maison* intime de François Ozon'.
138 Ince, 'François Ozon's Cinema of Desire', 113.
139 Ibid., 114.
140 Stéphane Delorme, '*Dans la maison*', *Cahiers du cinéma* 682 (October 2012), 55.
141 Campion, '*Dans la maison*'.
142 Colombani, 'Ozon, le prof et le petit démon'.
143 Tonet, 'Comment François Ozon s'est sauvé de chez lui'.
144 Colombani, 'Ozon, le prof et le petit démon'.
145 See Jonathan Rosenbaum, 'Work and Play in the House of Fiction: On Jacques Rivette', in *Placing Movies: The Practice of Film Criticism* (Berkeley: University of California Press, 1995), 142–52.
146 Delorme, '*Dans la maison*'.
147 Colombani, 'Ozon, le prof et le petit démon'.
148 See Douglas Morrey and Alison Smith, *Jacques Rivette* (Manchester: Manchester University Press, 2009), 111–12.
149 Later, in a further gesture to *Swimming Pool*'s repeated panning shots, we get an almost identical pan of Jeanne/Kristin Scott Thomas with Claude

seated in a similar disposition with regard to her. The repetition of the same saxophone refrain implies something about the ease with which a teenage boy's erotic fixation can switch from one woman to the next without taking account of their individuality.

150 Danièle Heymann, 'Doux vertige', *Marianne*, 6 October 2012.
151 Pierre Murat, '*Dans la maison*', *Télérama*, 10 October 2012.
152 Ibid.
153 See Ince, 'François Ozon's Cinema of Desire', 113 and n. 2, citing Asibong, *François Ozon*.
154 Schilt, *François Ozon*, 88.
155 Ince, 'François Ozon's Cinema of Desire', 132.
156 Fabien Le Tinnier and Timothée Picard, 'Éloge de l'impureté', in *Christophe Honoré: Le cinéma nous inachève*, ed. Jean Cléder and Timothée Picard (Lormont: Le Bord de l'eau, 2014), 178.
157 Douglas Morrey, 'Jean-Luc Godard, Christophe Honoré, and the Legacy of the New Wave in French Cinema', in *The Legacies of Jean-Luc Godard*, ed. Douglas Morrey, Christina Stojanova, and Nicole Côté (Waterloo, ON: Wilfrid Laurier University Press, 2014), 4. This essay presents an early version of the current argument focusing closely on *Dans Paris*. The current analysis summarizes the findings of the earlier work and adds detailed reference to *Les Bien-Aimés*. For another, even more detailed reading of the opening scenes of *Dans Paris*, see Gerstner and Nahmias, *Christophe Honoré*, 50–64.
158 Morrey, 'Jean-Luc Godard, Christophe Honoré, and the Legacy of the New Wave in French Cinema', 5–6.
159 See also, on this point, Simon Daniellou, 'La cinéphilie comme contemporanéité dans le cinéma de Christophe Honoré', in *Christophe Honoré: Le cinéma nous inachève*, ed. Jean Cléder and Timothée Picard (Lormont: Le Bord de l'eau, 2014), 34.
160 Christophe Honoré, quoted in Isabelle Vanderschelden, 'The "Beautiful People" of Christophe Honoré: New Wave Legacies and New Directions in French Auteur Cinema', *Studies in European Cinema* 7: 2 (2010), 143.
161 Notably in *L'Homme qui aimait les femmes* (Truffaut, 1977), also noted by Vincent Ostria, 'Aimer, désenchanter, chanter en Demy teinte', *L'Humanité*, 24 August 2011.
162 Originally released by Nancy Sinatra in February 1966 and covered by the French pop star Eileen later that same year, the song is thus ever so slightly 'anachronistic' when applied to a scene from 1964.
163 Jean Cléder, Aurélie Julien and Soazig Le Bail, 'Géographie de la création', in *Christophe Honoré: Le cinéma nous inachève*, ed. Jean Cléder and Timothée Picard (Lormont: Le Bord de l'eau, 2014), 118–19.
164 Lee Hill, 'The Third Mind of Christophe Honoré', *Vertigo* 14 (2007).
165 See, for instance, François-Guillaume Lorrain, '*Dans Paris*', *Le Point*, 28 September 2006.

166 Quoted in Gerstner and Nahmias, *Christophe Honoré*, 58, originally published in *The Guardian*, 13 December 2007.
167 In Cléder, Julien and Le Bail, 'Géographie de la création', 125.
168 Gerstner and Nahmias, *Christophe Honoré*, 30.
169 Louis Guichard, 'Interview with Christophe Honoré', *Télérama*, 27 July 2011.
170 Honoré, in Cléder, Julien and Le Bail, 'Géographie de la création', 122.
171 Guichard, 'Interview'.
172 Christophe Honoré, 'Triste moralité du cinéma français', *Cahiers du cinéma* 521 (February 1998), 4–5.
173 Gerstner and Nahmias, *Christophe Honoré*, 16.
174 Cléder, Julien and Le Bail, 'Géographie de la création', 123.
175 Jacques Rivette, 'Nous ne sommes plus innocents', reprinted in Frappat, *Jacques Rivette*, 66–8, first published in *Le Bulletin du Ciné-Club du Quartier Latin*, 1950.
176 Cléder, Julien and Le Bail, 'Géographie de la création', 124.
177 Daniellou, 'La cinéphilie comme contemporanéité dans le cinéma de Christophe Honoré', 43.
178 Bruno Blanckeman, 'Interview with Christophe Honoré', *Revue critique de fixxion française contemporaine* 5 (2012), 145.
179 Cléder and Le Cleac'h, 'Aimer les acteurs', 197.
180 As Honoré has admitted, see Guichard, 'Interview'.
181 Laëtitia Coindet and Timothée Picard, 'Dynamiques de groupe', in *Christophe Honoré: Le cinéma nous inachève*, ed. Jean Cléder and Timothée Picard (Lormont: Le Bord de l'eau, 2014), 153.
182 See, for instance, Hill, 'The Third Mind of Christophe Honoré'.
183 Richard Dyer, *Pastiche* (London: Routledge, 2007), 81.
184 Morrey, 'Jean-Luc Godard, Christophe Honoré and the Legacy of the New Wave in French Cinema', 7.
185 Vanderschelden, 'The "Beautiful People" of Christophe Honoré', 138.
186 Jean-Baptiste Morain, '*Les Bien-Aimés* de Christophe Honoré', *Les Inrockuptibles*, 25 May 2011.
187 Gerstner and Nahmias, *Christophe Honoré*, 12.
188 Louis Guichard, '*Les Bien-Aimés*: Christophe Honoré', *Télérama*, 24 August 2011.
189 Coindet and Picard, 'Dynamiques de groupe', 155.
190 Gerstner and Nahmias, *Christophe Honoré*, 62.
191 Ibid.
192 Ibid., 7.
193 Ibid., 4.

194 Daniellou, 'La cinéphilie comme contemporanéité dans le cinéma de Christophe Honoré', 37.
195 Morain, '*Les Bien-Aimés* de Christophe Honoré'.
196 Coindet and Picard, 'Dynamiques de groupe', 146.
197 Ibid., 150.
198 Ibid., 134.
199 Ibid., 149–50.
200 Cléder and Le Cleac'h, 'Aimer les acteurs', 195.
201 See Emily Barnett, 'Interview with Christophe Honoré', *Les Inrockuptibles*, 25 May 2011.
202 On this point, see Laurent Jullier and Giuseppina Sapio, 'Bernardo Bertolucci et Jacques Demy: Présences fantomales dans le cinéma de Christophe Honoré', in *Christophe Honoré: Le cinéma nous inachève*, ed. Jean Cléder and Timothée Picard (Lormont: Le Bord de l'eau, 2014), 20.
203 Coindet and Picard, 'Dynamiques de groupe', 137.
204 Ibid., 138–9.
205 Le Tinnier and Picard, 'Éloge de l'impureté', 162.
206 Hill, 'The Third Mind of Christophe Honoré'.
207 Le Tinnier and Picard, 'Éloge de l'impureté', 170.
208 Maule, *Beyond Auteurism*, 100.

Conclusion

On 19 May 2018, Richard Brody, film critic for the *New Yorker* and author of a fine biography of Jean-Luc Godard[1] tweeted: 'Great that Godard's new film gets a prize at Cannes, as did *Goodbye to Language*, but now, as then, the ending of *In a Lonely Place* comes to mind: "Yesterday, this would have meant so much to us."' What did Brody mean by this? Presumably that for a filmmaker as controversial, confrontational and often just plain confusing as Godard to be recognized by the world's most prestigious film festival (*Le Livre d'image* won a so-called Palme d'Or spéciale for its director) constitutes a considerable coup that, depending on your ideological purism, might be seen either as the incursion of a radical counter-cinema into the mainstream or as a bourgeois selling-out to the establishment. But the sense of Brody's citation from *In a Lonely Place* (1950) is that, today, this 'victory' quickly becomes lost in the glut of competing media stories. The tweet implies a rather melancholy sense that the time when cinema 'meant so much' is now definitively behind us and unlikely to come again. The very reference to Nicholas Ray's film, a key work in the canon of the *politique des auteurs* (Godard once famously opined that 'le cinéma, c'est Nicholas Ray'[2]), betrays Brody's loyalty to a bygone era of film criticism in which the defence of one's favourites and, with them, a certain conception of cinema could be considered a matter not just of personal honour but almost of life and death.

Another, perhaps more visible, sign of the increasingly unbridgeable distance travelled by film culture since the New Wave is the release of Michel Hazanavicius's film *Le Redoutable* (released in September 2017 in France and, in a neat marketing tie-in with the fiftieth anniversary of May 1968, in May 2018 in the UK). Based on Anne Wiazemsky's memoir *Un an après* (2015), it recounts Godard's relationship with his second wife from the reception of *La Chinoise* (released in France at the end of August 1967), through the events of May 1968, to their break-up in the early 1970s. The idea of making a film, in a broadly comical vein, about Godard and Wiazemsky's domestic, artistic and political misadventures in the years around 1968 would, I suspect, have been almost unthinkable until very recently. There have been fiction films about the events of May (themselves often the subject of heated debate, like *The Dreamers* [Bertolucci, 2003] or *Les Amants réguliers* [Garrel, 2005]) and sundry documentary accounts filmed in the immediate aftermath or much later. But something about Godard's cultural status, together with the mythical 'anticipation' enacted by *La Chinoise* with its famous tracking shot from university buildings to the immigrant-workers' shantytown on the edge of the Nanterre campus, should have rendered this material sacrosanct. The fact that it is Michel Hazanavicius, a parodist par excellence, who adapts the material only shows how ready we have become to laugh at the cultural seriousness and demagoguery of this era.

In *Le Redoutable*, Jean-Luc Godard is played by Louis Garrel, inevitably bringing his own cultural micro-history to the role as the son of Philippe Garrel (one of Godard's first and most faithful disciples in French cinema, as we learned in Chapter 1) and the broodingly handsome male star of both of the May 1968 movies mentioned above. Garrel mimics Godard's distinctive vocal delivery, adopting an inelegant lisp, and, although the impersonation is uncanny and impressively sustained, it is hard not to conclude that Garrel is also bringing elements of his own carefully cultivated persona to the role. The Godard of this film is, above all, a grump (we see him mostly being petty and argumentative, rarely, for instance, displaying any creativity), and, as such, he recalls Garrel's string of roles for Christophe Honoré in which the actor gave himself the challenge of rendering selfish and capricious characters likeable through the sheer verve of his performance. At times, though, the mise-en-abyme is properly vertiginous: in several scenes, Hazanavicius has Garrel address the camera and, paraphrasing some of Godard's less becoming rhetoric, denigrate the profession of the actor. This is something Godard did with Jean-Pierre Léaud in *La Chinoise* and, since Léaud has provided the acknowledged model for the development of Garrel's performance style, we find ourselves, in these scenes, looking at something like Garrel (actor) as Léaud (inspiration) as Godard (character) as Léaud (intertext) filmed by Godard filmed by Hazanavicius.

Le Redoutable is undoubtedly fond of its New Wave models, just as *The Artist* (2011) was beguiled by silent cinema. The film constitutes a knowledgeable and affectionate parody, and the account of the decline of Godard and Wiazemsky's relationship into jealousy, bitterness and recrimination is sensitive and ultimately moving. Still, Hazanavicius enjoys poking fun at Godard, as with the running joke about the breaking of his glasses during the events of May (this did really happen at least once, but it is shown or evoked no fewer than four times in the *Le Redoutable*). This tends to enshrine the cliché of the hapless intellectual out of his depth when plunged into the tumult of real political action. On the whole, the film presents the political arguments of the era as hopelessly dated and rich fodder for wry comedy. The doctrinaire positions of the time are assumed to be laughably reductive as when Jean-Pierre Gorin tells Godard, at a party, 'Either you're making revolutionary cinema or you're filming like a cop.' The public debates at the Sorbonne, peopled by jeering, long-haired extras, appear as quaint period pieces. The risk, then, is that political commitment and militant direct action come to be seen as amusing lifestyle accessories that are simply *passés de mode*, like miniskirts and turntables. This is particularly the case in a montage sequence where scenes of street riots are incongruously soundtracked by cheesy lounge music before segueing smoothly into erotic images of Anne (Stacy Martin) sunbathing in Cannes, their framing clearly recalling famous images from *Le Mépris* (1963). The Godard of *Le Redoutable* comes across less as a man undergoing a personal political crisis than as a simple victim of his own celebrity, a distinctly twenty-first-century problem. Anne continually reminds him of his status: 'You're Godard', she says, and 'I married Jean-Luc Godard, the filmmaker'. Among the clamorous crowds on the springtime streets, Godard is repeatedly approached by fans asking, 'Are you going to make more films like *À bout de souffle*?' Even a policeman politely comments that 'my wife and I really enjoyed *Le Mépris*'. One is insistently reminded of the fan in Woody Allen's *Stardust Memories* (1980) who expresses his nostalgic regret for the protagonist director's 'early, funny films'.

Le Redoutable is funny, and clever, in its multiple appropriations of Godard. The framing of individual images recalls shots from several of Godard's features, while also citing earlier films, just as Godard did (Jean-Luc and Anne go to see *La Passion de Jeanne d'Arc* [1928], as Nana did in *Vivre sa vie* [1962]), and Hazanavicius repeatedly plays with text on screen, like the early Godard, using book covers or surtitles to comment on the central couple's relationship like in *Une femme est une femme* (1961). The problem is that once the film's political context has been dismissed as a distant, if loveable, folly, then these cinematic *figures de style* are reduced to nothing more than period decoration. This is a manner of filmmaking to be parodied, like the spy movie conventions sent up in *OSS 117* (2006, 2009), but one mode of filmmaking can claim no cultural or moral primacy over the other. Indeed, despite the political backdrop of 1968 and its aftermath, Hazanavicius's steady focus on Godard and Wiazemsky's domestic deterioration seems ultimately to imply that the director was wrong to leave behind the intimate conjugal dramas of his New Wave period (in an interior monologue at the very end of the film, the Godard character admits that he 'lost his way'). But what this fails to recognize is that the forbidding political rhetoric and recondite montage patterns of Godard's work with the Dziga Vertov Group was prepared and made possible by the New Wave's resolute commitment to an ethics of film form. The language games that Hazanavicius gleefully recalls from the early 1960s work are not just games but serve to show both the groundlessness of our received sense of the world and the irrevocable linguistic alienation of interpersonal communication. It was the tireless exploration of these formal ideas across the 1960s that led Godard to question the most basic assumptions of both cinema and society such that his Maoist bifurcation can actually be seen not as a misguided following of fashion but as a logical consequence of his career-long theorization of image and sound in film form.

Do these two examples – *Le Redoutable*'s playful evocation of Godard-lite, plus Brody's shrugging acknowledgement of *Le Livre d'image*'s success – imply that the meaningful legacy of the New Wave may be at, or approaching, its end? If the New Wave is only a set of quirky personalities, sharp fashions, jaunty camera angles and good-looking couples, then it will soon lose its power to infuriate and inspire. How has this dilution happened? This book has suggested a number of key factors. Two elements that are essential to the identity of the New Wave – the energy of youth and the excitement of urban living – have undergone dramatic shifts in meaning in the decades since the 1960s, as discussed particularly in Chapters 2 and 3. Through a combination of profound shifts in the economy, technology and public health, youth has been transformed, for many young people, from a brief but open phase of possibility and experimentation to an indefinitely extended period of economic precarity, social pressure and sexual anxiety. Meanwhile, the closing down of public space through successive waves of privatization and securitization has increasingly made the city a space of corporate control and state surveillance, while the spiralling costs of rent and comestibles have rendered the interior spaces of the city equally inaccessible.

Another significant change impacting upon cinema in the time since the New Wave is the fragmentation of cultural experience and the consequent loss of common points of reference. As we saw in the last chapter of this book, Olivier Assayas, François Ozon and Christophe Honoré have all developed a notably citational form of cinema among whose terms of reference the New Wave figures prominently. Yet there is no clear sense of a movement emerging from this work, no shared purpose or common enemy. Both Assayas and Honoré have criticized a certain kind of Franco-French cinema, but they don't necessarily mean the same thing: the former blames the navel-gazing of intimate French drama, the latter the worthy subjects of social realism. Meanwhile, the commercial juggernauts of Hollywood are so far removed from the majority of French cinema – in their production models, their narrative formulae and their increasing disregard for live action – that it is almost difficult to accept them as arising from the same medium. (Witness, for instance, popular film review programmes on mainstream broadcast media in France, such as France Culture's *Le Masque et la Plume*, that frequently treat blockbuster CGI and comic-book adaptations as little better than jokes not worthy of airtime.)

No doubt the reason we love the French New Wave, the reason it continues to exert fascination over new viewers and the reason for its particularly long and fertile resonance in French and other cinemas lie in the movement's position at the hinge of classical and modern cinema. The New Wave is often held up as something like the culmination of modern cinema and elsewhere seen as instituting its postmodern era.[3] Yet the New Wave's classical roots remain close to the surface through its citational aesthetic. If the New Wave has been stubbornly associated with youth, indeed with adolescence, despite the relative lack of actual teenagers in these films,[4] it is surely because the movement stands as something like the adolescence of an art.[5] In the late 1950s, the cinema was still young enough that all of its major accomplishments could be comprehensively mapped by a few years' obsessive frequentation of the Cinémathèque. By the same token, then, the New Wave showed the audacity (and naïveté) of youth by believing it could overturn the established wisdom of cinema, rewrite the rules or begin again from zero. This is surely why some of the New Wave's most devoted followers and most original inheritors (Philippe Garrel, Leos Carax, to an extent Olivier Assayas) came to the movement in their own adolescence and, so to speak, never left it, since the energy and commitment of the Nouvelle Vague reflect the passion and certainty of those formative years. If there is unlikely ever again to be anything to resemble the spirit and impact of the New Wave in the future of cinema, it is because the culture of the moving image has become at once so dense and so diffuse, its points of entry so multiple and its modes of practice and reception so diverse, that strategies of subversion and resistance can only ever be local and context-dependent. The brief passage of the New Wave's comet and its long and brightly glowing tail remind us of a time, now seemingly light-years distant, when the cinema was everything.

Notes

1 Richard Brody, *Everything Is Cinema: The Working Life of Jean-Luc Godard* (New York: Metropolitan, 2008).

2 Jean-Luc Godard, 'Au-delà des étoiles', in *Jean-Luc Godard par Jean-Luc Godard, tome 1: 1950–1984* (Paris: Cahiers du cinéma, 1998), 119.

3 Compare Jean-Michel Frodon, *L'Âge moderne du cinéma français: De la Nouvelle Vague à nos jours* (Paris: Flammarion, 1995) and Susan Hayward, *French National Cinema*, second edition (London: Routledge, 2005), who sees the New Wave as instituting 'French cinema's age of the postmodern' (title of Hayward's chapter 4).

4 Keith Reader, '"Tous les garçons et les filles de leur âge": Representations of Youth and Adolescence in Pre-New Wave French Cinema', *French Cultural Studies* 7 (1996), 260–1.

5 I am, in a sense, adapting here Godard's concept of *L'Enfance de l'art*, discussed in Chapter 4.

BIBLIOGRAPHY

Adair, Gilbert. 'Rohmer's *Perceval*'. In *Éric Rohmer: Interviews*, edited by Fiona Handyside, 41–9. Jackson: University of Mississippi Press, 2013.
Alligier, Maryline. *Bruno Dumont: L'animalité et la grâce*. Pertuis: Rouge Profond, 2012.
AlSayyad, Nezar. *Cinematic Urbanism: A History of the Modern from Reel to Real*. New York: Routledge, 2006.
Amy de la Brétèque, François 'Éric Rohmer et son rapport à l'Histoire en particulier dans ses "tragédies de l'histoire"'. In *Rohmer en perspectives*, edited by Sylvie Robic and Laurence Schifano, 53–69. Paris: Presses Universitaires de Paris Ouest, 2013.
Anderson, Melissa. 'The Modest Gesture of the Filmmaker: An Interview with Agnès Varda'. *Cineaste* 26: 4 (2001): 24–7.
Andrew, Dudley. *Mists of Regret: Culture and Sensibility in Classic French Film*. Princeton: Princeton University Press, 1995.
Andrew, Dudley. *What Cinema Is! Bazin's Quest and Its Charge*. Chichester: Wiley-Blackwell, 2010.
Asibong, Andrew. *François Ozon*. Manchester: Manchester University Press, 2008.
Assayas, Olivier. 'Interview'. *Les Inrockuptibles*, 14 May 2014.
Assayas, Olivier, and Jean-Michel Frodon. *Assayas par Assayas*. Paris: Stock, 2014.
Assayas, Olivier, and Maggue Cheung. 'Dialogue entre un auteur français et une star chinoise'. *Le Monde*, 14 November 1996.
Assayas, Olivier, and Claire Denis, Cédric Kahn and Noémie Lvovsky. 'Quelques vagues plus tard'. *Cahiers du cinéma* special issue *Nouvelle Vague: Une légende en question* (1998): 70–5.
Assouline, Florence. 'Agnès Varda ne filme que les restes'. *L'Événement*, 6 July 2000.
Audé, Françoise. 'Entretien avec Noémie Lvovsky: Une belle personne'. *Positif* 408 (February 1995): 39–42.
Aumont, Jacques. *Amnésies: Fictions du cinéma d'après Jean-Luc Godard*. Paris: P.O.L., 1999.
Aumont, Jacques. *Le Cinéma et la mise en scène*. Paris: Armand Colin, 2010.
Aumont, Jacques. *Que reste-t-il du cinéma?* Paris: Vrin, 2012.
Austin, Guy. *Claude Chabrol*. Manchester: Manchester University Press, 1999.
Azoury, Philippe. 'Ozon boit la tasse'. *Libération*, 19 May 2003.
Azoury, Philippe. *Philippe Garrel, en substance*. Paris: Capricci, 2013.
Baignères, Claude. 'La quête de l'absurde'. *L'Aurore*, 17 March 1981.
Baignères, Claude. 'Tu causes, tu causes!' *Le Figaro*, 13 May 1996.
Baignères, Claude. 'Constat de néant'. *Le Figaro*, 19 May 1999.

Barnett, Emily. 'Interview with Christophe Honoré'. *Les Inrockuptibles*, 25 May 2011.
Baron, Jeanine. 'Leos Carax: "Le cinéma a été ma seule école"'. *La Croix*, 22 November 1984.
Bassan, Raphaël. 'Trois néobaroques français: Beineix, Besson, Carax, de *Diva* au *Grand Bleu*'. *La Revue du cinéma* 449 (May 1989): 45–50.
'B.B.' 'Bruno Dumont, l'ennui et la rédemption'. *Le Figaro*, 9 May 1997.
Belpêche, Stéphanie. 'L'émouvante mise à nu de Binoche'. *Le Journal du Dimanche*, 25 May 2014.
Bergala, Alain. 'Le vrai, le faux, le factice'. *Cahiers du cinéma* 351 (September 1983): 5–8.
Bergala, Alain. 'D'une certaine manière'. *Cahiers du cinéma* 370 (April 1985): 11–15.
Bernard de Courville, Florence '*L'Anglaise et le Duc*: Le réel et le tableau'. In *Rohmer et les autres*, edited by Noël Herpe, 169–81. Rennes: Presses Universitaires de Rennes, 2007.
Berry, David. 'Underground Cinema: French Visions of the Metro'. In *Spaces in European Cinema*, edited by Myrto Konstantarkos, 8–22. Exeter: Intellect, 2000.
Bescos, José. '*Les Doigts dans la tête*'. *Pariscope*, 11 December 1974.
Bescos, José-Maria. '*Diva*'. *Pariscope*, 25 March 1981.
Bickerton, Emilie. *A Short History of Cahiers du cinéma*. London: Verso, 2009.
Billard, Pierre. 'Ne ratons pas le premier métro'. *Le Point*, 23 March 1981.
Bingham, Adam. 'Identity and Love: The Not-So-Discreet Charm of François Ozon'. *Kinoeye* 3 (2003): 13.
Binoche, Juliette. 'A comme Anna'. *Cahiers du cinéma* 389 (November 1986): 21–4.
Binoche, Juliette. 'Juliette Binoche ou l'âge d'or d'une comédienne'. *Le Nouvel Observateur*,14 August 2014.
Bíro, Yvette. *Turbulence and Flow in Film: The Rhythmic Design*. Bloomington: Indiana University Press, 2008.
Blanckeman, Bruno. 'Interview with Christophe Honoré'. *Revue critique de fixxion française contemporaine* 5 (2012): 142–52.
Blumenfeld, Samuel. 'Vagues fantasmes au bord de la piscine'. *Le Monde*, 20 May 2003.
Bonnard, Olivier. 'Duel au soleil'. *Télé Obs Cinéma*, 20 May 2003.
Bonnaud, Frédéric. '*Les Glaneurs et la Glaneuse*'. *Les Inrockuptibles*, 23 May 2000.
Bonner, Virginia. 'Beautiful Trash: Agnès Varda's *Les Glaneurs et la Glaneuse*'. *Senses of Cinema* 45 (2007).
Bonner, Virginia. 'The Gleaners and "Us": The Radical Modesty of Agnès Varda's *Les Glaneurs et la Glaneuse*'. In *There She Goes: Feminist Filmmaking and Beyond*, edited by Corinn Columpar and Sophie Mayer, 119–31. Detroit: Wayne State University Press, 2009.
Borde, Dominique. 'L'écrivain et la nymphette'. *Le Figaro*, 19 May 2003.
Bory, Jean-Louis. 'Romance d'un jeune homme pauvre'. *Le Nouvel Observateur*, 14 May 1973.
Boujut, Michel. 'L'amour qui va vite mais qui dure longtemps'. *L'Événement du jeudi*, 27 November 1986.

Boujut, Michel. 'Le boudoir de Rohmer'. *Charlie Hebdo*, 12 September 2001.
Boulay, Anne. 'Au fond de la nature humaine'. *Libération*, 12 May 1997.
Boulay, Anne. 'Le pire pour moi, ce serait l'indifférence'. *Libération*, 18 May 1999.
Bouquet, Stéphane. 'Attache-moi'. *Cahiers du cinéma* 488 (February 1995): 24–5.
Bouquet, Stéphane. '*Irma Vep* d'Olivier Assayas'. *Cahiers du cinéma* 502 (May 1996): 56.
Bowles, Brett. '*The Life of Jesus (La Vie de Jésus)*'. *Film Quarterly* 57: 3 (2004): 47–55.
Bresson, Robert. *Notes sur le cinématographe*. Paris: Gallimard Folio, 1975.
Brincourt, Christian. 'Grand reporter'. *Le Nouvel Observateur*, 3 July 2003.
Briot, Marie-Odile. 'Le cycle infernal de la féminité (Sur *La Maman et la Putain*)'. *Positif* 157 (March 1974): 54–5.
Brody, Richard. *Everything Is Cinema: The Working Life of Jean-Luc Godard*. New York: Metropolitan, 2008.
Brunette, Peter, and David Wills. *Screen/Play: Derrida and Film Theory*. Princeton: Princeton University Press, 1989.
Bruyn, Olivier de. 'Une incertaine tendance du jeune cinéma français'. *Positif* 399 (May 1994): 48–50.
Calatayud, Agnès. 'The Self-Portrait in French Cinema: Reflections on Theory and on Agnès Varda's *Les Glaneurs et la Glaneuse*'. In *Textual and Visual Selves: Photography, Film and Comic Art in French Autobiography*, edited by Natalie Edwards, Amy Hubbell and Ann Miller, 209–34. Lincoln, NE: University of Nebraska Press, 2011.
Callahan, Vicki. *Zones of Anxiety: Movement, Musidora, and the Crime Serials of Louis Feuillade*. Detroit: Wayne State University Press, 2005.
Campion, Alexis. '*Dans la maison*'. *Le Journal du Dimanche*, 7 October 2012.
Carax, Leos. 'Journal d'un cineaste par Leos Carax'. *Libération*, 22 November 1984.
Carax, Leos. 'La beauté en révolte'. *Cahiers du cinéma* 390 (December 1986): 25–32.
Carayol, Cécile. *Une musique pour l'image: Vers un symphonisme intimiste dans le cinéma français*. Rennes: Presses Universitaires de Rennes, 2012.
Carayol, Cécile. 'Phénomène du minimalisme répétitif dans le cinéma français contemporain: Philippe Rombi, *Dans la maison* de François Ozon'. In *Musiques de films: Nouveaux enjeux*, edited by Séverine Abhervé, N. T. Binh and José Moure, 34–45. Paris: Les Impressions Nouvelles, 2014.
Carlson, Jerry W. 'Éric Rohmer, Historiographer'. In *The Films of Éric Rohmer: French New Wave to Old Master*, edited by Leah Anderst, 205–14. New York: Palgrave Macmillan, 2014.
Carroll, Noël. *On Criticism*. London: Routledge, 2009.
Cervoni, Albert. 'Un "néo-réalisme" français'. *France Nouvelle*, 16 December 1974.
Chauvet, Louis. 'Ce nouveau mal de la jeunesse'. *Le Figaro*, 17 May 1973.
Chauvet, Louis. Review of *Les Doigts dans la tête*. *Le Figaro*, 9 December 1974.
Chazal, Robert. '*Diva*: Amour et bel canto'. *France-Soir*, 16 March 1981.
Chazal, Robert. '*Mauvais Sang*'. *France-Soir*, 26 November 1986.
Chevrie, Marc. '*Boy meets girl*, de Leos Carax'. *Cahiers du cinéma* 360–361 (summer 1984): 73.
Chion, Michel. 'L'âge du capitaine'. *Cahiers du cinéma* 373 (June 1985): 75–7.
Chrostowska, S. D. 'Vis-à-vis the glaneuse'. *Angelaki: Journal of the Theoretical Humanities* 12: 2 (2007): 119–33.

Cléder, Jean, and Laura Le Cleac'h. 'Aimer les acteurs'. In *Christophe Honoré: Le cinéma nous inachève*, edited by Jean Cléder and Timothée Picard, 187–212. Lormont: Le Bord de l'eau, 2014.
Cléder, Jean, Aurélie Julien, and Soazig Le Bail. 'Géographie de la création'. In *Christophe Honoré: Le cinéma nous inachève*, edited by Jean Cléder and Timothée Picard, 115–32. Lormont: Le Bord de l'eau, 2014.
Clouzot, Claire. 'Contre-emploi et défense'. *Le Monde*, 29 April 1982.
Cohn-Bendit, Daniel. *Le Grand Bazar*. Paris: Belfond, 1975.
Coindet, Laëtitia, and Timothée Picard. 'Dynamiques de groupe'. In *Christophe Honoré: Le cinéma nous inachève*, edited by Jean Cléder and Timothée Picard, 133–55. Lormont: Le Bord de l'eau, 2014.
Colombani, Florence. 'Ozon, le prof et le petit démon'. *Le Point*, 4 October 2012.
Conway, Kelley. *Agnès Varda*. Urbana: University of Illinois Press, 2015.
Coppermann, Annie. 'La Diva'. *Les Échos*, 17 March 1981.
Coppermann, Annie. 'Feuillade revisité'. *Les Échos*, 14 November 1996.
Coppermann, Annie. 'La Terreur dans le boudoir'. *Les Échos*, 6 September 2001.
Coppermann, Annie. 'Deux femmes et un roman'. *Les Échos*, 21 May 2003.
Corless, Kieron, and Chris Darke. *Cannes: Inside the World's Premier Film Festival*. London: Faber & Faber, 2007.
Coutances, Jean. 'Une ronde vertigineuse'. *Télérama*, 25 January 1995.
Creton, Laurent. *Économie du cinéma*, fifth edition. Paris: Armand Colin, 2014.
Cruickshank, Ruth. 'The Work of Art in the Age of Global Consumption: Agnès Varda's *Les Glaneurs et la Glaneuse*', *L'Esprit créateur* 47: 3 (2007): 119–32.
Dall'Asta, Monica. 'The (Im)possible History'. In *For Ever Godard*, edited by Michael Temple, James S. Williams and Michael Witt, 350–63. London: Black Dog, 2004.
Daly, Fergus, and Garin Dowd. *Leos Carax*. Manchester: Manchester University Press, 2003.
Dambre, Marc. '*Arts* and the Hussards in Their Time'. *Film Criticism* 39: 1 (2014): 9–32.
Daney, Serge. 'Leos Carax, première fois'. *Libération*, 17 May 1984.
Daney, Serge. 'Sang neuf'. *Libération*, 26 November 1986.
Daniel, Isabelle. 'C'est au spectateur de devenir humain'. *Télérama*, 4 June 1997.
Daniellou, Simon. 'Le cinéphilie comme contemporanéité dans le cinéma de Christophe Honoré'. In *Christophe Honoré: Le cinéma nous inachève*, edited by Jean Cléder and Timothée Picard, 33–47. Lormont: Le Bord de l'eau, 2014.
Darke, Chris. 'Refuseniks'. *Sight & Sound* 11: 1 (January 2001): 30–3.
Darke, Chris. *Alphaville*. London: I. B. Tauris, 2005.
Darling, Lynn. 'The Curious Case of the Film *Diva*'. *Herald Tribune*, 6 August 1982.
Dastugue, Gérard. 'Musical Narration in the Films of Luc Besson'. In *The Films of Luc Besson: Master of Spectacle*, edited by Susan Hayward and Phil Powrie, 43–55. Manchester: Manchester University Press, 2006.
'D.B.' '*Mauvais Sang*'. *La Vie ouvrière*, 8 December 1986.
De Baecque, Antoine. 'Le livre ouvert'. *Cahiers du cinéma* 503 (June 1996): 27–9.
De Baecque, Antoine. *La Nouvelle Vague: Portrait d'une jeunesse*. Paris: Flammarion, 1998.
De Baecque, Antoine. *La Cinéphilie: Invention d'un regard, histoire d'une culture, 1944–1968*. Paris: Fayard, 2003.

De Baecque, Antoine. *Feu sur le quartier général! Le cinéma traversé: Textes, entretiens, récits*. Paris: Cahiers du cinéma, 2008.
De Baecque, Antoine. *L'Histoire-Caméra*. Paris: Gallimard, 2008.
De Baecque, Antoine. *Godard: Biographie*. Paris: Grasset, 2010.
De Baecque, Antoine (ed.). *Le Dictionnaire Eustache*. Paris: Éditions Léo Scheer, 2011.
De Baecque, Antoine. 'Rohmer/Politics: From Royalism to Ecology'. In *The Films of Éric Rohmer: French New Wave to Old Master*, edited by Leah Anderst, 117–30. New York: Palgrave Macmillan, 2014.
De Baecque, Antoine, and Noël Herpe. *Éric Rohmer: Biographie*. Paris: Stock, 2014.
De Baecque, Antoine, and Serge Toubiana. *François Truffaut*. Paris: Gallimard Folio, 2001.
De Baroncelli, Jean. '*Les Doigts dans la tête* de Jacques Doillon'. *Le Monde*, 9 December 1974.
Debord, Guy. *Commentaires sur la société du spectacle*. Paris: Folio, 1988.
De Gaspéri, Anne. '*Mauvais Sang* ne saurait mentir'. *Le Quotidien de Paris*, 26 November 1986.
De Gaspéri, Anne. 'La patate d'Agnès Varda'. *Le Figaro*, 16 May 2000.
Delcroix, Olivier. 'François Ozon jusqu'à l'obsession'. *Le Figaro*, 10 October 2012.
Deleuze, Gilles, and Félix Guattari. *Mille plateaux: Capitalisme et schizophrénie 2*. Paris: Minuit, 1980.
Delorme, Stéphane. '*Dans la maison*'. *Cahiers du cinéma* 682 (October 2012): 55.
DeRoo, Rebecca J. *Agnès Varda: Between Film, Photography, and Art*. Berkeley: University of California Press, 2018.
Desplechin, Arnaud, and Emmanuel Salinger. 'Interview'. *Cahiers du cinéma* 503 (June 1996): 30–5.
Devarrieux, Claire. 'La métaphore de l'alpiniste'. *Le Monde*, 9 April 1981.
Devarrieux, Claire. Untitled introduction to dossier on *Boy Meets Girl*. *Le Monde*, 15 November 1984.
Didi-Huberman, Georges. *Passés cités par JLG: L'oeil de l'histoire, 5*. Paris: Minuit, 2015.
Doane, Mary Ann. 'Film and the Masquerade: Theorising the Female Spectator'. *Screen* 23: 3–4 (1982): 74–88.
Dobson, Julia. *Negotiating the Auteur: Dominique Cabrera, Noémie Lvovsky, Laetitia Masson and Marion Vernoux*. Manchester: Manchester University Press, 2012.
Douchet, Jean. 'Le premier artiste d'après la Nouvelle Vague'. *Cahiers du cinéma* 523, special supplement *Eustache* (April 1998): 3–5.
Douhaire, Samuel. 'Dans le bain'. *Libération*, 20 May 2003.
Douin, Jean-Luc. 'La maladie d'amour'. *Télérama*, 26 November 1986.
Dubois, Colette. *La Maman et la Putain de Jean Eustache*. Crisnée: Yellow Now, 1990.
Dumont, Bruno. 'Notes de travail sur *La Vie de Jésus*'. *Positif* 440 (October 1997): 58–9.
Duran, Michel. '*La Maman et la Putain* (Eustache ou rasoir?)' *Le Canard enchaîné*, 23 May 1973.

Durmelat, Sylvie, and Vinay Swamy (eds.) *Screening Integration: Recasting Maghrebi Integration in Contemporary France*. Lincoln: University of Nebraska Press, 2012.
Dyer, Richard. *Pastiche*. London: Routledge, 2007.
Escoffier, Jean-Yves. 'La cérémonie du plan'. *Cahiers du cinéma* 389 (November 1986): 25–6, 30.
Farmer, Brett. 'Tracking the Vamp: *Irma Vep* and Postclassical Cinematic Anxiety'. *Postcolonial Studies* 3: 1 (2000): 43–52.
Faux, Anne-Marie. 'Éloge de la pauvreté'. In *Philippe Garrel*, edited by Jacques Déniel, 21–4. Pantin: Studio 43, 1988.
Ferenzi *(Sic)*, Aurélien. 'Interview with Éric Rohmer'. In *Éric Rohmer: Interviews*, edited by Fiona Handyside, 140–45. Jackson: University of Mississippi Press, 2013.
Fiant, Antony. 'Les bêtes humaines: Notes sur le cinéma de Bruno Dumont'. *Positif* 554 (April 2007): 48–55.
Fijalkowski, Krzysztof, and Michael Richardson (eds). *Surrealism: Key Concepts*. London: Routledge, 2016.
Fischer, Lucy. 'Generic Gleaning: Agnès Varda, Documentary, and the Art of Salvage'. In *Gender Meets Genre in Postwar Cinema*, edited by Christine Gledhill, 111–24. Urbana: University of Illinois Press, 2012.
Flamini, Roland. *Thalberg: The Last Tycoon and the World of M-G-M*. London: André Deutsch, 1994.
Flitterman-Lewis, Sandy. 'Varda: The Gleaner and the Just'. In *Situating the Feminist Gaze and Spectatorship in Postwar Cinema*, edited by Marcelline Block, 214–25. Newcastle-upon-Tyne: Cambridge Scholars Press, 2008.
'F.M.' 'Une histoire farfelue, ou les aventures d'un jeune postier'. *L'Humanité*, 11 March 1981.
Forbes, Jill. *The Cinema in France after the New Wave*. London: BFI/MacMillan, 1992.
Forbes, Jill. 'Psychoanalysis as Narrative in Films by Jean Eustache'. *French Cultural Studies* 14: 3 (2003): 249–56.
Fox, Alistair. 'Auteurism, Personal Cinema, and the Fémis Generation: The Case of François Ozon'. In *A Companion to Contemporary French Cinema*, edited by Alistair Fox, Michel Marie, Raphaëlle Moine and Hilary Radner, 205–29. Chichester: Wiley-Blackwell, 2015.
Fox, Alistair. *Speaking Pictures: Neuropsychoanalysis and Authorship in Film and Literature*. Bloomington: Indiana University Press, 2016.
Frappat, Hélène. *Jacques Rivette, secret compris*. Paris: Cahiers du cinéma, 2001.
Frodon, Jean-Michel. *L'Âge modern du cinéma français: De la Nouvelle Vague à nos jours*. Paris: Flammarion, 1995.
Frodon, Jean-Michel. 'Tour de force, tour de grâce'. *Le Monde*, 26 January 1995.
Frodon, Jean-Michel. 'Comment je me suis raconté'. *Le Monde*, 14 May 1996.
Frodon, Jean-Michel. 'Comment ils ont travaillé ... (avec Arnaud Desplechin)'. *Le Monde*, 13 June 1996.
Frodon, Jean-Michel. 'Le gai parfum de la dame en noir'. *Le Monde*, 14 November 1996.
Frodon, Jean-Michel. 'À bras le corps dans l'enfer du Nord'. *Le Monde*, 5 June 1997.

Frodon, Jean-Michel. 'Dans le regard d'une belle étrangère, un monde s'effondre'. *Le Monde*, 5 September 2001.
Frois, Emmanuèle. 'Arnaud Desplechin: "Misogyne? Tant mieux"'. *Le Figaro*, 11–12 May 1996.
Frois, Emmanuèle. 'Olivier Assayas: du cinéma dans le cinéma'. *Le Figaro*, 17 May 1996.
Frois, Emmanuèle. 'La petite grande'. *Le Figaro*, 20 May 2003.
Fumaroli, Marc. 'Cinéma et Terreur'. *Cahiers du cinéma* 559 (July–August 2001): 42–6.
Garrel, Philippe, and Leos Carax. 'Dialogue en apesanteur'. *Cahiers du cinéma* 365 (November 1984): 37–40.
Garrel, Philippe, and Thomas Lescure. *Une caméra à la place du coeur*. Aix-en-Provence: Amiranda/Institut de l'image, 1992.
Gatif, René. 'Comment je me suis emmerdé (au film de Desplechin)'. *L'Organe*, 15 December 2014 [first published 2001]: http://www.lorgane.com/COMMENT-JE-ME-SUIS-EMMERDE-au-film-de-Desplechin_a239.html.
Gautier, Éric, and Olivier Assayas. 'Le vol des bijoux'. *Cahiers du cinéma* 507 (November 1996): 37–41.
Gerstner, David A., and Julien Nahmias. *Christophe Honoré: A Critical Introduction*. Detroit: Wayne State University Press, 2015.
Gillain, Anne (ed.). *Le Cinéma selon François Truffaut*. Paris: Flammarion, 1988.
Gillain, Anne, and Dudley Andrew. 'Interview with Arnaud Desplechin'. In *A Companion to François Truffaut*, edited by Dudley Andrew and Anne Gillain, 3–22, 105–23. Chichester: Wiley-Blackwell, 2013.
Godard, Jean-Luc. *Introduction à une véritable histoire du cinéma*. Paris: Albatros, 1980.
Godard, Jean-Luc. 'C'est le cinéma qui raconte l'histoire: Lui seul le pouvait'. *Le Monde*, 8 October 1998.
Godard, Jean-Luc. *Histoire(s) du cinéma*, 4 vols. Paris: Gallimard, 1998.
Godard, Jean-Luc. *Jean-Luc Godard par Jean-Luc Godard, tome 1: 1950–1984*. Paris: Cahiers du cinéma, 1998.
Godard, Jean-Luc. *Introduction to a True History of Cinema and Television*. Translated by Timothy Barnard. Montreal: Caboose, 2014.
Godard, Jean-Luc, and Youssef Ishaghpour. *Archéologie du cinéma et mémoire du siècle: Dialogue*. Tours: Farrago, 2000.
Gombeaud, Adrien. 'Ozon, nouvelle saison'. *Les Échos*, 10 October 2012.
Gomez, Carlos. '*L'Humanité*, le film poil à gratter qui a scandalisé Cannes'. *Le Journal du Dimanche*, 24 October 1999.
Gomez, Carlos. 'Charlotte Rampling en eau trouble'. *Le Journal du Dimanche*, 18 May 2003.
Gorin, François, and Marc Cerisuelo. 'Conte de la Terreur ordinaire'. *Télérama*, 5 September 2001.
Guétin, Marie-Laure. 'Des décors révolutionnés: Le Pari(s) historique d'Éric Rohmer'. In *Rohmer en perspectives*, edited by Sylvie Robic and Laurence Schifano, 71–90. Paris: Presses Universitaires de Paris Ouest, 2013.
Guibert, Hervé. '*Le Monde* rencontre un film de Leos Carax'. *Le Monde*, 15 November 1984.
Guibert, Hervé. 'Le réalisateur: Une star pure et dure'. *Le Monde*, 15 November 1984.

Guichard, Louis. 'Radical et captivant'. *Télérama*, 27 October 1999.
Guichard, Louis. 'Interview with Christophe Honoré'. *Télérama*, 27 July 2011.
Guichard, Louis. '*Les Bien-Aimés*: Christophe Honoré'. *Télérama*, 24 August 2011.
Guichard, Sophie. 'Je l'aime, moi non plus'. *France-Soir*, 11 September 2001.
Guilloux, Michel. 'Quand le sujet entre dans le vif de lui-même'. *L'Humanité*, 13 May 1996.
Guilloux, Michel. 'Il voit le nord en peinture'. *Libération*, 27 October 1999.
Gunning, Tom. 'The Cinema of Attraction: Early Film, Its Spectator, and the Avant-Garde'. *Wide Angle* 8: 3–4 (1986): 63–70.
Gunning, Tom. 'Éric Rohmer and the Legacy of Cinematic Realism'. In *The Films of Éric Rohmer: French New Wave to Old Master*, edited by Leah Anderst, 23–31. New York: Palgrave Macmillan, 2014.
Hagman, Hampus. '"Every Cannes Needs Its Scandal": Between Art and Exploitation in Contemporary French Film'. *Film International* 9: 5 (2007): 32–41.
Hain, Mark. 'Explicit Ambiguity: Sexual Identity, Hitchcockian Criticism, and the Films of François Ozon'. *Quarterly Review of Film and Video* 24: 3 (2007): 277–88.
Halimi, André. 'Un cinéma nouveau'. *Pariscope*, 18 March 1981.
Hampton, Howard. 'The Strange Case of Irma Vep'. In *Olivier Assays*, edited by Kent Jones, 101–14. Vienna: Österreichisches Filmmuseum/SYNEMA, 2012.
Handyside, Fiona. 'Girls on Film: Mothers, Sisters and Daughters in Contemporary French Cinema'. In *Affaires de famille: The Family in Contemporary French Culture and Theory*, edited by Marie-Claire Barnet and Edward Welch, 221–37. Amsterdam: Rodopi, 2007.
Hardwick, Joe. 'The *vague nouvelle* and the *Nouvelle Vague*: The Critical Construction of *le jeune cinéma français*'. *Modern & Contemporary France* 16: 1 (2008): 51–65.
Harvey, David. *The Condition of Postmodernity: An Enquiry into the Origins of Cultural Change*. Oxford: Blackwell, 1990.
Hayward, Susan. *Luc Besson*. Manchester: Manchester University Press, 1998.
Hayward, Susan. *French National Cinema*, second edition. London: Routledge, 2005.
Heidegger, Martin. *Chemins qui ne mènent nulle part*. Translated by Wolfgang Brokmeier. Paris: Gallimard, 1962.
Heimermann, Benoît. 'Luc Besson en seconde'. *Le Matin*, 12 April 1985.
Herpe, Noël. 'Y aura-t-il un jeune cinéma français?' In *Le Jeune Cinéma français*, edited by Michel Marie, 30–7. Paris: Nathan, 1998.
Herpe, Noël. 'The Fall into Words: From *Contes des quatre saisons* to *L'Anglaise et le Duc*'. In *The Films of Éric Rohmer: French New Wave to Old Master*, edited by Leah Anderst, 65–72. New York: Palgrave Macmillan, 2014.
Herpe, Noël, and Cyril Neyrat. 'Interview with Éric Rohmer: Video Is Becoming Increasingly Important'. In *Éric Rohmer: Interviews*, edited by Fiona Handyside, 165–9. Jackson: University of Mississippi Press, 2013.
Hess, John. 'La Politique des auteurs (Part one): World View as Aesthetics'. *Jump Cut* 1 (1974).
Heymann, Danièle. 'Feux d'artifices'. *Le Monde*, 28 November 1986.

Heymann, Danièle. 'La mort, le sexe, la vie, bref, "l'Humanité" selon Dumont', *Marianne*, 25 October 1999.
Heymann, Danièle. 'La Révolution sur le visage d'une femme'. *Marianne*, 3 September 2001.
Heymann, Danièle. 'Avec *Swimming Pool*, Ozon risque la noyade'. *Marianne*, 19 May 2003.
Heymann, Danièle. 'Doux vertige'. *Marianne*, 6 October 2012.
Higbee, Will. *Post-beur Cinema: North-African Emigré and Maghrebi French Filmmaking in France since 2000*. Edinburgh: Edinburgh University Press, 2013.
Higham, Charles. *Howard Hughes: The Secret Life*. London: Sidgwick and Jackson, 1993.
Hill, Lee. 'The Third Mind of Christophe Honoré'. *Vertigo* 14 (2007).
Hillier, Jim. 'Introduction'. In *Cahiers du cinéma, Vol 1: The 1950s: Neo-Realism, Hollywood, New Wave*, edited by Jim Hillier, 1–17. London: Routledge and Kegan Paul/BFI, 1985.
Hochschild, Arlie Russell. *The Managed Heart: Commercialization of Human Feeling*. Berkeley: University of California Press, 1983.
Honoré, Christophe. 'Triste moralité du cinéma français'. *Cahiers du cinéma* 521 (February 1998): 4–5.
Hudson, Dale. '"Just Play Yourself, 'Maggie Cheung'": *Irma Vep*, Rethinking Transnational Stardom and Unthinking National Cinemas'. *Screen* 47: 2 (2006): 213–32.
Ince, Kate. 'François Ozon's Cinema of Desire'. In *Five Directors: Auteurism from Assayas to Ozon*, edited by Kate Ince, 112–34. Manchester: Manchester University Press, 2008.
Internationale situationniste. 'Le rôle de Godard'. *Internationale situationniste* 10 (1966). http://debordiana.chez.com/francais/is10.htm
Jameson, Fredric. *Signatures of the Visible*. New York: Routledge, 1990.
Jameson, Fredric. *Postmodernism, or the Cultural Logic of Late Capitalism*. Durham, NC: Duke University Press, 1991.
Jamet, Dominique. 'Elle court, elle court la maladie d'amour … ' *Le Quotidien de Paris*, 1 December 1986.
Jeancolas, Jean-Pierre. 'Un cinéma de la responsabilité: Esquisse de cartographie du cinéma français vivant en 1998'. *Australian Journal of French Studies* 36: 1 (1999): 12–25.
Jeancolas, Jean-Pierre. 'The Confused Image of *le jeune cinéma*'. *Studies in French Cinema* 5: 3 (2005): 157–61.
Jeannelle, Jean-Louis. *Films sans images: Une histoire des scénarios non réalisés de La Condition humaine*. Paris: Seuil, 2015.
Jeffreys, Sheila. *Anticlimax: A Feminist Perspective on the Sexual Revolution*. London: The Women's Press, 1990.
Jobs, Richard Ivan. *Riding the New Wave: Youth and the Rejuvenation of France after the Second World War*. Stanford: Stanford University Press, 2007.
Jones, Kent. 'Tangled up in Blue'. *Film Comment* 32: 1 (1996): 51–7.
Jones, Kent. 'Sad and Proud of It: The Films of Philippe Garrel'. *Film Comment* 33: 3 (1997): 24–5, 27–30.
Jones, Kent. 'Westway to the World'. In *Olivier Assayas*, edited by Kent Jones, 9–54. Vienna: Österreichisches Filmmuseum/SYNEMA, 2012.

Journot, Marie-Thérèse. *Le Courant de 'l'esthétique publicitaire' dans le cinéma français des années 80: La modernité en crise: Beineix, Besson, Carax*. Paris: L'Harmattan, 2004.
Jousse, Thierry, Nicolas Saada, Frédéric Strauss, Camille Taboulay, and Vincent Vatrican. 'Dix places pour le jeune cinéma'. *Cahiers du cinéma* 473 (November 1993): 28–30.
Julliard, Jean-François. '*Dans la maison* (Hôte-toi de là …)'. *Le Canard enchaîné*, 10 October 2012.
Jullier, Laurent, and Giuseppina Sapio. 'Bernardo Bertolucci et Jacques Demy: Présences fantomales dans le cinéma de Christophe Honoré'. In *Christophe Honoré: Le cinéma nous inachève*, edited by Jean Cléder and Timothée Picard, 19–31. Lormont: Le Bord de l'eau, 2014.
Kaganski, Serge. 'Dumont de piété'. *Les Inrockuptibles*, 27 October 1999.
Kaganski, Serge. 'Ciné brocante'. *Les Inrockuptibles*, 4 July 2000.
Kaganski, Serge. 'L'Anglaise et le continent'. *Les Inrockuptibles*, 4 September 2001.
Kaganski, Serge. 'Eaux troubles'. *Les Inrockuptibles,* 21 May 2003.
Kahn, Jean-François. 'L'aveu de la haine du peuple'. *Marianne*, 3 September 2001.
Kaupp, Katia D. 'Le réalisateur le plus "antifestival" va représenter la France à Cannes'. *Le Nouvel Observateur*, 14 May 1973.
Keathley, Christian. *Cinephilia and History, or The Wind in the Trees*. Bloomington: Indiana University Press, 2006.
Kelly, Ernece B. '*Diva*: High Tech Sexual Politics'. *Jump Cut* 29 (1984): 39–40.
Kendall, Tina. '"No God But Cinema": Bruno Dumont's *Hadewijch*'. *Contemporary French and Francophone Studies* 17: 4 (2013): 405–13.
King, Homay. 'Matter, Time, and the Digital: Varda's *The Gleaners and I*'. *Quarterly Review of Film and Video* 24: 5 (2007): 421–9.
Kracauer, Siegfried. *From Caligari to Hitler: A Psychological History of the German Film*. London: Dennis Dobson, 1947.
Lack, Roland-François. '"Sa voix"'. In *For Ever Godard*, edited by Michael Temple, James S. Williams and Michael Witt, 312–29. London: Black Dog, 2004.
Lalanne, Jean-Marc. 'Toutes les histoires. 1A'. *Cahiers du cinéma*, Special issue *Histoire(s) du cinéma*, supplement to no. 537 (July–August 1999): 6.
Lalanne, Jean-Marc. 'Les actrices'. *Cahiers du cinéma* 565 (February 2002): 82–3.
Lalanne, Jean-Marc. '*Sils Maria* d'Olivier Assayas'. *Les Inrockuptibles*, 20 August 2014.
Landrot, Marine. '*La Vie de Jésus*'. *Télérama*, 4 June 1997.
Larroque, Pierre-Jean. 'Le tissu déchiré de l'Histoire'. In *Rohmer et les autres*, edited by Noël Herpe, 213–17. Rennes: Presses Universitaires de Rennes, 2007.
Leavis, F. R. *The Great Tradition: George Eliot, Henry James, Joseph Conrad*. London: Chatto and Windus, 1979.
Le Berre, Carole. 'Comment Desplechin a tourné *Comment je me suis disputé* … ' *Cahiers du cinéma* 491 (May 1995): 38–43.
Lefort, Gérard. 'Les pieds dans le cru'. *Libération*, 4 June 1997.
Leigh, Jacob. *The Cinema of Éric Rohmer: Irony, Imagination, and the Social World*. New York: Continuum, 2012.
Le Morvan, Gilles. 'Les néons du néant'. *L'Humanité*, 10 April 1985.
Lequeret, Élisabeth. 'Le bel été de la Glaneuse'. *Cahiers du cinéma* 550 (October 2000): 32–3.

Le Tinnier, Fabien, and Timothée Picard. 'Éloge de l'impureté'. In *Christophe Honoré: Le cinéma nous inachève*, edited by Jean Cléder and Timothée Picard, 157–86. Lormont: Le Bord de l'eau, 2014.
Leutrat, Jean-Louis. 'Retour sur *Histoire(s)*, 4'. *Trafic* 73 (2010): 77–94.
Levieux, Michèle. 'La Mostra découvre une jeune réalisatrice'. *L'Humanité*, 15 September 1994.
Lévy-Klein, Stéphane. 'Entretien avec Jean Eustache (à propos de *La Maman et la Putain*)'. *Positif* 157 (March 1974): 50–3.
Libiot, Éric. '*Swimming Pool* de François Ozon'. *L'Express*, 22 May 2003.
Libiot, Éric. 'Le coup de la panne'. *L'Express*, 10 October 2012.
Livecchi, Nicolas. *L'Enfant acteur: De François Truffaut à Steven Spielberg et Jacques Doillon*. Brussels: Les Impressions Nouvelles, 2012.
Lorrain, François-Guillaume. '*L'humanité*'. *Le Point*, 22 October 1999.
Lorrain, François-Guillaume. '*Dans Paris*'. *Le Point*, 28 September 2006.
Lvovsky, Noémie. 'Je ne suis pas partie d'une histoire mais de l'idée de rébellion'. *Le Monde*, 26 January 1995.
Macia, Jean-Luc. 'Un trop-plein de cinéma'. *La Croix*, 28 November 1986.
Mandelbaum, Jacques. 'Biens sans maître glanés par maîtres sans bien'. *Le Monde*, 5 July 2000.
Mannoni, Laurent. *Histoire de la Cinémathèque Française*. Paris: Gallimard, 2006.
Marchand, Bernard. *Paris, histoire d'une ville: XIXe-XXe siècle*. Paris: Seuil, 1993.
Marie, Michel. *La Nouvelle Vague: Une école artistique*. Paris: Nathan, 1997.
Marie, Michel. '"Une famille avec des goûts communs mais des démarches personnelles ... ": Entretien avec Nicolas Boukhrief'. In *Le Jeune Cinéma français*, edited by Michel Marie, 38–47. Paris: Nathan, 1998.
Marie, Michel. *À bout de souffle*. Paris: Nathan, 1999.
Martin, Adrian. 'A Cinema of Intimate Spectacle: The Poetics of Philippe Garrel'. *Cineaste* 34: 4 (2009): 37–41.
Martin, Adrian. *Mise en scène and Film Style: From Classical Hollywood to New Media Art*. London: Palgrave Macmillan, 2014.
Mary, Philippe. *La Nouvelle Vague et le cinéma d'auteur: Socio-analyse d'une révolution artistique*. Paris: Seuil, 2006.
Maule, Rosanna. *Beyond Auteurism: New Directions in Authorial Film Practices in France, Italy and Spain since the 1980s*. Bristol: Intellect, 2008.
Mayne, Judith. 'Tous les garçons et toutes les filles'. *Studies in French Cinema* 5: 3 (2005): 207–18.
Monaco, James. *The New Wave: Truffaut, Godard, Chabrol, Rohmer, Rivette*. New York: Oxford University Press, 1976.
Morain, Jean-Baptiste. '*Les Bien-Aimés* de Christophe Honoré'. *Les Inrockuptibles*, 25 May 2011.
Morgan, Daniel. *Late Godard and the Possibilities of Cinema*. Berkeley: University of California Press, 2013.
Morice, Jacques. 'Valéria Bruni-Tedeschi (*sic*)'. *Cahiers du cinéma* 473 (November 1993): 40.
Morice, Jacques. '*Irma Vep*'. *Télérama*, 13 November 1996.
Morice, Jacques. 'Contre: étalage psy'. *Télérama*, 14 May 2003.
Morrey, Douglas. *Jean-Luc Godard and the Other History of Cinema*. Unpublished PhD thesis. University of Warwick, 2002.

Morrey, Douglas. *Jean-Luc Godard*. Manchester: Manchester University Press, 2005.
Morrey, Douglas. 'Jean-Luc Godard, Christophe Honoré and the Legacy of the New Wave in French Cinema'. In *The Legacies of Jean-Luc Godard*, edited by Douglas Morrey, Christina Stojanova and Nicole Côté, 3–14. Waterloo, ON: Wilfrid Laurier University Press, 2014.
Morrey, Douglas. 'The Lost Art of Keeping a Secret: Jacques Rivette's Film Criticism for *Arts*'. *Film Criticism* 39: 1 (2014): 51–66.
Morrey, Douglas, and Alison Smith. *Jacques Rivette*. Manchester: Manchester University Press, 2009.
Mulvey, Laura. 'Visual Pleasure and Narrative Cinema'. *Screen* 16: 3 (1975): 6–18.
Murat, Pierre. 'Ticket chic, effet choc'. *Télérama*, 17 April 1985.
Murat, Pierre. 'Arnaud ou le paradoxe'. *Télérama*, 12 June 1996.
Murat, Pierre. 'Plongeons avec Ozon'. *Télérama*, 21 May 2003.
Murat, Pierre. '*Dans la maison*'. *Télérama*, 10 October 2012.
Nacache, Jacqueline. 'Group Portrait with a Star: Jeanne Balibar and French "jeune" Cinema'. *Studies in French Cinema* 5: 1 (2005): 49–60.
Nacache, Jacqueline. 'Was There a Young French Cinema?' In *A Companion to Contemporary French Cinema*, edited by Alistair Fox, Michel Marie, Raphaëlle Moine and Hilary Radner, 184–204. Chichester: Wiley-Blackwell, 2015.
Neer, Richard. 'Godard Counts'. *Critical Inquiry* 34: 1 (2007): 135–73.
Neupert, Richard. *A History of the French New Wave Cinema*. Madison: University of Wisconsin Press, 2002.
Newsom, Chad R. '*Cahiers du cinéma* and Evaluative Criticism'. *The Cine-Files* 2 (2012).
Nowell-Smith, Geoffrey. *Making Waves: New Cinemas of the 1960s*. New York: Continuum, 2008.
O'Shaughnessy, Martin. 'Post-1995 French Cinema: Return of the Social, Return of the Political?' *Modern & Contemporary France* 11: 2 (2003): 189–203.
Ostria, Vincent. 'Aimer, désenchanter, chanter en Demy teinte'. *L'Humanité*, 24 August 2011.
Ozon, François. 'Je voulais realiser un film sur l'écriture'. *Synopsis* 25 (May–June 2003): 14–21.
Palmer, Tim. 'Style and Sensation in the Contemporary French Cinema of the Body'. *Journal of Film and Video* 58: 3 (2006): 22–32.
Péguy, Charles. *Œuvres en prose 1909–1914*. Paris: Gallimard Pléiade, 1961.
Penz, François. 'From Topographical Coherence to Creative Geography: Rohmer's *The Aviator's Wife* and Rivette's *Pont du Nord*'. In *Cities in Transition: The Moving Image and the Modern Metropolis*, edited by Andrew Webber and Emma Wilson, 123–40. London: Wallflower, 2008.
Pérez, Michel. 'Leos Carax: Les habits neufs du cinéma français'. *Le Matin*, 23 November 1984.
Pérez, Michel. '*Subway* de Luc Besson: Le metro aux heures creuses'. *Le Matin*, 12 April 1985.
Pérez, Michel. 'Un accès de fièvre de croissance'. *Le Matin*, 28 November 1986.
Péron, Didier. '*Irma Vep*, vampire dans le désordre'. *Libération*, 17 May 1996.
Péron, Didier, and Olivier Seguret. 'Interview with Arnaud Desplechin'. *Libération*, 12 June 1996.

Petit, Philippe. 'Le film qui enterre 1789'. *Marianne*, 3 September 2001.
Philippon, Alain. 'L'amour absolu du cinéma'. *Cahiers du cinéma* 336 (May 1982): 39–41.
Philippon, Alain. *Jean Eustache*. Paris: Cahiers du cinéma, 1986.
Philippon, Alain. 'Sur la terre comme au ciel'. *Cahiers du cinéma* 389 (November 1986): 15–17.
Philippon, Alain. 'Les ministères de l'art'. In *Philippe Garrel*, edited by Jacques Déniel, 17–20. Pantin: Studio 43, 1988.
Piazzo, Philippe. 'François Ozon: "On se définit aussi par ses fantasmes"'. *Le Monde (Aden)*, 21 May 2003.
Piazzo, Philippe. '*Swimming Pool* de François Ozon'. *Le Monde (Aden)*, 21 May 2003.
Pichon, Alban. *Le Cinéma de Leos Carax: L'expérience du déjà-vu*. Paris: Le Bord de l'eau, 2009.
Pierquin, Martine. '*La Maman et la Putain*/*The Mother and the Whore*'. In *The Cinema of France*, edited by Phil Powrie, 133–41. London: Wallflower, 2006.
Pigott, Michael. *Time and Film Style*. Unpublished PhD thesis. University of Warwick, 2009.
Planells, Martine. '*Subway*, sur le quai des adolescences'. *Le Quotidien de Paris*, 27 January 1985.
Plougastel, Yann. '*Subway*'. *L'Événement du jeudi*, 11 April 1985.
Powrie, Phil. *Jean-Jacques Beineix*. Manchester: Manchester University Press, 2001.
Powrie, Phil. 'Of Suits and Men in the Films of Luc Besson'. In *The Films of Luc Besson: Master of Spectacle*, edited by Susan Hayward and Phil Powrie, 75–89. Manchester: Manchester University Press, 2006.
Powrie, Phil. 'General Introduction'. In *French Cinema*, 4 vols, edited by Phil Powrie, vol. 1, 1–22. London/New York: Routledge, 2014.
Prédal, René. 'Agnès Varda: Une oeuvre en marge du cinéma français'. *Études cinématographiques* 179–186 (1991): 13–39.
Prédal, René. 'La déferlante'. In *Le Jeune Cinéma français*, edited by Michel Marie, 8–21. Paris: Nathan, 1998.
Prédal, René. *Jacques Doillon, trafic et topologie des sentiments*. Paris/Condé-sur-Noireau: Éditions du Cerf/Éditions Corlet, 2003.
Prédal, René. *Le Jeune Cinéma français*. Paris: Armand Colin, 2005.
Quandt, James. 'Flesh and Blood: Sex and Violence in Recent French Cinema'. In *The New Extremism in Cinema: From France to Europe*, edited by Tanya Horeck and Tina Kendall, 18–25. Edinburgh: Edinburgh University Press, 2011.
Rabine, Henry. 'Cannes: Un film français discutable et discuté'. *La Croix*, 18 May 1973.
Rachlin, Nathalie. 'L'exclusion au cinéma: Le cas d'Agnès Varda'. *Women in French Studies*, special issue (2006): 88–111.
Rampling, Charlotte. 'Retrouver ce chemin initiatique'. *L'Humanité*, 21 May 2003.
Rancière, Jacques. 'La Sainte et l'héritière: À propos des *Histoire(s) du cinéma*'. *Cahiers du cinéma* 536 (July–August 1999): 58–61.
Rancière, Jacques. *La Fable cinématographique*. Paris: Seuil, 2001.
Rancière, Jacques. 'The Saint and the Heiress: A Propos of Godard's *Histoire(s) du cinéma*'. Translated by T. S. Murphy. *Discourse* 24: 1 (2002): 113–19.

Rancière, Jacques. *Le Destin des images*. Paris: La Fabrique, 2003.
Rancière, Jacques. *Film Fables*. Translated by Emiliano Battista. Oxford: Berg, 2006.
Rancière, Jacques. *The Future of the Image*. Translated by Gregory Elliott. London: Verso, 2009.
Reader, Keith. '"Pratiquement plus rien d'intéressant ne se passe": Jean Eustache's *La Maman et la Putain*'. *Nottingham French Studies* 31: 1 (1993): 91–8.
Reader, Keith. '"Tous les garçons et les filles de leur âge": Representations of Youth and Adolescence in Pre-New Wave French Cinema'. *French Cultural Studies* 7 (1996): 259–70.
Remy, Vincent. '*Comment je me suis disputé ... (Ma vie sexuelle)*'. *Télérama*, 12 June 1996.
Revault d'Allonnes, Fabrice. 'Séparations (Gare, elle ...)' In *Philippe Garrel*, edited by Jacques Déniel, 27–31. Pantin: Studio 43, 1988.
Reynolds, Simon. 'From the Velvets to the Void'. *The Guardian*, 15 March 2007.
Richou, Pascal. '*La Vie de Jésus* de Bruno Dumont'. *Cahiers du cinéma* 513 (May 1997): 75.
Rigoulet, Laurent. 'Interview with Kristen Stewart'. *Télérama*, 30 July 2014.
Riou, Alain. 'Ozon du côté de Highsmith'. *Le Nouvel Observateur*, 15 May 2003.
Riou, Alain. 'L'effrontée de Cannes'. *Le Nouvel Observateur*, 22 May 2003.
Rivette, Jacques. 'Génie de Howard Hawks'. *Cahiers du cinéma* 23 (May 1953): 16–23.
Rivette, Jacques. 'L'Essentiel'. *Cahiers du cinéma* 32 (February 1954): 42–5.
Rivette, Jacques. 'The Essentiel'. In *Cahiers du cinéma, Vol 1: The 1950s: Neo-Realism, Hollywood, New Wave*, edited by Jim Hillier, 132–5. London: Routledge and Kegan Paul, 1985.
Rivette, Jacques. 'The Genius of Howard Hawks'. In *Cahiers du cinéma, Vol 1: The 1950s: Neo-Realism, Hollywood, New Wave*, edited by Jim Hillier, 126–31. London: Routledge and Kegan Paul, 1985.
Rochereau, Jean. 'La cantatrice et le postier'. *La Croix*, 14 March 1981.
Rochet, Didier. 'Pharaon simple flic'. *L'Humanité*, 19 May 1999.
Rochet, Didier. 'Humain, trop humain, le cinéma de Bruno Dumont'. *L'Humanité*, 26 May 1999.
Rohmer, Éric. *Le Goût de la beauté*. Paris: Cahiers du cinéma, 1984.
Rohmer, Éric. *L'Organisation de l'espace dans le Faust de Murnau*. Paris: Cahiers du cinéma, 2000.
Rohmer, Éric. 'Je voulais que la réalité devienne tableau'. *Cahiers du cinéma* 559 (July–August 2001): 50–8.
Rohmer, Éric. 'Le large et le haut'. *Cahiers du cinéma* 559 (July–August 2001): 59–61.
Rohmer, Éric. 'J'ai voulu faire mieux que les Américains'. *Le Nouvel Observateur*, 30 August 2001.
Rohmer, Éric. 'La Révolution numérique'. *Les Inrockuptibles*, 4 September 2001.
Rohmer, Éric. 'Éric Rohmer sous le signe du Lion'. *Le Figaro*, 7 September 2001.
Rohmer, Éric. 'J'aurais pu être beaucoup plus violent'. *Libération*, 7 September 2001.
Rohmer, Éric. *Le Celluloïd et le marbre, suivi d'un entretien inédit avec Noël Herpe et Philippe Fauvel*. Paris: Éditions Léo Scheer, 2010.

Ropars, Marie-Claire. 'The Search for the Neuter: Sexual Difference and the Status of the Subject in Contemporary Films, Masculine and Feminine'. *L'Esprit créateur* 42: 1 (2002): 122–35.
Rosello, Mireille. 'Agnès Varda's *Les Glaneurs et la Glaneuse*: Portrait of the Artist as an Old Lady'. *Studies in French Cinema* 1: 1 (2001): 29–36.
Rosenbaum, Jonathan. *Placing Movies: The Practice of Film Criticism*. Berkeley: University of California Press, 1995.
Rosenbaum, Jonathan. 'Trailer for Godard's *Histoire(s) du cinéma*'. *Vertigo* 1: 7 (1997).
Rouchy, Marie-Élisabeth. 'Irène Silberman: priorité au spectacle'. *Le Matin*, 11 March 1981.
Rouchy, Marie-Élisabeth, and Raphaël Sorin. 'Les *Cahiers* et Carax'. *Le Matin*, 26 November 1986.
Roy, Jean. 'Une volonté de fer'. *L'Humanité*, 26 November 1986.
Roy, Jean. 'Votons pour la grâce d'Éric Rohmer'. *L'Humanité*, 7 September 2001.
Royer, Philippe. 'Arnaud Desplechin chorégraphie les états d'âme de trentenaires'. *La Croix*, 12 June 1996.
Royer, Philippe. 'Les Flandres servent de cadre à une "Vie de Jésus" assez particulière'. *La Croix*, 4 June 1997.
Royer, Philippe. '*L'Humanité*, un film qui laisse à désirer'. *La Croix*, 19 May 1999.
Russell, David. 'Two or Three Things We Know about Beineix'. *Sight and Sound* 59: 1 (1989–1990): 42–7.
Sadler, Simon. *The Situationist City*. Cambridge, MA: The MIT Press, 1999.
Sainderichain, Guy-Patrick. '*Diva*'. *Cahiers du cinéma* 322 (April 1981): 66.
Saint Angel, Éric de. '*Diva* chez soi'. *Le Matin*, 25 December 1984.
Saint Victor, Jacques de. 'Ce sang était-il donc si impur?' *Le Figaro*, 12 September 2001.
Sayad, Cecilia. *Performing Authorship: Self-Inscription and Corporeality in the Cinema*. London: I. B. Tauris, 2013.
Schidlow, Joshka. '*Boy Meets Girl*: L'amour à vingt ans'. *Télérama*, 21 November 1984.
Schidlow, Joshka. 'Luc Besson tourne *Subway*: Métro, boulot, rigolo'. *Télérama*, 23 January 1985.
Schidlow, Joshka. ' ... Ou qui se détruit'. *Télérama*, 2 October 1985.
Schiller, Britt-Marie. 'On the Threshold of the Creative Imagination: *Swimming Pool* (2003)'. *International Journal of Psychoanalysis* 86 (2005): 557–66.
Schilling, Derek. *Éric Rohmer*. Manchester: Manchester University Press, 2007.
Schilt, Thibault. *François Ozon*. Urbana: University of Illinois Press, 2011.
Schwartz, Louis-Georges. 'Deconstruction *avant la lettre*: Derrida before André Bazin'. In *Opening Bazin: Postwar Film Theory and Its Afterlife*, edited by Dudley Andrew, 95–103. Oxford: Oxford University Press, 2010.
Seguret, Olivier. '*Subway*, ça rame'. *Libération*, 10 April 1985.
Sellier, Geneviève. *Masculine Singular: French New Wave Cinema*. Translated by Kristin Ross. Durham, NC: Duke University Press, 2008.
'S.G.' '*Sils Maria*'. *Le Nouvel Observateur*, 14 August 2014.
Shafto, Sally. 'Artist as Christ/Artist as God-the-Father: Religion in the Cinema of Philippe Garrel and Jean-Luc Godard'. *Film History* 14: 2 (2002): 142–57.
Shaviro, Steven. *Post-Cinematic Affect*. Winchester: Zero Books, 2010.

Shea, Louise. 'From Louis Feuillade to Johnny To: Olivier Assayas on the Future of French Cinema'. *French Forum* 34: 3 (2009): 121–36.
Sherzer, Dina. 'Gender and Sexuality in New New Wave Cinema'. In *Gender and French Cinema*, edited by Alex Hughes and James S. Williams, 227–39. Oxford: Berg, 2001.
Skorecki, Louis. 'Le silence de Leos Carax'. *Libération*, 9 December 1986.
Stewart, Kristen. 'J'adore les films qui parlent de la fabrication des films'. *Le Monde*, 25 May 2014.
Sutton, Paul. 'Olivier Assayas and the Cinema of Catastrophe'. In *Five Directors: Auteurism from Assayas to Ozon*, edited by Kate Ince, 17–37. Manchester: Manchester University Press, 2008.
Tarr, Carrie. *Reframing Difference: Beur and Banlieue Filmmaking in France*. Manchester: Manchester University Press, 2005.
Temple, Michael. 'Big Rhythm and the Power of Metamorphosis: Some Models and Precursors for *Histoire(s) du cinéma*'. In *The Cinema Alone: Essays on the Work of Jean-Luc Godard 1985–2000*, edited by Michael Temple and James S. Williams, 77–95. Amsterdam: Amsterdam University Press, 2000.
Temple, Michael, and Michael Witt (eds). *The French Cinema Book*, second edition. London: Palgrave/BFI, 2018.
Tesson, Charles. 'La Révolution selon Rohmer'. *Cahiers du cinéma* 559 (July–August 2001): 41.
Tesson, Charles. 'Le cou de Grace'. *Cahiers du cinéma* 559 (July–August 2001): 48.
Tesson, Charles. 'Sueurs froides'. *Cahiers du cinéma* 559 (July–August 2001): 47–9.
Tesson, Charles. 'Eau plate'. *Cahiers du cinéma* 579 (May 2003): 48–9.
Tester, Keith. *Éric Rohmer: Film as Theology*. Basingstoke: Palgrave Macmillan, 2008.
Théate, Barbara. '*Irma Vep*, la vampire chinoise'. *Le Journal du Dimanche*, 10 November 1996.
Tinazzi, Noël. 'La rédemption de Freddy, jeune paumé'. *La Tribune*, 4 June 1996.
Tinazzi, Noël. 'Les hesitations d'Ozon'. *La Tribune*, 21 May 2003.
Tonet, Aureliano. 'Comment François Ozon s'est sauvé de chez lui'. *Le Monde*, 10 October 2012.
Tonet, Aureliano. '*Dans la maison* intime de François Ozon'. *Le Monde*, 10 October 2012.
Torlasco, Domietta. 'Against House Arrest: Digital Memory and the Impossible Archive'. *Camera Obscura* 26: 1 [76] (2011): 39–63.
Torlasco, Domietta. 'Digital Impressions: Writing Memory after Agnès Varda'. *Discourse* 33: 3 (2011): 390–408.
Tranchant, Marie-Noëlle. 'La passion du cinéma selon Jean-Jacques Beineix'. *Le Figaro*, 8 March 1982.
Tranchant, Marie-Noëlle. 'L'heure du choix'. *Le Figaro*, 7 March 1985.
Tranchant, Marie-Noëlle. 'Olivier Assayas joue avec le chat'. *Le Figaro*, 14 November 1996.
Tranchant, Marie-Noëlle. 'Bruno Dumont et les larmes de Pharaon'. *Le Figaro*, 24 May 1999.
Tranchant, Marie-Noëlle. 'Révolution sans convention'. *Le Figaro*, 10 September 2001.

Tranchant, Marie-Noëlle. 'Olivier Assayas, phénomène nuageux'. *Le Figaro*, 19 August 2014.
Trémois, Claude-Marie. *Les Enfants de la liberté*. Paris: Seuil, 1997.
Truffaut, François. 'Une certaine tendance du cinéma français'. *Cahiers du cinéma* 31 (January 1954): 15–29.
Truffaut, François. 'Ali Baba et la "politique des auteurs"'. *Cahiers du cinéma* 44 (February 1955): 45–7.
Truffaut, François. 'A Certain Tendency of the French Cinema'. In *Movies and Methods: An Anthology*, edited by Bill Nicholls, 224–37. Berkeley: University of California Press, 1976.
Tulard, Jean. 'Une cruauté extraordinaire'. *Le Figaro*, 12 September 2001.
Tüzün, Defne. 'Abject's "Ideal" Kin: The Sublime'. In *The Sublime Today: Contemporary Readings in the Aesthetic*, edited by Gillian B. Pierce, 119–42. Newcastle-upon-Tyne: Cambridge Scholars Press, 2012.
Tweedie, James. *The Age of New Waves: Art Cinema and the Staging of Globalization*. Oxford: Oxford University Press, 2013.
Tyrer, Ben. 'Digression and Return: Aesthetics and Politics in Agnès Varda's *Les Glaneurs et la Glaneuse*'. *Studies in French Cinema* 9: 2 (2009): 161–76.
Vanderschelden, Isabelle. 'The "Beautiful People" of Christophe Honoré: New Wave Legacies and New Directions in French Auteur Cinema'. *Studies in European Cinema* 7: 2 (2010): 135–48.
Vanoye, Francis. *L'Emprise du cinéma*. Lyon: Aléas, 2005.
Varda, Agnès. 'Interview'. *Les Inrockuptibles*, 4 July 2000.
Varda, Agnès. 'Agnès Varda, glaneuse sachant glaner'. *Le Monde/Aden*, 5 July 2000.
Vassé, Claire. '*Oublie-moi*: Le boulet qui trace son chemin'. *Positif* 408 (February 1995): 37–8.
Vassé, Claire. 'Transgression des liens du sang'. In *Le Jeune Cinéma français*, edited by Michel Marie, 64–73. Paris: Nathan, 1998.
Vasse, David. *Le Nouvel Âge du cinéma d'auteur français*. Paris: Klincksieck, 2008.
Vaugeois, Gérard. '*Boy Meets Girl* de Leos Carax'. *L'Humanité-Dimanche*, 30 November 1984.
Vaugeois, Gérard. '*Subway* de Luc Besson'. *L'Humanité-Dimanche*, 12 April 1985.
Vernallis, Carol. *Experiencing Music Video: Aesthetics and Cultural Context*. New York: Columbia University Press, 2004.
Virgil. *The Aeneid*. Translated by Robert Fitzgerald. London: Harvill, 1993.
Warehime, Marja. 'Politics, Sex, and French Cinema in the 1990s: The Place of Arnaud Desplechin'. *French Studies* 56: 1 (2002): 61–78.
Weiner, Susan. 'Jean-Pierre Léaud's Anachronism: The Crisis of Masculinity in Jean Eustache's *La Maman et la Putain*'. *L'Esprit créateur* 42: 1 (2002): 41–51.
Wheatley, Catherine. 'Holy Motors'. *Sight & Sound* 24: 12 (December 2014): 44–8.
Wiles, Mary M. *Jacques Rivette*. Urbana: Illinois University Press, 2012.
Williams, James S. 'The Signs amongst Us: Jean-Luc Godard's *Histoire(s) du cinéma*', *Screen* 40: 3 (1999): 306–15.
Williams, James S. 'European Culture and Artistic Resistance in *Histoire(s) du cinéma* chapter 3A, *La Monnaie de l'absolu*'. In *The Cinema Alone: Essays on the Work of Jean-Luc Godard 1985–2000*, edited by Michael Temple and James S. Williams, 113–39. Amsterdam: Amsterdam University Press, 2000.

Williams, James S. *Space and Being in Contemporary French Cinema*. Manchester: Manchester University Press, 2013.
Wilson, Jake. 'Trash and Treasure: *The Gleaners and I*'. *Senses of Cinema* 23 (2002).
Witt, Michael. *Jean-Luc Godard, Cinema Historian*. Bloomington: Indiana University Press, 2013.
Wright, Alan. 'Elizabeth Taylor at Auschwitz: JLG and the Real Object of Montage'. In *The Cinema Alone: Essays on the Work of Jean-Luc Godard 1985–2000*, edited by Michael Temple and James S. Williams, 51–60. Amsterdam: Amsterdam University Press, 2000.
Yervasi, Carina L. 'Capturing the Elusive Representations in Beineix's *Diva*'. *Literature/Film Quarterly* 21: 1 (1993): 38–46.
Zea, Zahra T. *La Bande des quatre: Late Nineteenth-Century Literary and Artistic Sources in Late Nouvelle Vague Filmmaking*. Unpublished PhD thesis. University of Kent, 2016.

INDEX

À bout de souffle 6, 8, 55, 57–8, 67, 72, 79, 91–3, 105–6, 108–9, 132, 136, 233
Adieu au langage 231
Adieu Philippine 123 n.23, 137
Adjani, Isabelle 51, 75
Akerman, Chantal 13, 19, 30, 32, 93, 97
Aldrich, Robert 50, 195
Allen, Woody 204, 233
Alphaville 30, 58, 61, 137–8, 141
Amalric, Mathieu 91, 96, 99
Amants du Pont-Neuf, Les 45, 53, 71
Amants réguliers, Les 29, 232
Amours d'Astrée et de Céladon, Les 146, 158
An 01, L' 24–5
Anglaise et le Duc, L' 132, 145–59, 168–70
Année dernière à Marienbad, L' 173 n.20, 174 n.39
Antonioni, Michelangelo 34, 137
Apocalypse Now 134
Aragon, Louis 55, 136
Argento, Asia 192
Arte 90, 93
Artist, The 44 n.111, 232
Arts 2, 4, 17, 134
Ascenseur pour l'échafaud 2, 5
Assayas, Olivier 90–1, 93, 96, 185–93, 195, 198, 212–14, 219–20, 222 n.20, 234–5
Audiard, Jacques 92
Audran, Stéphane 195
Aumont, Jacques 113, 133–4, 140–1, 143–4
auteurism
    and biographical interpretation 4, 52–3, 55, 133, 164, 203, 217–18

and film historiography 7, 94
and film promotion 7, 46, 48–9, 52, 94, 167
and mise en scène 5, 72, 147
and romantic conception of the artist 28, 39, 49, 164, 196, 220
and world view 4, 39, 209, 215
as category of film production and distribution 7–9, 24, 45, 50, 90, 118, 185, 191, 194, 212, 217, 219, 222 n.20
Aznavour, Charles 3, 19

baby boom 2, 51
Baisers volés 91
Balibar, Jeanne 92, 97, 99, 124 n.54
Bande à part 28, 56, 133, 136
Band Wagon, The 173 n.20
Bardot, Brigitte 3
Baudelaire, Charles 163, 167
Bauman, Zygmunt 66
Bazin, André 5, 39, 92, 142–3, 147, 149, 169
Beaupain, Alex 218
Beau Serge, Le 2
Beautiful Blonde from Bashful Bend, The 138
Beauvois, Xavier 92, 111, 122 n.15
Bechdel test 103, 126 n.92
Becker, Jacques 139
Beineix, Jean-Jacques 45–9, 66, 74–5, 77, 95, 219
Belle de Jour 203
Belle Personne, La 217
Belmondo, Jean-Paul 3, 56, 58, 83 n.49, 131, 138
Benjamin, Walter 140, 163, 167
Bergala, Alain 47, 55, 65
Bergman, Ingmar 6, 134, 138, 195

Bergman, Ingrid 141
Bertolucci, Bernardo 232
Besson, Luc 45–6, 49–50, 67, 74–5, 77, 83 n.42, 95, 219
Biches, Les 195
Bien-Aimés, Les 198, 202, 209–11, 213–20, 227 n.157
Binoche, Juliette 53, 55, 58, 60, 189–93
Black Panthers 161
Blanchot, Maurice 175 n.54
Boarding Gate 192
Boetticher, Budd 134
Bohringer, Richard 47
Bonjour tristesse 136
Bonnaffé, Jacques 29–35, 37
Borderie, Clément 162
Bory, Jean-Louis 17–18, 23
Botticelli, Sandro 139
Boudu sauvé des eaux 135
Boulangère de Monceau, La 21
Bowie, David 58, 70, 78
Boy Meets Girl 46, 52–9, 69–71, 77, 79
Brakhage, Stan 186
Braunberger, Pierre 2
Bresson, Robert 18, 35, 55, 118, 134, 139, 142
Breton, André 162
Breton, Jules 160, 162
Brialy, Jean-Claude 3, 131
Britten, Benjamin 59
Broch, Hermann 144
Brody, Richard 231, 234
Brooks, Louise 58
Bruni-Sarkozy, Carla 124 n.54
Bruni Tedeschi, Valeria 97, 106, 108–10, 124 n.54
Buñuel, Luis 6, 194, 202–4, 217

Cahiers du cinéma 4, 7, 17, 48, 50, 52–4, 58, 62, 68, 91, 94, 134, 141, 158, 186, 188, 196, 205, 211–12
Cai Guo-Qiang 162
Camus, Albert 65
Canal Plus 90, 160
Cannes Film Festival 14, 92–3, 151, 231

Cantet, Laurent 95
Carabiniers, Les 8
Carax, Leos 45–6, 49, 52–9, 69–71, 77, 79–80, 85 n.86, 209, 220, 235
Carné, Marcel 47, 67
Carpenter, John 50
Cassavetes, John 90
Céline et Julie vont en bateau 101, 207–8
Céline, Louis-Ferdinand 17, 55, 204
Cent et une nuits, Les 131, 159
Chabrol, Claude 2, 14, 17–18, 27, 51, 59, 61, 72, 92, 96, 137, 145, 148, 194–5, 203, 217
Chansons d'amour, Les 202, 210, 213, 215–16, 218
Chaplin, Charles 59, 70, 135
Char, René 55
Chéreau, Patrice 102
Cheung, Maggie 186, 188–9
Cheval, Ferdinand 162
Chinoise, La 231–2
Chrétien de Troyes 145
Cicatrice intérieure, La 28–9
Cimino, Michael 137
cinéma du look 8, 45–7, 49–52, 60, 62–3, 67–9, 71–2, 74–5, 80–1, 119, 185
Cinémathèque Française 14, 28, 91, 139, 235
cinephilia 4, 14, 94–5, 121, 138–9, 141, 143, 171
Citizen Kane 47, 64
Classe de lutte 186
Classe operaia va in paradiso, La 16
Cléo de 5 à 7 20, 61, 67, 105, 110, 164, 171
Clouzot, Henri-Georges 196
Cocciante, Riccardo 137
Cochon, Le 17
Cocteau, Jean 47, 55, 134–5, 211
Coen, Ethan and Joel 90
Coeur fidèle 59
Cohn-Bendit, Daniel 29
Collard, Cyril 90
Comment je me suis disputé (Ma vie sexuelle) 93, 96, 98–105, 119–20, 122 n.15, 126 n.92

Coppola, Francis Ford 134
Costa-Gavras 137
Courbet, Gustave 116
Cousins, Les 61
Cousteau, Jacques 2
Créatures, Les 131
Cries and Whispers 134
Cure, The 135

Daguerréotypes 165
Dahan, Olivier 93
Daney, Serge 52, 54–5, 138, 218
Dans la maison 195, 203–9, 220
Dans Paris 209, 211, 213–15, 217–18, 227 n.157
Danton 151
Dardenne, Jean-Pierre and Luc 93, 95–6, 110–11
Dauman, Anatole 2
Davis, Miles 5
Dead Kennedys 77–8
de Baecque, Antoine 1, 15, 154
de Beauregard, Georges 2
Debord, Guy 71
de la Tour, Georges 59
Deleuze, Gilles 186, 188
Delon, Alain 3
Delpy, Julie 56, 85 n.86
Demoiselles de Rochefort, Les 210
Demoiselles ont eu 25 ans, Les 137, 159
Demy, Jacques 137, 159, 174 n.39, 210–11, 218
Deneuve, Catherine 131, 137, 210, 216–17
Denicourt, Marianne 92, 100
De Niro, Robert 131
Denis, Claire 93, 112
Deray, Jacques 196
Derrida, Jacques 143
De Santis, Giuseppe 137
De Sica, Vittorio 137
Désordre 185
Desplechin, Arnaud 92, 94, 96, 98–105, 119–20, 122 n.15, 125 n.64, 217
Destinées sentimentales, Les 187

Deux Anglaises et le continent 126 n.102
Deux ou trois choses que je sais d'elle 61
Devos, Emmanuelle 97, 99, 106, 124 n.54
Diaboliques, Les 196
Dickens, Charles 154
Didi-Huberman, Georges 132–3, 140
direction of actors 25–7, 36, 53–4, 102, 189, 192–3, 198, 202, 212, 219–20
Disney, Walt 50
Diva 46–9, 63–6, 68, 72–5, 80
Dix-sept fois Cécile Cassard 185
Documenteur 165
Doigts dans la tête, Les 24–7
Doillon, Jacques 8, 13, 19, 24–8, 30, 32, 38–9, 90, 102
Dorléac, Françoise 218
Dostoevsky, Fyodor 207
Douchet, Jean 15, 17–18, 207
Dreamers, The 232
Dreyer, Carl Theodor 139
Dreyfus, Jean-Claude 149, 157
Drôle de drame 47
Drôlesse, La 42 n.72
Duelle 222 n.17
Dumont, Bruno 93, 96, 111–21
Duras, Marguerite 34, 134
d'Urfé, Honoré 146
Duris, Romain 213, 215, 217
Duvivier, Julien 80
Dwan, Allan 195
Dyer, Richard 213
Dziga Vertov Group 14, 233

editing 3, 29, 46, 59, 61–2, 72, 79, 87 n.144, 102, 107, 149, 161, 164, 168
8 femmes 194, 203
Eisenhower, Dwight D. 67
Eisenstein, Sergei 72, 137, 143
Elle a passé tant d'heures sous les sunlights 28–38, 58
Elliott, Grace 145–6, 149, 151, 153–8
Enfant secret, L' 43 n.99

Enfants terribles, Les 135
Epstein, Jean 58–9, 135
Escoffier, Jean-Yves 53–5, 60
Eustache, Jean 8, 13, 15–23, 25, 28–30, 32, 36, 39, 100–2
evaluative criticism 7–8

Fanck, Arnold 191
Fassbinder, Rainer Werner 134, 195, 209
Faure, Élie 140, 176 n.56
Faust 154, 173 n.20
Fellini, Federico 6, 137
Fémis 94, 207
Femme qui pleure, La 32, 42 n.72
Ferran, Pascale 94, 96
Ferreira Barbosa, Laurence 93, 122 n.15, 127 n.119
Ferré, Léo 55
Feuillade, Louis 186
Fifth Element, The 83 n.42
Fille prodigue, La 42 n.72
film noir 1, 64, 73, 75, 157, 189, 195
Flandres 112
Flaubert, Gustave 207
Fond de l'air est rouge, Le 174 n.39
Ford, John 134
Forman, Milos 210
Fra Angelico 139
Frantz 220
Fresnais, Pierre 137
Freud, Sigmund 82 n.18, 135
Frodon, Jean-Michel 101, 108, 115, 155
Fuller, Samuel 55, 57

Gabin, Jean 139
Garrel, Louis 30–1, 211, 213–15, 217, 220, 232
Garrel, Philippe 8, 13, 19–20, 28–39, 43 n.93, 43 n.99, 44 n.111, 44 n.117, 58–9, 69, 100–1, 134, 220, 232, 235
generations
   as demographic category 51, 55, 81, 118, 138, 193, 204, 210, 216, 218, 220

in conflict 2, 14, 51–2, 63, 119, 190, 196, 216–19
of filmmaking personnel 3, 7–8, 13, 46, 55, 91–2, 94–5, 100–2, 113, 118, 122 n.14, 138, 175 n.42, 185, 187, 189–90, 193–4, 217, 219–20
Gens normaux n'ont rien d'exceptionnel, Les 127 n.119
Gesualdo, Carlo 139
Gigi 138
Gish, Lilian 20, 58
Glaneurs et la Glaneuse, Les 132, 147, 159–69, 172
Glaneurs et la Glaneuse, Les: Deux ans après 160, 162, 165
Godard, Jean-Luc
   and film historiography 8, 47, 131–3, 138–42, 144–5, 149–50, 168–70, 187
   and genre 50, 57, 79, 108, 148
   and May 1968 14–15, 171, 231–3
   and realism 5, 26, 32–3, 39
   auteur status 28, 30, 55, 92, 95, 132–5, 168, 171, 187, 219, 231–3
   cinephilia 54
   direction of actors 27, 36, 56, 220, 232
   film criticism 134, 140–1, 231
   intertextuality 20, 55, 57, 85 n.86, 108, 133–4, 149, 233
   modes of film production 2, 27, 30, 187
   montage 34, 83 n.49, 132, 135, 137, 140–4, 169, 173 n.20, 233
   narrative structure 3, 33, 55, 79, 94
   political interpretation of 17, 56, 61, 170, 233–4
   relationships with women 32–3, 59, 136, 187, 220, 231–2
   representation of women and gender 98, 210, 217
   rhythm 6, 20, 30, 72, 79, 107, 141
   sound 35, 55–6, 134, 136, 141
   stylized mise en scène 5, 56–7, 70, 83 n.49, 210

support for younger filmmakers 17, 85 n.86
Godelureaux, Les 61
Gomes, Miguel 44 n.111
Gorin, Jean-Pierre 233
Gozzoli, Benozzo 139
Grande Illusion, La 137
Griffith, D. W. 58
Groupe Medvedkine 186
Guattari, Félix 186
Guibert, Hervé 52, 218
Guitry, Sacha 19
Guy Debord, son art et son temps 71

Haine, La 120, 121 n.1
Hardly Working 138
Harvey, David 71
Hausner, Jessica 117
Haut bas fragile 92
Hawks, Howard 55
Hayworth, Rita 136
Hazanavicius, Michel 44 n.111, 231–3
Hebdige, Dick 51
Hegel, G. W. F. 100
Heidegger, Martin 174 n.34
Heroic Trio, The 186
Herrmann, Bernard 204
Highsmith, Patricia 198
Hill, Walter 50
Hiroshima mon amour 174 n.39
Histoire(s) du cinéma 57, 85 n.86, 131–45, 147, 149, 168–71, 172 n.4, 173 n.20, 175 n.54, 177 n.92
Hitchcock, Alfred 74, 134, 138, 141–2, 157, 194, 204, 206, 211
Hitler, Adolf 138
Holocaust, the 134, 138, 142, 170, 174 n.39
Holy Motors 45, 53
Homme qui aimait les femmes, L' 227 n.161
Honoré, Christophe 185, 195, 198, 202, 209–20, 232, 234
Hors Satan 118
Hughes, Howard 135
Hugo, Victor 140

humanité, L' 93, 96, 111–12, 116–20
Hussards, the 2, 17

In a Lonely Place 231
India Song 134
Ingres, Jean-Auguste-Dominique 59
Irma Vep 90, 93, 185–90, 192–3, 220
Isou, Isidore 186

Jacquot, Benoît 13, 19
Jacquot de Nantes 159, 171
J'ai horreur de l'amour 122 n.15
James, Henry 207
James, P. D. 198
Jameson, Fredric 47, 63, 66
Jarmusch, Jim 55
Jeanne la Pucelle 148
Jeffreys, Sheila 23
Jett, Joan 192
jeune cinéma français, le 8, 89–98, 101, 103, 105, 109–11, 118–21, 185
Jeune et jolie 220
Jeunet, Jean-Pierre 90
Joan of Arc 139
Joffo, Joseph 27
Jones, Rickie Lee 76
Jouvet, Louis 174 n.28
Jules et Jim 19, 110, 126 n.102
jump cuts 6, 72, 79

Kahn, Cédric 90, 92–3
Karina, Anna 3, 19–20, 33, 57–9, 136
Kassovitz, Mathieu 90, 120, 121 n.1
Kazan, Elia 134
Keaton, Buster 59, 70
King Lear 85 n.86, 137
Kleist, Heinrich von 145
Koltès, Bernard-Marie 218
Kosintsev, Grigoriy 134
Kristeva, Julia 165
Kubrick, Stanley 34

Lafont, Bernadette 3, 16, 18–20, 92
Lalanne, Jean-Marc 134–5, 139–40, 191
Lambert, Christophe 51
Lang, Fritz 64, 134–5, 138, 141, 157, 211

Langlois, Henri 14, 139
Lanzmann, Claude 134
Laplanche, Jean 162, 166
Lavant, Denis 52, 55, 78
Léaud, Jean-Pierre 3, 14–15, 18, 61, 91–2, 139, 187, 189, 232
Leavis, F. R. 140
Lebrun, Françoise 16, 20
Le Corbusier 60
Léon 83 n.42
Leopard, The 134
Lewis, Jerry 138
Lightning over Water 135
Lili Marleen 134
Limelight 59
Litnianski, Bohdan 162, 166, 170
Livre d'image, Le 231, 234
location shooting 2, 5, 19, 46, 60–2, 66–7, 73, 81, 92, 110, 145, 214
Luchini, Fabrice 203–4, 207
Lune dans le caniveau, La 48
Lupino, Ida 135
Lvovsky, Noémie 96, 105–8, 110, 119–21, 122 n.15
Lynch, David 212

M6 194
Machine à découdre, La 175 n.39
Madame Bovary 148
Malheurs de Sophie, Les 210
Malle, Louis 2
Malraux, André 2, 136, 140, 175 n.54
Maman et la Putain, La 15–25, 30, 39, 102
Mann, Thomas 190
Marchand, Guy 217
Marie, Michel 1, 5–6, 18
Mariée était en noir, La 101
Marie pour mémoire 28, 134
Marker, Chris 174 n.39
Marnie 141
Marquise von O, Die 101, 145, 158
Marseillaise, La 151
Martin, Stacy 233
Marxism 2, 13
Masculin féminin 17
Mastroianni, Chiara 210, 213–17
Mastroianni, Marcello 131

Match Point 204
Mauvaises Fréquentations, Les 17
Mauvais Sang 46, 51–4, 57–60, 69–70, 77–9, 85 n.86
May 1968 8, 13–17, 22, 24–5, 29, 123 n.38, 218, 231–2
Méliès, Georges 59, 147
Melville, Jean-Pierre 47, 135
Mépris, Le 8, 57, 98, 110, 131–2, 136, 210, 233
Métamorphoses 210
Meyer, Hans 58
Michelet, Jules 140
Miéville, Anne-Marie 33, 144
Millet, Jean-François 160, 162
Minnelli, Vincente 138, 173 n.20
Miracle Worker, The 134
mise en scène
  and ethics 113, 115, 150
  and rhythm 46, 74, 105, 111, 113, 188, 214
  and world view 4–5, 98, 113–14, 116, 120, 124 n.63, 141, 155–7, 159, 212
  as historical documentation 5, 62–3, 71, 81, 114, 143, 148
  as production design 45, 47–8, 63–6, 68, 70, 74, 116, 150, 155–7, 175 n.39, 208, 210, 213–14, 218, 233
  as self-conscious theatricality 18
  as spatial disposition 4, 46, 62, 104, 106, 121, 150, 154–5, 157, 159, 188, 193, 195, 212–14
  relation to auteurism 4–5, 113
misogyny 23, 103, 105, 168
Mocky, Jean-Pierre 174 n.39
Modern Times 135
Monaco, James 1, 3–6
Monory, Jacques 47
Moreau, Jeanne 131
Moretz, Chloe Grace 189, 191
Mouchette 118
Moullet, Luc 17
müde Tod, Der 138, 141
Mulvey, Laura 73
Munk, Andrzej 134
Mur murs 165

Murnau, F. W. 44 n.117, 154, 173 n.20
music, use in film 5, 19, 46, 55, 58, 73–8, 87 n.144, 107, 137, 144, 189, 195, 204, 208, 211, 213–14, 227 n.149, 233

Nadja à Paris 137
narrative structure 3–4, 14, 26, 33, 38, 45–6, 61, 66–7, 73–4, 78, 87 n.144, 91, 96, 102, 106–7, 110, 114, 116, 119, 162–4, 167, 195–6, 199–201, 206–7, 209, 214, 219
Neupert, Richard 2
Nico 29–33, 37–8, 43 n.93, 43 n.99, 59
Nietzsche, Friedrich 190
Nimier, Roger 2, 65
Noé, Gaspar 90
Non ma fille, tu n'iras pas danser 213
Noroît 148, 222 n.17
Notorious 141
N'oublie pas que tu vas mourir 122 n.15
Nuit américaine, La 30, 187
Nuit et brouillard 174 n.39

Occupation of France during the Second World War 27, 153, 170
Ogier, Bulle 92, 187
Opéra-Mouffe 165, 167
Ophuls, Max 174 n.28, 195
OSS 117 233
Oublie-moi 96, 105–10, 119–20, 122 n.15, 127 n.119
Ovid 210
Ozeray, Madeleine 174 n.28
Ozon, François 185, 194–209, 213, 215, 217, 219–20, 234

Pagnol, Marcel 19
Parapluies de Cherbourg, Les 174 n.39, 210
Paris
  growth 2
  in May 1968 14, 29
  modernization 60–1, 63, 71

  representation on film 6, 19, 46, 51, 60–1, 65–9, 73–4, 92, 105–6, 120, 145–6, 149, 154, 157, 213
Paris nous appartient 61, 66, 105
Parvulesco, Jean 152
Pasazerka 134
Pasolini, Pier Paolo 6, 134, 137–8, 204–6, 209
Passion 30
Passion de Jeanne d'Arc, La 20, 233
Péguy, Charles 140, 144
Penn, Arthur 134
Peppermint Frappé 14
Perceval le Gallois 145, 148, 158
Père Noël a les yeux bleus, Le 17
Perrier, Mireille 31–4, 55–6, 58
Personal Shopper 192
Personne ne m'aime 92, 122 n.15
Petits Arrangements avec les morts 96
Petit Soldat, Le 79, 187
Petri, Elio 16
Photo de famille 199
Piaf, Édith 19
Pialat, Maurice 90, 97, 100, 110
Picasso, Pablo 30
Piccoli, Michel 57, 131
Pickford, Mary 20
Pickpocket 118
Pierrot le fou 56–8, 79, 83 n.49, 133, 138, 210
Piscine, La 196
Pisier, Marie-France 217
Plages d'Agnès, Les 165
Pola X 45
politique des auteurs 4–5, 138–9, 194, 219, 231
Pons, Louis 162
Pont du Nord, Le 69
Portes de la nuit, Les 67
postmodernism 47, 55, 63–4, 66, 71–2, 80–1, 135, 150, 235
Potiche 220
Prédal, René 25–6, 89, 91–4, 102, 119, 171
Preminger, Otto 136
prime à la qualité 2
Proust, Marcel 31

INDEX 261

Quatre Cents Coups, Les 61, 92, 96, 101, 105, 124 n.63, 137, 139
quotation, within films 3, 52, 54–5, 57–8, 64, 80, 108, 133–4, 137, 139, 142, 144, 168, 171, 199, 233–5

Raiders of the Lost Ark 50
Rampling, Charlotte 195, 200, 225 n.96
Ramuz, Charles Ferdinand 55, 57
Rancière, Jacques 140–3
Ray, Nicholas 64, 135, 231
Rayon vert, Le 137
realism 2, 5, 18–19, 26, 45, 62, 65–6, 91, 97, 101, 111–12, 117, 120, 148–9, 169, 201, 213, 234
Rear Window 138, 204
Rebel without a Cause 64
Redoutable, Le 231–4
Reed, Lou 107
Reggiani, Serge 58, 78
Règle du jeu, La 30, 135
Rembrandt 162
Rendell, Ruth 198
Renoir, Jean 19, 134–5, 137, 151, 195
Réponse de femmes 161
Resnais, Alain 14, 24, 34, 95–6, 101–2, 173 n.20, 174 n.39
Révélateur, Le 36
rhythm 5–6, 30, 46, 71–3, 77–81, 98, 102, 107, 110–11, 119, 122 n.14, 155, 186, 188, 195, 197, 212, 214
Richard, Nathalie 186–7
Rimbaud, Arthur 52, 55
Ringwald, Molly 137
Rise and Fall of Legs Diamond, The 134
Rivette, Jacques 5, 14, 17, 26–7, 36, 61, 66, 69, 92, 94–5, 101–2, 110, 137, 148, 152, 176 n.66, 187–8, 207–8, 212, 217, 220, 222 n.17
Robbe-Grillet, Alain 217
Robespierre, Maximilien 158
Rochant, Éric 91–3

Rohmer, Éric 8, 17, 21–2, 26, 51, 54, 61, 95–6, 98, 101, 132, 137, 145–59, 168–71, 207
Rohrwacher, Alice 117
Ronet, Maurice 3
Rosetta 93, 110
Rosière de Pessac, La 17
Rossellini, Roberto 134–5, 137, 139, 147, 150
Rouch, Jean 18, 24
Roussel, Myriem 136
Rozier, Jacques 123 n.23, 137
Runaways, The 192
Russell, Lucy 149, 158

Sagnier, Ludivine 195, 198–200, 202, 210, 215, 220
St. Trinian's 205
Salut les Cubains 161
Sans toit ni loi 110, 164, 171
Sartre, Jean-Paul 153
Satie, Erik 73
Saura, Carlos 14
Schroeder, Barbet 2
Schubert, Franz 136
Schygulla, Hanna 131
Scorsese, Martin 90
Scott Thomas, Kristin 204, 226 n.149
Seberg, Jean 29, 31, 38, 43 n.93, 57, 136
Ségur, Comtesse de 146, 210
Seidl, Ulrich 117
Seigner, Emmanuelle 204, 208–9
Sellier, Geneviève 3
Seven Year Itch, The 47
sexuality
    representation on screen 3, 22–4, 39, 56, 98–100, 105, 108–9, 111–12, 114–17, 120, 157–8, 195, 199–201, 203–5, 208–9, 214–17, 220–1, 227 n.149
Shearer, Norma 136
Shoah 134
Signe du Lion, Le 61, 96, 105, 145
Silberman, Irène 48
silent cinema 20, 36–8, 56–9, 103, 135–6, 138, 186, 221 n.10, 232
Sils Maria 189–93, 198, 220–1

Sinatra, Nancy 227 n.162
Sirk, Douglas 195
Sitcom 185, 204
situationism 60–1, 63, 68, 71
Smith, Patti 107
Sonic Youth 189
sound, use in film 2, 5, 21, 35, 103, 201
Sous le sable 194, 209, 225 n.96
space, depiction on film 6, 72, 81, 154
  interiors 19, 35, 55–6, 61, 63–6, 69–70, 72, 98, 106, 149, 155–8, 204
  urban space 46, 51, 60–71, 106, 232
Spielberg, Steven 50
Splendor in the Grass 134
Stardust Memories 233
Stevenson, Robert Louis 154
Stewart, James 138
Stewart, Kristen 189–93
Strangers on a Train 141–2
Straub, Jean-Marie 35
Stromboli 147
Sturges, Preston 138
Subor, Michel 3
Subway 46, 49–51, 66–8, 74–7, 80, 83 n.49
Summer with Monika 138
Suspicion 141
Swimming Pool 194–205, 208–9, 220, 225 n.96, 226 n.149
Sze, Sarah 161

Tabu 44 n.111
Taken 45, 83 n.42
Tàpies, Antoni 162
Tarkovsky, Andrei 72
Taxi 83 n.42
Téchiné, André 93
Teorema 204
TF1 90, 177 n.92
Thalberg, Irving 135–6
Tirez sur le pianiste 50, 101
To, Johnnie 186
Tombeau d'Alexandre, Le 174 n.39
Toubiana, Serge 54
Touchez pas au grisbi 139

Tous les garçons et les filles de leur âge 93
Trauner, Alexandre 67
Trintignant, Jean-Louis 3
Triple Agent 145
Truffaut, François
  'Antoine Doinel' cycle 18, 51, 61, 139, 187
  autobiographical cinema 96, 101
  characterization 125 n.64
  children 27, 217
  cinephilia 54, 94, 168
  film criticism 26, 39, 119, 148, 212
  genre 50, 108, 148
  intertextuality 20, 108, 187
  May 1968 14
  mise en scène 5
  modes of film production 2
  narrative 3, 110
  politics 17
  rhythm 6, 20, 72
  tone 18, 26, 50, 98, 219
  women 59, 101, 211, 217, 220
Tsai Ming-Liang 212
Tweedie, James 4–6, 8, 39, 61–3, 71–2, 79–80
Twentynine Palms 112
Twilight 192
2 x 50 ans de cinéma français 131

Une belle fille comme moi 19
Une chante, l'autre pas, L' 14, 171
Une femme est une femme 8, 19–20, 58, 61, 233
Une femme mariée 57, 84 n.57
Une nouvelle vie 192
Un monde sans pitié 91–3, 123 n.23, 123 n.38
Un sac de billes 27
Utrillo, Maurice 162

Valéry, Paul 140
Vampires, Les 186–7
Vangelo secondo Matteo, Il 138
Varda, Agnès 3, 5, 8, 14, 20, 61, 67, 94–5, 97–8, 110, 131–2, 137, 145, 147–8, 159–68, 170–2, 187
Va savoir 92

Vent de la nuit, Le 29
Vernoux, Marion 92, 122 n.15
Vian, Boris 2
Vidor, King 58
Vie de Jésus, La 111–19
Vie ne me fait pas peur, La 96, 122 n.15
Vigo, Jean 135
Vincent, Thomas 111
Violette Nozière 148
Virgil 132
Visages villages 165
Visconti, Luchino 134, 137, 205
Vivre sa vie 20, 56, 58, 96, 110, 233
Vlady, Marina 136
von Stroheim, Erich 137

Wajda, Andrzej 151
Walsh, Raoul 50, 195
Warhol, Andy 32
Welles, Orson 34, 47, 134, 136
Wenders, Wim 55, 135
While the City Sleeps 135
Wiazemsky, Anne 31–3, 43 n.99, 136, 231–2

Wilder, Billy 47
women
   representation on screen 3, 20–3, 59, 79, 97, 101, 103–5, 109–10, 116, 126 n.92, 158, 189, 192, 194, 197–203, 208, 216, 220, 233
Wong Kar-Wai 212
Woo, John 188
Woolf, Virginia 144
Wrong Man, The 141

youth
   and social movements 13–14, 51, 62, 119, 234
   as filmgoers 50, 54, 216
   demographic trends 2, 6, 49, 51, 62, 68, 81, 138, 170, 234
   representation on film 5, 15, 27, 45–6, 49, 51–2, 60–1, 80–1, 90, 96–7, 111, 114, 119–20, 190, 199, 205, 216, 235

Zinnerman, Fred 137
Zonca, Érick 111

www.ingramcontent.com/pod-product-compliance
Lightning Source LLC
Chambersburg PA
CBHW062125300426
44115CB00012BA/1822